# Civil Disabilities

DEMOCRACY, CITIZENSHIP, AND CONSTITUTIONALISM

Rogers M. Smith and Mary L. Dudziak, Series Editors

# Civil Disabilities

## CITIZENSHIP, MEMBERSHIP, AND BELONGING

*Edited by*

## Nancy J. Hirschmann

*and*

## Beth Linker

**PENN**

UNIVERSITY OF PENNSYLVANIA PRESS

PHILADELPHIA

Published by
University of Pennsylvania Press
Philadelphia, Pennsylvania 19104-4112
www.upenn.edu/pennpress

Printed in the United States of America on acid-free paper
10 9 8 7 6 5 4 3 2 1

Library of Congress Cataloging-in-Publication Data

Civil disabilities : citizenship, membership, and belonging / edited by Nancy J.
Hirschmann and Beth Linker. — 1st ed.
    p. cm. — (Democracy, citizenship, and constitutionalism)
    Includes bibliographical references and index.
    ISBN 978-0-8122-4667-4
    1. People with disabilities—Civil rights—United States. 2. People with
disabilities—Social conditions—United States. 3. People with disabilities—
Legal status, laws, etc.—United States. 4. Discrimination against people with
disabilities. 5. Social integration—United States. 6. Citizenship—United States.
I. Hirschmann, Nancy J. II. Linker, Beth. III. Series: Democracy, citizenship,
and constitutionalism.
HV1568.C57 2015
305.9'080973—dc23
                                                            2014025621

# CONTENTS

# Disability, Citizenship, and Belonging:
# A Critical Introduction

Nancy J. Hirschmann and Beth Linker

Although the study of citizenship has garnered significant scholarly attention in the past several decades, disabled persons have been largely
overlooked.[1] But as this volume demonstrates, disability is central to understanding citizenship.[2] In the United States, most of the work on disability and citizenship has happened on the ground—through the blood and
sweat of disability activists—or in the courts, where legislation is interpreted
into fact. A major category of the modern welfare state, disability has been
fundamental to twentieth-century policy formation, health-care delivery,
and, more recently, antidiscrimination laws. Disability has also, by turns,
served as justification for eugenic sterilization and for exclusion from the
workplace and the nation-state as a whole, a prime mover for technological
invention, and an occasion for ever-greater inclusion in America's educational system.

The ubiquity and importance of disability to the development of civil
society in the past two centuries seems clear. In the United States, one can
trace the beginning of disability legislation to the concomitant mid-
nineteenth-century rise of industrialization and state reliance on a con-
scripted army. Disabled bodies could not conform to the needs of the
productive, capitalistic, imperialistic state. Therefore, welfare measures
were put in place but were rarely given priority, and the disabled quickly
came to be seen as a burden rather than an asset, an unsightly rift in the
fabric of humanity. The U.S. disability rights movement (DRM)—from the
1973 Rehabilitation Act to the 1990 Americans with Disabilities Act (ADA)

and the 2008 ADA Amendments Act—made great strides in resisting the devaluation of disabled persons by insisting on legislation that protected them against discrimination, secured equal opportunities in housing and employment, and mandated a built environment that would be conducive to freedom of movement for all kinds of physical impairments.

This narrative is one to which both scholars and activists themselves turn in order to understand the history and theory of disability and citizenship in the United States. It is an important narrative, but it often and somewhat oddly takes the meaning of citizenship—particularly as it pertains to disability—for granted. This may be because while most citizenship scholarship focuses on overtly political issues, such as rights to voting, due process, and equal protection of the law, citizenship for disabled persons has meant something both more basic and much larger. In the United States, for instance, it is undisputed that disabled persons born here and over the age of eighteen can vote—*if* they can get to the polling station, and *if* that polling station is accessible. Disabled persons can work—*if* they can overcome employer attitudes, and *if* the space in which they want to work is accessible, and so forth.[3] Those *ifs* are the heart of the matter, and they are about the distribution of power, regardless of whether that power is described in overtly political terms of "who gets what, where, when, and how," economic terms of "distribution to the least well-off," or humanistic terms of citizenship as "the signifying subject of the state."[4] The distance between legal signification and the lived reality of citizenship for disabled persons is often quite vast and leads us to conclude that legal categories of disability often pose not just practical problems for disabled persons but also ones of social standing.

This distance between law and lived reality, between ideal and practice, helped inspire us to publish this volume: the reiteration of exclusion of disabled persons from all aspects of the polity, social, economic, biological, cultural, epistemological, metaphysical, and political. This observation is found in disability scholarship from every discipline. As important as the hard-fought battles won by the DRM are, some scholars within the disability studies community still find the citizenship status of disabled people wanting, and rightly so. It is one thing to have a law on the books; it is quite another to see how that law becomes operationalized and interpreted in the courts. For instance, despite the intent to bring greater justice (and less discrimination) to the disability community, the ADA has been interpreted rather narrowly in the courts, and employers have won over 95 percent of the suits brought about under the act.[5] Furthermore, the difficulty of applying for and obtaining benefits from Social Security Disability Insurance (SSDI) and Supplemental Security Income (SSI), particularly when compared with the relative ease of applying for things like Social Security retirement benefits, give us reason to be suspicious whether the question of disabled citizenship is settled by law.[6] Richard Devlin and Dianne Pothier call this situation "dis-citizenship . . . a form of citizenship minus, a disabling citizenship" in which "many persons with disabilities are denied formal and/or substantive citizenship."[7] But in the process, disabled persons are also denied the informal hallmarks of citizenship; they are told that they do not belong. As disability historian Allison Carey puts it, they are "on the margins of citizenship."[8]

As feminists and critical race theorists have maintained, "citizenship" is a concept frequently designated for economically privileged white men. The concept revolves, too, around cultural perceptions and definitions of physical intactness. Citizenship has historically assumed "able-bodiness." This volume scrutinizes such an assumption by denaturalizing and problematizing both disability and citizenship simultaneously and examining the assumptions, fears, and prejudices that inform discriminatory practices in the first place. Drawing from a variety of disciplinary and interdisciplinary approaches, this collection of essays takes up an expanded notion of citizenship in order to better understand disability as an academic category of analysis, a lived experience, and a signifier of how membership and belonging are understood in societies invariably built on an imagined constituency of nondisabled persons.

Accordingly, for the most part, the chapters in this volume do not empirically explore various political practices of citizenship, such as voting, naturalization, or jury or military service, but rather examine the symbolic representations of what it means to "belong" as a disabled person within a political society in the Western context.[9] In this introductory essay, we aim to flesh out an enlarged notion of disability citizenship and provide readers with a guide to the essays that follow. To borrow from Mary Helen Washington's question about placing disability at the center of African American studies discourse, we ask: what does putting citizenship at the heart of disability studies—and the disabled subject at the heart of the concept of citizenship—"say about who is allowed to speak, who becomes representative, what is silenced or repressed, and finally who and what become the site of political resistance and value"?[10]

## Meanings of Disability, Meanings of Citizenship

To begin with, it is always important to note that neither citizenship nor disability is a static or universal concept. Readers new to disability will find a variety of definitions in any number of texts, ranging from the United Nations Convention on the Rights of Persons with Disabilities to activist websites to articles and books in a wide variety of academic disciplines. The authors of the essays in the present volume consider different specific instances of physical and intellectual disability, such as mobility impairment, blindness, deafness, tuberculosis, and cognitive and psychological impairment. So offering one overarching understanding of the concept may not be appropriate, and most of the essays here do not define what they mean by the term "disability." But all the authors—and indeed most disability scholars—subscribe to at least some form of the "social model of disability."[11] For readers new to disability studies, this model holds that disability is not a physical condition pertaining to a "defective" or "inferior" or "abnormal" body but rather a social condition brought about by social norms, practices, and beliefs; it is both socially produced and socially experienced. What makes something a disability is thus not bodily difference per se— not my impaired vision, or my deafness, or my weak or missing limbs, or my autism—but rather the social contexts in which they exist; disability is constituted by the interaction between environmental factors and the particularities of specific bodies. The fact that I have difficulty walking and use a wheelchair, for instance, does not in itself constitute a "disability": rather, the fact that most buildings have stairs rather than ramps and lack elevators and automatic doors is what disables my body from gaining access to the building. Because of the ways in which social relations, the built environment, laws, customs, and practices are structured and organized, certain bodies are disabled by those environments, while other bodies are facilitated and supported. "Impairment" is a term that refers to a natural part of biological life rather than an "abnormal" part and is generally incorporated into a person's sense of self. "Disability," by contrast, refers to what society, social conditions, prejudices, biases, and the built environment have produced by treating certain impairments as marks of inferiority. As

Devlin and Pothier put it, "Disability is not just an individual impairment but a systematically enforced pattern of exclusion."[12] "Disability" does not describe the body per se, but the body in a hostile social environment.

Among disability studies scholars, the social model has been an important corrective to the more dominant way of understanding disability, dubbed the "medical model," which views disability as a pathology found in a particular individual body that must be fixed or cured. Disability in this model is seen as both intrinsic to the body that "suffers" from it, which must be made to adapt to the preexisting environment; and simultaneously alien to the body, a hostile force that undermines the individual's true preferences. "The body" that is held up as the standard against which it is measured is what feminist disability scholar Rosemarie Garland-Thomson calls the "normate"—male, white, perfect in health and physical attributes, a standard that almost everyone fails to meet but nevertheless informs our assumptions about the body and how it should function in the world.[13]

The terms "social" and "medical" models are referred to throughout these essays, so the reader who is new to disability studies will want to keep this distinction in mind. For most disability scholars today, the social model is largely accepted as the preferred way of understanding disability, whereas the medical model tends to be disparaged. There are good historical reasons for this, particularly the poor treatment that persons with disabilities have often received at the hands of the medical community. The history of disability is one in which people with all sorts of impairments were institutionalized under deplorable conditions. Michel Foucault, for instance, tells us of "the great confinement" of the insane, a category that often included individuals with only physical impairments, starting in the seventeenth century in continental Europe.[14] Susan Schweik writes about nineteenth- and early twentieth-century U.S. "ugly laws" that prohibited disabled individuals from appearing in public, in part because of the belief that the well-to-do could not cope with the "horrors" of seeing "deformed" people on the street.[15] Many readers are familiar with twentieth-century horror stories like Willowbrook, the Staten Island institution for cognitively disabled children that kept them in such atrocious conditions that Senator Robert Kennedy called it a "snake pit."[16] Atrocities have continued in the twenty-first century; as recently as 2011, attendants at the Oswald D. Heck Developmental Center in New York regularly abused developmentally disabled residents and eventually killed a thirteen-year-old boy.[17]

Thus the medical model has not served disabled persons well. Increasing numbers of scholars, including some in this volume, believe that the medical model has something to offer; increasing numbers of scholars are now leaning toward a "hybrid" model.[18] But all disability scholars understand that the body's location in particular contexts of culture, language, law, politics, architecture, and custom always ensures that disability is socially constructed to a significant degree. The social model helps us recognize that the way society is organized and structured—its architecture, its values, its norms—helps turn the impairments some bodies experience into disabling conditions. But since society and social structures are always changing, disability must always change accordingly. In past times, moderate myopia could be severely disabling; now, eyeglasses are commonplace and even a fashion statement. Prosthetics and wheelchairs give amputees far greater mobility than in the past, and indeed in some cases, such as athletic competitions, such devices are seen as advantageous.[19] The variability of the physical conditions of disability, moreover, produces variability in how disability is seen, understood, and treated. Disability as a concept is something that has developed over time and continues to do so.

Similar variability characterizes the concept of citizenship. This might seem counterintuitive, for the concept of citizenship might seem to many, particularly from the United States and Western Europe, a fairly straightforward matter of deciding who is and who is not one. Many of us think of citizenship as individual rights conferred on us by a certain nation-state. Or, as sociologist T. H. Marshall put it, citizenship is "composed of the rights necessary for individual freedom—liberty of the person, freedom of speech, thought and faith, the right to own property and to conclude valid contracts, and the right to justice."[20] Because we often take citizenship to be defined by a circumscribed nation-state, the notion becomes almost indistinguishable from national identity.

Citizenship thus usually entails an attachment to a specific locality; we are citizens *of* something, generally a nation, but alternatively (or at the same time) of states, cities, towns, or even organizations.[21] But as Willem Maas observes, we live a "multilevel citizenship" on "nested and overlapping geographical levels: citizenship not only of the state but also of substate, suprastate, or nonstate political communities."[22] Indeed, citizenship is often applied to communities that are arguably apolitical. People who are considered "good citizens" include colleagues who are conscientious about service on university committees, neighbors involved in civic boosterism and civic pride in our local town or borough, and parents who help out in the local public schools and coach local sports teams. Citizenship implies belonging to a group, society, and culture: our neighbors, the parents of our children's classmates, the congregants of our churches, or the residents of our towns, our counties, our states, and our nation.

Such varieties of belonging already suggest that citizenship is not as simple and straightforward as some might think. And even the mainstream definition is complicated by the fact that people can be citizens of more than one state at a time, or of states and federations, such as the European Union or, indeed, the United States, where we are citizens of states and of the nation. Legal theorist Linda Bosniak calls citizenship "multivalent," containing "a basic ethical ambiguity" between aspirations of inclusion and realities of exclusion.[23] Lauren Berlant maintains that "citizenship is a status whose definitions are always in process."[24] Legal theorists Linda McClain and Joanna Grossman similarly view "citizenship as a non-unitary and evolving concept."[25] This can lead to a great deal of vagueness in how the term is used—sometimes as a synonym for "human being," sometimes as a stand-in for "local resident," and sometimes as a more specific legal category. Disability scholars Marcia Rioux and Fraser Valentine note that citizenship is "a messy concept" that "constructs a system of inclusion and exclusion, defining boundaries between who belongs and who does not, who enjoys the privileges (and duties) associated with membership and who is denied such privileges."[26] Hence "citizenship" as a term in both everyday language and scholarly discourse often holds a much broader meaning than the narrow confines of voting, military service, paying taxes, or even jury service. As philosopher Marilyn Friedman notes, "Citizenship is multiple and various. It can be an identity; a set of rights, privileges, and duties; an elevated and exclusionary political status; a relationship between individuals and their states; a set of practices that can unify—or divide—the members of a political community; and an ideal of political agency."[27] Supreme Court justice Ruth Bader Ginsburg noted in *United States v. Virginia* that "full citizenship stature" for all people entails "equal opportunity to aspire, achieve, participate in and contribute to society based on their individual talents and capacities."[28] These views are echoed by disability scholar Michael Prince, who maintains that "citizenship goes well beyond legal and governmental conceptions to embrace economic and sociological notions of participation, reciprocity, and autonomy"; it is constituted by "full membership in communities."[29] Indeed, community is vitally important to citizenship, particularly from a disability perspective. As T. H. Marshall notes, "There is a kind of basic human equality associated with the concept of full membership of a community—or . . . citizenship. . . . Citizenship requires . . . a direct sense of community membership based on loyalty to a civilization which is a common possession."[30]

But citizenship can also be a force that marginalizes some members and thus damages a genuine sense of community, setting up a dichotomy between a privileged class that grants citizenship and a subservient class on which this status may or may not be conferred. In the United States, as in many Western nations, white, Anglo-Saxon, property-owning men have often considered themselves the ones in charge of granting such status. Men bearing full rights of citizenship have been generally nondisabled as well, with the ambiguous exception of disabled war veterans, who are at once lauded as heroes and simultaneously pushed aside by an unaccommodating society.[31]

Even under a purely legalistic definition of citizenship, however, many of these de facto exclusions are not legitimate. Consider, for instance, that under the Fourteenth Amendment of the U.S. Constitution, "All persons born or naturalized in the United States, and subject to the jurisdiction thereof, are citizens of the United States and of the State wherein they reside."[32] Yet as the history of women's citizenship and the citizenship of racial minorities in the United States and Europe have shown, the legal doctrine of citizenship is often not enough to secure rights, and being "born" within certain geographic boundaries also is often not enough. (We set aside the naturalization clause because certain racial minorities were often excluded from naturalization, and disabled persons have been denied the right even to enter the United States, much less naturalize, as Douglas Baynton's essay in this volume shows.) Scholars in women's and African American studies have demonstrated that the technical designation "citizen" has done little to protect minority groups from having certain privileges inherent in their citizenship status denied. For instance, the Fourteenth Amendment legally designated women citizens as long as they were born in the United States, but it was another sixty-one years before they could vote, and even longer before they could universally serve on juries or in the military. They could even lose their citizenship by marrying non-American men, although men marrying foreign women did not lose theirs.[33] Similarly, although the Thirteenth and Fifteenth Amendments ended slavery and granted black men the franchise, gross discrimination continued under Reconstruction, and "separate but equal" became the law of the land in 1896, along with various pragmatic restrictions on black suffrage, such as "literacy tests," which began in the 1890s and continued through the 1960s, given disproportionately to blacks.[34] Recent voter-identification laws in various states similarly may hinder racial minorities from voting.

Scholars who study the history and theory of citizenship among these minority groups often refer to their status as that of "second-class citizenship," a term that refers to the discrepancy between theory and practice, as well as law and right. Women and African Americans had long been citizens "on the books," but for over a century they were not really treated as such. Their citizenship was—and arguably still is—ineffectual, for their political power and action always paled in comparison with those of the ideal Anglo-Saxon, male citizen.[35]

Throughout most of Western history, disabled people have also been treated as second-class citizens. Going further, we might suggest that disabled persons are perhaps even third-class citizens, for disability has historically served as a justification to deny the privileges of citizenship to both African Americans and women. Helen Meekosha and Leanne Dowse maintain that "the concept of a disabled citizen could be described as a contradiction in terms" because, as historian Douglas Baynton writes, "the *concept* of disability has been used to justify discrimination against other groups by attributing disability to them."[36] For example, antisuffragists prohibited women from voting because of the supposed innate "defects" of the female mind. Similarly, from slavery to Jim Crow laws to Hernstein and Murray's infamous book *The Bell Curve*, which was taken to suggest a possible genetic racial difference in intelligence, people have insisted that African Americans were inferior to whites, and that by virtue of their race, blacks were intellectually and morally disabled.[37] But suffragists and abolitionists rarely "challenged the notion that disability justified political inequality."[38] Instead, they put most of their political effort into disassociating themselves from the disabled, those they termed "defective," and "crippled." For much of American history, both the socially advantaged *and* the socially disadvantaged ostracized disabled people, making them the most marginalized of all minority groups.

This may be why disability was not covered in the 1964 Civil Rights Act; as Michael Bérubé reminds us, disability rights were seen as a "dilution of civil rights, on the grounds that people with disabilities were constitutively incompetent, whereas women and [racial] minorities faced discrimination merely on the basis of social prejudice."[39] Anita Silvers explains it the following way: "To make disability a category that activates a heightened legal shield against exclusion, it was argued, would alter the purpose of legal protection for civil rights by transforming the goal from protecting opportunity for socially exploited people to providing assistance to naturally unfit people."[40]

This history of exclusion has meant that disability has had a complicated and ambiguous status within the concept of citizenship. We seek an enlarged conception of citizenship to address this. Citizenship is a matter of entitlement, obligation, and belonging. Domenico Losurdo argues that the struggle to enlarge the notion of citizenship in the modern era has been tied up with the struggle to recognize the humanity of propertyless men, women, and racial minorities.[41] We share that aspiration for disabled persons and believe that this enlarged notion of citizenship intertwines the political and the social, legal status and human status. A citizen is someone who belongs to a particular group—whether a nation or other polity, organization, or community—and has certain entitlements and obligations thereby. The entitlements, though, are both a function and a means of the belonging. Thus denying those entitlements does more than take away an immediate good that the entitlement provides, such as income, education, or suffrage; it also takes away the belonging itself. Such denial is a signal of exclusion, an indication that you are not just different from others but an outsider, inferior, less than a citizen, even less than human. It is this denial and exclusion that disability scholars and activists seek to reject. We believe that this rejection entails an enlarged understanding of citizenship.

## Civil Disabilities: Membership and Belonging

The aspiration for an enlarged understanding of citizenship is central to the title of our book, *Civil Disabilities*. The term "civil" has multiple layers of meaning, ranging from those pertaining explicitly to legal categories of citizenship (particularly civil rights and civic association) to notions of politeness and consideration (civility, keeping a civil tongue in your head) and to colonialist discourses that disparage colonized cultures (as "barbaric" rather than "civilized"). It is one of those words in the English lexicon that evades a simple meaning, and that ambiguity pervades this volume in what we believe is a productive way. It signals that the legal conception of citizenship is insufficient for key purposes, albeit an important part of the disability story.

But "civil disobedience" is the phrase that our title most calls to mind, and Martin Luther King, Jr.'s famous "Letter from Birmingham City Jail" perhaps best captures the sense of the term we intend. For the reasons we expressed earlier, and that Silvers and others have pointed out, we are not suggesting that a direct analogy be made between black civil rights and that of disability rights—the former movement rejected images of disability and thus further stigmatized disabled citizens in its own struggle for citizenship status.[42] But King's essay offers a particular formulation of civil society and citizenship that we believe is useful for disability and is at least tacitly employed by the essays in this volume. (From a disability perspective, it may be particularly significant that for King, civil disobedience entails using "our very bodies as a means of laying our case before the conscience of the local and national community," because that is an inescapable part of disability claims for citizenship and membership. It is precisely the "differences" our bodies present that seem to make the struggle necessary in the first place.)[43] King shares with other theories of civil disobedience a challenge to state power and state authority at specific sites: the standard civil disobedience view is that the disobedience pertains to an unjust law, but not necessarily to an unjust regime. Indeed, part of the logic of civil disobedience entails a tacit recognition of the state's authority to punish one for one's transgression, "to arouse the conscience of the community over its injustice," as King put it.[44] In this sense, civil disobedience pertains to citizenship in the legal meaning.

But it also goes well beyond that aspect, particularly expressed by King, for acts of civil disobedience are also rebukes to the injustice of social relations. For instance, African Americans sitting at a "whites-only" lunch counter were claiming that they were entitled to equal protection of the law, that public establishments were not justified in having "whites-only" seating. But they were also making claims for humanity; they were saying that blacks were people, too, entitled to the same basic courtesies and recognition as white persons. As King noted, the actions of civil disobedience were meant to point out the ways in which the "I-thou" relationship was unsettled. By this he meant that the claim for recognition is a claim not just for legal rights of citizenship but also for humanity, for the recognition that I am here, that I belong, and you must recognize me as such. "We are caught in an inescapable network of mutuality, tied in a single garment of destiny," King noted. Indeed, at one point he even seemed to overturn the traditional notion of citizenship altogether when he said that "anyone who lives inside the United States"—thereby (perhaps unintentionally) including immigrants and others legally designated noncitizens—"can never be considered an outsider anywhere in this country." Rejecting "anything less than brotherhood," King centrally deployed notions of care for others, relationship, and community in the struggle for rights of citizenship.[45]

This intertwining of one's humanity and one's citizenship in the notions of community, membership, and belonging that we find in King's famous "Letter" are also central to one of the foundational texts in disability rights, Jacobus tenBroek's landmark 1966 article "The Right to Live in the World: The Disabled and the Law of Torts." One of America's earliest disability activists and academics and a leading expert in constitutional law, tenBroek challenged policy makers and legal scholars to give precedence to the blind, disabled body when they were considering civil rights and liberties.[46] Early in the essay he approvingly quoted a report from the U.S. House Judiciary Committee that "the badge of citizenship . . . demands that establishments that do public business for private profit not discriminate," as well as an amendment to the Vocational Rehabilitation Act that was "to provide the physically and mentally disabled persons of this Nation an improved and expanded program of services which will result in greater opportunities for them to more fully enter into the life of our country as active participating citizens."[47] Central to his argument is a critique of the ways in which most conceptions of citizenship (wrongly) assumed a kind of able-bodiedness that a significant part of the population did not and does not possess. Disabled persons, he argued, were not seen as "belonging" to the polity; their membership was compromised, as "crippled" (his term) as their bodies.

TenBroek's powerful and passionate challenge to the systematic marginalization of the blind entailed a claim not only for citizenship but also for full humanity for all disabled persons. Throughout the article, he intertwined his theory of citizenship with terms such as "human endeavor," "human dignity," and "human rights," asking, "Are persons after all not to be persons if they are physically disabled?"[48] Much as in the case of King, this was due to the context in which he wrote. Although the Social Security Act had been passed and various federal programs of vocational rehabilitation had been secured, tenBroek maintained that such laws were often ignored and, even when recognized, did not adequately address the needs of disabled persons.[49] Thus despite some advances in disability employment, tenBroek pointed out that blind Americans subsisted in a chronic state of destitution.[50] His focus on the "humanity" of disabled persons was thus an early recognition that for disabled persons, like all other excluded groups who have struggled to assert their membership and belonging in the American polity, such as African Americans and women, the call for recognition of our humanity is a call for "citizenship" in the enlarged sense.

Our invocation of the inspirational legacies of tenBroek and King does not lead us to be overly sanguine about what can be concretely achieved by the expanded notion of citizenship as membership and belonging that we are advocating here. Berlant argues that it is not simply a struggle for disabled persons to be included in an "us too" frame of mind. As she notes, citizenship has entered into a variety of areas that were heretofore not seen as public, with both good and bad results.[51] Such cautionary notes are all too familiar to disabled citizens who apply for SSI or SSDI, which require burdensome applications and state surveillance (although it is arguable that the situation is considerably better in other parts of the world, such as Scandanavia).[52] In the United States, at least, such benefits look less like what Marshall called a "social right" and much more like a charitable benefit administered by a suspicious and begrudging state. As Marshall noted about social rights in Europe as they emerged out of various poor laws, they were treated "not as an integral part of the rights of the citizen, but as an alternative to them—as claims which could be met only if the claimants ceased to be citizens in any true sense of the word."[53] Disabled persons are in many ways what Iris Young calls "subordinate citizens" because "through the logic of protection, the state demotes members of a democracy to dependents."[54]

Yet what Grossman and McClain call an "aspirational conception of citizenship" is relevant to disability struggles, for it "includes the complete rights, benefits, duties, and obligations that members of any society expect to share and aspires to goals of inclusion, belonging, participation, and civic membership."[55] Thus our focus on belonging and humanity is never entirely removed from law and rights. The economic rights of subsistence income and health care, along with the rights to work and to access all built environments (including polling stations), are what Marshall called social rights. These rights "range from the modicum of economic welfare and security to the right to share to the full in the social heritage and to live the life of a civilized being according to the standards prevailing in the society"—an account remarkably similar to Jacobus tenBroek's notion of "a right to live in the world."[56] Marshall's concept of "social citizenship" is "aspirational" in Grossman and McClain's sense precisely because it seeks to expand the concept of citizenship beyond strictly political rights to a broader set of rights that recognize our mutual embeddedness in larger social relations, not to mention the intertwining of politics with ethics, economics, and social status.[57] These social rights extend beyond the legal protections of due process to issues concerning economic welfare, such as employment legislation, social insurance, and health care, all of which have provided the foundation for various forms of disability accommodation, particularly those relating to subsistence income and the replacement of lost wages due to injury and disability. As Canadian disability scholar Michael Prince notes, such "income security programs and the tax system can be concrete expressions of social citizenship."[58]

Thus we maintain that the argument for citizenship and the argument for recognition of the full humanity of disabled persons—as workers, as members of families, as members of communities—are intimately related.[59] The late feminist philosopher Iris Young contended that "respecting individuals as full citizens means granting and fostering in them liberties and capacities to be autonomous—to choose their own ends and develop their own opinions. It also means protecting them from the tyranny of those who might try to determine those choices and opinions because they control resources on which citizens depend for their living."[60] Similarly, feminist disability scholar and activist Jenny Morris argues:

> Unless we have entitlements to action and resources to tackle these disabling barriers, we cannot achieve equality. . . . All of this is tied up with our right to exist. . . . If non-disabled people do accept our right to exist then they should also accept our common humanity and therefore our right to equality—as citizens and as human beings. We can't get equality or a good quality of life unless we are given entitlements to different treatment—to changes and resources which enable us to get equal access—to jobs, to housing, to leisure and political activities, and so on.[61]

For Morris and Young, the rights of citizenship are intrinsically tied up with one's claim to humanity; they are connected to one's status as a person, to one's very right to exist.

## Chapter Outline

It is this broader understanding of citizenship in terms of membership and belonging that we deploy in this book, and it is demonstrated, illustrated, drawn on, and referred to throughout the various essays in the volume. Some essays deploy obvious citizen tropes, such as the soldier disabled in the service of his or her country. Others talk about political mobilization, the representation of interests, officeholding, immigration, and identity politics. But most essays in this volume are concerned with the struggles of disabled persons to be recognized as members of their societies in the larger sense: entitled not just to the kinds of legal rights that tenBroek articulated in his expanded conception of civil rights, and not just the social and economic services that Marshall labeled "social rights," but to be accepted as members with a stake in our society, a right to claim that stake, and a right to be heard about their vision of what that stake entails—indeed, a right to be seen and treated as human beings.

The theme of citizenship must also be situated within the strong interdisciplinarity of this volume, which contains contributions from scholars of anthropology, English, history, history of science, music, philosophy, political science, and sociology. Part of the strength of the volume, we believe, is seeing how the issues and themes of disability and citizenship are developed differently by different disciplines and in different subject matters; the essays discuss archival research, biography, music, and film, as well as abstract theoretical texts. Thus structuring these essays in a particular order can take on a slightly random quality because any of the essays could go before any of the others with similar results. Readers should thus not feel bound by our ordering but should feel free to dip into whatever essay first captures their attention, knowing that whatever they choose next will deepen and complement the one preceding it.

Nevertheless, the job of editor requires us to order the essays, and we do so by following a narrative that moves from essays that highlight modes of exclusion and dehumanization to those that focus on strategies of inclusion and recognition. We start with Susan Schweik's essay, "Homer's Odyssey:

Multiple Disabilities and *The Best Years of Our Lives*," which digs below the surface of the highly acclaimed film to show how the double-amputee character Homer Parrish was made possible only through the "denial of politics," glossing over the reality that most disabled veterans deal with multiple disabilities. Focusing on the original book and screenplay on which the film was based, Schweik juxtaposes the "original" Homer with the filmic Homer. The original, textually based Homer sustained a traumatic brain injury and came home a "gargoyle of human form" who drooled, twitched uncontrollably, and demonstrated erratic behavior. Hollywood film producers and directors believed that American audiences could not bear such a sight, so they created the filmic Homer, a double amputee who could be easily "fixed" with a pair of prosthetic arms. Although often prized as a realistic film, *Best Years* in many ways denied the realities of wartime disability and, under the guise of inclusion and tropes of wartime heroism, excluded the realities of GI protests and rioting against housing conditions. Indeed, it may perhaps be a signature hallmark of disabled citizenship that the disabled soldier is simultaneously marked as a civil being and as the excluded other.

Ostensibly at the opposite pole from military veterans, one of the most obvious ways in which citizenship and inclusion have been regulated and surveilled is immigration. Douglas Baynton's essay, "Defect: A Selective Reinterpretation of American Immigration History," shows that disabled persons have been repeatedly denied entrance to the United States since the late nineteenth century. Immigration officials feared that blind, deaf, and "feebleminded" persons would be unemployable and thus likely to become economically dependent on the state. Baynton demonstrates, however, that many "defective" immigrants seeking to gain entrance to the United States enjoyed gainful employment in their home countries. Moreover, by taking disability as his primary analytic category for understanding immigration history, Baynton demonstrates a continuity in the history of immigration restrictions whereby physical and mental disability cuts across considerations of race, class, and gender and thereby becomes one of the most enduring and long-standing reasons for prohibiting entry into the United States. From this perspective, disability is a meta-analytic category by which to understand how citizenship is conferred and performed, as well as how civic exclusion is enacted.

In "The Disremembered Past," Susan Burch and Hannah Joyner revisit their previous work on the life of Junius Wilson, an African American man treated as a "lunatic" because of his deafness, wrongfully convicted of rape, and forcibly sterilized by castration at the age of twenty-three. The layers of exclusion in Wilson's life—from legal rights and protections, from intelligible communication with others, from bodily integrity—suggest the depth of the problems of citizenship within the history of disability, particularly when it is compounded by other categories of exclusion, such as race and class. Moreover, they suggest that "identifying" disability is itself an act of exclusion and show just how difficult it may be to establish a well-defined disability identity, so that certain individuals may be excluded from the political potential of disability identity altogether. More specifically, they point out that those who define identity in Deaf culture, for instance, have usually been European, white Americans.

These insights from Burch and Joyner lead us to turn from the documentation of exclusion to the struggle for inclusion, a theme central to Beth Linker and Emily Abel's "Integrating Disability, Transforming Disease History: Tuberculosis and Its Past." They explore the history of tuberculosis, long considered solely a disease within the medical sciences and humanities, and provide an account of how tuberculosis was understood to be a disability. But although abundant primary source records show how tuberculosis was categorized as a disability and recognized as such by the U.S. social welfare state, researchers have not considered the condition in this light because in the economy of medical and other forms of academic research, disease studies have enjoyed a privileged status over disability studies. As a result, those disabled by tuberculosis have been written out of disability and science studies almost entirely. But tuberculars frequently suffered from the same discrimination that people with other disabilities experienced, such as employment discrimination and stigma. The failure to understand the disability status of tuberculosis within various realms of academic scholarship further signals the troubled relationship between illness and disability more broadly.

The effort to include tuberculosis and other illnesses within the category of disability signals the thematic challenge of including disabled persons within larger communities, a subject similarly taken up by Faye Ginsburg and Rayna Rapp. Their essay, "Screening Disabilities: Visual Fields, Public Culture, and the Atypical Mind in the Twenty-First Century," in particular echoes the theme we have stressed here that citizenship must be understood culturally and socially, not just politically or legally, and so we must look in nontraditional places, such as the media, for involvement of disabled persons as citizens. They maintain that despite advances in disability rights over the past half century, most media outlets still exclude the disabled from public view. In their estimation, media representation is as vital as political representation to the fight for inclusion—and indeed is perhaps its foundation. They reveal the ways in which disability activists have attempted to scale up the media presence of the disabled in order not only to forge media-based kinship networks but also to challenge the ideas of normalcy on which notions of citizenship, personal value, and worth are based.

Alex Lubet moves us from film to music to demonstrate a different struggle for inclusion in "Social Confluence and Citizenship: A View from the Intersection of Music and Disability." Describing music cultures as "governments" with norms and rules that govern performance and self-presentation, Lubet shows how disabled performers have been excluded from musical performance and have struggled creatively to include themselves. By operating within different "social confluences" of musical norms, combined with physical ability, along with gender and race, different individuals' disabilities resulted in different relations to musical performance and different statuses of "musical citizenship." Comparing the stories of performers in the established domain of classical music, where the norms of performance are given and strict, with other genres, like jazz, that are more open to improvisation, Lubet shows that the norms of different genres of music create different possibilities for participation. For instance, whereas guitarist Django Reinhardt could develop an entire style of music that accommodated his disability, adapting his musical performance to his body, pianist Leon Fleisher had to find piano pieces for one hand, adapting his disability and his body to the requirements of classical music. Adding other factors of bodily presentment, such as gender, creates both marked and subtle differences in the "privileges of participation and level of inclusion."

The problems of and struggle for inclusion in these essays lead us to questions about the duality of inclusion and exclusion, a theme particularly prominent in essays by Catherine Kudlick and Allison Carey. Kudlick's "Our Ancestors, the Sighted: Making Blind People French and French People Blind, 1750–1991" explores the ways in which national and disability identity have intertwined in French history. She compares a late twentieth-century book on architecture for vision-impaired persons with an eighteenth-century Enlightenment text to consider both the nationalizing, and possibly colonizing, effort "to make the blind French," enabling them to appreciate the beauty of France's monuments and architecture, and the reciprocal effort "to make the French blind," to open up the understanding of sighted people to blind experience and to recognize their membership in French society. The former effort presumed an ideology of assimilation and sameness, following colonialist ideologies; like immigrants, blind persons needed to learn French culture in order to claim their status as citizens (or at least potential citizens). By contrast, the latter effort required attention to difference, celebrating the universal individualism, freedom, and equality of the Enlightenment. In uncovering the oppositional tensions in these seemingly parallel goals and placing blind people within the lexicon of nationalism and colonialism, Kudlick shows that efforts at inclusion are often accompanied by their political opposite, new forms of exclusion.

The dualism of inclusion and exclusion is further illustrated in Allison Carey's "Citizenship and the Family: Parents of Children with Disabilities, the Pursuit of Rights, and Paternalism." Focusing on parents of children with disabilities, Carey theorizes rights as relational and stresses the need to think of parental rights in relation to individual rights of disabled persons. Although able-bodied parents themselves—particularly if they are white, middle class, and heterosexual—do not usually have a contested relationship with citizenship, they must negotiate hostile laws, policies, and built environments on behalf of their children. Carey shows how parents negotiate this citizen/noncitizen tension by actively agitating for laws and social policies that secure rights for their children but also empower them as parents by further weakening their children's independent status. She notes that parents' claims for rights depend both on the citizenship status of their children, in claiming that society has obligations to help them care for these members of society, and on the denial of that status under the rubric of family privacy. The citizenship status of their children, accordingly, is constantly in flux, dependent on the strategies that their parents pursue.

These insights into the interrelationship of inclusion and exclusion lead us to the final essays in the volume, which take up different strategies for political and ethical inclusion of disabled subjects within the polity, within society, and within our understanding of "the human." Whereas Carey, like Ginsburg and Rapp, considers disability rights, Lorella Terzi in "Cognitive Disability, Capability Equality, and Citizenship" considers the duties that society and the able-bodied have toward disabled persons. Duties and rights are complementary in ethical and political philosophy; if I have a right to $x$, you have a duty not to interfere with my $x$, and the state may have a duty to foster $x$. Terzi considers this a "matter of justice." Focusing on the capabilities approach developed by Amartya Sen as an ethical framework for fighting extreme poverty in India, Terzi explores the ways in which debates over resource allocation to disabled persons are distorted by focusing on outcome equality—often impossible to achieve, thereby making claims dismissible—instead of "capability equality." Persons with cognitive disabilities pose a particular challenge because such persons are unable to participate in rational democratic deliberation. By seeing that disability is not just social but relational, constituted by the ways impairments are affected by contextual circumstances, the capabilities approach opens up participation to a more diverse realm that includes the use of surrogates and advocates. The use of "capabilities" to supplant and supplement "abilities" thereby has the potential to transform our understanding of "disability" as an ethical, linguistic, social, and political category of meaning and to enlarge our understanding and appreciation of the idea of "citizenship."

Nancy Hirschmann also takes up such enlargement in "Invisible Disability: Seeing, Being, Power." Hirschmann treats "invisible disability," a term more commonly used in reference to disabilities that are "hidden," such as dyslexia, as an interpretive device for understanding disability as a concept. She theorizes a variety of ways in which disabilities are made invisible, ranging from institutionalization to disbelief that a disability exists to the silencing of political voice. These various modes of invisibility affect the citizenship status of disabled persons in different ways, ranging from their literal exclusion from public debate and participation to the absence of disability perspectives in public and social policies. She considers whether invisibility can offer a subversive potential to reclaim citizenship. Recognizing the ambiguities and tensions of such a strategy, Hirschmann suggests that the civic status of the unseen and the unsettling ambiguity and anxiety that "passing" often generates can provide fruitful openings for shifting public discourse on and awareness of disability. When disability is invisible, the struggle for recognition takes on added complexity: on whose terms should the disabled be recognized?

Following up on Hirschmann's call for subversive political action, Tobin Siebers makes his own call for a return to identity politics in "Disability Trouble." Although "identity politics" is considered passé in some academic circles, Siebers's analysis of various critiques of identity politics finds in them not just hostility to disabled persons but a more metaphysical understanding of the ways in which "disability" is deployed as a metaphor and symbol for any sort of socially defined inferiority, such as gender, race, or sexuality. The only way not to be considered disabled, Siebers suggests—and hence the only way to be considered a deserving member of the political community—is to adhere to supposed "truths" about the nature of man, equality, freedom, and justice. In highlighting the hypocrisy of the rejection of identity as a viable political category, Siebers suggests that hostility to disability not only underlies hostility to other minority categories but also is so profoundly normalized that even members of those groups do not recognize it but instead participate in the exclusion of disability and disabled persons. Noting that identity politics is not just about "appreciating diversity" but about "changing the material and social conditions," Siebers argues that claims of citizenship go beyond the tokenism of passively "including" bodies and faces of different types to the active production of policies and laws that respond to the needs of individuals who are socially situated in positions of structural inequality.

These last three essays deploy theoretical categories, methodologies, and strategies most directly, but all the essays contribute to the theoretical project of contesting our understanding of disability and how it is and should be thought about in the context of an ableist world. The valuing or disvaluing of disabled bodies, the way such bodies are defined and classified, and the relationship of disabled bodies to rights and duties all contribute to our understanding of whether and how disabled persons are citizens, and how the concept of citizenship itself is affected when we make explicit acknowledgment of disability as a category for inclusion. The ways in which resources should be distributed, the physical landscape should be shaped, laws and policies should be written, court cases should be decided, moral philosophies should be developed, and theoretical categories should be imagined are all important contributors to a disability theory of citizenship based on the inclusion of bodily difference in the political, moral, and theoretical landscape. Although the present volume hardly develops a definitive view of disability citizenship, we hope that the essays presented here will spark ideas and suggestions in readers who will continue the project of fighting for a world in which disability is, after all, just another difference.

## CHAPTER 1

# Homer's Odyssey: Multiple Disability and *The Best Years of Our Lives*

Susan M. Schweik

"Multiple disabilities." Sometimes the phrase stands in for what otherwise gets called "severe disability." Always it indicates variety and combination. Usually it refers to qualities that are located in an individual body. My subject here is disability in representation, which is invariably a case of multiple disabilities. An impairment may be narrow and distinct. Think, say, of someone who has difficulty blinking. But disability never happens in the blink of an eye. Its effects are social, sustained, and intricate. Then, in the process of representation, from creation to reception, disability stories pile up and mix up; one story is brought to the creation or reception of another, one story inflects another, and, significantly, one story buries another. In any disability story there are many disability stories.

Everyone in the field of disability studies struggles to define disability, sometimes hoping that the plural "disabilities" will erase this need. But what happens when we interrogate how disability studies has used the plural? In this essay, I model a historical method for reading disability multiplicity, showing, in one example, how disability's ramifications extend into realms we label not only with the word "disability" but also with words such as "race," "class," "sexuality," and "gender." I will examine a linked series of texts that make use of disability as a narrative resource, demonstrating how these instances are embedded in very particular social networks of disability; each distinct network is formed out of close relations, connected to many other disability stories not just proximately but intimately. The interactions and intersections within these networks are not neutral; they are governed by power relations that allow some stories to be construed and some to be consigned to the archives of the misconstrued. But all of them are productive and exert their effects, either directly or deep in the warp of better-known texts.

The point of this exercise is not to bring to light better, more effective, more realistic, or more positive disability stories. To move from a single text and a single form or genre into a surrounding welter of stories is to move further and further away from clarity of pathos and prosthesis and to allow more fully for an embrace of what has been unassimilable, what has been confounding, what has been messy, what has been disabling in disability.[1] We have long and rightly objected to the sheer negativity in that word "severe" in the phrase "severe disability." But it may be useful to pursue a severe disability studies, one in which disability cannot be contained and appears in greater degrees. It may be useful to get even more multiple.

I will illustrate what I mean with an example from a text in which one of the most celebrated, singular characters in the history of disability performance appears: William Wyler's famous film of 1946, *The Best Years of Our Lives*. The history of *Best Years* provides a telling instance of how, in the course of representation, even representation under the aegis of disability studies, rich ecologies of disability can get winnowed down to one node only—to a single identified error, its lessons, and its fix.

Like many representations of returning U.S. veterans around 1946, *The Best Years of Our Lives* distributes disability among multiple characters.[2] We are briefly told in the film, for instance, that one of the three leading characters, Fred, was seriously injured overseas, and he is obviously traumatized.[3] But when the word "disability" appears near a reference to *The Best Years of Our Lives*, undoubtedly what immediately comes to mind is the spectacular disability of the man who played Homer, Harold Russell, a veteran bilateral hand amputee who was not a professional actor and who won two Oscars for his performance. After appearing in *Best Years*, Russell went on to become the leader of various veterans' organizations and chair of the President's Committee on Employment of the Handicapped.

*The Best Years of Our Lives* is what David Gerber calls a "reintegration drama," emerging as Americans worked through problems of the reintroduction of U.S. World War II veterans into civil society. Well over a million men had returned home from the war disabled in some form.[4] The broader problems, intertwined with disability in every way, were economic and structural. "As historians have documented," writes Sarah Kozloff, "overall the US government had learned from its disastrous handling of World War I veterans, when unemployment and homelessness culminated in 17,000 angry ex-servicemen camping out in Washington, DC in the 1932 Bonus March."[5] So 1944 saw the passage of the GI Bill of Rights, with its promise of better access to schooling and housing, and in the year before *Best Years* Congress was debating the Full Employment Act, guaranteeing veterans jobs. But that legislation passed only in a much-weakened version. "By October 1946," Kozloff writes, "when *Best Years* was in post-production, veterans accounted for half of the country's unemployed."[6] Harold Russell was chosen for this famous reintegration drama because of his already spectacular vocational adjustment; he had been the star of an in-house military rehab film made to inspire other disabled servicemen, the model for how not to give in to or to be the veteran problem.

The key disability studies analyses of this film come from David Gerber, in two important articles from the early 1990s, both of which center on Harold Russell's Homer and point out a key paradox. "Anger and Affability" (1993) examines how the character Homer's moments of melodramatic screen rage contrast with (but also give voice to the anger of) the relatively unruffled and matter-of-fact real-life public figure Harold Russell. A year later, Gerber returned to the subject and complicated the axis of anger and affability in a broader cultural register, exploring how the Homer who works in the service of veteran uplift (comes to terms, marries the girl next door, and so forth) also "personifies all the anxious projections about veterans. In developing the underside of Homer's character, Wyler was willing to exploit both the able-bodied audience's body anxieties and the well-established cultural archetypes of the physically disabled as freakish and menacing."[7]

Gerber's 1990s readings were contemporaneous with Kaja Silverman's psychoanalytic analysis in her *Male Subjectivity at the Margins*. Silverman read *The Best Years of Our Lives* in the context of other 1940s returned-vet films as texts of extreme dislocation that focus "obsessively and sometimes erotically on the physical and psychic mutilation of . . . veterans," emphasizing "male castration at the expense of the dominant fiction" and showing "sacrifice to be the inevitable price of all subjectivity."[8] Her analysis extended broadly, but like Gerber, she placed strong focus on Russell's character, Homer Parrish.

As Michael Anderegg has noted, Wyler's filmmaking routes audience attention to more general and sometimes less visible problems of veteran subjectivity through concentration on Homer. For instance, "Wyler films the scene where Homer recounts to the others how he lost his hands in a single take, keeping the three men together in a frame so that Homer's accident expands to become a communal experience, his physical mutilation only an overt sign of the psychological wounds they all share."[9] The delicate balance between group solidarity and Homer's intensely dramatic particularity had to be carefully negotiated; experienced star Fredric March objected that Harold Russell's hooks were stealing scenes.[10] It is primarily through the drama of Homer that disability in the film hits home.

As Beth Linker has demonstrated in *War's Waste*, this focus on the amputee was a very well-established strategy by the time of World War II. Linker makes clear that in modern rehabilitation culture as it evolved in the United States during and after World War I, amputees have been the gold standard for rehabilitative care, privileged models for successful renormalization and reintegration. For instance, Linker shows how U.S. presidents have always preferred to have their photographs taken with amputee soldiers rather than any other disabled veteran group; these photo ops, she argues, make for reassuring media stories about how war injuries can be fixed, elided, and forgotten. Such photo ops (and rehabilitation itself) also give legitimacy to the war machine: the United States can keep declaring war because, with the triumphs and miracles of rehabilitative medicine and technology, there appears to be no human cost for the citizens fighting the war.[11]

But in any disability story there are many disability stories. Other stories form a kind of band of brother plots or a narrative genealogy for *The Best Years of Our Lives*—a closer social network, and a more complex one, than the group of parallel returned-vet films with which *Best Years* is usually compared. They include two stories of "spasticity," one about a drooling, brain-injured veteran and one about a famous doctor. They also include stories of a scientist after a stroke, of a man's desire for other men, of strikes and demonstrations, of antiracist struggle, of disability organizing, and of a woman reading.

David Gerber has documented how William Wyler's interpretation of the character of Homer was negotiated with the actor, Harold Russell. The interactive, improvisatory process they developed included regular meetings to discuss the script development of Homer's character and, later, long closed-set rehearsals of critical scenes, with Russell playing a key role in the conversations that shaped the final product.[12] At the same time, as Gerber shows, Wyler pushed back on Russell, asking that he portray a character different from his own conception and performance of himself or Homer. At one point, the director "grew so impatient with Russell's problems portraying anger, confusion, and passivity that he actually threatened to require Russell to spend two weeks at a military hospital, where it was assumed that soon he would become bitter and miserable."[13] This complex dynamic between Wyler and Russell provides our starting point. Where else does Homer come from?

## MacKinlay Kantor

In November 1946, writer MacKinlay Kantor, seeking his share of credit for the success of *The Best Years of Our Lives*, published a piece in the *New York Herald Tribune* titled "Kantor Says Ex-G.I.'s Transmute His War Novel to Film Perfectly."[14] Kantor had been commissioned by Samuel Goldwyn to write a treatment for a film about soldiers returning from the war. Goldwyn had shelved the treatment, which Kantor had written in the very unusual form of blank verse; it had eventually been published as a blank-verse novel titled *Glory for Me*.

From the start, the film provoked both stories of collaboration and claims of competing authorship. Where Kantor emphasized the continuities between his version and the finished film, director Wyler emphasized the differences: "The three characters we have are not at all like the ones MacKinlay Kantor had in his book."[15] Kantor responded with an angry interview in which he expressed outrage at the omission of his name from film publicity and strenuously objected to Wyler's statement that the characters in the film bore little relation to his.[16]

Wyler told a different story. "Kantor's story was good for 1944–45, but we wanted a story that would stand up in 1946–47."[17] What exactly was the difference between what was needed in 1944 and what was needed in 1946? Wyler phrases this as a historical problem, but what follows in his account is not easily understood as the difference two more years made. A disability difference comes to the fore, as I will show.

Both of these men came to this debate with personal stories of war and disability. Before he began work on this project, Kantor had gone to England as a war correspondent and had ended up volunteering to fly as an aerial gunner. He had entered combat in this sidelong way because of his disability history: at the outset of the war he had just gone through the nineteenth operation on one of his legs, and as a result he was—as the author's biographical note on the dust jacket of *Glory for Me* put it—"physically unacceptable to the armed forces," in addition to being "well above draft age."[18] Wyler's story took the reverse form: the war had disabled him.


## William Wyler

It is well known that William Wyler was disabled, as well as a veteran. He had been deafened in one ear during the war by engine noise to which he had been exposed while shooting combat documentary film for the military.[19] One of his fellow filmmakers was killed during this stint of documentary filming. Wyler went through a period of total hearing loss immediately after the injury: "My hearing just went. . . . I couldn't walk straight when I got off. They thought I was drunk. I went to see the flight surgeon. He said, 'This is serious.'" His wife, Talli, described the conversation in which Wyler told her what had happened: "I heard an absolutely dead voice . . . toneless, without any timbre, without emotions. . . . He talked as if his life was over, not only his career." Wyler's friend Lillian Hellman reported of a visit to him in the hospital: "I'd never seen anybody in such a real state of horror in my life."[20] Wyler's biographer, Jan Herman, recounts the harrowing experience of disability oppression that Wyler then underwent:

> Finally, the Air Force sent him to a military hospital in Santa Barbara, where he submitted to psychiatric therapy with sodium pentothal treatments. Injections of the so-called "truth serum" were supposed to reveal whether his deafness had a psychosomatic component. The therapy consisted of intense scrutiny and deception. Psychiatrists told Wyler he was able to hear so well under the influence of the drug that he had understood what was being said in the next room. They even told that to Talli. "When I picked him up to bring him home from the hospital, he was in a padded cell," she recalled. "He could barely stand up. It was all I could do to get him out of the car." The drug treatment accomplished nothing. As compensation for his hearing disability, Wyler would get sixty dollars a month from the government for the rest of his life.[21]

But the disability knowledge Wyler brought to, and then discovered at, the set of *The Best Years of Our Lives* encompassed more than trauma; it also involved new experiment and transformation. At the start of the filming, he found that if he sat immediately under the camera and wore an amplified headset attached to the sound equipment, he had no trouble hearing. Herman writes that Wyler made direct links with Harold Russell to a shared prosthetic experience: "Pretty clever, no? I put on this innovation, like you with your hooks, and I can work" (287). As much as the mutilation and defilement Kaja Silverman has shown us how to find in *The Best Years of Our Lives*, Wyler was encountering a disability that defined itself as the putting on of innovation.

At the same time, Wyler brought to the set another less well-known disability story, one perhaps marked by less obviously clever innovations and conclusive lessons. He had grown up with a cognitively disabled older brother, Gaston, who lived with his parents and sometimes with Wyler till he died at the age of forty-one, two years after the filming of *The Best Years of Our Lives* (Herman, 9, 110–11). The questions of dependence and independence, of community support or isolation and exclusion, of stigma and loyalty, and of mental capacity and incapacity that emerge in the context of adult cognitive disability were active issues in Wyler's experience of his family. But if they frame the film, they are nowhere directly evident within it. Wyler had his own history with multiple forms of disability abjection, interdependence, and innovation, a history he discarded as much as he drew on it when he came to direct the relatively straightforward and narratively digestible movie that would be *The Best Years of Our Lives*.

### Glory for Me

A turn to MacKinlay Kantor's original verse treatment will show that the complexities and confusions of disability haunt the making of *The Best Years of Our Lives* even more than first appears—so much so that as Kantor approached his task, he could not even write it in conventional narrative form. The treatment Kantor wrote for the film upon being commissioned by Goldwyn took the form, rather, of a blank-verse novel. The allusion in the verse form to Homeric epic was obvious and was underscored by the naming of the character Homer (though undercut by his last name, Wermels, a name Harold Russell thought "crawly"; in the film his surname is converted to a generic WASP Parrish).[22] Goldwyn was bewildered by the blank-verse text, which Kantor titled *Glory for Me*, and he put the project to rest. When he resurrected it, he hired a new screenwriter, Robert Sherwood, to work with filmmaker Wyler.

The biggest shift between *Glory for Me* and *The Best Years of Our Lives* involves the disability representation of Homer. When Goldwyn turned over responsibility for development of the script to Sherwood and Wyler, his instruction was "Don't be too radical."[23] No matter how in-your-face the Harold Russell depiction of the character of Homer appears, it pales in comparison with the radical nature of his predecessor, Kantor's Homer.

Here is the first view of Kantor's Homer in *Glory for Me*:

This was a death—one piece of death,
Alive on its right side, and dying, jerking on the left,
It walked with pain and twisted muscles,
It was so young . . . it had a face without a beard.

. . . . . . . . . . . . . . . .

Its name was Wermels, Homer,
Seaman Second-Class,
But working as a gunner's mate the night torpedoes struck.
He went in as a child, as many went.
He came out as a monster.
In his brain a little telephone was doing things
And all so wrong, so very wrong indeed . . .
A little telephone spoke to his leg
And told it foolish things to do.
Spasticity, they diagnosed a dozen times,
But Homer's head was jerking nonetheless

. . . . . . . . . . . . . . .

He chattered like a monkey, with his lip drawn tight

. . . . . . . . . . . . . . .

But smiling still . . . his eyes so bright . . .
Like bits of broken teacup, or a twist
Of ribbon on a girlie's lingerie:
Pale blue, and rather soft and feminine and kind.

. . . . . . . . . . . . . .

He thought he'd talk, but no one listened.
He made his sounds alone, and no one listened,
But his eyes were bright.

. . . . . . . . .

And Homer beamed and drooled.

· · · · · · · · · · · ·

Homer was hoping for a bus.
How often did they run? He asked MPs:
They couldn't understand a word he said;
One stood, embarrassed, pitying,
While Homer asked for muss or uss
Or something strange.[24]

It is a commonplace in criticism on *The Best Years of Our Lives* to denigrate Kantor's version in comparison with the formal beauty and cultural impact of Wyler's film. *Glory for Me* is an obviously strange, strained text. But I think that we have reason still to take a long second look at Kantor's original. This brain-injured Homer speaks to our time, when traumatic brain injury is recognized as the signature injury of modern combat and as the leading combat injury now being seen.[25] As the verse novel continues, the experience of brain injury is represented from inside:

When you come out of War to quiet streets

· · · · · · · · · · · ·

You do not see yourself in malformation.
The men and girls who have no shells
Of War upon their backs—you count them well deformed.[26]

Who are these people? Do they pity me?

· · · · · · · · · · ·

I'm not a baby . . . dress myself . . .
They do not recognize
That I have seen the stars explode,
And felt the angry decks descend
Across more oceans than the pirates sailed.[27]

Why was the character changed in this way? Director William Wyler said, "We had a spastic case first, but I realized such a character would never ring true; that no actor, no matter how great his talent, could play a spastic with conviction."[28] Given Lon Chaney's roles in the past and Daniel Day-Lewis's famed "ringing-true" in *My Left Foot* in the future, Wyler's certainties on this question are not very convincing.[29] But the problem might have been more that an actor might have been too convincing. Harold Russell wrote that even if Goldwyn had been successful in finding an actor to portray a spastic sailor, "he would still be licked. The more realistically and convincingly it was played, the more unbearable it would be."[30]

Wyler, Goldwyn, and Sherwood agreed that audiences could not bear the sight of, and actors could not stand the role of, a brain-injured, spastic, drooling, speech-impaired Homer. Jan Herman phrases this as simple and obvious necessity: "The physical disability had to be altered."[31] Anderegg writes, "Homer Wermels, the spastic, becomes Homer Parrish, whose amputated hands have been replaced by prosthetic hooks. Undoubtedly, problems of 'aesthetics' entered into this decision."[32] The anxiety and embarrassment that those scare quotes around "aesthetics" register make clear that when disability is as multiple as Kantor's Homer's, it somehow both must be and cannot be understood as an aesthetic problem. Where disgust emerges (and it does) in the discourse around a spastic Homer, it usually does so shamefacedly, framed as compassion, as in this description of Kantor's character by William Wyler: "Unable to coordinate his movement, awkward, even grotesque, he finds homecoming sheer misery because his people don't understand him."[33] Harold Russell was more blunt. During the script's development, he objected to Sherwood that Kantor had made Homer "actively, aggressively repulsive, a gargoyle in human form."[34] Faced with this aggression, this severity, this multiplicity of disability, the film risked finding itself unable to coordinate its movement.[35] "The unfortunate but real grotesqueries of a spastic," explains Anderegg, "would have drawn attention away from the character to the physical disability in a way that Harold Russell's hooks do not."[36] For Fredric March, those hooks were scene-stealers, but next to Kantor's Homer's drool they turn into unobtrusive accessories. A grotesque Homer might have ushered the film into an "imaginative framework" like the ones of the "fantastic" films David Church has described, in which "the grotesque disabled body" moves "from the margins of representation and into the spotlight, much like the freak show performer on stage: an exploitative spectacle for sure, but one which might inadvertently point back toward our own cyborgian mode of spectatorship, revealing us all as part of the 'new flesh' so grotesquely intertwined with the disreputable pleasures of technology."[37] Instead, Homer's body in *Best Years* is finally less grotesque than classical, with its stylized, effective hooks offering compelling and reassuring refrains about where disability begins and where it ends. Amputation—

unlike the far more stigmatizing spasms, tics, and traumatic brain injury carried in Kantor's Homer's body—was, as Beth Linker brilliantly puts it, literally and metaphorically clean-cut.[38]

The omission of a brain-injured Homer and his replacement with amputee Homer might be seen as a kind of redoubled narrative prosthesis in Mitchell and Snyder's terms. Wyler could spot his Homer-to-be, Harold Russell, in military training films because those films were about literal prosthetics. Russell made *The Best Years of Our Lives* available for an intensive concretizing and emblematizing of the narrative prosthesis that the film so self-consciously enacted.

Clearly Goldwyn and Wyler prized a kind of realism in casting Harold Russell. As Russell himself put it: "Eventually I understood what William Wyler had seen in me: that I was *already* playing the part of Homer Parrish. Wasn't that the point of . . . my rehabilitation?"[39] This seeking an effect of the real was the source of Wyler's outrage when he learned that Goldwyn had hired an acting coach for Russell.[40] In their search for real impact through the impact of the real, however, Wyler and Goldwyn never considered casting a brain-injured vet; perhaps that would be too real. It is important to remember the Cold War context of the film, which was released only a year before the systematic beginnings of the Hollywood blacklist and the full-scale escalation of the Red scares of the late 1940s. By depicting a too-frightening injured veteran, the film could lead to greater unrest and an escalation of antiwar sentiments.[41]

One of the many consequences of this change from Kantor's brain-injured Homer to the Sherwood/Wyler version is the loss of a plot in the original that pointedly multiplies disability stories. At one point in *Glory for Me*, Homer comes across a book his girlfriend, Wilma, has been reading, *The Brain from Ape to Man*. He understands immediately that it is somehow about him, and he is furious at the implications: that he is atavistic, that he is animal. Then Wilma reads the right book, Earl Carlson's *Born That Way*, an autobiographical story that saves Homer. *Glory for Me* is at its center a parable of reading about disability.

### Earl Carlson

The book is by "a man named Carlson," *Born This Way*. Wilma tells Homer that it is

About a man . . . he used to be like you.
He wrote this book himself—a man named Carlson.
And I've read Helen Keller, too. But Carlson knows
Just how it feels to be like you,
And worse. He crawled around;
He couldn't walk, and he was born that way.

. . . . . . . . . . . . . . . . .

It's better, Homer, if it happens to you late:
You have a pattern formed. He says
You have a pattern formed. He says
You have to re-establish it—the pattern.
All the motions that you make,
You have to *will* them—think them out.
And you can do it, Homer.
Yes, you can.[42]

Kantor did not make this book up. The "man named Carlson" is Dr. Earl Carlson, a man with cerebral palsy who grew up in poverty as a significantly disabled child, nonverbal for years, and who eventually got his medical degree at Yale Medical School and became a famous specialist on cerebral palsy and an advocate for schooling for disabled children.

Carlson's book, the book Wilma is reading, is very much worth rereading for disability studies. As the quoted lines suggest, it is a medical treatment plan of sorts. Without a doubt it is part of the enterprise David Serlin has critiqued, a project of controlling and disciplining the disabled body in the name of normalization and "somatic respectability" under what Serlin calls "the presumptive logic of the modal subject."[43] But I think that we cannot rest with that analysis. Carlson's *Born This Way* (1941) is also a "nothing about us without us" manifesto: an assertion of disability expertise—an assertion of disability as expertise. Carlson tells various stories of "handicapped physicians" and disabled academics whom he knows, and he argues that his experience with cerebral palsy gives him "special advantage" in treating others with cerebral palsy:

There were those who felt that I would be like a blind man attempting to lead the blind. . . . I grew familiar with the stories of many handicapped physicians who had found ways to be useful to society by circumventing their handicaps. There was a blind heart specialist whose overdeveloped sense of touch enabled him to make better diagnoses of heart ailments through the use of his fingertips than an un-handicapped doctor. There was a famous psychiatrist who treated his patients from a wheelchair. . . . I could not be shaken in my conviction that my experience in overcoming my difficulties would give me a special advantage in helping other spastics to conquer theirs.[44]

If Carlson is the doctor ex machina in this plot, the one who can straighten Homer out, he is also a wrench in the works, a crip ex machina offering Homer, in Robert McRuer's words, a "seriously twisted way of knowing."[45] In Carlson's account, to a very significant extent, the famous medical model of disability studies is a social model, inflected with disability consciousness through and through.

### Frederick Tilney

Earl Carlson himself cites an important crip mentor, another forebear whose disability story we can add to Homer's family tree here: Frederick Tilney, his teacher, the disabled doctor who turns out to be the author of the other book that Wilma reads in *Glory for Me*, the textbook on evolution *The Brain from Ape to Man*. Here is the account by Carlson in *Born That Way* that Kantor's Wilma would have read, the lead that would send her (and might send Kantor's readers) to Tilney, in which Tilney extends disabled ways of knowing from a senior doctor to his junior:

Doubtless Dr. Tilney took such an interest in me because since his stroke he too had had handicaps to overcome. . . . He told me that as a matter of fact he got more work done after his stroke than he had before, and that the probable explanation was that natural left-handedness had been suppressed by training while a child. . . . The authorities of the medical school were somewhat doubtful about letting me go on, since they felt that my physical handicaps would bar me from practice and would even prevent my getting hospital training after graduation. Dr. Tilney's offer helped to eliminate their objections, and I was accepted as a regular student for the degree.[46]

Eliminating Homer's spasticity in *The Best Years of Our Lives* meant eliminating the traces of this spastic history, the great chain of crip science that seems to write itself whenever Frederick Tilney's name is invoked in this period, as in this excerpt from a 1940 memorial of Tilney in *Time*. Notice the spreading citations to disabled science that the asterisk marks, a footnote format not typical of *Time*'s style.

> In 1925, while working 15 hours a day, Dr. Tilney was struck by cerebral thrombosis (blood clot in the brain). For six weeks he *lost the power of speech. But his mind was as keen as ever, and he gave his colleagues detailed notes on the course of his disease. The devoted doctors at the Institute took turns sleeping in his house every night, came over in a band of five to carry his heavy, inert body from his study to his bedroom. Within a few months Dr. Tilney taught himself to scribble with his left hand, in six months wrote the entire manuscript of a two-volume masterpiece, The Brain from Ape to Man. When it was published in 1928, many scientists acclaimed it as the finest piece of evolutionary writing since Darwin.[47]

At the bottom of the page comes the subs(crip)t material connected to the asterisk: "*Pasteur also had a paralytic stroke, also did some of his most important work after his recovery. The late, great Brain Surgeon Harvey Cushing, a friend of Dr. Tilney, was crippled by a nerve disease during World War I, later recovered, went back to his six-hour operations."

All this disappears in Wyler's famous war film. In *Glory for Me*, unlike *The Best Years of Our Lives*, Homer's healing does not come finally or even primarily in that private, domestic space of dead citizenship, the if not completely able-bodied, then at least completely readjusted home.[48] It comes through a midcentury form of disability culture, in Earl Carlson and Frederick Tilney, necessarily mediated through the medical but not reducible to it. These modes of disability knowledge—passed on from Tilney to Carlson and from Carlson to Kantor to war-veteran readers and those close to them—are shut down at least as much as they are opened up by Harold Russell's spectacular Homer.

## "A Manuscript of a War Narrative"

James Agee's review of *The Best Years of Our Lives* in the *Nation* speaks for me. "At its worst," Agee wrote, "this story is very annoying in its patness, its timidity, its slithering attempts to pretend to face and by that to dodge in the most shameful way possible its own fullest meanings and possibilities."[49] Those fuller meanings and possibilities began to reveal themselves early, in the deeper archive of MacKinlay Kantor's work behind *Glory for Me*.

"A Manuscript of a War Narrative," a very early version of what would become *Glory for Me*, is held in Kantor's manuscripts in the Library of Congress. Not in blank verse, this narrative was Kantor's first attempt to tell the story of veteran return. He never published it but shelved it to start afresh with the verse version, *Glory for Me*. In this earlier narrative, the war-correspondent narrator, clearly modeled on Kantor himself, travels around the United States, as Kantor did, visiting women related to dead men whose planes have been lost on a mission that he flew with. "Yes," he says to Mrs. Jane Peel, one dead soldier's mother, "—I saw them die."[50]

Excavating the Homer/Kantor archive reveals body stories that show how, in Agee's terms, *The Best Years of Our Lives* pretends to face and by that means dodges its fullest meanings and possibilities. In a fragment of Kantor's earliest narrative version, a war-correspondent double for Kantor, Jackson, remembers meeting for the first time a soon-to-be-killed young soldier, Tommy Peel, the son of the mother he has just visited. The homosocial bonding and implicit homoerotic strains of *The Best Years of Our Lives* are a critical commonplace. But notice how much more fully, if no less anxiously and phobically, the meaning and possibilities of same-sex bonds are explored in this passage:

> Though he attributed spiritual homosexuality to himself in jest, he was more than a little puzzled by his feeling for Peel. . . . The thought of physical intimacies of an erotic nature with any member of his own sex was loathsome, but he desired the presence and companionship of these men he loved, with all passion. . . . Certainly such [here a word is crossed out and illegible] desires were normal and common in men of his warm-hearted, convivial

The fragment ends here, with the fullest meanings and possibilities for "men of his warm-hearted, convivial"—no identity position possible to specify—left open in the blank space outside the sentence.[51]

So let us add this to the Homeric family tree this blank space that potentially and impossibly queers—and simultaneously reinforces—nextness and kinness and lines of descent. It is as if homoerotic desire can occur only in the absence of disability: the dead boy Tommy Peel arouses it, maybe, but not the living amputee Homer. It is also as if an ethos of disability inclusion can occur only in the context of the blanking out and crossing out of passionate homosocial bonding and its intricate and potential relation to homosexual desire. By the time we get to *The Best Years of Our Lives*, Homer can be rehabilitated only into what Margot Canaday calls the "straight state," a remade nation where rehabilitation and reintegration are given over exclusively to married or marriageable men, while others are made into what David Serlin calls "anti-citizens."[52] Men who emerge, fit and improved, into family life and the postwar landscape are constituted as such only by contrast with men not only outside but antagonistic to the newly evolving good civil society. In order to arrive at full postwar citizenship, both spastic Homer and amputee Homer, at risk and antisocial, must marry into it.

## Dissenting Veterans

Even more overt threats to the state are suggested in other, later moments of revision of *The Best Years of Our Lives*, after Kantor was no longer part of the project. Robert Sherwood, the screenwriter who replaced Kantor and produced the final script of *The Best Years of Our Lives*, was a staunch New Deal liberal with close connections to FDR before Roosevelt's death.[53] Perhaps the most surprising suppression of material of all that happened under the regime of Goldwyn's rule "Don't be too radical" came from the Sherwood line. The material that was suppressed is not simply identifiable as a disability story, but it links the history of disability to other, multiple histories.

Sherwood's early draft of the script of *Best Years* included a scene of angry GIs rioting in protest at their housing conditions.[54] The possibility of armed veteran uprising was a live issue at the time.[55] So were housing shortages, poverty, and unemployment, urgent problems exacerbated by disability oppression where disabled veterans were concerned. The scene Sherwood drafted would have addressed these issues head-on. Goldwyn personally nixed it.

This kind of suppression of narratives of organized political dissent by veterans, and specifically by disabled veterans, was not unique to the process of making *The Best Years of Our Lives*. Let us turn to one more example of Homer's next of kin. Homer Parrish was not the only amputee-vet character on the screen in 1946. Edward Dmytryk's film *Till the End of Time*, an adaptation of Niven Busch's novel *They Dream of Home*, tells the story of a varied group of uneasy combat buddies arriving home together, very much like the former comrades in arms of *Best Years*. Busch's novel came out a year after Kantor's *Glory for Me*, but its film adaptation *Till the End of Time*, produced by Dore Schary, preceded the release of Wyler's film by a few months; Busch's wife, Teresa Wright, would have come to her performance of Peggy in *Best Years* with close knowledge of the story her husband had written. One of the men in Schary, Dmytryk, and Busch's version of the re-adjustment story is a disabled veteran named Perry Kincheloe. In the film he has lost both legs. In the novel on which the film is based, he has also lost one of his arms.

Martin F. Norden provides the standard disability studies summary of the plot of *Till the End of Time*, noting that "the film focuses primarily on able-bodied, All-American boy Cliff Harper (Guy Madison) but also fol-lows a cowboy gambler with a plate in his head named Bill Tabeshaw" (Robert Mitchum), as well as Perry, "an embittered 21-year-old who refuses to wear his prostheses." Perry's adjustment occurs when he is "stirred to action," Norden writes, "after his mother alludes to the post-disablement successes of Franklin Roosevelt. . . . Viewed from his mother's perspective, Perry emerges triumphant from his bedroom wearing his military dress uniform and both prostheses, and walking with two canes."[56] Noting that this is the first time in the film when Dmytryk films Perry from below, "be-stowing a certain heroic quality on the vet," Norden writes that Perry, in a scene similar to one in *Best Years*, "later demonstrates that he's lost none of his talent for fisticuffs by landing haymakers on several neo-fascists in a bar fight."[57]

Most critics use *Till the End of Time*, much as they cite *Glory for Me*, as a minor foil against which to set the great accomplishment of *The Best Years of Our Lives*.[58] In many ways, the film indeed seems timid in comparison. The lead character, Cliff, in Busch's book is explicitly identified as disabled; his experience of "attacks" of shaking is transferred in the film to a minor char-acter. From a disability studies perspective, it is important to note that the amputee in *Till the End*, Perry, is played by a nondisabled actor, Bill Williams, who does none of the strong cultural work assumed by Harold Russell in his groundbreaking performance. It is equally important to note that Perry is played by an actor unmarked by race—that is, by a white actor—while the Perry character in the original novel on which the film is based is repre-sented as "coal-black."[59] The opening scene of Busch's novel culminates clearly in a spectacle of staring, with race and disability equally at stake; after Perry is taken off a troop train at his hometown station through the train window on a stretcher, the chapter ends with a watching newsboy's exclamation: "'I seen a wounded guy,' he said. . . . 'I seen a wounded guy, I seen a wounded guy—I seen a wounded guy, an' he's a nigger.'"[60] None of this remains in the far more insipid film, although, as Perry's antifascist bar fight suggests, Schary and Dmytryk (and behind them David Selznick) were progressives with an investment in socially conscious filmmaking.

But a look at Busch's novel, the source text for *Till the End of Time*, brings us to a very different story of radical black disability, antiracism, and collective veteran activism. Toward the end of the novel, in our final view of Perry Kincheloe, he emerges out of his bedroom and into the public eye by his own choice, first putting on his uniform, a "triumph" his mother "had always longed for. At last she had seen her son in his fighting clothes." This is the equivalent of the filmic scene described by Martin Norden in which the white character Perry, brought to his senses and to proper relation to the ideal of citizenship by his mother's invocation of the disabled FDR, straps on his prostheses and stands tall in his uniform. In both versions, the messed-up vet with his muddied body, at once frighteningly excessive and utterly lacking, far too much in harm's way, assumes the proper military masculinity of what Aaron Belkin calls the "pristine soldier."[61] In the film, Perry's plot stops here, at the upright, end point of the normal individual. In the book, Perry's plot ends equally righteously but quite differently.

At this point in Busch's novel, Perry disappears as an individual character; instead, he is subsumed into a mass demonstration. This Fourth of July march is ranged in ranks, from "blind Negro veterans" through "Negro casualties who had eyes and little else—men with jaws, noses, and whole faces shot away," "legless Negroes," "'Section Eight' cases," and, last of all, "basket cases pushed along on special hand cars. The baskets were covered with canvas tops out of which the black faces of the men, one still bandaged, reared like seals." If this is a march of disabled black men, it is also a march that itself is disabled: "Nor did any of the various categories of hurt, amputated, crazed, blind, or maimed colored fighters move at a uniform pace: the placard-bearers kept going too fast for the less able-bodied." This march is many points removed from the way enjoyed by white, middle-class, nondisabled men who walk the walk of full citizenship.

The novel's response in part is open revulsion—"The parade of Negro casualties was something not fit for eye to see or mind to grasp"—but not only that. On the one hand, veteran black disability marks itself by ragged pace and sustained pathos manifesting as sound: "And always along the line rose the long breath, the indescribable deep sound of mourning, or protest, or sympathy, or maybe a combination of these emotions." On the other hand, it also marks itself with open signs, the placards that front the march: "THERE AIN'T NO JIM CROW BULLETS."; "FAIR PLAY FOR HORIZON'S COL-ORED WORKERS."; "END DISCRIMINATION." "Mourning" and "sym-pathy" give way to "protest," to fighting clothes. The signs refer to a struggle treated at length in the novel, racist violence driving black workers out of a Lockheed-like airplane plant, Horizon, that has culminated in a denial by the plant's president—"All reports of any racial friction at the plant were a lot of nonsense"—and encouragement to "buy extra bonds in celebration of the coming . . . anniversary of the nation's independence."[62] These march-ing men are organized, collective political and veteran agents, mobilizing the display of their wounds and their service as a strong demand for justice and authentic "independence." For a moment, the novel grants them real potential power.

But the threat they pose is finally displaced. By the end of the chapter, riot police appear—hardly surprising, in the face of the representation of forceful mass black action, even if it is mass crip black action. But they do not, although at first it seems so, emerge in the narrative in reaction to the march. Instead, the riot police are called out in response to the actions of another nonwhite disabled character, the Native American brain-injured-vet character Tabeshaw. In the Tabeshaw plot, dignified uplift is overcome by the "underside" that David Gerber has described: the "ominous messages" circulating in American culture "about veterans' anger, bitterness, violence, alcoholism, and personality disorganization."[63] Here the anxiety is so ex-treme, the anger against joblessness so uncontainable, that one seriously pissed-off Native American brain-injured man constitutes a full riot. The caps in the march placards are replaced by those of newspaper headlines: "MARINE VETERAN RUNS AMOK. William Tabeshaw, twenty-nine, dis-gruntled at being out of work, held up and robbed a grocery store." The news story overtakes "coverage of the extraordinary demonstration by the col-ored veterans."[64]

In the film version, extraordinary demonstrations disappear. They give way instead to the singular extraordinary body of (white, pristine) Perry. And the brain-injured Indian Tabeshaw, another of Homer Parrish's inter-esting relations, becomes—hilariously, depressingly—a cowboy. Soon after,

Harold Russell's riveting performance in *The Best Years of Our Lives* would grab public attention.

## Multiplying Disability

In *The Best Years of Our Lives*, Homer Parrish is brought full circle into health, normalcy, and sociality in the final white wedding scene, when the prosthesis meets the ring.[65] But that moment has been founded, as I have shown, on multiple other disability stories that have bitten the dust. The Homer brought into being by Harold Russell, Robert Sherwood, and William Wyler functioned undoubtedly as an icon of inclusion: (re)inclusion of veterans in postwar civilian society and full inclusion of disabled men in the ranks of workers, husbands, and fathers. I have been arguing, however, that this manifest, inclusive Homer came into being through—as—a process of exclusion: of brain injury and spasticity; of the abject disability of those "born that way"; of the disability expertise held by powerful disabled experts; of anything that might unsettle the normative straight family; of the politics of race, class, and economic inequity.

In the years after *The Best Years of Our Lives* came out, Harold Russell sought to use the fame his distinctive performance of Homer had brought him in order to call attention to an ever-widening circle of multiplying (disability) stories.[66] Thus his first autobiography, *Victory in My Hands*, culminates in narratives like the account of "'Hawaii,' a Nisei GI who had lost his right leg, arm and an eye at Cassino," in the service of Russell's antiracist critique.[67] His second autobiography moves away from his own story to an invocation of the man he says was "the most famous physically handicapped man" at the moment of *Best Years*' inception: civilian Paul Strachan, president of the first national cross-disability advocacy organization, the American Federation of the Physically Handicapped. Describing the public function he himself famously played as Homer as a kind of cover, a second-hand version of Strachan's achievement—"I was . . . a Paul Strachan of the veterans' movement"—Russell himself modeled the method I am seeking here.[68] He was not only enacting humility and honoring a predecessor. He knew that in any disability story there are many disability stories. The ones to which he gave capstone place involved direct challenges to normalization and an insistence on lives that evaded narrative simplicity and the simple closures of patriotism.

Critic Robert Warshow wrote in 1947 that the "disciplined clarity" of *The Best Years of Our Lives* allowed audiences to experience a satisfaction in a technique so complete and self-containing that it allowed audiences to relax into basic Hollywood and American myths while at the same time experiencing themselves as viewers with discriminating taste. "Where every statement is complete, clear, and limited, it can be with less difficulty made false." For him, the key falsehood in *Best Years* was "a denial of the realities of politics, if politics means the existence of real incompatibilities of interest and real *social* problems not susceptible of individual solution."[69] I have been arguing that Homer/Russell's disabled-body story functioned precisely as the epitome of this mystifying disciplined clarity. It did so because of the extreme affect produced by Russell's real amputation and his real prostheses; here is what Warshow had to say on this subject, describing what he called the "especially affecting" scene where Wilma's love for Homer proves true: "Everything about the sailor is especially affecting because the part is played by a man who really did lose his hands in the war. There was nothing else to be done, I suppose, but this is one of the elements that helps to make the movie spill over into the real world, carrying its falsehood with it."[70]

I have tried to show how there was, in fact, something else to be done with disability in the narratives that spilled over from the real world into the movie and back again—multiple, manifold things that were done, and that could be. On the one hand, we have an author (Kantor), a director (Wyler), and an actor (Russell), all of whom were disabled in complicated ways but ended up nonetheless with a neat and tidy narrative about a Homer who makes good, so good that his disability virtually disappears and becomes a nonevent. On the other hand, the history of *Best Years* shows just how wrong conventional assumptions are about a largely nondisabled film industry producing disability plots; disability events are everywhere once, as Douglas Baynton has famously reminded us, we begin to look for them.[71] Bringing their history to bear on thinking about and with Harold Russell's Homer helps spread limiting extremities of affect and counter the anatomies of falsehood that singular disability stories have bodied forth for U.S. culture, then and now.

What might it mean to produce a version of *The Best Years of Our Lives* for the twenty-first century? A new version might remake not only the film but also its making, reaching back to the rejected treatments and buried fragments of MacKinlay Kantor and the censored script of Robert Sherwood to tell more complex stories about war and disability. The film might lose in concentration, but it would gain something else in its foregrounding of multiple stories—veterans (brain-injured veterans), but also disabled civilians; patients, but also disabled doctors; men (and not only white men), but also disabled women; trauma, but also disability activism and broader (more multiple, more severe) sociopolitical perspective. It might gain, that is, the kind of brilliant "retardation" that Erich Auerbach identified in the original Homer in the first *Odyssey*. At the beginning of his *Mimesis*, which was published in the same year in which Harold Russell's Homer filled movie screens, Auerbach famously focused on the digressive scene in which Odysseus's nursemaid recognizes him after his return from the wars by his scar. The cause of "the impression of 'retardation,'" Auerbach wrote—that is, of a slowing while the story of the scar fully unfolds—"appears to me to lie . . . in the need of the Homeric style to leave nothing which it mentions half in darkness and unexternalized."[72] Perhaps we need a more Homeric Homer story, one that does not leave us all half in darkness about our bodies and our wars. It might help us recognize more of, and more about, our scars.

## CHAPTER 2

# Defect: A Selective Reinterpretation of American Immigration History

## Douglas C. Baynton

"Selection" is a fraught word for people with disabilities. Such terms as "prenatal selection," "selective reproduction," and "genetic selection" raise the specter of disability deselection based on normative assumptions about what constitutes a "good life" or "a life worth living." Reproductive selection today is generally framed as a matter of individual choice (although some ethicists maintain that it is largely an illusion that such choices could exist apart from social norms and pressures),[1] but eugenicists in the late nineteenth and early twentieth centuries saw social selection as an unalloyed good. They frankly advocated coercive methods, advanced normative assumptions as scientific fact, and regarded the elimination of what they termed "defectives" as common sense.

The intentional improvement of animal stock, what today is usually referred to as "breeding," in the nineteenth century was termed "selection." It was because of the familiarity of the term that Charles Darwin settled on "natural selection" to describe the means by which evolutionary change occurred. Although he worried that the term was "in some respects a bad one, as it seems to imply conscious choice," he believed that its utility as an explanatory device outweighed that disadvantage because "it brings into connection the production of domestic races by man's power of selection, and the natural preservation of varieties and species in a state of nature."[2] Eugenicists feared that natural selection, which worked to eliminate defects in nature, had become powerless under the conditions of modern civilization. Darwin himself made this point in *The Descent of Man* when he wrote that modern societies "check the process of elimination; we build asylums for the imbecile, the maimed, and the sick; we institute poor-laws," and, as a result, "the weak members of civilised societies propagate their kind." However, he hastened to add, this impulse arose from "the noblest part of our nature," and "to neglect the weak and helpless" would gain merely "a contingent benefit, with a certain and great present evil." He concluded that "we must bear without complaining . . . the weak surviving and propagating their kind."[3] Eugenicists did not entirely agree. Although allowing the weak to die was a line most eugenicists were disinclined to cross, allowing them to propagate was a different matter, and they believed that they had tools of selection that were both ethical and practical.[4]

Eugenics was primarily a nationalistic project. Although eugenicists spoke about the rights of individuals to be "well-born" and the advancement of the human race, most of their attention focused on the middle ground of the nation. American eugenicists carried on a decades-long debate over what methods of selection were best suited to creating "a superior national race."[5] Eugenic selection of worthy citizens occurred along two main tracks. The one most often associated with the eugenics movement was the curtailment of reproduction by undesirable citizens through institutionalization, sterilization, and public education campaigns that included fitter-family contests, school and college curricula, and a steady stream of books, articles, and sermons. Although federal courts became involved from time to time, this aspect of the eugenics movement was carried out mostly at the state and local level.[6] There was, however, another "field in which the federal government must cooperate," wrote Harry Laughlin, the director of the Eugenics Record Office at Cold Spring Harbor, "if the human breeding stock in our population is to be purged of its defective parenthood."[7] That field, the second main track of eugenic selection, was the restriction of immigration.

Immigration restriction represented the most complete and unambiguous expression of eugenic nationalism. Advocates of institutionalization and sterilization could include among their professed motives altruistic ones: to shelter vulnerable individuals, relieve parents of terrible burdens, prevent lives of presumed misery, and foster human progress. The popular writer Albert Wiggam was certain that Jesus, were he to return, would update the golden rule in light of modern eugenic science: "Do unto both the born and the unborn as you would have both the born and the unborn do unto you."[8] A pamphlet from the American Eugenics Society asserted that eugenics did not mean "less sympathy for the unfortunate" but instead a

"more concerted attempt to alleviate their suffering, by seeing to it that everything possible is done to have fewer hereditary defectives."[9] The physician Harry Haiselden could even claim that he practiced euthanasia for
disabled infants "because he loves them," and that death was "the kindest
mercy."[10] Immigration restriction, by contrast, was not plausibly defensible
as beneficial either to the individuals it affected or to humanity at large. It
promised only to keep defectives where they were: elsewhere. Moreover, institutionalization and sterilization affected mainly people who fell into the
categories of mentally or morally defective, while immigration restriction
eventually encompassed virtually all varieties of disability.

The concept of selection has an important but frequently misunderstood
place in the history of immigration policy. Scholars have commonly divided
the early regulation of European immigration into two broad categories, selective and restrictive, each with its own distinct rationale and purpose. Selective laws screened out undesirable individuals, mainly those with physical,
mental, and moral defects, while restrictive laws placed limits on racial or
ethnic groups, as well as reducing overall immigration. The periodization
that has followed from this division posits a selective phase, starting with the
Immigration Act of 1882 (the Chinese Exclusion Act of that same year is often cited as an exception),[11] and a restrictive phase that began in 1917 with
the passage of a literacy test or in 1921 with the first national quotas. The latter period has been treated as the more momentous and has been subjected to
much greater critical inquiry. Most accounts describe selection as a reasonable effort to protect the nation from harm and restriction as objectionable
because it was based on racism, nativism, and eugenics.

This interpretation is problematic in several ways. First, the term "selective" is generally treated as transparent and straightforward, and its charged
significance in the rhetoric of eugenics is overlooked. Second, making a distinction between laws that screened out inferior individuals and laws that
screened out inferior races misses the interconnected and mutually constitutive uses of the terms "defect" and "race" in eugenic thought. Eugenic
thinking was at the heart of federal immigration law from at least the 1890s
(although the term itself came into common use only after the turn of the
century). Finally, with a few notable exceptions, most discussion of immigration policy at the time did not make this distinction. Rather, selection
was seen as the means and restriction the end.

The laws during this period are better understood as forming a cohesive
whole, a decades-long legislative effort to find an effective method of exclud-

ing immigrants seen as defective. Lawmakers at first tried to restrict immigration via increasingly stringent inspection procedures and standards for admission. They assumed that this would reduce the numbers not only of defective individuals but also of nationalities and races (often conflated in nineteenth-century usage) understood as disproportionately prone to defect: for example, Jews, who were liable to neurosis and poor physique; Slavs, to feeblemindedness; and Italians, to emotional instability and outbursts of violence. When inspection and exclusion for individual defects proved incapable of checking the flow of undesirable immigrants, legislators finally turned to quotas based on national origin. This was not a departure from but rather a complement to the previous acts. The earlier laws based on inspection were expected to limit immigration from races prone to defect; conversely, national quotas were intended to further reduce the number of defective individuals. The overarching goal did not change. In immigration law, as in other realms, the issues of race and defect were deeply intertwined.[12]

The term "defect" in immigration debates corresponds in most instances to what today is termed "disability," but it was applied more broadly and with connotations specific to the time. It could signify any unwanted deviation from what was considered normal—mentally, morally, or physically. A defect might be a visible impairment or an ill-defined degeneracy that manifested itself in various ways, for example, in crime or poverty. Thus a writer in the *North American Review* in 1892 could refer to "paupers, criminals, or other defectives."[13] Defects of body, mind, and morality were assumed to be interrelated. A professor of medicine and criminal anthropology in 1904, for example, maintained that "defective physique . . . has not received the attention it deserves in the causation of crime."[14] Francis Galton, who coined the term "eugenics," advocated in 1905 the issuance of eugenic certificates for "goodness of constitution, of physique, and of mental capacity," stressing that these were not "independent variables."[15] A medical officer in the Immigration Bureau warned in 1906 that "there is to be expected in the case of poor physique, as an accompaniment of signs of physical degeneracy, some abnormality in the individual's mental and moral make-up."[16]

Given the inchoate understanding of heredity, which into the 1930s included neo-Lamarckian ideas about the inheritance of acquired characteristics, defects were assumed to be heritable. Moreover, defects were mutable, manifesting themselves in varied forms and having far-reaching effects on succeeding generations. The term for this phenomenon was "degeneracy,"

the tendency of defects to persist across generations, to mutate, and to me-
tastasize, such that a mild defect might within several generations become
a thoroughly corrupted nature. What was termed "moral imbecility," an
"absence of the moral sense often as complete as is the absence of sight in the
blind," was routinely associated with other defects: "Its influence in heredity
is far-reaching, liable to reappear in its own or in another form of defect."
Imbecility in all its forms had a "permeating, penetrating, disintegrating
power" and was "at once the most insidious and the most aggressive of de-
generative forces; attacking alike the physical, mental and moral nature, en-
feebling the judgment and will, while exaggerating the sexual impulses."[17]
An editorial in the *Boston Medical and Surgical Journal* could state without
fear of contradiction that "physical degeneracy is now known to go hand-in-
hand with mental and moral degeneracy."[18] This was the threat that immigration restriction was meant to counter. A great variety of immigrants were
rejected as defective, among them people with curved spines, hernias, flat feet,
missing limbs, short limbs, and impairments of vision, hearing, and mobility;
the excessively short or tall; hermaphrodites (intersexuals); men who suffered
from "feminism" (a hormonal deficiency resulting in underdeveloped sexual
organs); people with intellectual or psychiatric disabilities; freak-show performers such as Zip the Pinhead (microcephaly), Juggernaut the (limbless)
Human Cannonball, and the giant Delphi.[19]

Historians have either overlooked or misconstrued the central place of "defect" and "selection" in the history of immigration policy. Philip Taylor, for
example, explained that despite agitation against unrestricted immigration,
"very little was done" until national quotas were instituted in the 1920s; before then, "the categories of undesirables to be excluded were gradually extended," all of which "could reasonably be defended by arguments about
anti-social behavior of a rather obvious kind, or physical and mental defects
disqualifying the immigrant from any effective share in American life."[20] In
*Silent Travelers*, Alan Kraut explained that inspectors "guarded their country against disease and debility" and "barred those found physically or mentally unprepared for life in the tough, competitive society that demanded
fitness of body as well as of soul."[21] Given what we have learned about disability in recent years—the kinds of inexpensive, simple, and low-technology
accommodations that make employment accessible, and the importance of
social barriers and prejudicial attitudes in preventing accessibility—such
assumptions are no longer tenable.

Historians have noted that restrictionists attributed impairments to particular races or nationalities—inherited tendencies toward immorality, feeblemindedness, insanity, poor physique, alcoholism, emotional instability,
and so on—but usually only to condemn these attributions as a kind of slan-
der. Prejudicial attitudes concerning race and ethnicity have been closely
examined, while similar attitudes toward disabled immigrants have gone
largely unremarked. Even to those who, by training, are usually alert and
attuned to stereotypes, the rich, complex, and powerful imagery associated
with disabilities remains invisible.[22]

So much greater significance has been attributed to the quota laws that
in some instances, the preceding four decades of restrictive laws virtually
disappear from view. Categorical statements such as the following are not
difficult to find: "In May 1921 the era of open immigration to the United
States came to an abrupt end";[23] it was "1924 when free and open immigration ended";[24] "Immigration policy was famously open until the 1920s,
when eugenics arrived with a vengeance";[25] and "1924 marked both the end
of one era, that of open immigration from Europe, and the beginning of a
new one, the era of immigration restriction."[26] A chapter in a document collection on immigration is titled "Limited Naturalization, Unlimited Immigration—1880 to 1920."[27]

This period of ostensibly open and unlimited immigration began in 1882
(after passage of the Chinese Exclusion Act which, as historians of Asian immigration have often pointed out, was undoubtably restrictive) with an immigration act that mandated the exclusion of any "lunatic, idiot, or any
person unable to take care of himself or herself without becoming a public
charge." Lunatics and idiots were automatically excluded, while the capacity
of immigrants to live independently was for immigration officials to judge.
Their scope for judgment was narrowed in 1891 when "*likely* to become a
public charge" became the criterion, and further still in 1907 when officials
were directed to exclude anyone having a "mental or physical defect being of
a nature which *may affect* the ability of such alien to earn a living." The less
rigorous standard of "likely to become a public charge" was retained, however, for nondisabled immigrants.[28]

Among the ranks of the automatically excluded, lunatics and idiots were
joined in 1903 by epileptics and those who "have been insane within five
years previous [or] have had two or more attacks of insanity at any time,"
and in 1907 by "imbeciles" and "feeble-minded persons." The commissioner
general of immigration reported that year that "the exclusion from this

country of the morally, mentally, and physically deficient is the principal
object to be accomplished by the immigration laws."[29] In 1917, Congress
thought it prudent to consider one "attack" of insanity sufficient for exclusion and to add people of "constitutional psychopathic inferiority," which
meant the "various unstable individuals on the border line between sanity
and insanity, such as moral imbeciles, pathological liars, many of the va-
grants and cranks, and persons with abnormal sex instincts." Immigration
Bureau regulations distilled this into a clearer directive to exclude people
with "any mental abnormality whatever" and all "aliens of a mentally inferior type . . . without being under the necessity, as formerly, of showing that
they have a defect which may affect their ability to earn a living."[30]

Inspectors often spoke with pride of their ability to make "snapshot diagnoses" as immigrants filed past. Victor Safford maintained that it was "no
more difficult to detect poorly built, defective or broken down human beings than to recognize a cheap or defective automobile"; indeed, the skilled
examiner could often identify defects from "twenty-five feet away" by observing a "man's posture, a movement of his head or the appearance of his
ears, requiring only a fraction of a second."[31] S. B. Grubbs claimed that inspectors often "did not know just why they suspected at a glance a handicap
which later might require a week to prove."[32] Under questioning before a
House of Representatives committee, the assistant surgeon general of the
Public Health Service conceded that the "cursory" nature of inspection demanded that it be "mainly directed toward detection of the obvious physical
defects, such as the lame, the blind, the deaf, or for the purpose of detecting
mental defects."[33]

Under these circumstances, appearance mattered a great deal. Inspector
Allan McLaughlin explained in 1905 that "the gait and general appearance
suggest health or disease to the practised eye, and aliens who do not appear
normal are turned aside, with those who are palpably defective, and more
thoroughly examined later." For most, a normal appearance ensured an un-
eventful passage through the station. Others less fortunate had the mark of
their abnormality chalked in code on their clothing—L for lameness, K for
hernia, S for senility, X for mental illness, and so on—and were taken aside
for closer inspection, which might uncover problems that might or might
not be related to the abnormality that prompted it. Discovery of a problem
necessitated a hearing to determine on which side of the law an individual
stood. Those on the wrong side were returned to their port of departure,

often in the same ship that had brought them. In many cases, they had exhausted their resources, left jobs, and severed connections in preparation for the trip and had little to which to return.[34]

The precise number of those turned back for defects is difficult to pin down from available records, largely because of assumptions that linked disability and dependency. Until 1908, exclusions based on physical defects were mixed with nondefectives in the category of "likely to become a public charge." This was always the largest category of exclusion, but the criteria applied were never clear-cut. Lack of cash on hand by itself was not a primary factor, although it was taken into consideration. A 1911 congressional commission reported that "pauperism among newly admitted immigrants is relatively at a minimum, owing to the fact that the present immigration law provides for the admission only of the able-bodied," which suggests that disability was seen as the major factor in producing public charges.[35] After 1908, a rejected immigrant was counted in the category of "mental or physical defective" if he or she was deemed merely defective, but in the "public charge" category if he or she was both defective and a likely pauper.[36] In any case, taken together, exclusions in both categories grew from 0.6 percent of all immigrants in 1895 to 1.6 percent in 1910. They reached nearly 5 percent in 1915, when war in Europe dramatically reduced migration and allowed more careful inspection. By 1920, when immigration had rebounded, exclusions in these categories had fallen again, to 1 percent.[37]

These percentages seriously understate the impact of the laws, however. First, American immigration laws were widely advertised abroad, and many would not risk the journey knowing that they might be rejected. Second, not only were ship companies required after 1891 to return rejected immigrants to their port of embarkation at no charge and to pay a fine, but also the same provision applied if an immigrant was later discovered to have an excludable condition that initially passed unnoticed, up to a year after landing (increased to two years in 1903 and to three in 1907). Legislation in 1893 furthermore required a ship's surgeon to examine passengers and the captain to certify that none were defective. Shipping companies had strong incentives to refuse passage to questionable passengers.[38] Finally, ticket agents in Europe also became de facto inspectors because, as the superintendent of immigration noted approvingly in 1894, they were instructed to refuse tickets to "blind, deaf and dumb, and crippled persons" and fined for passengers subsequently rejected. A federal commission in 1911 conservatively estimated that ten times as many were refused transportation as were barred at U.S. ports.[39]

Histories of immigration policy that posit a selective and a restrictive phase attribute to each a distinct rationale: the former to screen out (alternatively, to sift, filter, strain, weed out, or winnow) undesirable individuals and the latter to reduce numbers overall and more particularly those of disfavored races. John Higham's *Strangers in the Land*, for decades after its publication in 1955 the standard work on immigration policy, was structured along these lines. Higham wrote that during the 1880s Congress "put aside plans for reducing the absolute number of immigrants and concentrated instead on regulation and 'selection.'" When legislation mandating a literacy test was passed by Congress but vetoed in 1907, he labeled it "the failure of restriction," concluding that no restrictive legislation "of any consequence became law for a decade after the essentially anti-restrictive measure of 1907."[40] This "anti-restrictive measure," in addition to prohibiting entry by idiots, imbeciles, feebleminded persons, epileptics, insane persons, and anyone with a history of insanity, also created the special provision for persons with any kind of "mental or physical defect," required that ship surgeons inspect passengers, and held ship captains responsible for affirming the absence of defective passengers.[41]

The first law that Higham considered restrictive in intent, because it mandated a literacy test, came in 1917. The distinction for Higham was that earlier laws were intended to screen individuals, while the literacy test was implicitly intended to target groups by race (which the quota laws later did explicitly).[42] Others have followed the same template, if not always the precise dates or terminology. In 1963, Marion T. Bennett maintained that the years between 1880 and 1920 were "generally called the Selective Period of qualitative controls," following which lawmakers "turned to numerical or quantitative restriction."[43] Edward Prince Hutchinson in 1981 agreed with Higham that the literacy test represented the "turning point in American immigration policy," when Congress made "a definite move from regulation to attempted restriction."[44] Roger Daniels, in 1990, declared the literacy test "the first significant general restriction ever passed"—adding later in his narrative, however, that "by 1917 the immigration policy of the United States had been restricted in seven major ways." The distinction between "major" and "significant general" restriction is unclear, but certainly Daniels did not see the exclusion of defectives as either. The seven major restrictions that he listed were those placed on Asians, criminals, violators of moral standards, persons with diseases, paupers, radicals, and illiterates.[45]

A variation on this approach was taken by Kenneth Ludmerer, who, in 1972, maintained that until the 1920s "federal policy embodied an economic, not a biological, view of immigration." The terms he used were somewhat different, but his argument was based on the same grounds, that the earlier laws prohibited "the entry of individuals (but not races) deemed undesirable—criminals, polygamists, anarchists, and the feebleminded." Leaving aside the incompleteness of this list, which omits many of the defects that were cause for exclusion, this interpretation assumes that when "the chief threat was considered to be the influx of degenerate persons, not degenerate races," policies were based on rational economic considerations; when the chief threat was degenerate races, however, policies were based on irrational prejudice rooted in eugenic thinking.[46]

The "public charge" provisions were often represented at the time as a question of ability to work and to avoid dependence on public assistance, and historians have generally taken this representation at face value. However, immigration officials never sought evidence that particular disabilities made people more likely to become public charges, and if so, which ones. It was at heart not an empirical claim but a cultural assumption that disability meant inability to live independently.[47] Women were similarly assumed to be homebound nonworkers and dependents despite the legions of working women and families dependent on them and were often rejected on that basis by immigration officials when they were unaccompanied by a male provider.[48]

Although the possibilities for workplace accommodations may be better understood today, they were not unknown at the time. Professionals in the growing rehabilitation movement condemned the "social arrangement that virtually condemns the cripple to mendicancy."[49] Henry Ford declared in 1914 that Americans "are too ready to assume without investigation that the full possession of faculties is a condition requisite to the best performance of all jobs,"[50] announced a nondiscrimination policy for disabled workers, and promptly hired thousands. The Red Cross Institute for Crippled and Disabled Men in New York City reported great success in finding employment for disabled workers in 1918.[51] Efficiency experts Frank and Lillian Gilbreth in 1920 advocated workplace reforms to "adapt the work to the man" by "rearranging the surroundings, equipment and tools . . . modifications of machinery, [or] changing the method by which the work is done." The chief obstacle, they argued, was the public's view "that the thought of a cripple re-entering competitive industrial life is repellent, that these people should be provided for by pensions in their homes."[52]

The reasons for unemployment among people with particular disabilities at particular moments in history are questions to be argued and demonstrated, not simply assumed. The design of industrial jobs was not a natural but a social artifact. Furthermore, whether or not legislators should be faulted for failing to recognize disability as a social rather than merely an individual problem, historians should place immigration restriction in context as one element in a society with systemic obstacles to independence for disabled people. Buildings, streets, transportation, and workplaces were designed for certain ways of functioning and not for others.

Even if we leave these questions aside, the economic explanation of restrictive policies is inadequate. In many cases, the defect for which immigrants were excluded entailed no impairment of function. For example, Donabet Mousekian, a photographer and Armenian refugee from Turkey, was rejected in 1905 for "feminism." As he said, "It won't do any harm to my working; what harm can I do to the U.S. by my being deprived of male organs?"[53] Many had been self-supporting in their home countries; Adrianus Boer, a skilled leather worker and saddle maker from the Netherlands, was rejected in 1905 for deafness in spite of having "always worked and supported the family without any outside help at all."[54] In some cases, an immigrant received a job offer before being deported; in 1913, the ironworker Moische Fischmann had fled an ongoing pogrom in his native Russia, and his brother, also an ironworker, brought a job offer from his own employer to the hearing, but Fischmann was deaf and so was turned away.[55] In many instances immigrants had family willing and able to support them if needed, such as Helena Bartnikowska, who, in 1908, was refused entry because, the inspector noted, "this supposed woman" was a "hermaphrodite."[56] Economic concerns were clearly part of the debate, but the argument that a selective policy during the early years of immigration law arose simply from practical economic considerations does not fit the evidence.

Although historians have distinguished selection from restriction, those engaged in the immigration debate at the time usually did not. Instead, they typically described immigration law as intended to accomplish restriction via selection. The 1882 act was understood as "restrictive" or "mildly restrictive."[57] Bureau of Immigration reports referred to "restrictive features" of the 1891 and 1893 laws, which were "framed to sift the incomers."[58] A brief surge in immigration early in 1893 was explained as immigrants rushing "to arrive before the restrictive measures" of the 1893 law took effect,[59] while the bureau predicted in 1894 that the "volume of immigration will be restricted" and its quality "will continue to improve" as a result of the law.[60] The prediction was vindicated the following year, the decline being steepest from "countries usually furnishing many of the most undesirable immigrants."[61] The report of 1897 trumpeted a decrease since 1891 "for which credit, in large part, must be given to restrictive legislation."[62]

In short, the laws were functioning as designed—simultaneously selective and restrictive—to keep out defective individuals, nudge in a satisfactory direction the racial balance of immigration, and reduce total immigration. The bureau's understanding of how the laws were working was not idiosyncratic; in 1892, the president of the New York Chamber of Commerce lauded the "restrictive laws" that excluded "lunatics, idiots," and others before calling for a literacy test to further restrict the number of immigrants and "improve their quality." In 1893, the chairman of the Senate Committee on Immigration recommended "further measures of restriction," and a year later the commissioner of Ellis Island pronounced the "sifting" and "winnowing" under the recent law "a great success as a restrictive measure."[63] A writer in the *Atlantic Monthly* backed him up, affirming that the efficacy of the law in "limiting the number and determining the quality of immigrants" had been "conclusively proved."[64]

As it later turned out, the laws excluding the unfit did not live up to the hopes of the restrictionists; immigration began to increase again after the turn of the century, and the market for new ideas to address the problem continued to be lively. Among the proposals was the literacy test, which, after twenty years of failed attempts, was finally enacted in 1917. The interpretation that this represented a turning point toward a policy of restriction may come from the report of the Dillingham Commission of 1911, the first comprehensive study of immigration to the United States, which described existing laws as merely selective and recommended a literacy test to restrict total volume. The commission, however, was departing from common usage, which did not change after the report was issued. Moreover, in places the report blurred the distinction just as other writers and officials had typically done. For example, the report's "Minority View" described the literacy test as "a selective test" and elsewhere quoted advocates who argued that it would weed out undesirables but "not permanently cut down the number of our immigrants to any considerable degree."[65] A Senate report described the test as likely to "tell most heavily against those classes of immigrants . . .

excluded by existing law, and is therefore a continuance of the present policy of the United States which has met with general acceptance."[66] That is, it was not restrictive of numbers overall and did not represent a break from past practice.

Historians may also have included the literacy test with racial quotas under the mantle of restriction because of its association with the Immigration Restriction League, which had promoted it ever since its founding in Boston in 1894. League publications, however, promoted it as a more practical and effective method of restriction but still an extension of earlier methods, "far more selective than any other test proposed." Moreover, they argued that "it is certain to improve the quality of the aliens; but it is not certain to very largely diminish their numbers." Its constitution defined the goal as "further judicious restriction" and "further exclusion of elements undesirable for citizenship."[67] The two principal founders of the league, Prescott Hall and Robert DeCourcy Ward, both described their support for the literacy test as a question of efficacy. Hall wrote in 1904 that current laws were theoretically sound but "practically" incapable of solving the "main problem of the proper selection of immigrants." Writing in that same year, Ward similarly favored the "further restriction of immigration" with a new method for "selecting" desirable immigrants, maintaining that "inspection of the incoming aliens on the dock" was inadequate to the task. The literacy test was the best solution chiefly "because the measure will be practical."[68]

Historians have generally understood the literacy test as a proxy for race. That it was a proxy for other matters was widely conceded at the time. Rather than race, however, its advocates frequently and openly described it as an effective screen for individual fitness.[69] When race was invoked, it was in the context of a tendency toward defect in certain races, for it was commonly said that "illiterate races are generally inferior in physique," as well as prone to insanity and violence.[70] Hall insisted that although for the purposes of studying the effects of immigrants on society, "it is convenient to consider them by nationalities," nevertheless, in practice, "each individual must be judged on his own merits without race proscription or prejudice."[71] Ward similarly argued that with appropriate policies "we can pick out the best specimens of each race to be our own fellow-citizens and to be the parents of our future citizens," and he took pains to stress that "it should be most emphatically stated that no one should object to the coming of the better classes of Italians, Austrians, and Russians, even in fairly large numbers."[72]

Ward and other restrictionists did write a great deal about race. Ward stated in 1904, for example, "We have spent too much time studying the economic sides of the question," and "There is a racial side which is even more important than all the economic aspects put together." This seems to suggest that he would next advocate immigration restriction on the basis of race, but he did not, instead urging more effective methods of selection. When Ward wrote that the "question before us is a race question," he meant that inferior types were outbreeding superior types, that the "highest stratum" would eventually be "eliminated in the course of natural selection," and that this would "profoundly affect the character of the future American race." It was not a problem of foreign races per se so much as it was the decline of the American race due to an influx of inferior individuals. He believed that the debate had focused too much on the economic costs of defective immigrants in the present and that the important issue was the genetic future of the nation.[73]

Evolutionary thinking of the time posited two levels of competition, one in which individuals competed for survival and another in which groups—families, communities, races, and nations—competed. Eugenicists generally believed that within each race the fittest individuals would rise to the top. Thus if the best of other nations came to the United States, that would enhance its standing in the competition of nations. The problem was that the best of other races did not as a rule emigrate, but rather the worst. Charles Davenport, the founder of the Eugenics Records Office at Cold Spring Harbor in 1910, insisted that "no race per se . . . is dangerous and none undesirable." Instead, he advocated investigating the pedigree of prospective immigrants; those with family histories of "imbecile, epileptic, insane, criminalistic, alcoholic, and sexually immoral tendencies" should be refused entry.[74]

One of the literacy requirement's early advocates, the chairman of the Senate Immigration Committee, William Chandler, believed that it would sift out more of the "degraded immigrants" but insisted that "no indiscriminate opposition to the admission of all foreigners of any particular races (except the Asiatic) is contemplated by any one."[75] As late as 1920, just a year before Congress passed its first racial quotas, Harry Laughlin still insisted that regulation should take the form of nonracial, selective laws, although he conceded that since strict selective laws would disproportionately affect people from inferior nations, they would appear racist even if they were not.[76] Advocates of the literacy test readily conceded that it was a blunt instrument, that illiteracy did not in itself make an immigrant undesirable, and that the test would bar many desirable immigrants along with undesirable ones; nevertheless, they favored it as "the only immediate practicable means of reducing the immense volume of immigration as well as improving the average quality."[77]

That the literacy test was intended as a proxy for screening out defective types of individuals is evidenced by the other proposal most advocated by restrictionists: the physical test. Support for a physical test was, like that for the literacy test, of long standing. The commissioner general in 1898, for example, had argued for a physical standard to provide "intelligent, discriminating restriction."[78] The issue gained prominence, however, when William Williams, commissioner of Ellis Island, took up the cause in 1903. Over the next several years, Williams used lectures to university and civic groups, newspaper articles, and annual reports to advocate a physical exam to exclude those "of low vitality, of poor physique . . . and unfitted mentally or morally for good citizenship." The problem was that excluding defectives still required finding that they were likely to become public charges, but "it is obviously impossible to exclude on this ground all persons whose physical condition is poor." Williams's concerns were not confined to the question of self-support. He granted that the laws already screened out "mere scum or refuse," but further measures were needed to eliminate those who, while not clearly "riff-raff," were far from desirable. He therefore urged legislation to make immigrants of "poor physique" excludable on that basis alone, without the necessity of claiming that capacity for self-support was impaired. This would significantly reduce immigration, especially by "undesirable and unintelligent people from Southern and Eastern Europe." However, like most restrictionists, he emphasized that it was not national origin or race per se that was the problem, but that too many people from certain parts of the world were defective.[79]

Williams's proposal received widespread support. In a memorandum the following year, the commissioner general explained (with admirable syntax) that "a certificate of this nature implies that the alien concerned is afflicted with a body but illy adapted [sic] . . . to the work necessary to earn his bread . . . undersized, poorly developed [and] physically degenerate, and as such, not only unlikely to become a desirable citizen, but also very likely to transmit his undesirable qualities to his offspring, should he unfortunately for the country in which he is domiciled, have any."[80] Both Hall and Ward of the Immigration Restriction League wrote articles, as well as letters to Congress and the Immigration Bureau, to advocate legislation taking up Williams's proposals. Ward described poor physique as the greatest threat posed by immigration to the fitness of the American stock. Hall suggested that the physical and literacy tests were similar proxies that would tend to eliminate the same degenerate types of immigrants.[81] Williams's efforts were rewarded when the provision excluding persons with a mental or physical defect, regardless of any impact on capacity for self-support, was incorporated into the Immigration Act of 1907.

Although one of the attractive benefits of excluding the physically deficient was that it would apply especially to unwelcome races, the principal motive was to exclude individuals considered defective. The most undesirable were from "Greece, South Italy and Syria, as well as most Hebrews, Magyars, Armenians and Turks," according to one official, but "strict enforcement of the present medical laws will automatically exclude these races to a sufficient extent, admitting the few who are fit."[82] The commissioner general emphasized in 1910 that physical inspection was needed "to preserve and improve the American race" because the "strength of a nation is the combined strength of its individual members."[83]

Race indeed mattered to restrictionists, but it was the "American race," the "American of tomorrow," that figured most conspicuously in their rhetoric. And although they thought that certain races contributed a disproportionate share of defective blood to American veins, the primary problem was defect rather than race. The popular writer Montaville Flowers maintained that "citizenship in our land is not primarily a question of race, but it is a question of individual fitness which may be determined by the national and racial inheritances of their fatherlands."[84] The biologist Edward M. East bluntly stated the essential equation for restrictionists: "If in the future the proportion of people of Grades A and B increases, the nation will prosper; while if the proportion of people of Grades D and E increases, the nation will decay." He concluded that the "eugenic ideals" of selective reproduction and immigration were "the sole and final means of keeping a nation from deterioration."[85]

Many worried about the scale of immigration, but defect figured more prominently. If "hordes" of immigrants were a problem, the real catastrophe, according to the New York surgeon Arthur Fisk, was that "an ever increasing horde of degenerates from all nations is entering our fair land, who are debasing the physical, mental and moral being of the nation."[86] The economist Irving Fisher, founding president of the American Eugenics

Society in 1921, emphasized that population growth or decline was in itself neither good nor bad: "The eugenist is interested in the quality of human beings rather than their quantity." The main problem was that the United States was "a dumping ground for relieving Europe of its burden of defectives, delinquents and dependents." He argued that if "indiscriminate immigration is dysgenic, a discriminating exclusion must be eugenic," and he advocated "having aliens examined in their home countries for mental and other defects." The main eugenic demand was for a better means of selection, not reduced numbers.[87]

It became increasingly clear over the years that physical inspection could not accomplish the desired end in the face of ever-rising numbers of immigrants. The sheer scale of immigration overwhelmed the system. To adequately inspect the thousands of immigrants pouring into the country would be too difficult, time consuming, and expensive. The assistant surgeon general of the Public Health Service told the House of Representatives in 1920 that "a complete medical examination requires at least an hour [and] one examiner could not handle more than 20 immigrants a day." Given the several thousand immigrants landing at Ellis Island most days, the existing facilities were inadequate; instead of the forty medical examiners currently assigned there on any given day, one hundred fifty would be required.[88]

The literacy test has been interpreted as a deliberate but veiled attempt to exclude certain races, but the fact that it was considered a "blunt instrument" suggests otherwise. If it were aimed at racial groups, it would be a sharp instrument indeed, cutting out only selected individuals from within races. It was a blunt instrument because it was considered a less precise but also a less difficult, time-consuming, and expensive alternative to individual inspection. When it finally came in 1917, its advocates were again disappointed. It was efficient and practical, as promised, but in the twenty-some years since it had first been proposed, public education and literacy in Europe had improved markedly. The test had little effect.

For forty years, Congress, the press, and restrictionists grappled with the problem of how to allow desirables in while keeping undesirables out. For a decade before passage of the first quota bill in 1921, advocates built on the public consensus that had formed in favor of excluding defective individuals to advance laws restricting undesirable races. They quoted expert opinion that immigrants from southern and eastern Europe contributed a disproportionate share of hereditary feeblemindedness.[89] A physician and specialist in "medical sociology" warned about "the slow-witted Slav," the "poor physique" and "neurotic condition of our Jewish immigrants," and the "degenerate and psychopathic types, which are so conspicuous and numerous among the immigrants."[90] The sociologist Frederick Bushee maintained that the "immigration of southern Italians brings a large superfluous population of hot-headed men who are fit only for unskilled labor," and moreover that "the high rate of infant mortality among the Italians indicates small physical stability." Similarly, "the Irish have not that toughness, that power to resist disease, shown by some of the other nationalities," and their "physical instability is shown by the exceptionally large number of defectives among them."[91] A Public Health Service physician and later professor of tropical medicine at the University of California, Alfred C. Reed, asserted that the "Greeks offer a sad contrast to their ancient progenitors, as poor physical development is the rule among those who reach Ellis Island, and they have above their share of other defects," while Jews have a "predisposition to functional insanities," and "the proportion of defectives to total landed is greatest among the Syrians." In short, "no one can stand at Ellis Island and see the physical and mental wrecks who are stopped there . . . without becoming a firm believer in restriction."[92]

Public advocates echoed the experts. After observing immigrants disembarking at Ellis Island, one wrote that "the physiognomy of certain groups unmistakably proclaims inferiority of type." He could see that "in every face there was something wrong. . . . There were so many sugar-loaf heads, moon-faces, slit mouths, lantern-jaws, and goose-bill noses that one might imagine a malicious jinn had amused himself by casting human beings in a set of skew-molds discarded by the Creator." Their bodies were inferior to those of earlier immigrants: "South Europeans run to low stature. A gang of Italian navvies . . . present, by their dwarfishness, a curious contrast to other people. The Portuguese, the Greeks, and the Syrians are, from our point of view, undersized. The Hebrew immigrants are very poor in physique . . . the polar opposite of our pioneer breed."[93] The issues of race and defect became inextricably intertwined. Undesirable races were made so by their heavy burden of defective heredity, and defective individuals, should they become sufficiently numerous, had the potential to drag down any race.

Beginning with the Emergency Quota Act of 1921 and continuing with the National Origins Act of 1924, immigration policy shifted emphasis. The 1921 act limited annual immigration from any country to 3 percent of the number identified to be of that nationality in the 1910 U.S. census. The 1924

Immigration Act reduced the number to 2 percent and substituted the 1890 census. As long hoped, an immigration law finally achieved severe reductions in immigration from southern and eastern Europe. It did not replace existing laws but complemented them—excluding defectives disproportionately affected immigrants from inferior nations, while quotas on those nations likewise reduced the numbers of defectives. Like the literacy and physical requirements, the quota laws were not a departure but a continuation of the search for an effective means of excluding defective people.

This "restrictive phase" was simultaneously a "selective phase." Most obviously, the earlier laws remained in place, and selection by physical inspection continued. More important, if Congress had intended quotas merely to restrict numbers, it would have based them on the populations of countries of origin or some other neutral formula or set an annual cap after which no immigrants would be accepted. Instead, it devised a system that selected immigrants of desirable nationality and race and deselected those of undesirable ones. Desirable nations had far more generous quotas than those considered undesirable (so high that they would rarely be filled). The quota laws were a continuation of selective policy by other means.

In 1925, Secretary of Labor James J. Davis looked back over the history of immigration policy and reflected on the present. The major reason, as he saw it, that Americans had chosen to gradually narrow their gates to immigrants over the preceding four decades was that they believed that their country had "become an asylum for the alien insane, defective, and degenerate." Inspection alone had proved unable to cope with the "great wholesale pressure of immigration which would completely swamp us." The best argument in favor of quotas, he believed, was that they slowed immigration to the point that careful and rigorous selection was possible. If that were possible to accomplish without quotas, the "retail method of selection" would be "the fairest test of fitness" and "the better way of selecting our guests and future citizens." He believed that "most civilized races contribute good, sound strains of family and individuals." Race had never been the central issue, he insisted, but it had to be acknowledged that "such races are spotted with defective, degenerate, and inferior lines and stocks."[94]

The advent of federal immigration laws reflected both the growing nationalism of the period and the expanded powers accorded the national government, but the content of those policies reflected particular and evolving notions of citizenship. Although immigration policy was shaped by varied and often conflicting interests and constituencies, it offers a valuable measure of how Americans defined the worthy citizen. Because citizens performed multiple roles, these policies were continually reshaped in ways intended to protect and enhance economic well-being, political order, cultural values, social cohesion, health, and safety. Thus the many categories of exclusion discussed in histories of American immigration law during this period: disfavored races and nationalities, criminals, violators of moral standards, the sick, the poor, political radicals, and illiterates. In recent years, studies on the roles of gender and sexuality have further complicated our understanding of the workings of immigration law.[95] In short, the picture is complex.

The fundamental role of defect in the history of American immigration law has received far less critical inquiry than its prominence in the laws would seem to demand. Defects that today would fit comfortably in the category of disability were the most prominent issues in the restriction debate and in legislation before the 1920s. Furthermore, most of the other categories of exclusion were also understood as varieties of defect. An undesirable race was one in which defects proliferated; the diseased were often those whose degenerate constitutions made them susceptible; criminals and the otherwise immoral were feebleminded or "moral imbeciles"; deviant sexuality was a mark of degeneracy; political radicals were mentally unsound; poverty was symptomatic of inborn psychopathic inferiority. Even the capacities to adopt democratic norms and to assimilate in American society were frequently cast as qualities lacking in many immigrants and carried in the blood.[96] All defects were potentially heritable and at odds with any notion of useful American citizenship.

The history of immigration policy has focused primarily on the analytic categories of race and ethnicity, followed by class and economic interest. To the extent that eugenics has been included in the story, it has been to decry its invidious application to ethnoracial groups. This may well be a result of its close ties to the larger field of immigration history, which has developed largely as the study of ethnic groups, an emphasis reflected in the title of the leading journal in the field, the *Journal of American Ethnic History*. It may also have to do with the fact that class, race, and ethnicity deal with recognized and politically salient groups. Although people with disabilities also formed groups, networks, and organizations built around shared values and common interests, these were neither large nor widely known and were typically organized around particular disabilities. There were no calls for defectives of the world to unite, no pandisability associations. In his 1922 polemic against the eugenics movement, G. K. Chesterton lamented that "there is no trade union of defective children," and that therefore opposition to eugenics amounted to "protests so ineffectual about wrongs so individual." Chesterton feared that this same dynamic would make the injuries inflicted on disabled people less visible in history, "trivial tragedies that will fade faster and faster in the flux of time."[97]

Defectives did form a large and powerful group, however, in the thoughts of eugenically minded Americans, where the defective population assumed frightening and ever-growing proportions, even while uncounted others from abroad clamored to add to it.[98] The exclusion of "the defective" was not merely a matter of rational economic choice but rather of the survival of the nation. As their fears increased, defect became a crucial element in defining the undesirability of others and making a compelling justification for their exclusion. Assumptions about the inheritance of acquired characteristics, the mutability of defects across generations, the threat of "degeneracy," and the conviction that defective types were reproducing faster than anyone else meant that a great deal hung in the balance. This was the meaning and the import of "selective" immigration in a eugenic nation.

CHAPTER 3

# The Disremembered Past

Susan Burch and Hannah Joyner

Historians remember. We try to "recapture the past" and hold those events "in mind for attention or consideration."[1] Remembering can be, according to the *Oxford English Dictionary*, "recall[ing] the memory of (a person) with some kind of feeling or intention." It is through remembering that we as humans construct who we are and where we have come from. Historians have assisted that process by preserving and analyzing what is left of the past: the stories passed down to us in their entirety, as well as the fragments that help us rebuild what has been forgotten. The dictionary's definition suggests that "remember" can also mean "mention favorably" or "commemorate."[2] Recent generations of scholars have drawn critical attention to the past, have mentioned marginalized groups favorably, and in so doing have provided subtle and complex ways to commemorate the past. As with all historical work, our scholarship benefits from and builds on our predecessors' efforts.

With this in mind, we suggest that historians have not merely remembered; we also have misremembered, dismembered, and even disremembered the past. When we isolate specific identity vectors (such as race or gender) or specific social forces (such as oppression), the accounts produced are just as incomplete as if we had only considered one class of human being. This misremembers the past.

We have deconstructed, we have dismembered, the lives of people in the past, turning them into neat theoretical categories rather than trying to understand the messy complexity of their lived experiences. Historian Glenda Gilmore addresses this issue: "The subfields of the discipline [of history]—

African American history, women's history, social history, southern history, political history—are drawn by and for historians. Analyses that separate these subfields misrepresent the way people actually lived their lives."[3]

Toni Morrison offers the terms "disremembered" and "rememory" as a way to approach a more complete understanding of the past. Our reliance on certain kinds of evidence (often text based and produced by people of privilege) inherently limits the disciplinary reach to examine and struggle with lives that exist beyond the page. Although oral history and other methodological innovations have closed some of this gap, many histories remain fractured and incomplete, or disremembered.

The word "disremember" comes from Morrison's powerful novel *Beloved*, where it is used by the character Sethe to mean a deliberate effort to escape from painful memories. Although the disremembered history may be forced out of consciousness, it is never truly dead and continues to inform the present. As historians such as Fitzhugh Brundage, Estelle B. Freedman, Janice Brockley, Benjamin Madley, and others have shown, confronting the atrocities of our pasts productively challenges scholars and mainstream society to reconsider who we have been and why.[4] It is only through acknowledgment of those horrors and analysis of their impacts that we can begin to bridge the distance between scholarly work and historical experiences as they actually were lived. This struggle makes more obvious their effect on individuals, as well as communities, across geographic, temporal, and social boundaries. It fosters new ways to understand how the shadows of these difficult pasts shape how and what we preserve as history, why we interpret that history the way we do, and how our interpretations are used.

In our times, "dis" (or often "diss") means "treat with disrespect," "disparage." To "diss" someone is to refuse to give them their due. "Disremembering," then, means treating parts of our past, perhaps certain people or communities in our past, as if they did not deserve to be treated as full and equal human beings. Examples of disremembering abound: the absence of people with disabilities and disability-related terms in most historical indexes, the marginal space inhabited by disabled people in most studies of American (or other) histories even though disabled people represent the largest minority in the world, and the tendency not to preserve sources by or about disabled people.

"Dis" also refers directly to disability. Historians who have theorized categories of identity, such as gender and race, have spent very little time critically engaging issues of disability as a cultural category. As scholars like

Paul Longmore, Kim Nielsen, and Katherine Ott have shown, most references to disabled people draw on a Western biomedical interpretation of disability.[5] Simply put, this tradition regards disability exclusively or primarily as a pathology that resides in the individual. Advocates of this model examine and express disability as a defect that requires medical intervention in order to "cure" or mediate what is viewed as an inherent "problem." But, as critical disability studies scholars regularly demonstrate, disability and normalcy are culturally and historically contingent categories. Attitudes, beliefs, and environment significantly shape the meaning of disability, as they do many other aspects of human identities. Adhering to a sociocultural interpretation of disability, critical disability scholars have drawn attention to dynamic, relational, and highly contextual historical understandings of disability. This engagement recognizes that people with disabilities have a rich history that is fundamental to the broader understanding of the past.[6]

How to "re-member" history matters a great deal. As Gerda Lerner suggests, contributory scholarship ("add a woman and stir" historical works) produces a limited form of understanding of women and of the past; similarly, most disability historians resist "add a disabled person or group and stir" scholarship.[7] Frequently, work emanating from critical disability studies recenters the research focus to consider the perspectives and lives of men, women, and children who have had—or were perceived to have had—disabilities. It seeks to integrate these histories within the broader historical landscape and dissolve the boundaries—perceived, acculturated, and material—that commonly separate disabled people from broader community narratives.

Our work is not the full answer to Morrison's call to engage more directly with traumatic, complex, and deeply human experiences from the past, but it does offer one response: we seek to bring her idea of disremembering into dialogue with disability history. What a disability studies approach can teach us is that we do not need to look for a cure for all troubling issues. There is great benefit to an honest attempt to appreciate the past, reckon with it, struggle mightily with it at times, and, perhaps most importantly, include even the messy parts rather than whitewash them or erase them altogether.

Three interrelated goals motivate this essay. First, we envisage a theoretical framework for deaf cultural history that more closely approximates the lived realities of these often marginalized communities and their relationship to broader mainstream society. Eschewing "identity hierarchies," this project examines deaf history with close attention to myriad forces shaping identity and human experience. These forces include (but are not limited to) race, ethnicity, gender, sexuality, socioeconomic status, disability, age, and place. Rather than considering factors shaping identity as meeting at the intersections, we view them as deeply interdependent, constantly shaping, inflecting, complicating, and otherwise amplifying the meaning of one another. Interdependence rigorously struggles with the reality that individuals and groups simultaneously embody numerous and complicated characteristics; gender, sex, race, ethnicity, class, and disability are only some of the major features that make us who we are at any given time. An interdependent approach to historical identity also draws attention to the powerful role context plays in bringing out, negotiating, and interpreting various components of an individual's or group's identity. This recognizes the highly relational character of identities perceived, performed, and claimed as well. This essay also attempts to expand and complicate traditional deaf cultural histories by acknowledging and critically examining experiences of removal. This fundamental addition reinforces the theoretical and lived claim that deaf—and disability—identities are socially constructed; it honors and emphasizes that relationships among individuals, groups, and the state color the meaning of "deaf" and "disability." In so doing, it invites scholars to consider what and who else remain in the margins—perhaps we should say the locked wards—of our historical work.

The third goal is cumulative. We are trying to revisit histories of people who have been removed from the broader national U.S. narrative. We want to re-member people into the histories they lived. We seek to demonstrate that an interdependent framework that goes beyond typical category-bound analyses or systems-based interpretations can be useful and perhaps even necessary. And we argue that this framework and this application open us to new understandings of the past.

When historians try to re-member stories from the past, they often rely on theoretical concepts to help them gain access to particular histories. One approach, intersectionality, posits that analyzing the points of intersection of categories of identity can help us understand systems of oppression.[8] For example, works by important and pioneering historians, such as Evelyn Brooks Higginbotham, Vicky Ruiz, and Ellen DuBois, illustrate the value of engaging with race, gender, and class.[9] But these works, like most intersectional historical studies, reveal fairly selected applications, commonly limiting the focus and recognition to these three categories. As Wendy Brown has argued, intersectionality theory also does not take fully into account the ways in which race, sex, gender, and class are fundamentally different systems.[10] Importantly, Brown, too, limits the focus of the critique to these categories, overlooking other central aspects of identity, including age, disability, and geographic location, to name just a few. This deliberate focus on (at most) race, gender, and socioeconomic class inaccurately suggests that such factors as disability are discrete and can be isolated. It assumes that identity factors intersect in certain instances but potentially not in others. In addition, it skews historical understanding by privileging select forces and experiences, essentially reinscribing a hierarchical model of identity. Race, class, and gender are not the only factors that affect identity. Age, disability, location, time period, national origins, faith traditions, and a vast constellation of other points of identity are always present, even if they are less scrutinized or less understood. Struggling with the reality that all these factors—and others— shape any given society invites a more dynamic and humanized understanding of how our social systems are constructed.

As historians, our interests are not only the creation of social systems. We also seek to understand the experiences of real people who created their lives within those social systems. Understanding the lives of individuals requires us to ask questions that cannot fit neatly into an intersectional approach. Shaped by complex and dynamic relations between and among persons and between groups, individual life stories often defy broad categories and problematize any systemic framing. Instead of intersectionalty, we argue that interdependence is a more useful conceptual tool to help us understand the lives of the people in the past. Identity is dynamic: categories like race and gender and disability constantly shape, inflect, complicate, and amplify the resonance of one another and change their meanings in different times and places.

Narrowing the lens and focusing on individuals and the contexts in which they created their lives reward us with stories that are complicated, personal, diverse, embodied, shifting, and interactive. We acknowledge that individual life stories do not necessarily represent broad populations or experiences, but microhistory and biography give us the chance to ask "large questions in small places."[11] Intense study of the particular offers assets not available in broader historical and theoretical analysis. The unique qualities of an individual's story make very real the ways interdependent forces shape lives.

We have chosen to explore these specific questions of identity interdependence by returning to a subject about which we have written in a different context: the disremembered history of an African American deaf man, Junius Wilson, who lived in North Carolina during the twentieth century.[12] Wilson's story gives historians a lens to view traditional historical topics, such as the changing meanings of race or the development of institutions in this southern state. Focusing on personal experiences of large social contexts reveals elements of those contexts that might otherwise be obscured. In addition, Wilson's story suggests new avenues of analysis and underscores the importance of historicizing disability, as well as pointing out the centrality of the theme of removal—a theme we will develop further in this essay.

Junius Wilson was born in Castle Hayne in 1908 and entered the racially segregated North Carolina State School for the Colored Deaf and Blind Children in Raleigh in 1916. North Carolina, the first southern state to create such an educational institution, established its school for black deaf youth in 1868. For several decades, this segregated school provided space for deaf people and signing (nondeaf) relatives of different races and ethnicities to serve as teachers. Adult children of Chang and Eng Bunker (the original "Siamese twins"), all of whom were graduates of the white school, taught at the institution. Brothers Thomas and David Tillinghast, master signers and prominent figures in the white deaf cultural world, were leading instructors at the North Carolina school.[13] Two black deaf teachers—Thomas Flowers and Blanche Williams, graduates of northern residential schools for the deaf—joined the faculty in the 1890s and remained for nearly two decades.

By World War I, all the deaf teachers had left the school. The white deaf school had been reestablished across the state in Morganton, and administrators changed the institution's communication policies. This meant that black deaf children at the school had few adult deaf role models or a consistent means to transmit a codified sign language. Separated geographically from white deaf schools and other black deaf schools, Raleigh's students developed and shaped a signed communication that increasingly differed from the American Sign Language used by earlier generation of educated deaf faculty. Hearing, nonsigning black teachers, often graduates of nearby Shaw University, had to learn "Raleigh signs" from the students in order to conduct their classes. Over time, the Raleigh school community became a microcosmic linguistic group whose means of communication was truly accessible only to its immediate community. Raleigh school signs were not fully understandable by deaf people, black or white, outside this school.[14] Of course, nonsigning hearing people could not understand the language developed at the Raleigh school.[15]

Even with these limitations, Raleigh signs were fundamentally important to Junius Wilson and his peers from the deaf school. Through signs, deaf people not only gained access to knowledge but also acquired the foundations of a cultural identity. When Wilson crossed the threshold of the school, he entered a distinct world and in time began to adopt a new cultural identity: that of a black deaf North Carolinian. Signature qualities of this historical acculturation included a sign name, a deaf-centered folklore and forms of humor, intimate physical proximity to other signers, and various ways to command attention, share information, and navigate the world.

Along with most other children who attended deaf residential schools, Junius Wilson embraced cultural deafness, including aspects of that culture that often made hearing people uneasy: yelling, stomping feet, or slapping tables to catch the attention of others; standing in close physical proximity to others; and sustaining eye contact. Hugging or touching one another also was a celebrated element of deaf culture. As generations of students have attested, the many hours together, particularly outside the classroom, combined with a shared linguistic identity and code of values and beliefs, promoted a tight-knit community. Across these generations, students shared information and experiences that profoundly shaped their worldviews and senses of self and community.[16]

It was not uncommon for students to be barely able to read or write when they left school. Until 1932, no student formally graduated from this school.[17] Wilson managed to stay almost eight years before his dismissal. On October 24, 1924, the deaf teenager was sent back to Castle Hayne because of "unsatisfactory conduct and progress." When the school took students to the State Negro Fair in Raleigh, he "slipped away . . . and stayed 2 nights and 1 day."[18]

Removal from the school incurred additional costs for someone like Wilson. Disability discrimination compounded Jim Crow oppression and made it difficult for the black deaf male teenager to find work, contribute to the family economy, fit into his kinship community, or even communicate in any significant way with others in Castle Hayne. Race, gender, age, disability, place, and socioeconomic status (to name just a few factors) all informed the complex, dangerous, and vulnerable place Wilson inhabited in the 1920s.

In Castle Hayne, Wilson's behavior was a significant problem for his family; his staring, touching, and unintelligible noises were interpreted as animalistic. These behaviors were common at deaf schools but alien in this nondeaf environment. Tensions mounted. It was logical for the family to fear that these behaviors could be misinterpreted by white bosses and, perhaps more disturbingly, by white women. Race riots across the nation had spiked in the years after World War I. Ku Klux Klan membership gained momentum in this era as well. The threat of violent retribution for real or perceived infractions of Jim Crow haunted black communities across this region.

In this complicated context, a neighbor and adopted kin, Arthur Smith, came to the conclusion that Wilson's possible conflict with the white population could represent a genuine danger for the family. Ultimately, he took matters into his own hands. In 1925, he accused Wilson (apparently falsely) of attempted assault with intent to rape an African American woman. Police officers arrested the deaf teenager and removed him to the Wilmington jail.

Uninformed of Wilson's hearing status, the jailer, jury, and judge—all white nondeaf men—misinterpreted his deafness as mental incompetence, first viewing him as "feebleminded" and then as "insane."[19] According to the trial report, the doctor who evaluated Wilson never mentioned his deafness. He assessed Wilson's inability to respond "appropriately" to his voiced questions and directions as indications of mental incompetence and perhaps of trickery. Emphasizing the charges brought against Wilson, the prosecutor elicited from the physician authoritative confirmation that the teenager was a danger to himself or others. Unable (literally) to speak on his own behalf and absent others who understood his signed form of communication, Wilson—a young black man accused of a sex crime—was read by the jurors as incompetent and deviant. Consequently, they deemed him unable to stand trial in a criminal case and had him removed to the Criminal Ward of the State Hospital for the Negro Insane (later renamed Cherry Hospital) in Goldsboro. In 1931, the superintendent of the mental hospital further misjudged Wilson, drawing on the original charges and supplementing them with fabricated diagnoses in his petition for the inmate's forced sterilization. Granted this by the Eugenics Board, he performed the castration himself. Taking advantage of Wilson's otherwise "healthy" body, W. C. Linville then sent the inmate to labor on the hospital farm. Wilson worked there, uncompensated, for roughly thirty years.

In 1947, twenty-one years after Wilson's removal to the asylum, Wilson's younger sister, Carrie, and his father, Sidney, came to the campus and tried to obtain his release. They argued that Wilson's mother needed her son to build her a home in Castle Hayne, and that it was time for him to be (re)integrated into his kinship community. The hospital refused their request. Wilson did not see his family members for almost fifty more years. He ultimately spent over seven decades in the institution, surrounded mostly (and most of the time) by people who did not understand his signed communication.

Civil rights activism ultimately affected Wilson's life as the hospital desegregated in the mid-1960s. With the subsequent closing of the institution's farm, Wilson and his peers were removed from this comparatively privileged space—the metal-covered brick farm dormitory and the vast cultivated and natural land surrounding it—and sent to the main campus. In the next decade, disability civil rights activists successfully campaigned for the release of inmates in psychiatric institutions. More diverse options for treatment in this period contributed to more than 90 percent of institutionalized men, women, and youths leaving locked wards across the United States. North Carolina's effective deinstitutionalization rate was similar: 86.7 percent.[20] During the 1970s and 1980s, staff doctors also formally concluded that Wilson was sane. At the same time, an investigation by a caseworker revealed that the criminal charges had been dropped. Technically, there were no legal grounds to keep Wilson there. Yet he was, for twenty more years. Why?

Bureaucratic policies, compounded by disabling attitudes, shaped the rationales given for holding Wilson at the hospital. For example, over the years, by working odd jobs, Wilson had accumulated several thousand dollars that was kept in a hospital account. Although he himself did not have direct access to the money, its presence ironically disqualified him from the federal programs like Medicaid that would have supported housing for him outside the hospital if he had been released.

Ableist and audist beliefs also strongly shaped Wilson's role and place at Cherry Hospital. Many staff members assumed that Wilson's deafness eliminated any ability for him to live independently. As a hospital employee explained in a 1975 questionnaire about Wilson's mental and physical status, the deaf inmate was "unable to care for himself because of his handicapps [sic]."[21] Another wrote in Wilson's medical file that "although the patient appears to be able to adjust to some extent in the hospital setting, it is doubtful in view of his being a deaf-mute whether he would be able to adjust to a

community setting."[22] A fellow staff member insisted, "I don't think attempts should be made to get him in the community because for sure it
would disrupt his whole life."[23]

Most of the Goldsboro hospital employees we interviewed had little or
no exposure to broader deaf cultural communities and—like many people
outside deaf cultural societies—held narrow views about deaf people's capabilities. Affirming their role as caregivers, many hospital staff judged Wilson unprepared for the outside world and insisted that it would be cruel to
release him. One explained, "This is his home and I do not think he should
be sent away from his home."[24] Instead, *they* signed forms that made Wilson
a "voluntary" patient at the hospital in this period.

During the 1980s, hospital officials became increasingly aware of Wilson as a deaf person. At this time he underwent several evaluations in which
specialists who knew sign language suggested that the hospital accommodate him with actual sign language. These men and women read Wilson
"through deaf eyes" and offered starkly different descriptions of the deaf man:
"a loner, intelligent, quiet." In one conversation with a signer, Wilson was
asked, "Where are you from?" He fingerspelled back clearly "Castle Hayne."
The evaluator asked for clarification: "Near Wilmington?" He nodded in
affirmation.[25] This exchange was among the first in Wilson's six decades at the
institution in which he could communicate beyond mere gestures with his
interviewer.

Unfortunately, in 1986, Wilson suffered a stroke that incapacitated his
dominant right arm. This impaired his ability to communicate; it also
marked him as a person with multiple disabilities. His inability to perform
tasks that had previously earned him money and certain privileges informed the decision to remove him from these roles and the locations that
he had claimed as partly his. This had material and personal consequences.
Goods that he had been able to acquire, such as chewing tobacco, candy, and
soda, were no longer available to him. Opportunities to spend time around
familiar staff and friends disappeared because he was forced to remain in
the geriatric ward. The judgment of Wilson as increasingly (and differently)
incompetent and nearing the end of his life motivated hospital staff to seek
new legal guardianship for him.

In the early 1990s, John Wasson, the assistant director for social services
in New Hanover County, became Junius Wilson's legal guardian. Wasson
interpreted Wilson's medical files through a decidedly different lens than
had generations of doctors, nurses, social workers, and health-care techni-

cians. He concluded that Wilson was a victim of racism and bureaucratic inertia. Consequently, he and a team of lawyers brought suit on Wilson's behalf, seeking the black deaf man's release from the locked ward.

In 1992, North Carolina settled the lawsuit. The agreement provided for the elderly man's continuing care. It gave him a small house on the grounds of the institution where he would live out his days semi-independently. Although his moving-in day was delayed by the discovery of asbestos in the cottage during its renovation, by 1994 Junius Wilson was, at least in theory, a free man living in his own home.

To Wasson and other members of Wilson's health support team, Wilson, who by this time had spent almost three-quarters of a century within the institution, did not appear to have the life skills or physical health to assimilate fully into mainstream society. The hospital hired Everett Parker to be a companion for Wilson. Parker had been a student at the Colored Department of the North Carolina State School for the Colored Deaf and Blind Children in Raleigh a few years after Wilson had been expelled. The two men communicated in Raleigh sign language, but Wilson's long isolation in the hospital and the effects of a stroke compromised his vocabulary and ability to process complex thoughts.

In this period of Wilson's life, staff at the hospital regularly described him as a gentle, childlike man who spent most of his days watching television, working jigsaw puzzles, going with his caretakers to lunch at Hardee's, and entertaining friendly visitors. By most accounts, Wilson did not express bitterness or resentment about his situation. It is unclear how much he even understood about the reasons for his incarceration at Cherry Hospital. Junius Wilson died on March 17, 2001.

The story of Junius Wilson's life involves multiple removals—from and to kinship and cultural communities and to and from particular institutions. State interventions to remove certain people and place them in specific settings reveal the resonant and complex interplay of numerous factors shaping identities and status and invite us to consider the meaning of belonging from diverse vantage points. We seek to draw critical attention to these stories to expand the interpretations of who belongs in twentieth-century U.S. social and cultural history and in so doing to provide new ways of remembering the past.

The origin story that deaf communities celebrate commonly begins with young deaf children, isolated from language and an inclusive and authentic

community, finding their true home upon arrival at residential schools for
the deaf.[26] According to the traditional American narrative, within these
residential school environments, young deaf people and deaf adults shared a
codified language of signs, American Sign Language (ASL), through which
they discovered and transmitted folklore and humor. Here they learned
about deaf heroes and were exposed to ways of understanding and behav-
ing. Deaf people cultivated artistic expressions and developed friendships,
partnerships, and enemies, as well as a sense of belonging that crossed generations and oftentimes physical boundaries.

Generations of culturally deaf people have recounted with sincere appreciation the many ways these distinct cultural hubs provided sanctuary,
opportunity, identity, and kinship. Since their founding in the early nineteenth century, state-supported residential schools for the deaf have provided enriched lives in a very real sense for deaf boys and girls across the
United States. As deaf studies scholars Carol Padden and Tom Humphries
have documented, many culturally deaf people "believed they were 'res-
cued' by schools for the deaf, and their memories are of leaving behind un-
bearably lonely homes for an environment of friends and adults who could
sign and communicate with them."[27]

Generations of older students typically comforted the new arrivals in a
ritual poignantly marking the crossing over into the deaf cultural world.
The long reach of experience and the formative experience of life at residential schools can be seen in social rituals within the deaf world. Historically,
when culturally deaf people first became acquainted, conversations began
with the question "Which school did you attend?" Removal to an upbring-
ing within the residential school system has long been considered a fundamental characteristic of deaf cultural identity.[28]

Forces mostly outside deaf cultural worlds (including both policy makers and hearing parents) primarily determined that deaf people belonged in
residential schools, but the rise of deaf cultural communities contributed to
young adult deaf people and older deaf people claiming that deaf children
did in fact belong in deaf schools. In this way they asserted some authority
and agency in the matters for themselves and others like them. These adults
and youths also argued that deaf people belonged to a distinct community,
often created or initially experienced in schools but spreading out far beyond
campus gates as the years went by.

"Belonging" in the deaf cultural world had its own limitations and
boundaries. Sometimes the interpretation of deaf culture was expressed in a

hierarchical fashion: "Deaf trumps all other identities," or "deaf-same." Differences rooted in other identity factors, such as race, class, gender, sexuality, or other disabilities (especially cognitive and psychological disabilities), might be sublimated or denied, and thereby the power of any movement toward social justice along lines other than being deaf was blunted. Monolithic stories of deaf culture as a space where "everybody belongs" do not accurately represent the lived experiences of all individuals. Although constricted boundaries can protect and support, they can also contain and control. As novelist Chimamanda Adichie has insightfully warned, dominant narratives present cultural and material dangers because "they make one story become the only story."[29] We agree with Adichie that single stories flatten lived experiences and obscure the texture, diversity, and complex beauty of individuals and ultimately of groups and societies. This applies also to deaf cultural history and to those who tell its stories.

American deaf studies scholars and cultural advocates usually downplay any negative experience of removal from home to a new life in residential school and focus their attention instead on celebrating the unique development of cultural communities that flourished within campus walls.[30] This universalizing story nevertheless neglects a significant dimension: removal. This experience importantly marked both deaf children and their families. Deaf newspapers and other sources occasionally referenced grief-stricken parents who had "great affection" for their offspring.[31] The deaf children's prolonged absences must have contributed in profound and subtle ways to the remaining family members' understandings of community, home, kinship, and deafness.

Even as children benefited from a rich deaf cultural environment, the marks of removal also shaped their young lives. For young boys and girls, attendance at residential schools typically meant physical removal from their original kinship communities and transportation across significant distances from their homes. Such removals could be bewildering to the children, as well as their family members. Limited communication between deaf sons and daughters and their relatives—a common feature in American history—exacerbated confusion, fear, and wonderment, marking entire families across generations.

Anecdotal evidence details young boys and girls loaded onto trains with notes pinned to their clothing giving directions for their removal to the school.[32] Others, brought by families to the residential campuses, were left without understanding why. Some, like Herbert Andrew Childress, concluded that their families no longer loved them.[33] As they toured their new homes, children confronted completely foreign environments: crowded dormitories, the smell of institutional life, and regimented daily schedules. Even the use of American Sign Language could seem distant or forbidding at the beginning.[34]

In a particularly dramatic retelling, deaf actor Bernard Bragg described his experience of removal in the 1930s when his deaf mother brought him to the New York School for the Deaf (Fanwood):

> I asked again where we were going but she gave no reply. For the first time I began to feel a sense of fear and foreboding. I stole glances at her face, but it was immobile and her eyes were fixed on an unseen place somewhere ahead. We rode for a long time, and then we stopped and found ourselves in front of an enormous building. . . . We walked into the building, and once inside I was immediately struck by a medicinal, institutional smell. This did not look like a hospital, or like any other building I had seen before. My mother bent down, turned me toward her, and said: "This is where you will get all your education. You will live here for a while. Don't worry, I will see you again later." Then she couldn't seem to say anymore, she hugged me quickly, give me a kiss, and then, inexplicably, left.[35]

Unlike most of his deaf peers, Bragg had grown up already communicating in American Sign Language. Still, feelings of loss, fear, silence, and separation—among many emotions—indelibly marked this threshold moment in the Bragg family. His experiences at this time mirrored those of many deaf youngsters.[36]

Reflecting on stories from deaf schools across the twentieth century, scholar Carol Padden affirms the haunting impact of removal on some alumni: "Their own experience as children in such schools has left an indelible impression on their adult lives. They remember the . . . long separation from parents and family, and living for months with other children without love or affection from adults."[37] As Mary Herring Wright and Thomasina Brown, both former students at the North Carolina State School for the Colored Deaf and Blind Children, recalled, the initial separation from their families was excruciating. During the drive to the train station, Wright remembered, "I hurt and ached all over and couldn't stop crying." When the train arrived, "Papa pulled me [Wright] away from Mama as I cried and hung on."[38] Thomasina Brown's experience, as shared with her daughter, Maxine Childress Brown, was both frightening and heartbreaking. Confused when a teacher took her hand and walked her away from her family, young Thomasina tried to break free and later "wept uncontrollably" on her bed in the dorm room. She grieved for months. Her parents, Martha and Clarence, also were brought to tears at the parting. Like many other parents, they wanted their child to benefit from a residential school education, but they keenly felt the personal cost of the decision.[39]

Life stories of people like Mary Herring Wright and Thomasina Brown, however, rarely appear in deaf cultural history publications. This deaf world (or at least this historical telling of the deaf world) included predominantly white European Americans who usually did not identify as having additional disabilities, and most of the individuals we know about in the nineteenth and early twentith centuries were academically successful. In other words, we have primarily told the stories of elite culturally deaf Americans. Southern deaf African American children, as one identifiable group whose history has been disremembered, generally came to deaf cultural communities much later or in different ways than their white peers. Southern states did not establish schools for any black children until after the Civil War. For example, Virginia founded its school for white deaf children in 1839 but established the School for the Negro Deaf and Blind Children in 1909. White deaf children could attend school in Louisiana from 1852 on, but black deaf children had no in-state option until 1938. Before creating their own institutions, some southern states either ignored African American deaf children's educational needs altogether or sent small numbers of them to northern institutions. The lack of sports teams, newsletters, and formal organizations for black deaf people reflected and compounded their isolation from the broader deaf world. Indeed, deaf African Americans were categorically barred from membership in southern state associations for the deaf (and also from the two leading national deaf organizations, the National Association for the Deaf and the National Fraternal Society for the Deaf). Their historical experiences vividly illustrate complicated and sometimes unexpected results of interdependent identity forces. Their stories especially remind us that removals and belongings are dynamic, relational, living, and complicated practices.

Closer attention to the interdependent factors that shape identities, communities, and historical moments reveals a longer and more richly textured story in deaf cultural and general U.S. history. For example, even regimented placement within the schools speaks to specific constructed ideas about these interdependent factors. All students had to be of a certain age to qualify for admission and to remain at the school. Young deaf girls slept, bathed, dressed, and gained vocational training in spaces separate from young deaf boys. In the South, deaf children—boys and girls—studied and lived in separation from their deaf peers of other races. Resources, teacher training, and basic expectations differed significantly by region and racial composition of schools.

Wilson's tragic story complicates not only the conventional views of both the cultural deaf world and the racial caste system of Jim Crow. Scholars of southern history have shown us ways in which race unified small communities like Castle Hayne in the face of crushing oppression; but in this instance, disability undermined racial ties and led to Wilson's expulsion from his family.

Likewise, Wilson's age and his being deaf shift ideas about his racialized gender. At the time Wilson was sent to the residential school, he would have been unable to provide much to the family economy, and state laws required that he attend school. Although he grew up in the Jim Crow South, the little boy likely was too young and too dependent to be seen as threatening. Perhaps he was viewed as worthy of charity as a disabled young person. Perhaps he was even seen as a person with potential. It appears that both the state and his family felt that he belonged at the residential school more than he did in Castle Hayne.

When he became a young black man, however, his culturally deaf behaviors may have appeared especially threatening in a Jim Crow context. After returning home from the North Carolina school, the teenager would have been expected to contribute financially to the family economy, but this proved impossible to fulfill. Wilson was read as a sexual being, and his deaf actions, such as staring, yelling, and perhaps touching others, took on a sexualized meaning. In this setting, myriad interdependent factors—perhaps most notably sexuality and gender, race and class, disability and age—contributed to what happened to Junius Wilson.

We want to stress the impact of Wilson's removals: from biological home to school, from school to home, and from home to hospital. These removals inflicted losses more profound than most. He was removed from kin who knew him and from cultural kin from the school who could communicate with him. In essence, he lost the cultural and social capital that had sustained him.

Repeated and compounded removals also marked Wilson's time at the Goldsboro institution. His transfers from the criminal insane ward to the hospital farm community and then to and from various locked wards map his shifting statuses from a menacing "black savage" to a compliant inmate. With removal to the geriatric ward and ultimately to a cottage on the hospital grounds, Wilson acquired different roles and statuses: as an insider community member and as a charitable ward of the state and ultimately as a noninmate of the institution and as a victimized American citizen.

Material consequences accompanied these shifting statuses. Each time administrators removed the deaf man from one ward or building to live in another, Wilson needed to establish a means of communicating with those around him. Unequal power relations complicated information exchanges. Wilson's frustrated outbursts often received medical judgments. Some staff described the deaf man's signs as "crude gestures." Others developed their own gestures to encourage compliance. For example, one employee in the 1970s apparently created a sign to mean "work time." In both American Sign Language and Raleigh signs, the same sign meant "cannot" or "can't."[40] It would be reasonable for Wilson to respond with confusion or frustration over such conflicting messages, as well as the limited access to full communication he daily experienced. Unequal power relations complicated these information exchanges, however. Wilson's irritated outbursts sometimes cost him cherished privileges, like access to the television, chewing tobacco, or his favorite chair. Pathologizing his responses, staff ignored the implications of their own limited understanding of Wilson and of his means of communicating.

Information created by the hospital during Wilson's long incarceration largely charted a story that increasingly deviated from Wilson's actual past. Slivers of Wilson's family history—names, letters, addresses, and an effort to gain his discharge—were lost under new pages in the inmate's medical files. Staff regularly created their own explanations of Wilson's presence at the psychiatric hospital. One nurse interpreted unanswered hospital letters to relatives sent in the 1970s as evidence that they were unable or unwilling to take Wilson back. Others assumed that Wilson had no family left. Employees regularly expressed the general belief that inmates generally were "better off" at the hospital. "They have three hots, a roof and a warm bed," one asserted, "so they have no reason to complain."[41]

The changing labels for Wilson reflect external cultural beliefs, shaped by time, place, and readings of his aging, raced, classed, and disabled body.

Such markers were always dynamic, shaped in part by those so labeled. In this case, as in many others, our access to how Wilson understood any of this remains frustratingly elusive. This is a dismembering and a disremembering that haunts us.

The changing interpretations of how Junius Wilson was judged and categorized by others, including by us today, serve as a cautionary tale to consider categories and concepts like "race" and "disability" (as well as "citizenship" and "belonging") in constant relation to the very human ways these are experienced. It is particularly important that we as scholars and activists not remove from our collective history people who have been removed to or from institutions. Junius Wilson and the countless other institutionalized men, women, and children continued to have lives, and there is much to learn from their individual and collective histories. Wilson and many other institutionized people were, as scholar C. Richard King has described it, "diagnosed, categorized, compared and evaluated with reference to dominant psychological and cultural norms."[42] Across this experience, they were understood not merely as pupils, inmates, or wards but as specifically identifiable people, strongly marked, by medicalized, racialized, gendered, classed, ableist, and age-based understandings.[43] Wilson and others clearly dealt with oppression and struggle, but their stories also reveal a spectrum of human interaction, including dynamic, complicated, and shifting self-definitions and changing roles in community.

Our essay is part of an effort to do the kind of re-membering that Toni Morrison calls for in *Beloved*. As she writes, the process of rememory invites repeated returns to sites of historical loss, recollecting, and haunting, as well as to a place where healing can begin. Junius Wilson and the countless other men, women, and children whose lives have been marked by disability teach us the importance of acknowledging the experiences of people often pushed out and removed from the histories shared, preserved, and remembered. They invite us to consider what and who else remain in the locked wards of our past.

CHAPTER 4

# Integrating Disability, Transforming Disease History: Tuberculosis and Its Past

Beth Linker and Emily K. Abel

Tuberculosis has a cherished, if still contested, place in medical history. Through a multitude of books and articles dating back over one hundred years, historians have debated the efficacy of biomedicine, the social welfare state, and systems of public health aimed at prevention. On one side of the debate stand the historians who see tuberculosis as a quintessential story of medical triumph. Selman Abraham Waksman, George J. Wherrett, Thomas M. Daniel, and Leonard G. Wilson speak of medical miracles, celebrating antibiotics and the demise of tuberculosis.[1] On the other side of the debate are those scholars who insist on seeing tuberculosis, as Henry Sigerist wrote in 1943, as an "extremely social disease."[2] British physiologist Thomas McKeown made this point explicit in *The Modern Rise of Population* (1976) and *The Role of Medicine: Dream, Mirage, or Nemesis?* (1976), insisting that improved living standards and nutrition rather than the rise of laboratory science and public health measures accounted for the decline in tuberculosis rates.[3] The McKeown thesis—along with the AIDS epidemic and a 1993 World Health announcement declaring tuberculosis a global emergency— set off a new flurry of historical research that still continues today.[4]

We, too, take up tuberculosis history, but to different ends. Tuberculosis histories, especially those that helped establish the social history of medicine in the 1970s and 1980s, have exhibited cutting-edge analysis, insisting on the need to speak for the "public interest," but there have been some scholarly oversights along the way.[5] For starters, most tuberculosis histories of the past forty years focus almost exclusively on the pulmonary form of the disease, playing into the well-entrenched myth, as Susan Sontag put it, that tuberculosis is a disease of one organ, the lung.[6] Although it is true that pulmonary tuberculosis was and is the most prevalent form of the disease, the tubercle bacillus can settle into other organs of the body, such as the cervical lymph nodes, the skin, the spine, and other long bones. In their 2010 *Tuberculosis Then and Now*, historians Linda Bryder, Flurin Condrau, and Michael Worboys admit to the lack of scholarship concerning nonpulmonary tuberculosis, acknowledging that "important histories remain to be written about other forms of tuberculosis, particularly of forms in which bones and joints were affected."[7]

Part of the purpose of this essay is fill that gap. Our goal, however, is more ambitious than merely plugging a hole in the existent historical scholarship. In what follows, we look at the history of tuberculosis, both pulmonary and nonpulmonary, from a disability perspective. Rather than couching the history of tuberculosis in terms of public health success or failure, or in how medical ideas and diseases are constructed, we aim to look at how those with tuberculosis made claims on the state, and how the modern U.S. welfare system responded to those who manifested the disease after the germ theory had been established. By taking a disability perspective, we place historical emphasis on long-term care and benefits, on what happened after those with tuberculosis (who often referred to themselves as tuberculars) left the sanatorium or the clinic and attempted to reintegrate into their family lives and work. One advantage of this mode of analysis is that it allows us to look at all variants of tuberculosis and not be constrained by modern-day biomedical distinctions among different types of the disease. A disability perspective also enables us to examine all forms of state intervention—from public health interventions and military benefits to welfare funds—without reifying the tendency within medicine (and medical history) to privilege curing and eradication over caring narratives.[8] Disability provides a meta-analytic umbrella, a paradigm that can account for all forms of bureaucratic and medical interventions, as well as the multiplicities of lived experiences.[9]

To a certain extent, disability narratives already exist in the established canon of tuberculosis history, though not self-consciously so.[10] Stigma has been discussed in numerous studies.[11] The word "disability" even occasionally appears here and there, specifically in relation to how certain persons with tuberculosis qualified for state disability funds beginning in the twentieth century.[12] Still, when disability is mentioned in these works, it remains little more than an afterthought or a side note, not the crux of the story.

By looking at the first half of the twentieth century in the United States, we demonstrate how tuberculosis came to be defined as a prototypical disability, affecting how the U.S. social welfare system would take shape and how citizenship and rights would be negotiated for those with tuberculosis. Although "citizenship" is a capacious term that is contingent on place and time, scholars have demonstrated that economic independence and employment largely framed early twentieth-century conceptions of citizenship. The storybook ideal of citizenship, Allison Carey writes, "exudes intelligence, independence, and the ability to contribute to the national well-being through hard work."[13] By contrast, disability is assumed to lead to dependency, a vice that stands in opposition to the ideal citizen.[14] Because citizenship is bound up with the problem of the unequal distribution of resources in society, disability forces one to contend with difficult and rather dehumanizing questions, such as "who is considered a burden and who a resource, who is expendable and who is esteemed."[15] At base, disability throws into relief the biological basis of citizenship and thus how tenuous and vulnerable this status is.[16]

Because our historical actors understood tuberculosis as a disability, our account sheds light on how those afflicted with tuberculosis crafted their own identities in relation to the state, where rights and entitlements are contested, normalized, and propagated. Scholars have, of course, pointed out the ways in which tuberculars were stigmatized, especially in the era of increasing public health surveillance; a disability perspective, however, deepens our understanding of the ways in which tuberculosis threatened an individual's sense of belonging in relation to not only the nation-state but also friends, hometown communities, and families.

Those with tuberculosis found themselves in a unique and tragically ironic double bind regarding their particular form of disability. Because tuberculosis was thought to be exacerbated—and in certain cases brought about—by poor working conditions and overtaxing the body, those who contracted it could not simply redeem themselves or their citizenship through rehabilitation and work therapy as easily as other disabled persons could. To be sure, social workers and medical experts prescribed work therapy to tuberculars, but always with a note of caution. Too much work, especially manual labor common among the working poor, could make one sick again, and thus tuberculars could be blamed for failing to properly maintain their able-bodiedness. Too little work inspired worries that the tubercular was lazy and would forever be a public charge, a burden to friends and family. Such mixed messages did little to stop many tuberculars from seeking gainful employment and in some cases succeeding even in the face of blatant discrimination. Nevertheless, the debilitating stigma of tuberculosis was nearly impossible to shed because the norms of medical science and those of the social welfare state conflicted. Both working and not working could be considered deviant forms of behavior.

## Pulmonary Tuberculosis Through the Lens of Disability

Disability is a mercurial concept, just as disease and illness can be. Like most concepts, the meaning of disability changes over time and is shaped by context and place. The actual word "disability" has been in use since the sixteenth century to describe, in the most general way, any given incapacity or weakness. Before the twentieth century, however, the English-speaking world tended to rely more frequently on such words as "crippled," "lame," "freak," or "maimed" to describe the disabled, often derogatorily.[17] At the turn of the twentieth century, during the heyday of eugenics, "defective" became the word du jour, but as the movement fell into disrepute by mid-century, so too did its favored terminologies. The word "disability," by contrast, gained ground throughout the twentieth century, largely because of its usage in the emerging social welfare state.[18]

By the turn of the twentieth century, "disability" became a household word for many American families because the U.S. military had been using the term as a label to indentify veterans who qualified for federal monetary assistance since the U.S. Civil War. Union soldiers injured by war received "disability ratings" and subsequent cash payments according to an actuarial schedule that the federal government (via the Pension Bureau) used to assign monetary worth to body parts or functions lost in battle. According to the schedule, loss of a body part was correlated to the impact this loss would have on a man's ability to perform manual labor. If a Union soldier lost both arms, for example, he would receive a "totally disabled" (100 percent) rating, for it was assumed that he was unable to perform manual labor. If, by contrast, a Union soldier lost only a finger, he would likely be deemed 25 percent disabled.[19]

Amputation was not the only kind of disability covered, nor was it the most common. Between 1862 and 1888, some of the most frequently cited disabilities that warranted payment from the Pension Bureau included chronic diarrhea, asthma, epilepsy, hernia, rheumatism, malaria, and, last but not least, tuberculosis (known as "consumption" at the time).[20] Even though today's scholars within both medical history and disability studies tend to see a clear line differentiating disease and disability, the two have had an intimate relationship for centuries. Regarding the economy of disability, Pension Bureau officials saw little difference between limb loss and tuberculosis since the rating schedules included both. Approximately one-third of total disability pension disbursements between 1890 and 1907 went to soldiers with chronic cases of consumption.[21]

Knowing that consumption cost the federal government large sums of money in veteran payouts, World War I military officials barred men who had incipient tuberculosis from the draft in 1917, categorizing the disease as a preexisting and permanent disability akin to deafness, flat feet, epilepsy, and weak heart.[22] Despite this precaution, nearly 20,000 soldiers sent overseas came home with active tuberculosis.[23] By the early 1920s, approximately one-third of all World War I disability claimants were veterans who had tuberculosis, whereas only 5 to 7 percent of claimants had orthopedic disabilities, such as amputated arms and legs.[24] These figures were rarely publicized or discussed because they made the nation look weak. Disablement as a result of disease "lacked the heroic luster of wounds won on the battlefield" and instead raised suspicions of national fragility, a nation-state susceptible to widespread infection, and, in the case of tuberculosis and venereal disease, "suspicions of immoral and culpable behavior."[25]

Veterans with tuberculosis constituted such a significant proportion of disability claimants mainly because they had tremendous difficulty finding work. As information about the communicable nature of tuberculosis spread during the early twentieth century, employers fired workers suspected of harboring the disease. In the private sector, upper-class people refrained from bringing washing or sewing to women whose families were afflicted.

But more than fear of contagion was at play. People with pulmonary tuberculosis were hindered both by virtue of the medical advice doled out and by the fact that the postwar labor market offered few jobs that could accommodate their particular kind of disability. Doctors often instructed those with early stages of the disease or "arrested" conditions to find "light jobs," but such employment frequently was unavailable to the many manual laborers who suffered from tuberculosis. In 1923, an official of the Los Angeles County Department of Charities complained that tuberculosis patients "are referred to us by the clinics as being able to do light work and we don't know what that light work is. We haven't got it for them to do."[26] The less strenuous jobs that existed rarely paid a living wage. After receiving a tuberculosis diagnosis in 1925, Daniel Smith, a Tennessee carpenter, moved to Los Angeles. When his condition worsened, he found work as a night watchman. According to Becky M. Nicolaides, the job "allowed him to lie down and rest during his shift," but he did not earn enough to support his family.[27] One physician who evaluated veteran disability claims in New York contended that for tuberculosis, "psychology, sociology, and medicine are mingled as in no other medical problem."[28]

In response to both job-market constraints and rising veteran pensions, the U.S. government instituted programs in physical and vocational rehabilitation for soldiers injured during World War I.[29] In newly outfitted hospital-based rehabilitation units, soldiers with tuberculosis worked alongside gunshot-wound victims and amputees, as well as the deaf and blind, learning new workplace skills, such as woodworking, watchmaking, stenography, truck gardening, and retail work. The primary tenet behind the rehabilitation movement was that disabled soldiers would recuperate with an explicit vocational goal in mind. Ideally, the injured soldier would reenter the workforce and earn a living wage, with his war-inflicted physical impairment "cured" or at least imperceptible to any potential employers.

The military's conceptualization of pulmonary tuberculosis as a disability soon filtered into the civilian sector. Shortly after World War I ended, Congress passed the Smith-Fess Act of 1920 (also known as the Civilian Rehabilitation Act), which extended physical and vocational rehabilitation to civilians and subsidized state coverage of people with tuberculosis. With Smith-Fess in place, Edythe Tate Thompson, the chief of the California State Bureau of Tuberculosis, urged that a special fund be appropriated exclusively for the rehabilitation of tuberculosis patients and ex-patients in California.[30] A large proportion of the recipients of California's pension program for mothers, for example, were wives and children of men with tuberculosis.[31] In 1932, the California State Bureau of Tuberculosis reported that nearly one-quarter of the physically disabled people aided by its Rehabilitation Department were classified as having tuberculosis.[32]

The Civilian Rehabilitation Act also profoundly affected tuberculosis institutions. Medical historians commonly describe the rise of sanatoriums in the years after the germ theory as an extension of the new public health movement; once tuberculosis sufferers were understood to harbor dangerous germs, they were depicted as "menaces" who had to be isolated from their families and the rest of society. But the most pressing goal of the day-to-day operations of many U.S. sanatoriums was rehabilitation, not isolation.

Restructuring his institution to reflect the new ethic of rehabilitation, Hermann Biggs, chief medical officer of the New York City Department of Health, insisted that municipal sanatoriums restore those with pulmonary tuberculosis "to permanent usefulness in the community."[33] In line with this goal, Biggs began to institute policies that would preclude sanatorium admission to those individuals who had advanced cases of tuberculosis. Viewed as pariahs, those with late stages of disease were lumped together with "chronic alcoholics, and the persistently incorrigible" and thus were warehoused in large city hospitals.[34] As his biographer, Charles-Edward Armory Winslow, explained, Biggs believed that "there were individuals . . . whose lives were so worthless to the community that it would be an unpardonable waste of public funds to give them the benefit of sanatorium care."[35]

In order to fully rehabilitate his patients, Biggs instituted a work cure at the municipal sanatorium at Otisville instead of relying on the "rest cure" that better-off patients received at private facilities.[36] Although it had long been debated whether work or rest produced the best outcomes, federal vocational rehabilitation legislation favored those who advocated work therapy. Because medical and social welfare experts commonly believed that the dependent spirit was a psychological trait easily nourished by periods of enforced idleness, work therapy also was instituted in a wide array of institutions caring for disabled people at that time.[37] Hospital schools for crippled children, asylums for the feebleminded, and military rehabilitation units all compelled patients to work as soon as possible.[38] Like Biggs, Thompson urged administrators of Olive View, a Los Angeles County sanatorium, not to squander their efforts on the "hopelessly ill," patients who would never be able to work regardless of how much rehabilitation they received.[39] She insisted that advanced cases of tuberculosis be placed instead in low-cost facilities, "leaving more time to be spent on the rehabilitation of patients who show that they are suitable for training."[40] The Los Angeles Tuberculosis Association bolstered Thompson's view, claiming that the vocationally oriented training program at Olive View would make "ex-patients normal, self-supporting members of the community."[41] For tubercular people, as for other disabled groups, normality was the only acceptable state, and labor-force participation was the only way to achieve it.

But even the "hopeful" cases of pulmonary tuberculosis faced stigma. Some state legislators complained that incipient cases of pulmonary tuberculosis overwhelmed the health-care system because they required care for months or even years. Others complained that because the disease frequently led to impoverishment, patients and their families consumed a greatly disproportionate share of both public and private assistance.[42] Concerns about the high cost of paying for tuberculosis victims also dominated immigration policy. Amy L. Fairchild argues that the main reason immigration authorities categorized tuberculosis as an "excludable condition" was not fear of the germs victims spread but rather the belief that they were "likely to become a public charge."[43] Disability, not disease, precluded admittance to the United States. "When categories of citizenship were questioned, challenged, and disrupted" throughout American history, Douglas Baynton writes, "disability was called on to clarify and define who deserved, and who was deservedly excluded from, citizenship."[44]

Similar considerations underlay the campaign to stem the tide of invalids moving into southern California at the time.[45] During the late nineteenth and early twentieth centuries, the southwest region of the United States was an especially popular destination for tubercular people. According to reigning beliefs, the climate had a beneficial effect on the disease, and city boosters circulated stories of miracle cures. After the turn of the century, however, southern California gradually withdrew its welcome. Advocates of a statewide quarantine against the tubercular argued not only that they posed a danger to the rest of the population but also that they too often were poor people who quickly exhausted their funds and crowded both the relief rolls and public institutions. When efforts to quarantine California failed, officials began to send indigent invalids home. In 1917, a physician at a city tuberculosis clinic noted that, with the help of the Los Angeles County Department of Charities, he had "deported back to their home town or city many tuberculars." As he explained, "It is a far cheaper method of caring for them than it is to allow them to stay in the County Hospital until they die."[46]

Partly as a result of Los Angeles' negative campaign, the flow of health seekers gradually diminished in the 1920s and 1930s. Tuberculosis-control efforts now focused on the burgeoning Mexican population. Historians familiar with the consequences of associating immigrants and disease will not be surprised to learn that Los Angeles officials exploited white fears by inflating statistics about the prevalence of tuberculosis among Mexicans and portraying them as deviants. But the criticism of tubercular Mexicans had another dimension as well. Construed as outsiders who had no legitimate claim to public resources, Mexicans were condemned for overwhelming government coffers when they took advantage of whatever services were directed toward them. The identification of tuberculosis with Mexicans contributed not only to the campaign to restrict their immigration in the 1920s but also to their expulsion in the 1930s.

Discriminatory hiring practices made it especially difficult for Mexicans to find the light work doctors recommended. Members of that group represented more than 30 percent of the patients at Olive View Sanatorium; however, a report of its rehabilitation program between 1928 and 1936 acknowledged that "the rehabilitated group, with almost ninety percent white is a selected group as regards to race."[47] One reason may have been that the program prepared patients for white-collar occupations; Los Angeles employers, however, restricted Mexicans to manual jobs.[48]

Although women (minority and white) were less likely to enter the paid workforce, those who did encountered similar problems. In 1933, the executive secretary of the Los Angeles Tuberculosis and Health Association discussed the case of a "discouraged" woman whose "tuberculosis condition was quiescent and wanted employment which would enable her to make a modest living which would not break her health again." She had "been forced to work far beyond her strength in laundries and in janitor service after which experiences she would not be able to be out of bed for several days." The association "arranged for her to do a few hours work each day in a nursing home."[49] It is not clear, however, that she was able to support herself through this part-time employment.

A major value of a disability perspective, then, is that it directs our attention to the primacy of welfare and citizenship in the history of tuberculosis control. As various historians have noted, experts involved in the new public health effort dispensed advice that had strong moralistic overtones. Because the discovery of the tubercle bacillus made disposal of sputum an urgent issue, educational circulars provided detailed "scientific" instructions about hygiene. The science of hygiene, however, shaded easily into moralistic tracts about neatness and order. Nurses supervising tubercular people, for example, reported not just whether sputum cups were overflowing but also whether beds were made, children's faces washed, and rooms kept tidy.[50]

But traditional welfare concerns infused the tuberculosis program in other ways as well. The social service component of tuberculosis care was designed according to the tenets of welfare policy, not according to medical criteria. Thompson repeatedly cautioned administrators of hospitals and sanatoriums not to make their facilities so attractive that patients would be encouraged to stay longer than needed. When most wards of Los Angeles General Hospital moved to a new building, Thompson urged that tuberculosis patients continue to be housed in the old facility. She explained, "It would appear that in the new hospital, they are having a great deal of difficulty in discharging patients as they are more comfortable than they have ever been in their lives." If convalescent patients received "fewer comforts . . . their stay would not be quite as long."[51] Bryder recounts a similar balancing act in the British context. When Great Britain passed legislation giving monetary allowances to tuberculars, at first the welfare funds were "designed as a disincentive to work." But soon fears of malingering arose, at which point the minister of health realized that "the financial help should not be so great that the patient had no incentive to achieve his financial independence," but it could "not be so small that the patient is driven to exertion for which he is not yet [physically] fit."[52]

Back in the United States, Thompson insisted that all monetary assistance be tied to social control. When a bill was introduced in the California legislature to provide a $35 pension to convalescent patients, she wrote that "if it passed, it might make discipline and recovery impossible" because recipients would depart the sanatoriums where strict regulations governed their behavior.[53] In addition, she frequently suspected people of trying to manipulate the system, simulating tuberculosis symptoms to claim benefits to which they were not entitled. The importance sanatorium administrators placed on encouraging the work ethic further demonstrates the influence of welfare concerns. And, as we have seen, social workers were central actors in tuberculosis programs, providing the resources poor people needed to follow medical recommendations; tuberculosis patients had to adhere to dominant cultural norms in order to qualify.

Viewing pulmonary tuberculosis as a disability compels us to entertain other questions about the U.S. health-care system. As noted earlier, a major concern of historians of tuberculosis has been to understand the impact of the germ theory on late nineteenth- and early twentieth-century public health programs. We might also ask how tuberculosis sufferers fared in a system that increasingly was geared toward acute ailments. At a time when medical prestige was attached to the display of technical prowess, did more and more doctors spurn the tubercular? In 1924, a prominent Los Angeles physician explained why his colleagues were willing to provide free care in the surgical ward of the public hospital but not in the outpatient tuberculosis clinic: "When a man goes over to the County Hospital and gives his time, there is a certain amount of reaction or kick that he gets out of the thing. . . . He gets an immense and valuable education for himself." Tuberculosis sufferers, by contrast, provided little interest.[54] In 1939, Edythe Tate Thompson acknowledged that care of sanatorium patients in California involved a great deal of "drudgery" for physicians.[55] Indeed, in 1936, when the planners of the eventual Social Security Disability Insurance program insisted that medical professionals serve as arbiters of disability claims, physicians were, as Deborah Stone puts it, "reluctant imperialists."[56] Later, in congressional debates, physicians testified that they could not "objectively determine" disability, that it was too "elusive" a category that encompassed everything from chronic headaches, arthritis, pulmonary illness, and neurotic conditions to anxiety and heart disease. One doctor in particular claimed that "disability is almost . . . a philosophy . . . People with backaches, anxiety, and neuroses are legitimately disabled even though their condition is not medically demonstrable."[57]

What happened to tuberculosis wards as hospitals transformed themselves, in Paul Starr's words, "into awesome citadels of science"?[58] Some evidence suggests that pressure for the establishment of sanatoriums came not only from tuberculosis advocates but also from hospital administrators, eager to shed responsibility for a large chronic patient population. In 1923, a Los Angeles doctor noted that "the county hospital is not equipped for tuberculosis cases and does not want them."[59] Physicians who specialized in treating the disabled (usually orthopedists or physiatrists who specialized in rehabilitation services) often found themselves poorly remunerated in comparison with other medical specialties defined by specific diseases and body systems. In his work on British orthopedists, historian Roger Cooter demonstrates that "rehabilitation medicine . . . was overwhelmingly state funded and poorly remunerated and therefore low on the professional hierarchy" throughout most of the twentieth century.[60]

Unlike health care for acute conditions, long-term care involves a combination of social and medical services. Moreover, according to late nineteenth- and early twentieth-century beliefs, good shelter, ventilation, nourishing food, and rest were more beneficial to tuberculosis patients than medical interventions. The New York Charity Organization Society, the city's major philanthropic agency, raised funds to provide clients with new beds, special diets, clothing, trips to the country, and occasionally even help in moving to sunnier and better-ventilated apartments.[61] Because Los Angeles lacked a major charitable organization, the Los Angeles County Department of Charities was primarily responsible for furnishing aid to the tubercular poor. The assistance available in both localities, however, was far from adequate.

The inadequacy of charitable services became even worse by the 1930s at the height of the Great Depression. Soon after the original Social Security Act was passed in 1935, Congress added disability-insurance amendments in order to offer a safety net for blind persons, as well as other disabled persons, including tuberculars, provided that the applicant could "medically demonstrate" permanent disability.[62] The amendments were put in place in order to protect wage earners and their families against loss of income due to disabling diseases and physical injuries.

But the framers of Social Security—most of whom were able-bodied, white males—grudgingly included disability insurance, partly for fear that there would be too many fraudulent claimants and partly because the permanently disabled were seen as economic burdens, especially compared with the temporarily disabled who received short-term aid through workmen's compensation.[63] Jacobus tenBroek, a famous lawyer and blind rights advocate, railed against the treatment of the disabled and the lack of federal programs and funding to secure their rights as citizens. Writing in the 1940s, tenBroek asserted that "in California, no more than two hundred blind men and women were (by official estimate) actually at work in normal occupations." "Thousands upon thousands," he claimed, "who were able and willing to work were without jobs, forced to live on public aid grants which in most states were beneath the level of minimum subsistence."[64] Even when blind persons received vocational rehabilitation through the Social Security Administration, tenBroek argued, the services were "ineffectual and rudimentary."[65]

Like those who were permanently blind, tuberculars usually eked out a living by laboring in sheltered workshops or piecemeal jobs without any chance for upward mobility or ever securing a position in the competitive employment marketplace. Few other physical disabilities, however, had the same kind of fraught relationship with work as did tuberculosis. Compared with more permanent and predictable disabilities, such as blindness, deafness, and amputation, tuberculosis was, as mentioned earlier, believed to be a fluctuating disability, an unstable physical condition that was unpredictable and presumably exacerbated by work.[66] Although certain U.S. employers were just beginning to adjust workplace environments in the early twentieth century for "crippled" employees, accommodating tuberculars proved to be more challenging.[67] Changing the physical environment and machinery of the workplace—for example, industrial limb attachments for amputees and aural sensory adaptations for the deaf—did not hinder worker productivity once such accommodations were in place. With proper accommodation, those with relatively stable disabilities could ostensibly work at the same speed and efficiency as nondisabled people.

Fluctuating and unpredictable disabilities, such as tuberculosis (and conditions more common today, like chronic fatigue syndrome), could not be physically accommodated in the same way.[68] On the contrary, accommodation for such disabilities usually required time off or worker slowdowns, demands that employers (and often fellow employees) saw as unjust and economically unviable, hindering a business's productivity and output. It is little wonder, then, that many tuberculars attempted to keep their medical histories secret from employers. Not only did tuberculars have to fear the shame of being infectious at one point in their lives, but they also had to worry about the additional stigma of being perceived as unreliable workers, failing to comply with the demands of a marketplace society that prized consistency and productivity above all else.

### The Neglected Other: Bone Tuberculosis

Another way to read tuberculosis through the lens of disability is to consider the history of bone tuberculosis, when the bacillus settles into the spine and invades and softens the body of the vertebrae, leading to severe curvatures and hunchbacks. Before the acceptance of the germ theory in the late nineteenth century, physicians and the general public saw little relation between bone and pulmonary tuberculosis. Bone tuberculosis most often affected children. It was rarely fatal, although it invariably led to permanent disfigurement. Pulmonary tuberculosis, by contrast, affected adults the most. Although pulmonary tuberculosis could be a terminal disease, those who did recover rarely dealt with permanent, visibly apparent deformities.[69]

In many ways, then, the disability experiences of these two groups of people were significantly different, even though in the immediate post-germ-theory years, medical experts and state welfare workers lumped them together because of their shared biological marker. Once bone tuberculosis and pulmonary consumption were known to share the same biological origins, treatment regimes merged accordingly. Some children with bone tuberculosis underwent rehabilitation in sanatoriums already established as sites for care of adult pulmonary tuberculosis. (These children, however, often inhabited separate wards because bone tuberculosis, unlike pulmonary tuberculosis, was not considered communicable.) Other children took up residence in specially designed seashore hospitals in the belief that abundant sun and salt water could help hasten the healing process.[70] The basic rehabilitative tenets—rest, good nutrition, healthful environment, and a heavy dose of occupational/work therapy—remained intact, though, for all tuberculars, no matter the type of the disease.

Still, sanatorium stays for children with bone tuberculosis were, on the whole, much longer than those for adults with pulmonary tuberculosis. Bone tubercular children often recovered through the use of body casts and traction devices, making for years of prolonged bed rest and institutionalization.[71] Gloria Paris provides a case in point. Upon receiving a diagnosis of hip tuberculosis at the age of five in 1936, Paris lived in the sanatorium for nine years. During her first year of treatment at the Homer Folks Memorial Hospital in New York, Paris remained immobilized, permanently attached to a leg traction device. Although traction had, in Paris's account, "greatly reduced" the severe and persistent hip pain she had been experiencing, the tuberculosis continued to fester and progress, absorbing the entire neck of the femur.[72] By her second year in the sanatorium, Paris was put in a spica body cast in the hopes that it would better immobilize the joint while allowing her to move around the sanatorium in a wheelchair. Paris underwent eight more years in a constant cycle of casts and traction before she was deemed physically able to return home, where her working-class, Italian immigrant family was expected to support and care for her.

Such long-term removals from family, school friends, and the rhythms of everyday, noninstitutional life proved challenging for both tubercular children and their relatives. When Paris was first discharged at the age of fourteen, she had to move in with her mother's elderly aunt and uncle because her natal home did not have the space to accommodate her physical limitations and orthopedic appliances. Even when she eventually moved back home, she felt severed from family life. Because she had spoken only English in the sanatorium, she had difficulty communicating with her Italian-speaking relatives and friends and could only watch when her siblings conversed with ease. Her physical limitations, combined with her mother's refusal to let Paris help with the housework, made her feel "useless and unwanted."[73] In the sanatorium, she felt "well-adjusted to living away from home," but once home, she felt like an outsider, marginalized from her biological kin.[74]

Institutionalization disrupted conventional kinship networks in myriad ways, as is evinced in Paris's case and those of countless other disabled children and adults who came before her.[75] The question of belonging—whether at the level of the family, the institution, or the state—concerned many bone tuberculars as they grew into adulthood.[76] Writer Andrew Solomon explains that although disabled children share some traits—a "vertical identity"—with their biological parents (for example, race and religion), they also experience a "horizontal identity," a sense of self that comes through participation in a subculture outside the family.[77] Vertical identities are often taken for granted as conventional forms of belonging, but horizontal identities challenge presumptions of what constitutes a family. Although the two kinds of identities can coexist, a crisis often arises when the horizontal identity is given primacy over the vertical. The best historical case study of such a crisis can be found in the Deaf community during the Progressive Era when the oralism campaign—a movement that aimed to eliminate sign language in favor of speaking and vocalization—reached its peak.[78] Oralists insisted that the best place for deaf children to live was in the home of their hearing, biological parents; leaders of the Deaf community maintained that hearing-impaired children belonged in residential institutions where they could be immersed in Deaf culture and sign language. Kinship, Deaf leaders argued, was determined "not by blood but . . . by culture."[79]

Although institutionalization frequently brought questions of identity to the fore among many disabled children, it was by no means a necessary condition. Take the example of Katherine Butler Hathaway, born to an upper-middle-class family, who convalesced at home when she was diagnosed with tuberculosis of the spine in 1895 at the age of five. She spent the next ten years strapped to her bed by iron traction frames, "pinned down," in her words, "to boards like specimen butterflies."[80] Hathaway's recuperation took place in her parents' house in Salem, Massachusetts, under the medical care of several well-known orthopedic surgeons from Harvard University. Still, despite her material comfort, Hathaway writes that she felt "intrinsically separate" from everyone around her.

Hathaway's sense of isolation arose from both physical barriers and the aesthetic exclusion onlookers imposed on her.[81] Hathaway writes of the profound loneliness she would often experience from being tucked away in an upstairs bedroom. Although physical isolation contributed to such feelings, Hathaway contends that the company of others often exacerbated her sense of solitude. "Certain grown-up callers insisted on coming burlingly [*sic*] upstairs," looking at Hathaway with pity in their eyes. Childhood friends would take "ghoulish pleasure in staring" at the traction device; they would whisper among one another about the leather halter pulley system that encased her head and kept it immobile through the intricate rope-and-weight system that hovered above her.[82]

Even when medical treatment and convalescence were over, Hathaway had to negotiate a world in which social prejudice against visible physical deformities was pervasive. This was a time when cities across the nation adopted municipal laws prohibiting "unsightly" persons from the streets (otherwise known as "ugly laws").[83] This was also the heyday of the American eugenics movement, when those deemed unseemly or unfit could be sterilized and, in cases like that of the Bollinger baby, euthanized.[84] Although those with sufficient financial means rarely found themselves subjected to such draconian measures, the extremes of the eugenics movement colored and defined social attitudes, affecting the everyday lives of people with bone tuberculosis.

Hathaway's aestethic exclusion ultimately made it impossible for her to identify with anyone around her except one particular family employee: the working-class, "gnome-like" locksmith who had also suffered from spinal tuberculosis as a child and who came to the Hathaways' house for regular maintenance calls. The locksmith so haunted Hathaway that she entitled her memoir *The Little Locksmith*. A short, hunchbacked man whose "chin was almost down to his chest," the locksmith, Hathaway writes, "refused to belong to our world or anybody else's. He acted as if he lives all alone in a very private world of his own."[85] When Hathaway first saw her back after being released from bed at the age of fifteen, she felt "hot with shame," for she had "turned out . . . like the little locksmith" despite the years of medical intervention and promises.[86] Feeling a connection to the locksmith, a horizontal bond that stood in contrast to her vertical identity as a member of a well-heeled, Anglo-Saxon, New England family, Hathaway felt that "a hideous disguise had been cast over her"; "I . . . was confused by it," she wrote, "confused by my own identity."[87]

As Hathaway entered adulthood, the biggest affront to her identity was that she was perpetually treated like a child. When her siblings began dating, Hathaway noticed that nobody ever said, "When Katherine gets married," or "Why hasn't Kitty got a beau yet?" or "We must get a beau for you, Kitty," presumably because no one thought of her as marriageable, let alone a grown woman with sexual needs.[88] "I lived inside my cage," Hathaway writes, "close to the others, among them, touching them, laughing and talking with them; yet by an unspoken understanding it was taken for granted that I was not to have what was apparently considered the most thrilling and important experience in grown-up life": sexual intimacy and marriage.[89] Even after graduating from Radcliffe College and acquiring her own home in Castine, Maine, Hathaway still felt like a "very small childish spinster."[90]

Others with bone tuberculosis similarly faced infantilization. Randolph Bourne, the famous early twentieth-century New York intellectual, who also had bone tuberculosis as a child, struggled to gain an education and respect from his peers.[91] His wealthy uncle assisted Bourne's sister in gaining admission to a university at a time before women's higher education was the norm, but the uncle refused to help Randolph, assuming that his nephew's stunted and deformed body would preclude him from entering the world of university degrees and gainful employment. Romantic relations also eluded Bourne. Although he was a self-proclaimed feminist who enjoyed the company of many close women friends, he was rebuffed whenever he made gestures of physical intimacy. One of his female friends recalled, "He had only to venture an inch over a forbidden line to have [his women companions] fly from him like shy birds." Another woman acquaintance remarked, "I always took it for granted he was cut off from the whole range of experience by his deformity."[92] As a result of both his stature and the taboos revolving around sex and disability, Bourne was considered an asexual being, not quite fully adult.

In contrast to the mythology popular in nineteenth-century literature that adults with pulmonary tuberculosis had boundless sexual desire and lives filled with romance, those with bone tuberculosis were treated as if time had stopped at the moment of diagnosis, when they were young children. Although bone tuberculosis survivors were rarely candidates for sterilization, they were often urged to avoid reproduction. Experts with a eugenics bent worried that diseased and deformed bodies would taint offspring. Others worried that the physical demands of reproduction would be too great for the supposedly frail tubercular body, especially the female tubercular body, to handle. None of the memoirists under review here had children except Paris, who did so against medical advice. Although several physicians told Paris that she would be unlikely to "recover from the disease process," and that if she were to have children, she should limit herself to one child by means of a cesarean section, she went on to birth three children, all vaginally.

The most significant difference between pulmonary and bone tuberculars lay in the ability—or lack thereof—to pass as "normal" able-bodied adults. Bryder documents the extremes to which pulmonary tuberculars would go to hide their medical histories once they had left the sanatoriums and workhouses. Confronted by a public health officer about her previous disease state, one pulmonary tubercular told the state official that she wished to "keep her past a secret from her family" and asked that the officials stop inquiring after her.[93] Other tuberculars who found jobs after recovery sometimes lost their positions once employers found out their health history.[94]

Despite the challenges that systems of state surveillance posed, pulmonary tuberculars could nevertheless pass in various parts of their daily life because they usually displayed little or no outward sign of their tuberculosis past. By contrast, those who contracted bone tuberculosis as children bore permanent bodily stigmata into adulthood and thus could rarely pass as "normal." Bourne's tubercular past, for example, resided on his face, which was twisted from mouth to ear, and his back, which was noticeably hunched and curved. Paris spent a majority of her adult life with braces and orthotics to accommodate her leg length difference and scoliosis. By late middle age she needed the assistance of canes and then eventually a scooter to get around. Hathaway's contorted spine made her feel as if she belonged "to the company of the queer, the maimed, the unfit."[95]

Bone tuberculars were thus often rejected from employment and housing, as well as from many other forms of belonging (including U.S. citizenship), before they even had a chance to prove themselves as adults. According to historian Paul Longmore, magazine editors often refused to take Bourne to lunch, fearing that his appearance would offend other well-off New York diners. During a brief time in France, Bourne found that "concierges ... repeatedly refused him lodgings, until after two days he finally found a vermin-ridden flat."[96] His experience was not unique. One British tubercular man from 1911 described how "depressing" it was "to find how frightened people are of becoming us." "I am being turned out of rooms," he recounted, "and this will make my fourth move in this particular town."[97]

Like many severely affected pulmonary tubercular migrants and immigrants, bone tuberculars met rejection at state and national borders. Of the two types of tuberculosis, however, bone tuberculosis was more easily detected because it could be seen with just a cursory visual inspection. Ellis Island commissioner William Williams encouraged the exclusion of immigrants who had bone tuberculosis or any sign of "poor physique," a category that included individuals who exhibited "frail frame, flat chest," and "deficient . . . muscular development."[98] Baynton recounts the story of one prosperous immigrant, Abraham Hoffman, whose curved spine placed him at risk of deportation because he was thought likely to become a public charge.[99]

The stigma that bone tuberculars experienced occurred at virtually every level of society, including social welfare programs intended to assist the neediest citizens. Most welfare records did not include bone tuberculosis as a category separate from pulmonary tuberculosis and thus rendered bone tuberculars and their unique needs invisible to the system. We do know, however, that during World War II in Great Britain, the Office of Public Assistance prohibited nonpulmonary tuberculars from applying for funds; over 90 percent of the payouts to tuberculars went to applicants with mild cases of pulmonary tuberculosis.[100] Within the welfare system both in the United States and abroad, social workers favored tuberculars who were most likely to recover enough—that is, to pass as healthy and able-bodied—to find gainful employment and no longer require money from the state. But people with bone tuberculosis never had a possibility of full recovery. Thus within the category of tuberculosis itself, state officials created a hierarchy of impairment, making a clear distinction between the worthy and unworthy disabled that was based largely on aesthetics.[101]

Looking at the history of tuberculosis through the lens of disability, then, uncovers a complicated picture of how the condition has been articulated, defined, and parsed in the past, rendered not simply as a disease but as a lifelong impairment. In "The Tyranny of Diagnosis," Charles Rosenberg writes that the naming of disease is "central to how we organize health care delivery, think about ourselves, debate and formulate social policy, and define and manage deviance."[102] The same can be said for the naming of disability, especially in the twentieth century, when disease and disability became fused in a complicated web of social welfare programs.

A disability approach transforms traditional disease histories by expanding them to include actors outside the clinic and larger political issues, such as social welfare, citizenship, and belonging. When pulmonary and bone tuberculosis are both viewed as disabilities and compared as such, one thing becomes clear: those who were perceived to be the least disabled (that is, incipient pulmonary tuberculars) often enjoyed greater benefits, material and otherwise, than those who were considered permanently disfigured and impaired (bone tuberculars). Historians of medicine must be cautious not to play into such entrenched hierarchies; their focus on pulmonary tuberculosis (as well as on acute disease) has tended to perpetuate the idea that certain types of impairments are more worthy of attention than others. Interrogating disease and disability hierarchies—how they come about and what kinds of meanings they take on—is fertile ground for further inquiry. And, significantly for our case study, it reignites the important political vision of early tuberculosis historians who insisted that history speak to and for the public interest.

## CHAPTER 5

# Screening Disabilities: Visual Fields, Public Culture, and the Atypical Mind in the Twenty-First Century

Faye Ginsburg and Rayna Rapp

I started working at *Sesame Street* as a writer in 1970. . . . In 1974 my son was born with Down Syndrome. The world changed in an incredibly dramatic way. I was devastated by the news. I had no idea what to do. The doctor advised us to send him away to an institution and tell our friends that he had died. The nurse came in and told us—and this is 32 years ago—that there is something very controversial you can try. It's called early intervention. Maybe he will be able to sit up. . . . At least you will have given it your best shot.

When I got home, I turned on the television and I realized that families like mine were absent. This must have been what it was like for African Americans. We were absolutely invisible. We are absent from women's magazines as well. I felt so disenfranchised. It was a terrible lonely feeling.

Pretty soon I realized my son, Jason, was quite bright, learning the alphabet at two–three years. We have clips of Jason on *Sesame Street* spelling at three years of age. . . . 400,000 people had Down Syndrome at that time in the US. I got lots of mail . . .

> Inclusion and visibility are just as important as
> curriculum, for people to see themselves. . . . *Sesame*
> *Street* now has a better record of inclusion than any other
> television show on the air.
>
> —Emily Kingsley, scriptwriter for Sesame Street
> and disability activist[1]

Emily Kingsley's pioneering work as a disability media activist inspired our chapter exploring images of disability in public culture as they shape claims to recognition beyond the strictly legal arena. In early twenty-first-century America, cultural and political understandings of people with disabilities cannot be grasped apart from the accelerating circulation of popular and medicalized media imagery. We are tracking an emergent phenomenon across a variety of locations that are off the map of mainstream media, where people with disabilities are virtually invisible. *Sesame Street*'s pioneering role in featuring children with disabilities since the 1970s is still the exception. Almost 20 percent of Americans ages five through sixty-four are living with a disability, but only 0.5 percent of words on mainstream television are spoken by a person with a visible disability.[2] At the same a time, people with disabilities are increasingly turning to other kinds of technologies, especially social media, which are far more accessible and are rapidly remapping the contemporary public sphere.

This chapter draws on our broader ongoing research on cultural innovation and learning disabilities; we analyze how young people labeled with atypical cognition—including diagnoses such as learning disabilities, dyslexia, attention-deficit/hyperactivity disorder (ADHD), and Asperger's syndrome—are mediated across multiple social arenas. These range from multimedia platforms to classrooms to brain research labs. In our ethnographic fieldwork, we engage with children and young adults, teachers, scientists, media makers, and a range of disability activists.[3]

The road to recognition in public arenas often starts at home, as Emily Kingsley's case vividly demonstrates. We have found that the social infrastructure for achieving recognition as a person with a disability in public is often first organized through the intimate world of family and kinship, biological and otherwise. The cultural practices of everyday inclusion that are the ultimate goal of disability rights, we suggest, are often initially generated in this most fundamental arena, as is the case for many disability activists and their allies. Eventually "scaling up" the insights and transformations they experienced as members of families living with difference, many of them contributed to a broader movement for civil rights for people with disabilities. Their advocacy practices have increasingly employed a range of media forms; these include documentaries, websites, and other outreach tools that enable a sense of kinship that can reach beyond the family. This ability to recalibrate to the scale of larger social arenas can give new forms of significant but undertheorized public recognition to previously marginalized communities, establishing a sense of kinship beyond the family; we call this process "mediated kinship." This term indexes the social relations built through the scaling up that media encourage, enabling a sense of kinship with those marked as disabled to reverberate through media worlds.[4] This term indexes how media encourage a public sense of kinship with those identified as disabled.

Mediated kinship emerges as a neighboring field to the formal, institutionalized discourse of disability rights, offering a critique of normative American family life that is embedded within everyday cultural practice. Across many genres, a common theme is an implicit rejection of the pressure to produce "perfect families"; rather, embodied difference is incorporated into the domain of reconfigured kinship relations. These mediated spaces of public intimacy are crucial for building a social fund of knowledge more inclusive of the fact of disability, foundational to an expanded understanding of cultural citizenship.[5] Such media practices provide a counterdiscourse to the stratification of families that has marginalized those with disabilities. It is not only the acceptance of difference within families but also the embrace of relatedness that such models of inclusion present to the body politic.

Kinship emerges beyond the biological frame as groups of people living with similar diagnoses—autism, Down syndrome, ADHD—recognize one another through these media practices. An emergent sense of kinship and identity makes these spaces potentially radical in their implications for an expanded understanding of personhood and politics. As sites of information and free play of imagination, these cultural forms contribute to a more inclusive social landscape beyond the genealogical or familial. In any polysemic tradition, there are many ways to materialize a sense of relatedness among citizens— what Benedict Anderson has called an "imagined community" foundational to civil society.[6] A variety of media practices, from *Sesame Street* to analog photographs to websites, can increasingly be understood as signifiers beyond blood and other bodily substances that can produce a sense of kinship among those with disabilities and their supporters. How, we ask, is familial sentiment—and ultimately the kind of recognition that expands possible public inclusion of those with disabilities—built through the substance of media as much as DNA or blood that we more conventionally identify with family relations?[7] Because media of all sorts have the capacity to circulate beyond the confines of face-to-face worlds, their political consequences can be substantial, as Emily Kingsley understood more than forty years ago.

## From the Ugly Laws to Visual Activism

None of the transformations we have indexed could have occurred until quite recently. It was only forty years ago that most American cities abolished their "ugly laws," which made it illegal for persons with "unsightly or disgusting disabilities" to appear in public; such legislation laid the groundwork for normalizing both eugenics and institutionalization in the early twentieth century.[8] This paradigm radically changed with the passage of the Americans with Disabilities Act (ADA) in 1990 and its 2008 amendments, which mandated public accessibility and inclusion for all citizens and built on earlier groundbreaking federal initiatives, especially the Individuals with Disabilities Education Act (IDEA) of 1975.

In America, disability rights legislation was forged in a larger social crucible, self-consciously part of the legacy of the prior civil rights movement for racial equality. Additionally, advances in medicine played a significant role, resulting in the increased survival of vulnerable babies and children with a higher incidence of disabilities than in the general population. By the 1970s, deinstitutionalization meant that increasingly, these young people were raised at home. As a result, families became responsible for providing their care; for some, this life-changing experience of "reinventing the family" growing out of the intimacy of kinship and caretaking moved beyond the household and often catalyzed activism among family members, as our examples in this chapter make clear. The rallying cry "Nothing about us without us" (first used by disability activists in 1990s Eastern Europe) aptly describes how people with disabilities are progressively more visible as well as politically present in public culture, demanding recognition on their own terms as rights-bearing citizens.[9]

In this chapter, we highlight our research on the increasing proliferation and circulation of media representations of young people with cognitive differences, from television characters to Internet activism to laboratory imaging. Most of the work we discuss here embraces, whether explicitly or implicitly, a cultural model valorizing "all kinds of minds," a widely used phrase made popular by the late learning-disabilities expert Mel Levine.[10] However, the expansion of such liberatory visual representations of neurodiversity is at times overshadowed phenomenologically by quotidian efforts to categorize and regulate cognitive difference, from insurance and medical forms to special-education paperwork. In other words, civil disability victories such as the passage of the ADA and the renewals of the IDEA have had paradoxical consequences. As people with disabilities have access to enhanced forms of public support, they are also increasingly subject to escalating bureaucratic categorization, their enforced pathway to medical diagnoses and qualifying for state-sponsored services. Elsewhere, we have termed this complex nexus of benefits and burdens that comes with the naming of disability entitlements "the paradox of recognition."[11]

## Seeing Disability I: Portraits, Festivals, and Alternative Epistemologies

New scholarship in disability studies and visual culture has opened lively discussions on how the circulation of image-based media is deeply implicated in the creation of a more inclusive sense of citizenship—civil disabilities—for nonnormative social actors. Visual theorist W. J. T. Mitchell reminds us: "Whatever disability studies becomes, it will have much to teach us about visibility and temporality, about forms of mediation, representation, and their evolution over time."[12] Almost a decade after Mitchell's influential essay, Rosemarie Garland-Thomson, in her book *Staring* (2009), showed what we might call a recent "see change." She introduces the idea of "visual activism," a term that describes how, increasingly, people with disabilities and their allies put themselves in the public eye, saying "Look at me" instead of "Don't stare."[13] Among the many artists she discusses are painters such as Doug Auld and Chris Rush, both of whom turned to portraiture of people with disabilities. For example, Auld's remarkable series of oil paintings, *State of Grace*, celebrates the humanity and beauty of burn survivors he met at St. Barnabas Medical Center in New Jersey.

In 2002, I presented the idea of painting portraits of burn survivors to the Burn Center at Saint Barnabas Medical Center in Livingston New Jersey. . . . The young people that have volunteered for this series have all endured physical pain and personal tragedy. They have developed a strong sense of "self" at an early age in order to survive public alienation due to their appearance. Many of them lost family members in the fires that they survived. My motivation to paint them is rooted in the desire to explore the parameters of beauty in our society. These paintings document their visual facts while interpreting the less tangible aspects of inner beauty and personal character.[14]

Arizona artist Chris Rush's portraits of subjects with cognitive disabilities were made when he taught patients with a range of impairments at a local hospital. He was struck by the fact that he rarely saw any representations of people like his students in public art exhibitions and started to remedy the situation through his own paintings. At the opening of his 2010 show titled *Stare*, Rush described "an invitation to stare, especially at the images of obviously disabled individuals, . . . encouraging viewers to confront and appreciate the unfathomed beauty and interest inherent in every human being, bar none."[15]

A third artist whom Garland-Thomson discusses inverts the usual social positions of starer and staree. Kevin Michael Connolly is a champion skateboarder and photographer who was born without legs. His online exhibition *Rolling* highlights his photographs of people's reactions to him as he traveled the world on his skateboard. He explains:

Everyone tries to create a story in their heads to explain the things that baffle them. For the same reason we want to know how a magic trick works, or how a mystery novel ends, we want to know how someone different, strange, or disfigured came to be as they are. Everyone does it. It's natural. It's curiosity. But before any of us can ponder or speculate—we react. We stare. Whether it is a glance or a neck-twisting ogle, we look at that which does not seem to fit in our day-to-day lives. It is that one instant of unabashed curiosity—more reflex than conscious action—that makes us who we are and has been one of my goals to capture.[16]

Such intervention through visual culture "stretches our shared understanding of the human variations we value and appreciate and invites us [instead] to accommodate them."[17] The radical nature of this insight and the fact that the work she discusses is from the twenty-first century are compelling testimony to rapid and recent changes in public culture.

Disability scholars and filmmakers Sharon Snyder and David Mitchell interpret work with similar ideas in their writing on disability film festivals worldwide.[18] They argue that exposure to a broad range of disabilities that occurs at such festivals can produce what they call "aesthetic reprogramming" for audiences who watch an array of films that embrace the "new normal" as part of everyday life. They invite all to stare in Rosemarie Garland-Thomson's sense, vicariously experiencing the remarkable variety of lives with a difference. This sense of alterity occurs whether it is via documentaries or fictional accounts with characters played by disabled actors whether wounded warriors, or stutterers, or people with autism, Down syndrome, ADHD, cerebral palsy, blindness, deafness, brain injury, or depression. Mitchell and Snyder regard such film festivals organized by and for counterpublic communities as dynamic sites where distinctive features of that world come into formation.[19]

> As one of the few public spaces within which to actively fashion alternative disability identities, film festivals challenge internal and external orthodoxies that tend to quickly sediment within politicized identity gatherings. They not only serve the important function of historical recovery; they also seek out a variety of perspectives on the meaning of disability from older and younger generations of disabled people and non-disabled allies. Disability film festivals actively disrupt static boundaries of disability identity—even with respect to disabled peoples' concepts of their own collective makeup.[20]

Such public exposure, they argue, can lead potentially to an embrace of "the permutation of the species"—disability in all its diversity—as newly evolving concepts of "being disabled" emerge in such settings, even as they "resist articulating a shared identity based on collective coherence of experience, affect, or diagnosis." Their analysis reminds us that such film festivals serve as utopian spaces of both mediated kinship and cultural citizenship compared with the darker side of prejudice that is not so easily overcome.

Nonetheless, they are increasingly sites for community and consciousness building among disabled people and their supporters. As many social movement theorists have argued, these are the under recognized but essential scaffolding on which new sociopolitical formations are built.[21]

This sense of a utopian space of possibility is palpable at every screening at one of our research sites, the Reelabilities New York Disabilities Film Festival, which has grown expoentially since its inception in 2008.[22] This festival, which now has spread to thirteen other cities (the number is still growing), features outstanding films from all over the world. Far from simply expanding the range of available "entertainment," such events enhance collective recognition and are powerful community-building projects.

For example, the closing-night film in 2011, *Wretches and Jabberers: Stories from the Road*, was sitting and standing room only, with the requisite off-screen adaptations for "cripping" the viewing space that are central to disability inclusion: audio description for those with visual impairments, signing for deaf audience members, seating that allowed for at least ten power chairs in the room, a few guide dogs, and a high tolerance for unruliness. The documentary features Tracy Thresher and Larry Bissonnette, two men with autism who have limited oral speech but much to say. As young people, both faced lives of isolation; their capacity for communication went completely unrecognized. It was not until adulthood, when each learned to communicate by typing with the help of newly invented assistive technology—giving them a way to express their thoughts, needs, and feelings—that their lives changed dramatically. After more than ten years of advocating for people with autism in the United States, they went global, helping people with autism in other countries break through the isolation they both knew so well. Thus the film both represents and is part of the forging of mediated kinship and a new arena of public visibility and activism across national boundaries for those with communicative limitations.[23]

The sense of being part of another kind of global community was central to the response generated by the 2012 opening-night film, *Ocean Heaven*.[24] This 2010 Chinese–Hong Kong feature was written and directed by Xue Xiaolu and was based on her experiences working with young people with autism. The film stars martial-arts blockbuster celebrity Jet Li, in his first full dramatic role, as a single father with terminal cancer who is the sole caretaker of his autistic son. Jet Li embraced this part, a pro bono labor of love given the salary he can command, because of his nephew with autism and his recent creation of a philanthropic foundation. The goal of both Xue

Xiaolu and Jet Li was to build awareness, support, and inclusion of people with autism, a kind of politics of recognition[25] that resonated far beyond the realm of entertainment. Over the course of the film, the completely dependent son is slowly transformed as the father insists that he learn to manage his own life, with imaginative interventions and the support of an unexpected community that emerges around him. A significant subtext of the film is the crucial and frequently neglected transition—at least in the United States and apparently in China—as young adults with cognitive disabilities age out of available school programs and other child-focused services while facing the inevitable aging of their caretakers at home. The film dramatizes the limits of familial care and implicitly makes an argument for public recognition of the humanity, needs, and rights of those with disabilities. It also became a form of mediated kinship as it circulated widely throughout China and beyond, inviting audiences to experience vicariously the dilemmas of caretaking and disability across the family cycle and showing people with disabilities and their supporters as agents of their own social integration.[26]

## Seeing Disability II: Visualizing All Kinds of Minds

Public representations of disability are usually associated with popular forms of visual culture, such as film and television; our research takes into account how disabilities are routinely envisioned in medical and scientific imaginaries dedicated to the investigation of cognitive difference, such as neuroscience and psychiatry. We are especially interested in how ideas, imagery, and notions of personhood that emerge in one field are taken on board in others, always reframed by the institutional and disciplinary logics of the particular arena in question. We find that these trajectories are often entangled in ways we think of as interocular,[27] a concept describing the accelerating circulation of meanings, scripts, and images as they transfer across locations—for instance, linking the scientific and the popular—and reframe public understandings in the process. Drawing on this idea in our fieldwork, we examine the transfer of meanings across a range of sites that have considerable cultural power for the general public. Images of the brain, for example, currently hold particular fascination for understanding cognitive differences to a wide array of interested parties including neuroscientists, families of diagnosed children, and research subjects, who interpret neurodiversity according to their own paradigms.

In a functional magnetic resonance imaging (fMRI) lab in Manhattan, for example, we have observed scientists researching differences in neural networks of the brains of children with a range of conditions, such as ADHD, autism, and dyslexia, as they seek new material evidence for atypical cognition. Lab boundaries are linguistically permeable; the language of neurodiversity, neuroplasticity, and (most recently) neurotypicals flows across scientific, familial, and social movement discourse. Lab work moves forward a public image of what neuroscientist Miguel Nicolelis calls "neural democracy"; he highlights how diverse neural networks "cooperate" across regions of the brain to produce different behaviors.[28] Diversity in brain wiring thus becomes one more form of human difference: the brain of a child diagnosed with autism or Tourette's syndrome, for example, is assumed to be wired fundamentally differently than the brain of a child without the diagnosis. Unlike the framework that prevailed as late as the 1970s, in which such diagnoses might lead directly to institutionalization, the scientists we are studying are part of an emerging regime of neuroscientific scrutiny, enabled by fMRI, that recognizes these diagnoses as part of the spectrum of human diversity.

This attitude is especially comforting to families who enroll their diagnosed children as research subjects in neuroscientific studies. The language of neuroplasticity, neurotypicality, and neurodiversity removes blame for a child's school or social failure from the parents (overwhelmingly, the mothers). The materiality of brain scans speaks back to Leo Kanner's classic "refrigerator mother" theories of autism (1943), or popular blame of ADHD on too much television and sugar consumption.[29] If a child's school problems are lodged in dysfunctional neuronal connections, not bad parenting, this enables a relative or teacher to accept childhood differences with more compassion. Parents of children widely perceived to be "difficult" or "odd" are particularly prone to laboratory collaborations: their children are genuinely valued, actively recruited, and noted for their individuality in the lab. For example, one researcher is conducting an fMRI study of children with frequent temper outbursts, currently considered a precursor to the controversial diagnosis of childhood bipolar disorder and attendant use of potent antipsychotic pharmaceuticals. The researcher's protocol included giving mothers small video cameras to record outbursts at home, which she later correlated with the differential brain states that she was studying. When some of the children stopped "tempering" when they realized that they were being filmed, several enterprising moms continued subtly recording on their cell phones at the dinner table and uploaded their files to the lab. Neuroscientists appreciated not only the creative moms but also the savvy children; this was not a response the distraught mothers were accustomed to receiving. One parent said, "My daughter is valued here, she can be useful to scientists and we know they appreciate her."

Lab scientists see atypical children as located "on the spectrum" of human variation; parents, in turn, inscribe their kids into fMRI studies as a form of mediated kinship, taking the personal initiative to participate in what they imagine to be possible explanations, if not cures. But at the same time, differential diagnostic categories are reinforced without interrogation: research subjects are sorted into "diagnosed" and "healthy controls" without concurrently offering treatment options, thus adding modern modes of material evidence to much older mechanisms for sorting "the normal and the pathological."[30] Yet the categories of normal and pathological brains are everywhere leaky.

In a particularly striking moment of the sort that fieldwork often provides, we experienced interocular frisson while conducting routine lab observations around Halloween. In the lab, we noticed that the children in the fMRI magnet were choosing to watch a *Simpsons* Halloween episode in which Mr. Burns directs his sidekick, Smithers, to remove a subject's brain, shouting, "This isn't rocket science, it's only brain surgery." We found this an astonishing choice by the scientists to offer to their impressionable research subjects whose brains were being scrutinized, but the scientists simply saw it as a seasonal Halloween video for their subjects. To them, apparently oblivious of the nuances of popular culture and media effects theory, what the child watched was irrelevant as long as they could scan a brain both in action and in resting state. But both brains—cartooned on television and imaged through fMRI—are dancing cheek-to-cheek. More profoundly, families who have volunteered their children with atypical cognition for brain studies also comment on images taken from scans. "It looks so normal, just like any other brain," one mother, for example, opined. She added in frustration, wishing that fMRI might lead more quickly to treatments: "So how am I supposed to know what's wrong with him?"

Ideas and images about the neurological bases for atypical learners are not restricted to the laboratory. They leak out with remarkable speed and power into public domains, with serious consequences for children diagnosed with cognitive disabilities. For example, they are apparent in a curriculum designed to provide teachers with strategies for accommodating the 13 to 15 percent of U.S. students now labeled as needing special educational services. We have participated in training sessions for teachers in New York City and have observed how this curriculum is used in popular school programs such as the aforementioned "All Kinds of Minds," which offers a nonstigmatizing way to recognize and acknowledge cognitive differences in the classroom; these programs come with an arsenal of commodified curricula to address the needs of nonnormative learners, including books, games, webinars, online assessment and teaching tools, and blogs. This model relies heavily on a neurodevelopmental perspective that builds on the same kind of scientific materiality as that of the neuroscientists scanning children's brains in the fMRI machine. However, this educational approach—supported by a range of media—also emphasizes the need to develop a worldview from the classroom out that accepts cognitive difference as a normal part of the human experience and embraces inclusion as a foundational educational principle. Its explicit agenda is to contest prior representations of children sent for special education as inferior to those deemed normal.

Disability as both diversity and pathology made a brief but dramatic appearance in New York City's public landscape in 2009. New York University's Child Study Center previewed an advertising campaign that showed "autistic children" as alleged kidnap victims with signage mimicking a ransom note that read, "Parents: we've got your child."[31] Ostensibly aimed at raising awareness of the profound implications of an autism diagnosis, the ads were quickly and successfully contested by many, spearheaded by the Autism Self Advocacy Network. These signs, they argued, were deeply offensive and falsely implied that there is (or should be) a cure for autism. The work such images perform as they move from laboratories to schools to public culture is highly interocular, sometimes contested, and socially consequential. The accelerating speed with which such images circulate in and beyond the medical/scientific arena reframes public understandings of cognitive difference as an aspect of daily life.

## Seeing Disability III: Reframing Civil Disabilities

The inclusive reframing of "all kinds of minds" across multiple domains has been taken up in advocacy campaigns. For example, activist filmmaker Dan Habib has launched a movement in the United States to help build a national conversation around issues of educational inclusion. His work was inspired by his son Samuel, born with cerebral palsy, who "brought the disability rights movement into our home." Habib began photographing their journey searching for an educational placement in their small New Hampshire town, and soon a documentary film was in production. *Including Samuel*, exemplary of mediated kinship, extended the questions Habib had about his son's unpredictable future to address the status of disabilities in American public schools, a fundamental concern of civil rights. In addition to his son, he profiled four other students with a range of disabilities at different life stages to ask questions about the possibilities and limits of inclusive education from kindergarten through college. Since its completion in 2008, *Including Samuel* has been screened across the country and has been widely publicized, not just for its compelling story but also for its visionary as well as practical advocacy. The film is now used by thousands of schools, parent organizations, nonprofit groups, universities, and state agencies around the United States. The *Including Samuel Project* website extends the activism to the creation of collective counternarratives by inviting fellow travelers to upload their stories of disability and inclusion, thus creating a kind of counterpublic virtual community. Habib calls all this activity the "Including Samuel Effect." This story is one example of a recurring phenomenon that we see in our research. Like many parents of cognitively "atypical" children, the Habibs are not only rethinking the intimate world of kinship but are also taking their insights beyond the home. One of the many cultural innovations they have developed is a Movie Party Tool Kit for kids with disabilities and their siblings and friends to educate their peers and challenge hegemonic hierarchies. In one school, teens initiated an "I Am Norm" campaign, with labels worn by everyone, emphasizing the impossibility of a singular standard for normalcy. Thus, with the medium of a simple stick-on label and a catchy slogan, students reframed the discursive understanding of the school community.[32]

Mediated kinship is apparent on social media platforms used by people diagnosed with autism and other forms of cognitive difference. The design of these venues is particularly appropriate for displaying the worldviews, intelligence, and communicative skills of people on the autism spectrum. Their communicative capacities might once have gone unrecognized, especially if they did not use oral speech or found face-to-face interaction overwhelming. As Australian educator and communication rights activist Rosemary Crossley famously put it, "Not being able to speak is not the same as not having anything to say."[33] The capacity of such media as blogs or You-Tube to disaggregate different dimensions of communication has made them particularly appealing to many people on the spectrum. Consider the compelling example of Amanda Baggs, an autistic woman and neurodiversity activist. In her 2007 YouTube video *In My Language*, Baggs makes riveting use of the medium, immersing the viewer virtually into how she experiences the world in a way different from neurotypicals. Explaining her work, Baggs writes: "The first part is in my 'native language,' and then the second part provides a translation, or at least an explanation. This is not a look-at-the-autie gawking freakshow as much as it is a statement about what gets considered thought, intelligence, personhood, language, and communication, and what does not."[34] The first part shows Baggs engaged in a variety of repetitive gestures around her apartment—playing with a necklace, typing at her keyboard, moving her hand back and forth in front of a window—to the sound of a wordless tune she hums off camera, creating a meditative effect. Baggs, who stopped speaking verbally altogether in her early twenties, provides the "translated portion" of the piece from which the preceding quote is taken halfway into the video. Her spoken voice is rendered via an augmentative communication device, a DynaVox VMax computer. Her typed words emerge into spoken speech—as well as in yellow subtitles—via a synthetic female voice that, in the words of one interviewer, "sounds like a deadpan British schoolteacher."[35] This YouTube video has received almost 1,250,000 hits as of March 2014, with the majority of the more than 5,500 comments expressing gratitude and a sense of relatedness, illustrating what we are calling "mediated kinship." One woman commented: "Thank you for posting this video i have two autistic sons who are non verbal to the normal world i seem to understand them just fine . . . this video was completely normal for me as with a few of the others you have posted i understand them completely but only because my son's have taught me your language . . . but to learn it you have to care enough to listen."[36]

Perhaps because Amanda Baggs's video appeared early in the life of You-Tube and during a period of intense interest in the "autism epidemic," her virtual interventions attracted considerable attention, including that of CNN's celebrity medical expert and neurosurgeon, Dr. Sanjay Gupta. In April 2008, Gupta visited and interviewed Baggs at her Vermont home, greatly enhancing her public visibility in the mainstream media. He chronicles the transformation in his own understanding of the personhood of Baggs (and people like her), whose humanity he clearly had not recognized in the past. After this encounter, he noted the remarkable access that was opened to her by media platforms such as YouTube or blogging: "The Internet is like a 'get out of jail for free' card for a new world of autistics. On the Internet, Amanda can get beyond names and expectations. She can move at her own pace, live life on her own terms."[37] In other words, the YouTube platform has enabled Baggs to inaugurate a profoundly important counterpublic discussion on the rights of nonneurotypicals to represent themselves in their own language. Like other neurodiversity activists, she makes a claim for public recognition of a particularly stigmatized form of difference.

Some of the benefits of having an extension into virtual reality are practical, especially for the many Americans with disabilities who are unemployed because of discrimination and workplaces that are less than accommodating.[38] Seshat Czeret has a painful disability that makes it difficult for her to leave her home or participate in community life. However, in the online virtual 3-D immersive world of Second Life (SL), where participants interact via avatars they create, she runs a successful business designing virtual clothing, paid for by other Second Life participants' avatars, electronic figures manipulated by their creators and users. She describes her use of SL not as escape into fantasy but as a way for her to make a living, be part of a community, and "escape from persecution."[39]

In 2007, a remarkable community of support for people with disabilities on SL emerged, largely due to the efforts of disability activist Alice Krueger and fellow travelers who have joined her. Before becoming involved with Second Life, Krueger

> worked part-time from home as a technical writer and editor for an education research firm for five years using adaptive office equipment. As a woman with Multiple Sclerosis, she found it increasingly difficult to participate in her real life community. No longer able to leave home to work, volunteer, or socialize with friends, she turned to virtual worlds to fulfill these basic human needs. Ms. Krueger is the mother of three young adults with disabilities and has been a special education teacher. Ms. Krueger's avatar in Second Life' is Gentle Heron. Gentle can stand and walk without crutches.[40]

The community that Krueger/Gentle Heron founded with two other disabled friends began in June 2007 when they began thinking about how important the concept of community was for those who faced barriers to participation in the physical community in which they lived. They began asking other disabled people what their idea of "community" was and what they expected from being a member of a community. From this research, the friends determined that people with disabilities want the same things everyone else does.

> They want companionship and friendship, especially with people who understand the limitations placed on them by their disabling conditions. They need to learn more about their own conditions, about health and well-being, and about resources available to make their lives better. They want a chance to be employed or to do volunteer work since both give back to our community. And, they want to have fun. . . . People who are disabled are often socially isolated, even physically isolated, within their geographic communities. So the three friends . . . decided to explore virtual reality as a setting within which to build a supportive community.[41]

Within its first eight months, the community grew to 150 members and quickly earned a reputation as the primary group supporting people on SL with real-world disabilities. After a wide-ranging discussion, they became Virtual Ability, a nonprofit corporation, in January 2008.[42] Virtual Ability has six SL properties that together reflect the concerns first articulated by its founders, including a new-resident orientation and training to teach people with disabilities or chronic illnesses how to navigate Second Life; information on physical, emotional, and mental health; interactive displays; links to outside resources, events, and personalized assistance; and a space for hearing-impaired users, as well as for military amputees and their families.[43]

Unlike most other participants with avatars in Second Life and other virtual communities, those involved in Virtual Ability do not regard their participation in Second Life as a game or a form of entertainment. Their goal is to provide a support community for people with disabilities and their fellow travelers so that they can participate more fully in civic community life. They do not see the boundary between virtual and real life as significant.[44] The creation of a supportive environment includes thinking "beyond ramps."[45] Second Life has become more accessible to people with different kinds of disabilities by rethinking the actual technological interface to accommodate a variety of forms of embodiment.[46] There is still considerable ground to cover before "disability in its digital incarnations may unfold in new, unexpected, and fairer ways to the genuine benefit . . . of people with disabilities."[47]

Back in the nonvirtual world, people with "invisible" cognitive disabilities, such as dyslexia or ADHD, sometimes have more difficulty creating community because they are not readily visible to one another. We are conducting fieldwork with a group that has a game plan for remedying that problem: Project Eye to Eye (E2E). Founded in 1997 at Brown University, E2E is now a national organization of students with learning disabilities (LDs) who have made it to college, where they "come out" and bond via a mentoring program they run with middle-school kids who are also labeled LD.[48] This is the first national organization created for, about, and, most importantly, by young adults with LDs. It currently has more than fifty chapters and a grant to expand. Since 2009, E2E staff have carried out systematic outreach to a number of corporations to create awareness and potential job opportunities for young adults transitioning from educational settings to the workplace. E2E chapters run "Beyond Normal Art Clubs" to enhance children's self-esteem by demonstrating the skills, creativity, and humor that the young adult E2E mentors developed along their own slower route to success. In projects such as yarn collages, which put the student at the center surrounded by supporters, and projects in which they make masks that show their present vulnerabilities and later their future strengths, middle schoolers are taught to be proud of their different ways of thinking and aware of the community that supports them. By making art from their experiences as "kids with a difference," they also are able to go public about learning disabilities that many have tried to hide. Their art is on view in an end-of-term exhibit for the whole school, mounted by each chapter. At the annual organizing institute where new E2E leaders are trained, a T-shirt is always given out. In the year when we attended, the T-shirt proclaimed: "Special Education: A Revolution, One Classroom at a Time."

The remarkable cultural innovations in everyday life and public culture that disability advocates and their supporters have created across a range of visual platforms in the past several years exemplify the creation of new forms of sociality, scaling up from the intimacy of family life. This is what we have

come to understand as mediated kinship, the scaffolding on which a counterpublic domain of recognition is built. These practices are essential to the
expansion of the place of disabilities as part of civic life, changing quotidian
life's "doxa," the ancient Greek word adapted by Pierre Bourdieu to refer to
the cultural structures that render "the natural and social world as self-
evident."[49] We conclude with some examples that remind us how the exclusions of disability from everyday life are deeply naturalized in hegemonic
American civil society. The quotes that follow come from events we attended
where activists took center stage both to present their own projects and to
point to the work that lies ahead.

At the Reelabilities Film Festival in 2012, we joined an invitational
screening to watch a documentary film in progress on the struggles to include actors with disabilities as a regular aspect of film, television, and advertising.[50] Afterward, actress, composer, and disability activist Anita
Hollander reported the findings of I AM PWD, a watchdog action group assessing the state of disability inclusion in the performing arts in the United
States.[51] As a vocalist and a member of the group carrying out the inquiry,
she chose to sing the findings to the tune of Gilbert and Sullivan's "Modern
Major General." Her first verse made the case succinctly:

There's NBC & ABC & CBS & FOX-TV
There's Showtime, AMC, & TNT and ABC Fam'ly
Films are shooting, plays producing, LA to Schenectady
But where do we see any performers with disabilities?[52]

Despite the humor of her performance, the situation itself is a sober one, as
the statistics we cite at the beginning of this chapter on the virtual invisibility of actors with disabilities on American television make clear.[53] Given
these grim numbers, it is no surprise that people with disabilities have taken
up more easily accessible media forms to signal their claims as participants
in the public sphere whose particularities need to be accommodated. As
Amanda Baggs phrased it more colloquially: "We're here. We're weird. Get
used to it."[54]

The turn to media by disability activists provides the means for society
to get used to the public presence of this form of difference. This is clearly an
ongoing battle. Thus it is appropriate to end, as we began, with Emily Kingsley, the indefatigable advocate for the inclusion of disabilities in arts and
public culture for nearly half a century. Despite the revolution she helped

catalyze at *Sesame Street* forty years ago, the battle is as present as the arrival of the daily mail. She explains:

> Every day I go through catalogues I get in the mail to see if there is a model with a wheelchair. I do a disability check [to see if there is any representation of people with disabilities. Mostly they aren't there.] Why aren't we in advertising?
>
> I have a form letter on my computer that I use every week:
>
> To Whom it May Concern:
>
> I will not be ordering anything from your catalogue. People with disabilities are America's largest minority. No one realizes we have pocketbooks.
>
> We have not yet gotten our voice, yet we are 57 million people strong. We have not yet found our Martin Luther King.
>
> —Emily Kingsley[55]

Such letters penned in frustration over the lack of recognition of "life with a difference" are not in vain. Over the past two decades, inaugural efforts by major corporations have been normalizing the presence of people with disabilities as part of the social landscape.[56] Pampers pioneered the use of Down syndrome babies as diaper models in the 1980s; Bennetton created a provocative 1998 campaign using children with disabilities wearing its clothes; television commercials for McDonald's display a disability-inclusive kitchen staff; and a 2012 Target campaign featured a little boy model with Down syndrome. The attention these efforts garner from disability advocates attests to their significance, as well as their infrequency. Indeed, disability activists have used YouTube crusades and media parodies to protest their invisibility in the commercial mediascape and to insist on their presence as both consumers and citizens.[57] People with disabilities are almost 20 percent of the population, not including their families and friends, a large potential consumer market that has been virtually ignored.

Doxa change is an uneven and ongoing task that requires vigilance, creativity, and moxie.[58] We have been struck by the ways in which traditional and especially social media offer opportunities for recognition and community building to those whose mobility or communicative capacities may require cultural innovation. The cases discussed here make clear that a shift in the zeitgeist is evolving across a range of media practices, from the scientific to the artistic to the activist and communitarian. We argue that the increasing public presence of representations by, for, and about people with disabilities is helping build an emergent counterpublic of nonnormative bodies and "all kinds of minds." It is in this informal, interocular experience of an everyday that incorporates a disability imaginary on the multiplicity of screens that shape our lives in the twenty-first century that a truly inclusive sense of cultural citizenship is in the process of being forged.

## CHAPTER 6

# Social Confluence and Citizenship: A View from the Intersection of Music and Disability

Alex Lubet

## Social Confluence: A Musical Example

Among the most famous musicians with a disability was the great jazz guitarist Django Reinhardt. When Reinhardt was in his teens, he was burned over much of his body, and the third and fourth fingers on his left hand became essentially immobile.[1] Although this forced Reinhardt to radically transform his technique and imposed some limitations, particularly on his ability to play chords, he nonetheless became one of the most important and influential jazz guitarists of all time.[2] This was possible only because of the broad interpretive latitudes that jazz permits. Jazz Artists are expected to be creative: to improvise, to devise their own parts, and often to arrange or compose. Reinhardt did all these.

Had Reinhardt worked exclusively in an idiom in which he was expected to play parts devised by others based on a generic notion of instrumental technique that did not take his (or anyone else's) impairment into consideration, he would have had to change professions. Within the social confluence of jazz performance, Reinhardt's impairment was widely recognized—it is a significant aspect of his notoriety—and its limiting impact, particularly on his ability to play chords that used three or four fingers, was known. His facility in playing melodic lines with extraordinary speed seems to have been unimpeded, although his impairment is readily apparent when one plays notated transcriptions of his solos because his improvised melodic choices were often particularly idiomatic to his two-finger technique.[3] Reinhardt was at once physically impaired in a manner that affected his playing and splendidly accommodated by the protocols of the music, which permitted him to create his own parts according to his ability rather than excluding him because of his disability. Within the social confluence of jazz, Reinhardt was able to excel as a disabled virtuoso whose adapted guitar technique was of his own invention and suited to the unique aspects of his impaired body.

In this essay, I suggest that Reinhardt's story is a paradigmatic illustration of social confluence theory. Social confluence theory is a concept I introduced in *Music, Disability, and Society* that extends the concept of culture propounded by anthropologist Arjun Appadurai and represented in music in the work of ethnomusicologist Mark Slobin.[4] These scholars question whether "cultures" as autonomous populations can exist in the modern/postmodern, globalized, technologically advanced world. Rather, they see "cultures" as the praxes of affinity groups. Individuals are understood as belonging to and moving among multiple affinity groups and as a result claiming and being ascribed to multiple identities. For example, Appadurai specializes in the Indian diaspora and observes that its members may claim, among others, both their Indian identity and the identity of the nation-state of which they are citizens. They may claim additional identities based on such affinities as work (an employer or a profession) or education (an institution or a field of study). Any of these identities might be manifested by a variety of praxes. Indianness, for example, could be expressed by preferences in food or sport enjoyed together with others of shared Indian identity.

Social confluence theory expands Appadurai's idea slightly but significantly.[5] It argues that an individual's identity can change repeatedly and frequently, depending on the encounter of the moment. The term "confluence" comes from geography, where it refers to the joining of two rivers to form one, as when the Mosel River runs into the Rhine at Koblenz, Germany (Koblenz derives from the Latin word "confluentes"); "social confluence" similarly takes on and is affected by the daily encounters with others who can shift the direction of our identities. And like rivers (to push the metaphor further), our identities are always moving, shifting, changing, and absorbing what enters us.

The idea came to me when, on a single day in 2000, I experienced four "encounters" related to my return to work after the first of my spinal surgeries:

with my university's Disability Services, my doctor, my attorney, and my guitar. In each encounter—each "social confluence"—the part of my identity that is my disability status was defined differently, ranging from able-bodied at Disability Services, where I was told that there was no legal obligation under the Americans with Disabilities Act (ADA) to provide accommodations, to incapacitated in my practice as a guitarist. At Disability Services, I was told that I was legally able-bodied under the unamended ADA (and thus did not qualify for accommodations) because of the possibility, however remote, that my condition could be remedied by surgery and was therefore temporary. My doctor, who mentioned such surgery in his accommodation letter to Disability Services, regarded it as unlikely to provide relief and therefore inadvisable, and my disability as permanent. My attorney, using Minnesota workers' compensation law as his criterion, rather than the ADA, determined that I was "permanently partially disabled," a status that would be confirmed in court two years later.[6] As a guitarist, I came to realize that the nerve damage to my right arm and hand would render conventional classical technique at a professional level impossible and in effect incapacitate me within the social confluence of classical guitarists. I was eventually accommodated by Disability Services, although I was told that this was not a legal obligation under the ADA, and I was never provided an explanation of its change of heart. I play guitar more than ever now, but almost exclusively my own music and highly personal interpretations of others' works, with my idiosyncratic technique that showcases my left hand and keeps things simple for my right.

My experience illustrates a series of social confluences. Each encounter, often contrasting or even conflicting with the one before it, caused me to experience my body as a socially located entity in a different way: not only as a legal subject, as a university professor of music, and as a musician but also, through these categories of identity and affinity, as someone whose disability status would be assigned in different ways by others and experienced in different ways by me. Social confluence theory posits that it is within the confluence rather than, for example, the nation-state, tribe, ethnicity, family, or individual that the primary unit of identity in contemporary globalized, information-oriented society is found. In other words, I am arguing that the essential social structure within which an individual or affinity group finds identity (assigned or self-assigned) is the social confluence. The significance of this grounding of identity in the encounter rather than in more fixed structures is in its sense of fragmentation, of identities continuously transformed, indeed remade, by context. Unlike Gertrude Stein's concept of her hometown, Oakland—"There is no there there"[7]—social confluence theory argues that identity is a function of the situational "there." Although social confluence theory is potentially applicable to any aspect of identity or affinity, it was originally demonstrated with examples of different views of disability status. Individuals and groups with embodied impairments were regarded as having radically different degrees of disability, depending on context. As I will show further (and as has been illustrated, if only provisionally, in my own history), in music, disability status, the window through which the impact of social confluence will be observed here, can vary widely depending on the protocols of performance and composition in different kinds of music. In this essay, I apply it to the various "cultures" of different kinds of professional music making, as I will explain.

Had Django Reinhardt been a classical guitarist whose repertoire consisted largely or entirely of works of other composers, the norm within that profession, he would have had to stop playing professionally. The standard classical guitar repertoire and all standard classical repertoires, with only minor exceptions that I will discuss later, demand two typically able-bodied hands. Although his technique as a jazz player was stunning, he would not have been able to play even the simplest classical pieces, which require four mobile left-hand fingers. Thus, within the social confluence of professional classical guitarists, after his accident, Reinhardt would have become totally incapacitated, completely disabled, and unable to function.

Had Reinhardt abandoned his chosen profession after his accident and sought other work, his disability status would have varied according to social confluence. (And, of course, as an active guitarist with a disability, he encountered nonmusical confluences during times when he was off task in which his disability status.) Let us imagine that instead of a mid-twentieth-century French Roma, he was a contemporary American with the same hand impairment. Had he been injured on the job (Reinhardt was not), he would have been considered "permanently partially disabled" under workers' compensation. Under the ADA, his impairment might not have been regarded as impeding performance of "major life activities," and thus he would likely have been denied disability accommodations under the original 1990 ADA. The act was amended in 2008 to broaden its coverage,[8] but more case law is needed to determine how many more people with disabilities will benefit. There are numerous additional disability laws and policies that affect such concerns as employment, education, and public accommodation. (My situation with Disability Services and the ADA was different in that it was the permanence of my impairment, rather than its severity, that was questioned. Had permanence not been an available point of contestation, though, I suspect that severity might have entered the argument.)

Each of the examples of my disability status in four social confluences concerns rights of participation. Three of the cases are straightforward, nation-state legal issues concerning the ADA and workers' compensation. The fourth, my ability to play guitar at a professional level, concerns participation in a community of artists on a particular instrument. Musicians, particularly those with a background in ethnomusicology, understand that professional guitarists constitute a cultural system with its own praxis, protocols, and rules for participation and exclusion, which can be construed as a self-policing unit, a sort of informal guild (musicians have a formal labor union as well, of course), and thus a "government," inhabited by musician-citizens. In this essay, I use the concept of social confluence to examine the notion of citizenship as it operates in Western classical music, jazz, and electronic dance music. Each of these musical idioms—musicians refer to them simply as "musics"—is not only a style but also comprises communities that are sometimes formalized as institutions and that are governed by codes of rules with varying levels of formality, from ones that are explicitly published to those that are unwritten but nonetheless well-understood and persuasive traditions. The idea of musics not simply as sounds but as communities with cultural praxes is well understood and accepted in ethnomusicology, sociology of music, and anthropology, and it is from this understanding that I refer to musics as "governments" whose participants I describe as "citizens." To engage with a music is thus to participate in a social confluence.

I will consider the attitudes of the cultural systems embodied in these three musics toward disability as regards rights and privileges of participation and level of inclusion. All focal examples concern performers/composers, as opposed to other, less foregrounded participatory roles, such as administrator, patron/donor, and audience member. Musics, which function as communities with legal systems, formal or informal, are thus understood as governments, their performer-participants as citizens, and the citizenship rights and responsibilities of disabled musicians as the focal concern.

Although my previous example, guitarist Django Reinhardt, may be the best known of all musicians with a physical disability/mobility impairment and an artist whose particular impairment serves well as an example of social confluence theory, both in his own musical idiom, jazz, and beyond music, in such realms as workers' compensation and the ADA, his instrument, at least as played by disabled musicians, does not appear in all the musical cultures required to make the cross-genre comparison necessary to understand various musical governments. (Neil Young and Joni Mitchell are both mobility-impaired polio survivors, but their disabilities do not loom nearly as large in their legends as Reinhardt's, nor do they so dramatically impact their performance.) In the interest of consistency and nuanced comparison, I use keyboardists with mobility impairments as the principal point of departure in the comparison of the three musical idioms, although, as will be seen, the keyboards used vary. A unique feature of keyboards that makes this comparison particularly apt is that they may be operated with one hand, two hands, or no hands, and the hands used to play may be fully able or impaired. In each of the musical idioms considered, there is an initial focus on a noted professional keyboardist, and each of them uses his hands differently. All the featured performers are male, an attribute that is more than coincidence because disability policy and much of the government of music are highly gendered, and gender issues are discussed, including the marginalization or exclusion of women. Fuller consideration of each of the musical idioms will extend to additional performing media—other instruments, voice, DJing, and dance—for reasons including and extending beyond full gender representation.

Before I proceed to the examples of music cultures as governments, an explication of how "citizenship" is conceived and implemented within these cultural systems is in order.

## Music as a Site of Citizenship

The idea of citizenship is typically associated with nation-states and smaller governmental units within them. But there are also larger, transnational confluences of government, such as treaty organizations and a body of international law. My purpose here, though, is to consider other confluences of government. Although heretofore examples of social confluence have concerned individuals (in particular, my own example and that of Django Reinhardt), it needs to be noted that these are presented in the manner of case law, intended to be broadly applicable to all in analogous circumstances. Confluence theory does not apply only to personal identity but also to any social formation, ranging from the individual to large institutional structures.

In some instances, the idea of government as applied to social conflu-ences neither readily nor at all associated with nation-states is perfectly clear and requires little or no explanation. Most readers have engaged with the governance of institutions of higher learning on an ongoing basis. Often these are patterned on nation-state systems and include such elements as a president (with a chief of staff and other advisers), senate, and judiciary. Aca-demic professional organizations are also easily understood as governments, and little imagination is required to recognize the governance of academic publishing, whose instruments of rule include peer review and citation styles. Research methods, particularly in the sciences, and the protocols of class participation—what is a syllabus if not a code of conduct?—are similarly strongly prescribed. In all these examples, participants are bound by rights and responsibilities that are the privileges and duties of citizenship.

Non–musicians might require some suspension of disbelief to imagine music cultures as governments whose participants function as citizens, but the idea has been propagated and well known within music scholarship for decades, if not precisely in the terms used here. The study of music as an as-pect of culture is at least as old as anthropology, a parent discipline of ethno-musicology. Since the 1970s, music scholars have taken a logical next step in examining musical institutions as distinct cultural systems. Among these scholars and the institutions they have considered are Christopher Small (symphony orchestra). Henry Kingsbury (conservatory),and Bruno Nettl (university school of music).[9] Given the fixed locations, long histories, legal standings, and sharply defined memberships and hierarchical orderings of such institutions, as well as their strongly rule-bound natures—something true as well of the Western classical music that is their sole or dominant dis-course—it is both easy and enlightening to understand them as governments populated by citizens. Other musics, marginalized or nonexistent in the aforementioned cultural systems and institutions and often associated with and made by marginalized populations, while typically having less estab-lished power structures and institutions and thus less formal governance and established statutes, are nonetheless, I argue, governed by informal and often unarticulated but mutually understood codes of conduct and membership.

Although Nettl addresses the role of marginalized musics and musicians within university schools of music, beyond academia, such musics also oper-ate according to their own protocols in ways that have, to my knowledge, not heretofore been contemplated as governmental frameworks, as I do here. Before I proceed to examples of the government of disability within various musical cultures, some explication of what is meant here by "marginal" is necessary.

The previously mentioned works of Small and Kingsbury concern themselves with musical institutions nearly or entirely devoted to the Western classical music tradition. Historically, that music culture has been associated with privilege. In contemporary Western and some Asian nations, Western classical music remains associated with and even wields a degree of genuine power; that is, it holds sway over significant resources. Classical music dominates the music education system, public and private, from kindergarten through college. Its large performing institutions, such as symphony orchestras and opera companies, are with great consistency the largest and richest musical nonprofit organizations. Symphony and opera orchestras have long been among the few sites in which musicians' unions have been demonstrably successful in defending workers' rights and livelihoods, with some of the best contracts in all organized labor, although there are indications that, at least in the United States, their power and influence, like those of all other unions, are waning. This is evidenced in Minnesota, where the St. Paul Chamber Orchestra was locked out by management for most of the 2012–13 season and returned to work after capitulating to nearly all of management's demands, and where the Minnesota Orchestra locked out from October 2012 to February 2014, resumed their duties while taking a 15 percent pay cut.

In the for-profit music industry, however, it is classical music that is marginal in terms of buyer interest and market share. The music industry is, of course, dominated by popular music, which is, however, the most marginal idiom in music education and the nonprofit world. Popular music is a lesser presence in the non-profit world presumably because popularity breeds profit, although, in the United States, music that is no longer very popular ("oldies") is a fixture during pledge weeks of the Public Broadcasting System, and formerly popular music, such as jazz, has a history of being reassigned to the category of "classic." Jazz is often referred to as "America's classical music and as "art." (However, there is, curiously, a repertoire known as "classic rock" that is universally understood to be "popular" and not "classical.") Jazz has thus gained a foothold in American music education and with it a sense of government by means of formalized pedagogy, which has also transformed considerably the way the music, at least that of the "governed," students in sanctioned jazz education programs, sounds.

"Popular" music is not a particular repertoire, style, or sonic outpouring of any particular affinity groups, and popularity is an extremely volatile attribute. It is not only the popularity of musical styles that is volatile but also the means of dissemination, which have evolved from physically made, mostly disc recordings to downloads to streaming services, presenting significant challenges to corporations, unions, performing rights organizations, and a legal system (as in the case of sampling) that have not always been well equipped logistically or psychologically and intellectually to keep up with ever more rapid developments in technology.

Popular music also requires both the cultural input and massed purchasing power of marginalized groups, who often originate and dominate popular styles. Paradoxically, popular styles often sustain the contradiction of (to quote Jack Black in *School of Rock*) "sticking it to the man"[10] in their content and being "the man" in their status as a major industry. For all the reasons discussed here, as well as the anarchic and hugely volatile nature of "the market," the governments of popular music cultural systems are rarely, if ever, formally articulated.

## Western Classical Music: Virtuosity as Standardized Physical Capacity

For most of his career, classical pianist Leon Fleisher has lived with focal or musician's dystonia, a task-specific neurological condition that affects his right hand.[11] For most of that time, he could not play with his right hand at all. Since 1996, a combination of Botox treatments and Rolfing has restored his ability to play two-handed, albeit within limits.[12] He can perform only certain works, not the most virtuosic, and in recital he has sometimes stopped playing a two-hand piece and informed the audience that he will be substituting a work from the extremely limited left-hand-only repertoire.

My consideration of Fleisher is as a concert pianist within the social confluence of professional classical piano soloists who has other identities/ affinities in confluences. As an artist, he is subject to the government of professional classical music performance, in which concert pianists are a subset with some unusual characteristics. As a citizen of this government, Fleisher's "passport" is marked with a special designation. As Neil Lerner observes, artists with such limitations are never "pianists" but always "one-handed pianists."[13] There is no similar classification for other classical instrumentalists, with the exceptions of other keyboards, such as harpsichord and organ. (Unusually, perhaps uniquely, Douglas Fox (1893–1978) was a one-armed organist who was organist and director of music at Clifton College in Bristol, England, for whom English composer Oliver Horsley Gotch composed a set of 24 preludes and fugues for left hand and pedals.)[14] "One-handed pianists" can perform only a minuscule repertoire, much of which was commissioned by war-wounded amputee pianist Paul Wittgenstein and some by Fleisher. Although it may at first seem that this limited repertoire is only a consequence of impairment rather than an instance of disability law/policy, jazz pianist Horace Parlan, as I will shortly discuss, demonstrates that this is not the case.[15] Nor is it the case that Fleisher was anatomically incapable of playing with his right hand. Focal dystonia rendered typical use of his impaired right hand impossible, but it is the protocols of classical music, in particular the technical demands of the sanctioned two-handed repertoire, that forbade use of his right hand. In other endeavors, including other kinds of music and on other instruments (especially in idioms other than classical music), people often use their impaired hands, and Fleisher has used his right hand as a conductor. In fact, it is unusual for a person not to use an impaired limb as best one can. It must also be noted that two-handed classical pianists are permitted to play and do play one-handed repertoire. Although that license may seem unremarkable, in other traditions, for example, in Ukraine (according to folklorist Natalie Kononenko) and Japan (as documented by disability historian M. Miles), there have been musical occupations designated as the exclusive domains of disabled people, specifically the blind.[16]

Like all classical concert soloists, professional pianists are required to be virtuosi, that is, to possess great technical prowess. After developing focal dystonia, Fleisher became particularly noted for his performance of the *Piano Concerto for the Left Hand* of French composer Maurice Ravel, a work commissioned and often performed by amputee pianist Wittgenstein. As can be witnessed in a performance of that work by Fleisher,[17] it is indeed a dazzling display piece in which, if it is only heard and not seen, its one-handedness might evade listeners' notice. For classical concert pianists, virtuosity, even if it is disabled virtuosity in a handful of cases where one "good" hand remains, is the law.

Like citizenship under many governments, the confluence of classical soloists has a gendered legal system that affords greater opportunities for disabled men than for disabled women. (I have considered only Western classical music performance here; I will discuss composition, an activity distinct from performance in both classical music and electronic dance music, at length in the section on the latter.) One of the responsibilities of female soloists is visual spectacle. Men are expected to dress like the music director (assuming that the conductor is male, as is nearly always the case) and the rank and file of the orchestra, thus taking on a kind of invisibility that facilitates undisrupted focus on musical sound. But women are also re-quired to concern themselves extensively with the complex implications, both practical and semiotic, of wardrobe choices[18] and even to market them-selves in a sexual manner,[19] which in extreme cases has included posing nude.[20] Visible physical disability would not work in women's favor in this regard, and data show that this is reflected in visibly physically disabled women's exclusion from the classical soloist ranks.

The two best-known classical soloists among disabled women are deaf percussionist Evelyn Glennie and double leg amputee violinist Rachel Barton Pine.[21] Glennie's disability is visible only insofar as she performs barefoot, which improves her perception of sonic vibrations.[22] Barton Pine's disability is concealed by clothing.[23] Although she used a wheelchair in the years after the accident that caused her injuries, she now walks with a prosthetic leg. Women's citizenship in the classical musical world, far more than men's, depends on their ability to maintain a passably able-bodied appearance—adapting their disability to the requirements of performance. Both Glennie and Barton Pine make good use of their disability narratives in their pub-licity narratives, but only, it seems, because their stories are illustrated by an acceptably (close enough to) nondisabled experience. By contrast, al-though classical music "governs" its citizens more strictly than jazz, as a man, Fleisher is able to adapt his performance to his disability. Neither Glennie nor Barton Pine needs to perform accommodative repertoire that emphasizes their impairment. The confluences of gender with disability and classical music thus travel in different directions in that gender influ-ences the way in which their disabilities interact with the musical polity in which they operate.

## Jazz: Virtuosity as Idiosyncrasy

Jazz pianist Horace Parlan developed polio as a child and became signifi-cantly paralyzed on his right side. His right hand is essentially immobile. Unlike Fleisher and other one-handed classical pianists with hand impair-ments (as opposed to amputees like Wittgenstein), Parlan plays with both hands. He is a big man with large hands and is able to employ his immobile

but strategically positioned second and fifth fingers in the manner of per-
cussion mallets, as used on vibraphone, marimba, and xylophone. He has
had a major career, perhaps remarkable less for his many solo performances
and recordings than for his employment as a sideman in the ensembles of
such jazz immortals as Charles Mingus and Archie Shepp, who would have
had their pick of two-handed pianists but chose Parlan for his gifts rather
than rejecting him for his limitations.[24]

Unlike "one-handed" classical pianists such as Fleisher, who do not use
their impaired hand at all, Horace Parlan is permitted, if not encouraged or
even required, to play two-handed, as did Oscar Peterson after a severe
stroke that greatly limited use of his left hand.[25] That disabled jazz pianists
like Parlan and Peterson use their impaired hands is due to that music's very
different expectations of its citizens.

Jazz mandates considerable interpretive latitudes of performers. Typically, performers are expected to improvise, invent, or arrange much of
their own music within limits that are often defined by compositions that
are less than thoroughly notated. This is in contrast to classical music, for
which fastidious notation enables certain works to become the "master-
pieces" of the "great composers" and thus canonized. Loyalty to the notated
score takes on a role analogous to belief in biblical inerrancy. Regardless of
whether a work of classical music is regarded as canonic, the canonic paradigm of fidelity to notation and the "composer's intentions" (whether these
can ever truly be known or not) is a law that does not exist in jazz. In jazz,
musical invention, improvisation in particular, is a duty of citizenship. All
performers create their own music in accordance with their idiosyncrasies
of embodiment, whether they are disabled or not.

Still, jazz does not enable participation by all, regardless of disability status. Jazz performance demands not only invention but also virtuosity, formidable technical prowess. Jazz differs from classical music, however, in its
greater acceptance of "disabled virtuosity." Both Parlan and Reinhardt had
atypical limitations on their playing owing to hand impairments that rendered impossible gestures that would be simple for performers with two
fully able hands, but both artists are or were capable of extraordinary technical accomplishments based on what their hands could do, far beyond the
range of many players. A classical pianist with Parlan's impairment could
play only the one-handed repertoire. A classical guitarist with Reinhardt's
impairment could probably not play the extant repertoire at all.

As with classical soloists, disability and gender interact differentially in jazz. As Sherrie Tucker observes, female jazz musicians had not only musical work but also "glamor as labor."[26] The data support the argument that, as in classical music, the extra, added obligation of spectacle has served to disenfranchise women with visible physical disabilities from jazz almost entirely. The only exception of whom I am aware among prominent artists is singer Ella Fitzgerald, who, owing to diabetes, became a double leg amputee late in life; and failure to fully recover from surgery severely limited the frequency of her performances[27] and ended her recording career.[28] It seems unlikely that Fitzgerald could have launched her career with that limitation. Although blind singer and pianist Diane Shuur's impairment is sensory rather than mobility related, she at once conceals and reveals her impairment by wearing dark glasses when she performs,[29] an accessory used by nearly all prominent blind musicians regardless of genre (classical and crossover tenor Andrea Bocelli is the notable exception).[30]

## Electronic Dance Music: The Equalizer of (Dis)Abilities?

The distinction between the roles of composition and performance is arguably more pronounced in Western classical music than in any other idiom (even though many classical composers have also been performers). This division of labor could theoretically offer opportunities for people with mobility impairments to realize their musical ideas in notation and recording, even if they are unable to sing or play. However, this has rarely been the case. Composer Frederick Delius became paralyzed (and blind) late in life and continued composing with the help of his assistant Eric Fenby,[31] but I am unaware of any classical composers who began careers with comparable upper body mobility impairments, despite the feasibility of doing so. (Musicologist Susan Feder writes that American composer John Hausserman [1909–86], who had cerebral palsy since a child, "dictated his compositions painstakingly by playing a single note at a piano which an assistant confirmed at a second instrument."[32] But it is not clear that this was a lifelong practice, or one that was adopted later in life, when Hausserman, an accomplished organist, became even more severely disabled and a wheelchair user, owing to an auto accident.)[33] The history of professional blind musicians, beyond the focus of this essay, is quite different and somewhat more encouraging.[34]

I have argued elsewhere that the classical music cultural system idealizes flawless bodies and that the roots of this idealization in Western culture are ancient and referenced in both Hebrew and Christian scriptures.[35] The abhorrence of flaws is evidenced, for example, in one-handed pianism, in which the impaired hand has no role. Musically, it is hidden, nonexistent, or even functionally amputated. The abhorrence of physical impairment is much in evidence in the life of German baritone Thomas Quasthoff. Quasthoff was denied admission to any German conservatory because of his inability to play the piano owing to his attenuated limbs, a result of his mother's thalidomide use during her pregnancy.[36] Metaphorically, classical music's emphasis on technically flawless performances of a quasi-sacred canonic repertoire enforces the same value system on another level.

Although world-class soloists like Quasthoff and violinist Itzhak Perlman (a polio survivor who uses crutches and a motorized scooter) have been able to surmount the obstacles that have confronted them,[37] the same cannot be said of artists with less spectacular gifts. For example, in my career of forty-plus years as a musician and educator, I have never seen (live or recorded) a rank-and-file band or orchestral musician, amateur, student, or professional, who uses a wheelchair onstage, although most instruments in these ensembles can be played from that position. (Perlman uses crutches onstage.) I posit that this stigma on physical disability contributes to the failure to develop composition as an opportunity for those who cannot perform. Quasthoff's being denied a holistic conservatory education, with the training a composer requires, is testament to the manner in which physically disabled potential musicians, including potential composers, are discouraged.

The prospect of composing without the mobility required for performance has become increasingly realistic as music technology has improved. Although seemingly this has made no difference in classical music, where there are many able-bodied nonperformer composers, providing opportunities for mobility-impaired composers, often nonperformers, has been a significant part of the work of the Vancouver Adapted Music Society (VAMS).[38] Most of the VAMS studio's technology can be operated with the head (including breath) only, such that even artists without any limb mobility are able to compose.

In 2013, a project whose technology is more advanced and even more enabling than that of the VAMS studio was launched. *Smirnoff* [the sponsor] *Mindtunes* formed an artistic collaboration between the United Kingdom's "drum 'n' bass veteran" DJ Fresh, French neurotechnologist Julien Castet, and three disabled musicians, Andy Walker, Mark Rowland, and Jo Portois, to create an electronic dance track "using only their minds."[39] The three disabled musicians, whom press coverage refers to instead as "fans," have severe mobility impairments. Walker and Portois are quadriplegics with acquired disabilities, without ability to move their limbs.[40] Rowland has cerebral palsy, with extremely limited limb movement, and uses a speech-synthesis communication device like that perhaps most familiar from its use by physicist Stephen Hawking.[41] Rowland is an active musician whose personal studio contains technology of similar sophistication to that of VAMS. Portois is a former DJ who explains that his disability makes that work too difficult. Walker is clearly tech-savvy but gives no evidence of prior musical experience.[42]

According to *Fact Magazine*, "Castet 'uses an ElectroEncephaloGraphy device (EEG) to measure the electrical activity of the brain, turning brainwaves and emotions into musical beats', a press release explains. Here's where Fresh comes in, arranging these beats into a whole track."[43] I have taken some literary license here to characterize all the digital controllers used here as "keyboards," although DJ Fresh, who is not disabled, does use a piano-like keyboard controller. In several remarkable scenes, sliding potentiometers, controlled by brain waves, appear to move by themselves.

The liberatory power and potential of this technology in granting these disabled artists "full citizenship" within the social confluence of electronic dance music (EDM) is an intriguing question with implications beyond music. The notion of musical "technique" as physical prowess in controlling the voice or an instrument is clearly not operative here. Notably, nondisabled DJ Fresh states that he has never played an instrument well but is able to make music successfully because of digital technology.[44] Unfortunately, none of the *Smirnoff Mindtunes* videos nor any article I have found details sufficiently either DJ Fresh's role versus the contributions of Walker, Rowland, and Portois or the degree to which Castet's technology enables severely mobility-impaired artists to create music without assistance. Doubtless, the videos Smirnoff released are intended more to fascinate than to inform. Nonetheless, it is clear that older technologies, such as those used by VAMS and by Mark Rowland before this project, have gone a long way toward eliminating any need for physical prowess in music making and that Castet's invention has great promise for enabling disabled musicians even further. Although someone with mobility impairment comparable to Stephen Hawking's would likely be unable to operate VAMS technology, it seems that only the ability to think about music is required to work with Castet's.

However, it is not only the ability to create music that confers citizenship within a particular confluence, but also acceptance of disabled musicians within that community. EDM offers a paradoxical combination of simultaneous openness and rejection. In addition to the elimination of the need for physical prowess, the native musical vocabulary synthesized consists of sounds that have little or no association with particular acoustic instruments (arguably, percussive sounds are exceptions). One resultant effect is that listeners do not envision or otherwise imagine embodied—able or not—human performance on familiar instruments; there is no equivalent to air guitar. In EDM's native public space, dance clubs, the DJ is the exception to the rule of invisibility, but the DJ's art is so unlike acoustic instrumental or vocal performance that she or he proves the rule by calling attention to it even more than were no human music-making agent present at all.

It might seem, then, that EDM could be a great equalizer of opportunity for disabled musicians. The *Mindtunes* videos offer a difference of opinion among the disabled musicians.[45] Rowland, who was an active musician before the project, had already fully embraced the genre. But Portois had been a DJ and laments that this is now "too difficult."

On another level, there is the question whether EDM is primarily a musical idiom or an implement for facilitating dance as the foreground activity. In the dance club, EDM's native habitat, even beyond the nonembodied nature of its sound dissemination and the lack of evocation of human performance (which are obviously closely interrelated), there is the relative lack of interest in the identity of the music makers. The music is more than merely ambient but less than the focus of attention. The documentary *DJ Fresh & Mindtunes* concludes with the premiere of the track at a club. As Rowland says, no one in the club was aware of the identities of the artists, but the response was "phenomenal." The film does not reveal how much the club patrons were made aware of the artists' identities, although, in addition to the music, the presentation includes a projection that identifies the track as *Smirnoff Mindtunes*.

The anonymity of EDM composers could indeed serve as an equalizer of able-bodied and disabled artists, but for the unfortunate reason that it hides disabilities rather than mandating acceptance. But it is also important that this mixed-media genre (music and dance) is, to an extreme, about dancing and thus shifts the issue of disability acceptance to that performance medium, in which EDM appears to have little or no potential to advance community integration for people like Walker, Rowland, and Portois.

A discussion of the potential of EDM as a social confluence in which disabled musicians might enjoy full citizenship cannot be complete without considering the actual impact and limits of the *Smirnoff Mindtunes* project, including the impressions of its disabled participants. According to the video documentary, the full proceeds from iTunes downloads of the track the musicians created are being donated to the Queen Elizabeth Foundation "to build a state of the art assistive technology group home." Julie Tugwell, of the foundation, speaks of how "it's been fantastic working with Smirnoff, DJ Fresh, and Julien" and how "we're very lucky that DJ Fresh has donated the proceeds from iTunes." It is unclear why, among the artists, the decision to donate royalties and the credit for donating should belong to DJ Fresh alone. In her remarks, Tugwell gives no acknowledgment of the contributions of Walker, Rowland, and Portois other than to praise "people making their own decisions and being part of this wonderful project."[46] This does not sound like full citizenship.

Toward the video's close, the disabled musicians are unanimous in expressing a tremendous sense of loss that the project has ended. This seems wrong and unnecessary. Rowland, whose inability to speak singles him out for special regard, even from Walker and Portois, despite being the most knowledgeable and experienced musician of the three, is also the one who says, through his communication device, that "it's such a positive project on the *professional* and *social* level of disabilities" (emphasis mine), and that "I think that the whole disability movement needs this type of platform." It is interesting that the artist regarded as most disabled by virtue of his speech— that is, his sonic—disability is also the one whose (synthesized) voice is the most political. Regrettably, Rowland's vision of the potential of the project seems to have been, at best, put on hold.

The emancipatory potential for mobility-impaired people of the technology used in this project, as well perhaps as that of electronic dance music and related idioms whose aesthetics do not include physical prowess and "technique," has yet to be realized and may not be if technological advances are not accompanied by a parallel shift in cultural attitudes toward people with disabilities. One indication of how far this particular social confluence and the larger cultures within which it resides have to go is that in the documentary videos released by *Smirnoff Mindtunes*, Walker, Rowland, and Portois seem to be bit players in their own story.

As elsewhere, citizenship in EDM is deeply gendered. According to the *Huffington Post*'s Sarah Gates, as well as communications studies scholar Kembrew McLeod, female club DJs endure both outright discrimination and are subject to the same burden of glamor as labor and pressure to display themselves sexually as in other musical confluences.[47] The challenges able-bodied women face are apparently insurmountable by visibly physically disabled women. In that context, it is thus hardly surprising that the disabled musicians recruited for the *Smirnoff Mindtunes* project are all male.

## Musical Citizens

Using social confluence theory, this essay has examined three musical cultures as governments with their own protocols of citizenship. For consistency, a focus on professional keyboard artists with physical disabilities that limit mobility and inhibit live performance was employed. The primary examples were all male, less for consistency than because female artists with comparable mobility impairments could not be found. Reasons for the absence of female artists with disabilities and differences in women's access to citizenship within the three musical confluences were also discussed.

Artists with mobility impairments were chosen because of availability of data and a more pervasive history of discrimination in music than other disabilities, such as blindness (which offers many more examples but less disablement within musical confluences).[48] A study of mental disability, including substance addiction, would have been unfeasibly complex. Keyboards were chosen both for the availability of examples and because of the flexibility with which they may be operated: played, programmed, or a combination of playing and programming.

Of the confluences considered, only classical music has stable institutions and protocols through which statutes can be verified through documentation rather than inferred. For example, the requirement that all applicants to German conservatories be able to study piano was used to deny entrance to baritone Thomas Quasthoff. In jazz and EDM (and to some degree in classical music as well), "rules" needed to be determined through observing praxis.

The essential question of citizenship for a disabled artist (rather than an audience member or administrator or service provider) within a music confluence is the degree to which one is permitted to participate. Permission to participate intersects with ability to participate, but they are not identical.

Possessing the skills and knowledge to execute the responsibilities and exercise the full rights of citizenship, or the ability to obtain such skills and knowledge, by no means guarantees that citizenship will be conferred. Music confluences are as prone to arbitrary discrimination as any others.

Ability to participate as a performer within a music confluence, that is, to assume the responsibilities of citizenship, is a function of how that culture regards "technique," which has historically been understood as the physical prowess required to play an instrument or sing. Within the confluence of professional classical pianism, virtuoso technique is required. Virtuosity is standardized through formal training and the expectation that professionals be able to play a shared repertoire. One ramification of the standardization of piano technique is that since each individual's impairment limits functionality differently, impaired hands are not used. Artists with a hand injury are then "demoted" to the rank and title of "one-handed pianist" and provided only a minuscule repertoire, as was long the case for Leon Fleisher (whose partially restored right-hand facility enables him to play some two-hand repertoire some of the time).

Virtuosity is fundamental to the ethos of jazz as well, but it is understood differently. Jazz virtuosity requires individualism, not standardization. Pianist Horace Parlan's story is one of full citizenship, borne out by a distinguished career and many admirers familiar with his work but unaware of his impairment. Doubtless, as listeners, they have heard what Parlan can do without considering what he cannot. (Although Parlan's disability has largely gone unnoticed, it is an important part of guitarist Django Reinhardt's legend, and his prowess is all the more admired because of it.)

Composing or "producing"[49] EDM tracks (unlike live DJing) does not require physical prowess. In using the equipment developed for *Smirnoff Mindtunes*, it appears that only the ability to think is required to compose and record, so even musicians with severely limited mobility are enabled to make music. At this time, the technology appears to have been used only to create a single track, by DJ Fresh and his disabled colleagues Andy Walker, Mark Rowland and Jo Portois, and it is unclear when or whether it will be made available again and to whom. The anonymity of EDM tracks in their native environment, dance clubs, negates neither that DJs are celebrities and visual, embodied, performative presences nor that dancers are as well. With regard to the ultimate wide acceptance of disabled artists within the musical confluence of EDM, the seemingly unlimited potential for mobility-impaired musicians to create tracks must be weighed against the music's powerful association with social dancing, an activity that is powerfully associated with able-bodied physicality.

All three musical confluences examined here both erect obstacles and propose pathways to full citizenship for mobility-impaired musicians. An ideal environment would fully honor the possibility of composition as a process distinct from physical, real-time performance, an idea most associated with Western classical music. That environment would, like jazz, celebrate virtuosity as personal idiosyncrasy. It would be a conceptual space where music making does not demand physical prowess, like the composition phase of EDM.

All the musical governments surveyed here retain an ethos of ableism, a demand that at least some performative roles be played by actors of marked physical prowess. An ideal musical confluence would challenge essential aesthetic tenets of all the musics considered here (and all musics of which I am aware). The potential for emancipation lies in part in the advanced technologies evidenced in the *Mindtunes* project. But it is also essential to embrace the physicality of disabled people, the idiosyncratic physical prowess of artists like Parlan and Reinhardt.

One hopeful recent development has been the nascent inclusion of "adaptive music" in medical practice.[50] Although artists such as Parlan and Reinhardt have been adapting their performance techniques to their impairments for decades and there is evidence that indicates that there has always been such adaptive praxis,[51] there are now also allies within the medical and rehabilitation professions who, in their practices, assist musicians who acquire disabilities to continue to perform and enable potential musicians with disabilities to identify suitable performance media, playing and singing techniques, and assistive technologies. Ultimately, a musical ethos will need to emerge that both regards physical prowess as optional and simultaneously celebrates the idiosyncratic varieties of physical prowess of musical performance by artists with all manner of bodies.

## CHAPTER 7

# Our Ancestors the Sighted: Making Blind People French and French People Blind, 1750–1991

Catherine Kudlick

In 1991 the Museum of Science and Industry in Paris published an intriguing architecture book titled *Des clés pour bâtir* (*Keys for Building*).[1] Clearly, much effort and money had gone into its conceptualization, design, and production. Each of its sixty pages contains a combination of large print and Braille accompanied by masterful tactile illustrations depicting important architectural concepts, such as lintels, reinforced concrete, buttresses, white light, and numerous other terms too complex even for my top-of-the line French-English dictionary. The book has no preface but rather gets right down to business, as if every architecture book catered to people with vision impairments: "To build houses, temples, skyscrapers, bridges, or cathedrals," it begins, "the architect must consider use, resistance, beauty, and the cost of these works." It then continues: "This will determine the choice of materials, assembly, form, and how it will be carried out. Here you will find a few examples of assemblies or structures that humankind has progressively developed to solve problems of resistance, that is, solidity and stability."[2] The book is both simple and complex. Some places—and indeed the entire format—initially appear to cater to children. Others (such as one rather detailed discussion of triangulation) seem better suited to someone with a sound background in geometry or perhaps even astronomy. I bought *Keys for Building* in the museum bookstore for about twenty U.S. dollars. It was just one of many science offerings for patrons, albeit the only one in Braille.

Why would anyone publish something like this? Who was its intended audience? Was *Keys for Building* really for blind and visually impaired people, or did it serve another purpose for sighted ones? What made it so French, and why would it be impossible to imagine a tactile book with similar content coming out in America?

The answer, I argue, lies in a unique conflation of historical forces linked to specifically French ideas about marginality, assimilation, and visual culture, ideas far from the medical and institutional approaches that dominate most studies of "the blind." My analysis challenges what disability studies scholars often refer to as the "medical model" that casts disabilities as ahistorical and apolitical products of abnormal pathological conditions awaiting a cure. *Keys for Building* was not created by health professionals with the aim of rehabilitating blind patients. Nor was it inspired by "special education" aids so often associated with helping disabled clients. No physicians had a hand in determining the content, and no advanced academic degrees lent the book an aura of expertise. To be sure, medical doctors were important shapers of modern French policy and identity by being unusually prominent as legislators and social commentators throughout the nineteenth and twentieth centuries. But because *Keys for Building* is rooted in the embodied experience of blindness, the book's lessons, and indeed its healthy physicality, lie outside medical interests and understanding. Put another way, in this chapter I offer a history of the body that places medicine under quarantine.[3]

At the same time, I want to expand our thinking about what constitutes a "social model." Although the book is decidedly not *for the blind* in a medical or rehabilitation sense, it has definite qualities of having been carefully thought through and produced as an object of beauty that speaks directly to blind people and intrigues sighted ones. In dealing with such a text as physical and conceptual, my concern goes beyond how visually-impaired people become marginalized or categorized as "disabled" in French (or other) society. And it is only partly about the conscious links activists draw between the need for alternative text formats such as tactile books and the full social inclusion of outsiders with print-reading disabilities. Above all, building on the premise that disability should be understood as another "other" on a par with race, gender, and social class, I explore how blind people transcend these categories by teaching everyone something unexpected about citizenship's inner workings.[4]

To accomplish this, my chapter offers a close textual and contextual reading of *Keys for Building* as a product of France's historically complex notions of belonging. Ideas that celebrate social equality, universality, and assimilation while still maintaining clear distinctions between "us" and "them" began to permeate French society and culture during the eighteenth century and persist down to the present. Linked to expanding definitions of human rights, the great Revolution of 1789 laid the groundwork for promoting this type of inclusion as "citizenship." Blind people—a term I use to refer to those who primarily access the physical and cultural world through means other than vision—offer a unique entry point. At times I fold them into the broader category of people who live with a variety of disabilities, an artificial, problematic grouping if ever there was one, but one with surprising staying power.[5] Conceptually, many elements were in place to frame people with disabilities within other discourses of human rights, such as those pertaining to women, slaves, and religious and other minorities.[6] Moreover, as an unsighted minority being defined within a political framework built on ideas of "enlightenment," "transparency," and "spectacle," blind people introduce both obvious and obscure complications. Can people understood solely in terms of their being unable to see truly be members of a nation rooted so deeply in vision? Historians have not yet approached citizenship from this perspective, either theoretically or practically, even as scholars have become more excited by visual culture's central relationship to the polity.[7] The long-term history behind *Keys for Building* suggests an odd phenomenon whereby blind people remained largely invisible at the same time at which they became emblematic of a society grappling with new forms of participation.

To be sure, much of what I say here may be limited specifically to French culture and society. The country that translated so much of Enlightenment thinking into practice through revolution offered particular ways of seeing and seeing through disability. Still, this analysis can contribute to scholars' attempts to understand what citizenship, membership, and belonging might mean not just for French people or disabled people but for everyone. Certainly France's approach to human rights, citizenship, and visual culture influenced other modern Western political cultures that consciously or unconsciously incorporated some features and rejected others while dealing with their own complex relationships to difference.[8]

Starting from the premise that *Keys for Building* offers a rare peek into inclusion as a visceral process, this chapter traces two paths with potentially contradictory destinations. One involves making blind people "French" by rendering what is taken for granted visually—in this case the built physical landscape so central to French culture—through touch while still preserving a basic conceptual framework linked to sight. The second makes the French "blind" by helping sighted French people understand how their fellow visually impaired citizens apprehend, comprehend, and interact with French culture nonvisually and thereby drawing attention to other means of inculcating assumed national values. The book, which ultimately turns out to be a tactile celebration of the beauty of Parisian monuments, offers a path toward assimilation for blind people much like that for France's colonial subjects while also suggesting genuine possibilities for subverting it by proposing something completely new.

## Making Blind People French

The French have long been associated with an impulse to erase cultural differences in favor of a universal bourgeois ideal. Articulated by French Enlightenment *philosophes*, put into practice by the 1789 Revolution, and expanded over the next two centuries, this arrogant generosity reflects the confidence of the nation's triumphant bourgeois elites. It both stems from and bolsters a belief that a particular set of Enlightenment values is synonymous with civilization itself: rationality, tolerance, individualism, equality, democracy, progress, secularism, and transparency. Enshrined in documents such as the Declaration of the Rights of Man and Citizen (1789), such ideas have been exported around the world in what we today call "human rights."[9]

Claiming to be the birthplace of such values, France believed that it had a responsibility to enlighten others.[10] This would become known as a *mission civilisatrice* (civilizing mission). A broad education was the weapon of choice. Education went beyond the basics of reading and writing to inculcate the previously mentioned values associated with French culture. Accordingly, French history is full of examples of teaching the less fortunate, from the poor and working-class women of the early nineteenth century to the subjects of its vast colonial empire well into the twentieth. The process was so thorough and seamless that for a time French bourgeois ideals triumphed as unquestioned universal assumptions for everyone. The civilizing mission rests on a web of contradictions and paradoxes, of which the most glaring and important for purposes of this chapter is that universal values can be universal only if there is an underlying belief that not everyone is capable of holding them.

*Keys for Building* can be read as an example of this civilizing mission applied to blind people.[11] The book might seem to suggest that a blind person, like the schoolchild in Mali or Senegal who allegedly memorized phrases such as "our ancestors the Gauls," should embrace important aspects of Frenchness, however foreign they might be to actual lived experience. By teaching blind readers the importance of architectural features that most people associate with sight, *Keys for Building* can at one level be seen as an attempt to train visually impaired French citizens to appreciate what they cannot literally see. But can we really think of blind people in the same vein as colonial subjects? Or might such an approach be an exaggeration? In his controversial and passionate study *The Mask of Benevolence*, Harlan Lane offers an intriguing, if problematic, starting point for thinking about this question by considering how society treats Deaf people.[12] Lane draws direct parallels between hearing professionals and colonial authority. "Like the paternalism of the colonizers," he explains, "hearing paternalism begins with defective perception because it superimposes its image of the familiar world of hearing people on the unfamiliar world of deaf people" (37). He sets up a model to show how, in his words, "Hearing paternalism likewise sees its task as 'civilizing' its charges: restoring deaf people to society." He further asserts that "hearing paternalism fails to understand the structure and values of deaf society" and notes that "the hearing people who control the affairs of deaf children and adults commonly do not know deaf people and do not want to. Since they cannot see deaf people as they really are, they make up imaginary deaf people of their own, in accord with their own experiences and needs" (37). To drive home his point, Lane provides two tables that reveal how colonizers and what he called "the audist establishment of professionals" used similar adjectives to demonstrate the inferiority of their charges. Terms such as "childlike," "stubborn/insolent," and "unsocialized" pepper both tables. Other assertions implied that deaf people, like colonized subjects, suffered from limited intellectual ability and psychological instability and were inferior to their rescuers because they lacked language, culture, and a distinctive history (34, 36).

However schematic, Lane's parallel between Deaf people and colonial subjects would seem to make less sense for blind people. After all, unlike the blind (almost always spelled with a lowercase *b*), the Deaf (spelled with a capital *D* to emphasize an identity) share a rich common language and accompanying culture. Moreover, as work by various scholars has shown— including Douglas Baynton's chapter in the present volume—Deaf people have been actively colonized and oppressed, with schools for the deaf forbidding the use of sign language, deaf people being institutionalized as cognitively disabled, and other oppressive measures. Still, I believe that Lane's observations serve as a useful entry point for thinking about the blind if we consider another form of literacy equally important to the French: "visual culture."

Blind people must live in a decidedly visual world, but although most modern nations share this obsession, no culture has been more consistently linked with it than France. In his influential book *Downcast Eyes*, Martin Jay suggests that the vision and visual culture that began with the Greeks was absorbed into French thought, where it enjoyed a central place well into the nineteenth century. The inherent visuality of Catholicism played an especially vital role; certainly, if one thinks about ornate Catholic churches compared with plain Protestant ones, it is not hard to imagine why Paris became synonymous with the visual arts and fashion in a way that far surpassed Berlin or London. In a similar vein, the luxury and spectacle of the French court—particularly once it moved to Versailles under Louis XIV— also played a part in solidifying the relationship between visual display and power. In their quests for Truth, Enlightenment thinkers and subsequent revolutionaries both built on and perpetuated the centrality of the visual— and therefore vision—by stressing the importance of observation and transparency. By the end of the nineteenth century, vision became a means of selling everything from art to a way of life. With their garish shop windows and dramatic displays of goods, Parisian department stores stood at the forefront of creating links between visual culture and commodification. Thus, in France, with its capital known as "the City of Light," power and the visual became synonymous in many ways, large and small. Not surprisingly, French politicians across the spectrum have offered vision to others as they touted French glory. Charles de Gaulle famously proclaimed France "the light of the world" on more than one occasion. Meanwhile, in his 1980 inaugural address, socialist François Mitterand promised that "a just, generous France . . . can illuminate the path of mankind." More than simply being the stock-in-trade of all political rhetoric, such word choices reveal a deeply rooted attachment to vision and the visual, ultimately linked to France's civilizing mission.[13]

Although it is not uniquely French, the nation's popular culture has an especially strong connection to the visual that makes it easy for anyone unfamiliar with blind people's alternative forms of appreciating the world to be dismissive or wary. To be sure, many forms of visual beauty remain difficult to access through other senses; signature architectural features might be out of reach, not to mention that, depending on circumstances, the latest dress or hairstyle might be untouchable for different reasons. Although the scores of visual metaphors present less of a problem for most blind people, their prevalence might undermine the other senses and hence anyone who relies on them. Given this context, it is easy to comprehend how blind people might be understood as exiles or as subalterns in visual culture, even if inattention or lack of education means that virtually everyone, regardless of visual acuity, could be constantly missing important visual features.

*Keys for Building* can be read as an attempt to instruct French blind people about this visual culture. Indeed, the detailed illustrations relegate even the most complex textual explanations to a subordinate role. To teach the principles of architecture, the book offers a series of tactile images that represent buildings as a process of creation that combines science and art. Thus the first image depicts how various elements, such as rain, ice, wind, and sun, interact with materials, such as wood, iron, and stone. Readers learn about bricklaying, stonemasonry, and principles of welding through tactile pictures. They also learn how architects account for forces such as resistance and equilibrium when they design bridges, archways, and eventually whole buildings.

The illustrations and the supporting text build unmistakably toward an architectural climax: the city of Paris. After learning about arches, for example, readers see these ingenious principles applied to the Arch of Triumph. Domes culminate in the Pantheon, flying buttresses in Notre Dame, ironwork in the Eiffel Tower. The book takes readers up to the present day in pages where they learn about the Pompidou Center, the Arch at La Défense, the Montparnasse Tower, and, of course, the Museum of Science and Industry that created the book. The last pages present a side-by-side comparison of each major Parisian monument to offer a sense of each one's relative size. And to familiarize themselves with the relative locations, readers can flip to the final page for a tactile map of Paris with each monument schematically placed in its proper part of the city and labeled on the facing page. What begins as a primer on architecture, then, ends as a tactile civics lesson that demonstrates grandeur culminating in Paris as the ultimate and ongoing achievement of French civilization.

Because Paris has such a grip on the French popular imagination, making the capital the book's culminating lesson has particular symbolic power from the perspective of a civic education project. Indeed, much of French history focuses on the tensions between Paris and the rest of the country as everyone tries to sort out the extent to which Paris is France and vice versa. Every French schoolchild learns the lesson, first crudely and later with more subtlety: beginning in the Middle Ages, given an added boost by Louis XIV, and accelerating after the 1789 Revolution and Napoléon, successive French governments sought to rationalize power by concentrating it in one place. Given the capital's unparalleled primacy, and given the French penchant for touting their national glory, it seems only fitting that the city and the nation became fused as one. Such ideas seeped into the country's formidable literary tradition, where for much of the nineteenth century novels with a character making his way from the provinces to the great metropolis became staples of French literature.[14]

Keys for Building takes its readers on a similar journey, instructing and introducing them—like the newly arrived provincial youth—to the glories of the capital. This quirky little architecture book embodies the idea that being functionally literate in French culture requires having a particular intimacy with the visible highlights of Paris, whether one has been there or not. Now blind people have joined their sighted French counterparts because they can comment with (literal) firsthand knowledge about the construction and composition of the city's monuments, their relative sizes, and even their locations. More than the modern sightseeing tourist, the blind reader of Keys for Building has taken an important step toward assimilation.

To develop this notion of a "civilizing mission" that I have imposed on a book whose creators never stated this as their goal, it is instructive to explore a case where such a mission did play a part, and where disability themes loomed large. Consider the work of Father Jacques Ghys, a forward-looking Catholic priest interested in the French perspective regarding relations between the metropole and the Islamic world as it played out in immigrant experiences of the 1950s and 1960s.[15] In addition to founding a number of social service agencies dedicated to helping newly arrived Algerians, he began a monthly journal catering to France's helping professions called the Cahiers Nord-Africains (or North African Notebooks). The publication took up a number of topics, many of which share a certain benevolent paternalism with the disability field: affordable housing, social psychology, job placement and retention, impact of social legislation, family problems, teaching methods, and health and social services.

Written by "experts" for "experts," the articles suggest important links between immigration and disability. This insider view of the issues posed by the arrival of so many North Africans in France after World War II conveys much of what Harlan Lane described when he likened colonizers to hearing professionals. The tone's admixture of paternalism, self-satisfaction, and adventurous engagement with the lives of people whom others ignore characterizes the writings of many who work with the disabled. Accordingly, some articles display impressive foresight, such as one surprising passage labeled "Some Traits of the North African Mentality," which noted, "Because [immigrants] are so used to being exploited [by Europeans], we [teachers] must be sure to explain why we are there." Elsewhere, the journal offered exposés on various aspects of North African life, even urging its readers to learn as much Arabic as possible. Other articles display jaw-dropping condescension with clear links to disability: "Upon their arrival our [Algerian] students reveal constant spasming and clumsy body movements due, among other things, to inadequate or irrational eating habits, as well as to traumas stemming from failure or the fear of failure." Other passages about the inferiority of the colonial subjects in "creativity" and "cultural development" suggest that disability is an ever-present concern. Indeed, if one leafs through the pages of the *Cahiers*, one is led to believe that Father Ghys—and surely the helping professionals he tried to reach—approached immigration writ large much like a disability.

Intriguingly, the *Cahiers* also provide tools for drawing the equation in the opposite direction, that is, approaching people with disabilities like immigrants. A special issue in 1954 explores how to educate newly arrived Algerians, from young children to working adults. It includes grammar lessons reprinted from a textbook called *Ali apprend le français* (*Ali Learns French*), some of which share underlying similarities with *Keys for Building*. Although Ali does not learn about Paris and its monuments in the few exercises reproduced in the volume, he nonetheless masters important lessons about his new country. Thus he learns about bread baking (bread being the staple of the French diet) and restaurant etiquette (he should order coffee at the end of a meal and tip the waiter 10 percent of the total bill). The primer also teaches Ali about transportation systems, winter, personal hygiene, visits to the doctor, and—interestingly, because it represents one of the first lessons taught to blind people in mobility instruction—the four cardinal directions of north, south, east, and west. Perhaps the most revealing chapter discusses "La France," where students read that they now live in one of

Europe's most important countries and one of the most beautiful to boot "because of the richness of its soil and the variety of the countryside." Ali, who presumably comes from a hot and dry Muslim country where alcohol consumption is forbidden, also learns about great verdant forests, Mont Blanc and the Alps being covered with snow year-round, and Bordeaux and Champagne, "where famous wines are made." Like the imagined blind reader of *Keys for Building*, Ali meets a France he should know, but one that might never truly accept who he is.

These texts offer provocative insights into the French approach to expanding citizenship and social membership to those deemed to be outsiders. There is, of course, the idea of helping one's fellow citizens by bringing them up to speed, by educating them in prevailing values and practices. But juxtaposing colonialism and disability introduces a more problematic side that is largely overlooked in regard to blind people but becomes more apparent once we place them alongside discussions of other Others.[16] Most obviously, we find the issue of paternalism, of doing something for the less fortunate as a gesture of social largesse rooted in a feeling of superiority that reinforces the disabled person's inferiority and problematic nature. More subtly, we must confront what lies behind the desire to assimilate in the first place, again a question that has been more deeply explored in relation to other forms of marginalization. Over thirty years ago, leading French disability theorist Henri-Jacques Stiker explained the danger in his pathbreaking analysis *A History of Disability*: "This act [of rehabilitation, which in French is "reeducation"] will cause the disabled to disappear and with them all that is lacking, in order to assimilate them, to drown them, dissolve them in the greater and single social whole. . . . The problem of our society is not a failure to integrate but of integrating too well, of integrating in such a way that identicalness reigns, at least a rough identity, a socially-constructed identity, an identity of which citizens can be convinced."[17] By creating a class of "dis-disabled people," this process of inclusion strives to make them identical but without making them truly equal.

In sum, we have much evidence for understanding *Keys for Building* as an example of the French civilizing mission applied to blind people. Interpreted in this way, the book can be read as yet another example of asserting France's assimilationist goals. That Ali and his imaginary blind friend should grow up to know about Paris and its distinctive characteristics reflects a benevolent, paternalistic desire to extend a helping hand to the less fortunate who need enlightenment. These same impulses also suggest a fear of difference, or at least a belief that France's "others" bring nothing valuable to the nation from their own unique experiences. As Stiker explains, "Disability cannot be a confrontational position, a force for social change, a mutant or revolutionary minority. . . . The disabled should always adapt to society as it is."[18] Put another way, the idea that disability offers a useful perspective remains so foreign that it is completely unthinkable; the disabled can never help, they can only be helped. So even as our tactile book offers the keys to enter the exalted world of the visual, the door never truly opens. This becomes clearer when one poses a fundamental question never raised in *Keys for Building*, but one that the beautiful multisensory object cannot help but ask: who would ever dare to hire a blind architect?

## Making French People Blind

The first part of this chapter offered a reading of *Keys for Building* as an oppressive tool within a colonialist and assimilationist framework that formed blind people as subaltern citizens of French visual culture. But perhaps this is not really true, since in this second part I want to argue just the opposite: by situating the book within a different historical context, we can read it as a subversive and potentially revolutionary document. This requires going back to the Enlightenment. Earlier I stressed the influence of Enlightenment thinking on erasing cultural differences in favor of higher universal bourgeois ideals. But this period of intellectual and political foment also championed self-determination, individuality, equality, cosmopolitanism, and democracy. As much as *Keys for Building* can be read as an unusual example of the French desire to assimilate its others, the book's very existence suggests a certain audacity. It might even be seen as a desire to celebrate, even elevate, a form of cultural difference the French have overlooked. A little Enlightenment could be a dangerous thing, especially in the hands of people who both wittingly and unwittingly challenged vision's supposedly indispensable place in French culture.

On this alternative reading, the genesis of *Keys for Building* could be found in one of the Enlightenment's boldest but least-known books: *An Essay on the Education of the Blind*, published in 1786.[19] Believed to be the first tactile book produced in multiple copies, the *Essay* consisted of 118 pages (including notes) of raised large-print letters that could be read by both blind and sighted people. It was the brainchild of Valentin Haüy (1745–1822), a

sighted paleographer and linguist who would become known as "the Father
of the Blind."[20] In the 1780s, this middle-aged man, fluent in nearly a dozen
classical and living languages, had already enjoyed a successful career as a
translator of official documents when he began to take an interest in educating blind people. Working collaboratively, Haüy produced the *Essay* as a tes-
timonial plea to the king and other luminaries to open the world's first
school for blind children.

Until this book and the establishment of Haüy's school two years before
the *Essay*, no blind person in the Western world had a ready means of reading, writing, or becoming educated. (Louis Braille, born in 1809, would enter the successor to Haüy's school, the Institut National des Jeunes Aveugles,
in 1819 and would teach there until his death in 1852.) Only a handful of
blind individuals from across Europe had been lucky enough to be born
into wealthy families who could provide someone to read to them. Even
fewer had the wherewithal or the ingenuity to invent their own systems for
writing. Instead, the overwhelming majority of blind people—a considerably larger segment of the population than they are today—remained illiterate, uneducated, and unemployed, often relegated to a life of begging on
the streets.[21]

Haüy's call to educational arms that sought to bring literacy to blind
people epitomized the spirit of the Enlightenment. The *Essay* was only one
of a growing number of treatises that promoted education as a panacea for
social and political ills. Influenced by Denis Diderot's important 1749 *Letter
on the Blind for the Benefit of Those Who See*, Haüy's embossed book came
out in a climate that celebrated human perfectability.[22] Already the Abbé de
l'Épée (1712–89) had become a celebrity at court, showing off the ability of
his deaf students to use sign language in elaborately staged performances
designed to raise money. Moreover, the *Essay* must be understood in the
context of the Enlightenment's championing of minority rights. Although
historians have yet to present them like this, the calls for educating blind
and deaf people paralleled demands for religious toleration, women's rights,
and the abolition of slavery.

It would be easy to read *An Essay on the Education of the Blind* as yet
another example of sighted opportunism at the expense of blind people.
Haüy tugged at the heartstrings, notably in the preface—the part not presented in embossed letters and hence illegible to the people it discussed—
referring to "the young unfortunates, deprived of the benefit of light" and to
the eye as "the organ that contributes the most to our enjoyment of all that

society has to offer." Laying it on especially thick in his dedication to the king (also not in raised letters), Haüy explained that his aim was to help those "whose existence stretches before them in what can only be called a darkened dungeon."[23] To be fair, in late eighteenth-century France, such a description may not have been far from reality for the vast majority of impoverished blind people. Even so, Haüy no doubt drew on the most egregious stereotypes in order to win support for his cause.

The *Essay* has a Janus quality of being simultaneously on the defensive and the offensive. An early chapter addresses a series of imaginary objections that might be raised about the book and its methods. What if embossed letters become illegible with too much use? Aren't tactile books impractical because of their bulkiness and weight? Is it true that the blind read so slowly? Patiently, Haüy answered each concern by providing detailed explanations. At the end came the blunt Enlightenment precursor of the politically incorrect question "What good would it do to teach blind people to read raised letters?" Implicit in this fourth objection, however, seemed to be a concern that lay at the heart of what Haüy sought to combat: "Why publish books for them to use? They'll never read our books. And will the knowledge that they'll gain from learning the principles of reading result in any advantage to Society?"[24]

Haüy, the former translator of numerous foreign languages, picked up on the "us-and-them" quality of the questions and retorted with prickly ones of his own: "What does it matter to you that different peoples publish books every day?" he began; "Do you read Chinese, Malabar, Turkish, Quipus of Peru, or however many other languages that are so necessary to those who understand them? Indeed! You'd be nothing but a blind person in China, on the banks of the Ganges, in the Ottoman Empire, or in Peru."[25] Haüy surely had the intelligence and experience to know that blind people spoke and read the same French as sighted ones. Still, it is noteworthy that he so easily relied on the Enlightenment's love of far-away peoples to both normalize and exoticize the blind. Blindness, Haüy seemed to suggest in an early precursor to twentieth-century claims that would be made by the Deaf, is a culture, with its own language, one interpreted through touch rather than sight, just as sign language is interpreted through sight rather than through sound. Because language occupied such a central place in Enlightenment and revolutionary discourse, it made rhetorical sense to suggest this connection and to piggyback on the popularity of the Abbé de l'Épée's deaf students performing at court.[26]

More than a defense of educating the blind, however, the *Essay* also served as a radical precursor to *Keys for Building* by laying the groundwork for their assertiveness and ultimate independence. Through its structure, its content, and its very existence, the *Essay* offered a means by which blind people could, quite literally, take matters into their own hands. Indeed, its lengthy subtitle was *An Exposé on the Various Means, Confirmed by Experience, to Enable Them to Read Through Touch, to Print Books in Which They Can Learn Languages, History, Geography, Music, and to Learn Different Skills and Trades.* By explaining to the king in considerable detail how he would teach what the book's front matter described as "the most unfortunate class of humanity," Haüy gave those unfortunates exactly the tools they needed to execute his plan and even to move beyond it on their own terms. The *Essay*, produced and published by Haüy's first students, provided explicit instructions about how to manufacture a tactile book. Early chapters covered the basics, from paper selection and the choice of tools for embossing to the positioning and height of tables used in the printing process. Later ones offered techniques for rendering music, geographic maps, mathematical equations, and basic drawings through the use of thin wires, sand, and other everyday objects.

Imagine the impact this must have had on Haüy's blind students who produced the words as embossed letters they could read. Although I lack archival evidence to substantiate this, it seems clear that one of Haüy's goals was to bring blind people into the French polity, to make them full (and productive) members of society, for the *Essay* was self-replicating. Each time a team of blind students completed a book, they reproduced not just the information but the process for creating others just like it. In a seamless way, then, the *Essay* blended the practical and intellectual knowledge that would allow students to become educated and to challenge the deep-rooted prejudices that had dogged blind people for centuries. As contributors to the production of knowledge, Haüy's pupils engaged in the Enlightenment project of spreading literacy, information, and rationality that would be evidence of their productivity and broader participation in society.

Haüy proved even more subversive in his marketing. Having been a keen observer of the Abbé de l'Épée's carefully orchestrated performances of deaf pupils, the Father of the Blind eagerly hosted similar events. But in addition to the popular demonstrations of blind students playing musical instruments, doing handicrafts, and reading passages from the embossed books they produced, Haüy introduced a truly revolutionary exercise. "We call your attention to the experiment that we had the pleasure of watching on several occasions, and to which the Public can bear witness," the *Essay* noted, "where a blind child taught a sighted one how to read." In case the point was lost on the king or potential patrons, a footnote elaborated, "During the lesson the Teacher had a book with white pages that contained embossed type, while the Student looked at the same edition with print letters."[27] By turning the tables in this way, Haüy placed blind people in an unimaginable position of authority. No longer would it be possible to think of the blind solely as the beneficiaries of sighted people's largesse. While the sighted world quickly forgot this lesson, one day blind people would revive it, as will become clear below.

*An Essay on the Education of the Blind* thus laid the physical and potentially subversive foundations for tactile books that would evolve over the next two centuries. During the 1800s, the tactile book came into its own as a pedagogical tool that reflected broader modernizing trends. France's blind men and women found themselves buffeted by the same forces that Eugen Weber traces in his classic study *Peasants into Frenchmen*.[28] Like schools that educated Bretons, Basques, and other diverse groups, Haüy's National Institution for Blind Youth in Paris would try as best it could to increase literacy in the name of national consolidation. But the school's mostly sighted officials and teachers confronted unique obstacles if they wanted their students to survive in a world that was relying increasingly on visual forms of literacy. After all, by definition, a blind school defied France's modernizing impulse to replace traditional oral cultures with a more uniform printed one. Unfortunately, the embossed books inspired by Haüy's *Essay on the Education of the Blind* could not meet such challenges because it was difficult to read them quickly, and they were very expensive to produce and distribute.

The invention of Braille in the 1820s would solve this problem but introduce new ones. Derived from an experimental code that would allow French army officers to read messages at night without alerting the enemy, the elegant system reduced letters to a series of raised dots small enough to be read instantly by the tip of one finger rather than having to trace a large embossed letter.[29] Tellingly for the relationship between disability and citizenship, the country's first widely produced Braille book was a short history of France that appeared in 1837—another attempt to "make the blind French," one might reasonably postulate. The Bible soon followed (France before God), although owning a copy required a serious commitment of time, space, and money because the embossed text of an average page of Braille, though considerably shorter than Haüy's raised letters, is five times larger than a printed text. Moreover, before the advent of computer embossing in the 1980s, it routinely cost at least one hundred fifty times more to produce Braille than a print book. And until this same information revolution made it increasingly easy for blind people to create and consume texts in a variety of formats on their own terms, the need for expensive specialized paper and machines virtually guaranteed that the fabrication of tactile books would be controlled exclusively by organizations and institutions run by sighted professionals. Blind pupils might produce the books in workshops, but the increasingly supervised world of nineteenth-century pedagogy gave them little say in matters of design and content.

Yet the potential for subversiveness lay at the heart of Braille. Indeed, its history helps corroborate sighted people's discomfort with ceding control over books they could not read. Based on a fifteen-year-old boy's restructuring of a French military code originally devised so Napoléon's soldiers could pass secret information at night, the system appeared foreign and impenetrable. The fact that Braille proved difficult for sighted people to master by touch, particularly compared with embossed books like Haüy's *Essay*, increased its subversive potential and the resulting sighted anxiety. In a world distancing itself from the "lower senses" by replacing them with sight, a reliance on touch suggested something crude and uncivilized. And there were always concerns about the ability of blind students to communicate inappropriate information without the knowledge of their teachers.[30]

It is beyond the scope of this essay to discuss how Braille won over school officials and triumphed over other systems being invented simultaneously throughout the world.[31] Let me just make a couple of points that will help link this history to *Keys for Building*. First, although Braille was not an actual language but rather a means of transcribing a previously existing language (in this case French), its eventual triumph gave it a similar power to be a tool for both assimilation and subversion. Second, once tactile books became more widespread thanks to reading systems such as Braille, the door was opened for thinking more about how to render images tactually.

But placing *Keys for Building* within the context of Braille's ascendancy tells only part of the story. Because reading and writing engage different processes than images, the book's tactile illustrations force us to deal with more visceral concerns related to touch being so little understood compared with sight. "Touch brings the blind many sweet certainties which our more fortunate fellows miss, because their sense of touch is uncultivated," deaf and blind Helen Keller explained in her sensuous meditation *The World I*

*Live In*. "When they look at things, they put their hands in their pockets. No doubt that is one reason why their knowledge is often so vague, inaccurate, and useless."[32] This might help explain the comparatively rare scholarly attention devoted to touch, not just as part of history but also in terms of practice: this "lower sense" remains undertheorized as it hides in the realm of being taken for granted.[33] As a result, translating an image from the visual to the haptic proves extremely difficult without conceptual tools or even a vocabulary to pose questions and offer solutions for how it might be done. It also suggests why the history of tactile books must be understood in the context of a more complex, costly, commercially limited process of production and distribution. Simply put, even though touch is basic and direct, tactile images are rarified and abstract.

The first tactile books with illustrations emerged in the 1840s, and tended to be crude, basic renditions.[34] Coming on these books later in the century, several sighted observers likened them to early Egyptian petroglyphs or even cave paintings. Such comments that equated the blind with cavemen may have been inspired by recent exciting archeological discoveries of Spain's Altamira Cave in 1880.[35] But seeing them as primitive holdovers might also be the result of the natural assumptions of superiority made by those dependent on sight. In a world that assigned blind people almost no professional role, sighted experts who designed tactile picture books for the blind might well have underestimated the capacity of their readers to interpret more complex imagery. Still grappling with the difficulty of translating vision into touch, they may have settled for the simplest solution, much as Haüy had done with relief letters until Louis Braille came along.

In tactile books published before the 1950s (when new techniques made it possible to offer a wider variety), certain images recur again and again. Perhaps because blind people could not easily touch the real thing, depictions of wild animals proved especially popular. The researcher Yvonne Eriksson reports tactile pictures of elephants, birds, galloping horses, alligators, bats, and snakes. Hot-air balloons were also popular, as were body outlines and muscle structures for blind people learning to be masseurs.[36]

Then there are the images that pull one up short because they seem to offer a direct view into the values of their day. In one book Ericksson discusses from the 1930s, an illustration depicts how to offer a toast, while another presents the various (Western) positions for saying a prayer. What made these images more important than any other from the infinite range of possibilities, such as how to greet a woman or how to cheat at cards?

Illustrators, whoever they were, surely made decisions based on a compromise between the feasibility of producing an image and its broader social utility and acceptability.

Learning to raise a glass and learning to pray share a number of attributes. Both constitute gestures that are relatively easy to depict. In addition, each one provides blind people with direct access to a behavior that could be awkward to learn in person. More abstractly, toasting and prayer suggest a ready means by which the individual might link herself or himself to the collectivity by demonstrating how to participate in a common social experience, a form of social citizenship. Many blind people would appreciate learning these conventions in a country that placed such a high premium on assimilation.

But surely blind people displayed impressive ingenuity in creating images of their own. Eriksson speculates that over the past two centuries a uniquely informal and diffuse cottage publishing industry existed that produced tactile images. Little is known about these ephemeral books, many of them produced in single copies, that relied on everything from thread and buttons to wax, twigs, animal hair, and push-pins to represent human forms, borders between nations, the orbits of the planets, or an elephant's tusk. We will probably never know about most of them because an unsuspecting sighted person coming on such collages might assume that they were child's play or an eccentric's trash. Meanwhile, the remaining ones might be hidden under the stacks and stacks of uncataloged papers locked away in the few remaining institutions for the blind. Although history might not preserve the physical evidence, we can assume that blind people were as inventive as anyone else.[37]

### Toward a Subversive Citizenship

Ultimately, *Keys for Building* is as much a product of this rogue, subversive world as it is a weapon of France's civilizing mission. Both readings turn blind people from destitute outsiders into citizens: one presents the elegant tactile book as an effort at colonization, making the blind "French," while the other highlights the book's innovative approach as a means for expanding notions of citizenship and inclusion by celebrating blind ways of knowing. As these seemingly contradictory readings reveal, social constructions of disability intersect with citizenship in ways that both help and hurt disabled subjects.

Significantly, the two impulses of civilizing and subversion are by no means mutually exclusive. Taken together, they challenge the tendency to see blindness, like disability more broadly, as the unique purview of medicine and instead reveal the many other domains—political, social, economic— that define blind people's capacity and worth. Locating blind people within the larger sighted culture and developing the means for their integration into this decidedly visual world, *Keys for Building* joins other remarkable texts whose inclusion of "outsiders" pushes a society to change in new and unanticipated ways. Attention to the interdependent duality of subversion and citizenship invites scholars from various vantage points to bring greater nuance to how we think of such ideas as "embodiment," "rehabilitation," and even "cure." By reading something like *Keys for Building* from radically different perspectives, we have a sense of greater possibilities beyond opposing interpretations, ones that can actually be complementary and interactive.

At the end of his 1957 meditation *The Colonizer and the Colonized*, the Jewish Tunisian writer Albert Memmi offers insights that can help us read *Keys for Building* in both ways to get at these greater possibilities. After dissecting the colonial system with remarkable simplicity and finesse, Memmi concludes with a chapter titled "The Two Answers of the Colonized." One path leads to assimilation. "The first ambition of the colonized," he explains, "is to become equal to that splendid model [of the colonizer] and to resemble him to the point of disappearing in him."[38] He strives, like the ideal Ali and his blind friend, to be more French than the French by making wine his drink and Paris his city. But, as Memmi predicts, the colonized cannot really succeed because contempt for the colonial subject is central to the very idea of colonization. Thus even the Alis or the blind people who can lift a glass to the Eiffel Tower as the grandest of Parisian monuments never have a real chance to assimilate. If they did, France would cease to be France because it is dependent, as all identities are, on maintaining a tension between insiders and outsiders.

Memmi's other path for the colonized suggests embracing the colonizer's criticisms and turning negatives into positives. "Not only does [the colonized] accept his wrinkles and his wounds," Memmi exclaims, "but he will consider them praiseworthy. He offers himself as a whole and agrees that he is what he is."[39] Certainly he would appreciate Andrew Potok's observation that "diversity in all its forms provides not only fascination but strength," and he might even applaud the blind writer's celebration of what is "exuberantly impure."[40]

Rather than fleeing or seeking isolation, Ali and his blind friend might one day come to assume that their differences actually have something to offer. The result might even be something like *Keys for Building*.

Having subjected this lovely book to extensive scholarly analysis, let me end my meditation on blind people and citizenship by turning to the 1991 object's creators at the Cité des Sciences in Paris. Like Haüy's *Essay on the Education of the Blind*, *Keys for Building* is the product of an extensive, collaborative effort. This time, however, a brilliant blind woman called the shots. A former geography teacher at the National Institute for Blind Youth (the successor to Valentin Haüy's school), Hoëlle Corvest worked at the Museum of Science and Industry until her retirement in 2011. A Québécoise who emigrated to France, Corvest had learned for herself the pros and cons of assimilation and no doubt something about what it means to grow up within competing cultural imperatives such as those at play in francophone Canada during the 1960s and 1970s.

Corvest led the interdisciplinary team of blind and sighted researchers that created this fascinating book and a growing list of others.[41] It would be an understatement to say that they were conscious of what they were doing, at least from the perspective of visual culture. Pursuing what she called a "grammaire graphique" or "picto-grammar," the team poured over every bump, line, and curve in order to parse out what it means to know, and how one comes to know it. The goal was not to give blind people sight, as so many tactile books attempt, but rather to give them knowledge. Corvest could spend hours talking animatedly about how the team determined basic concepts, and about how blind and sighted illustrators thrashed out the best way to render pictures that would make sense in two such radically different areas of perception. Corvest thought of it as translating between two different psychological relationships to space. "Until blind people entered the conversation," Corvest told me, "our sighted project members had never thought so carefully about what it meant to see; for the first time we blind people were forcing them to emphasize the object, not the person looking at it."

By presenting the nonvisual as a natural and fundamental way to apprehend the world, *Keys for Building* highlights a form of understanding perfected by blind people. Blindness need not be a diminished state. Rather, it can introduce new forms of understanding that might actually prove useful in a three-dimensional world, such as that of architecture. Since the field draws on concepts of three-dimensionality, in many instances it might well benefit more from touch than from vision. By injecting a sense of wonder and awakening curiosity in both blind and sighted readers, *Keys for Building* makes a compelling case for that previously unimaginable blind architect.

Most strikingly, the book does not present this as exotic knowledge. Nowhere does it proclaim that it is of or for blind people. In fact, the word "blind" does not appear anywhere in its pages. To recall Memmi, this book is what it is. Yes, it offers subtle lessons to blind people on how to assimilate into France's cherished visual culture. But it also celebrates difference. In the most fundamental way, then, *Keys for Building* provides the tools for launching an unapologetic revolution in how to see the world.

But who will wield these tools, and to what end? This practical, very political question is pertinent because very few people in France today know about these pathbreaking books. Although it was created for a late twentieth-century French audience (recall that I bought it in the Museum of Science and Industry's bookstore for a reasonable price), *Keys for Building* has remained an isolated, rarified object. In fact, it probably enjoyed less publicity than Haüy's precursor, *An Essay on the Education of the Blind*, which circulated surprisingly widely at a time with far fewer possibilities for production, distribution, and promotion. There is no easily targeted market for a book that hovers awkwardly between what seems to be a child's primer and a tour de force of collaborative expertise, especially for a book that engages a sense that few think to perfect. At the same time, the practice of reading is changing. This includes today's blind people, who, thanks to electronic devices and audiobooks, for the first time in history join their sighted peers suffering from information overload. They—also like their sighted peers—engage less and less directly with books as physical objects; since 1960 Braille literacy in the United States and France has dropped from 50 percent to around 10 percent.[42]

So how can such an object offer new thinking about citizenship if so few people know it exists? How can it educate blind people about French visual culture and sighted ones about their blind compatriots if they never encounter it? In another essay, the problem of measuring the reaction and empirical effects of *Keys for Building* would in itself be a powerful argument to make. The book's limited reach could be taken as further evidence about the ambivalence of French society regarding the citizenship status of its blind inhabitants. Still, my deliberately provocative reading seeks to inspire explorations of similar processes that may be at work through other objects and projects, processes related to what it means to expand notions of citizenship both wittingly and unwittingly. At the same time, I have tried to suggest ways in which disability as an analytic concept figures into the complex processes of colonization and internalized colonization. Besides, *Keys for Building* is a text that will speak to whoever does read it, blind or sighted; as French literary critics and theorists have taught us, texts have lives that extend well beyond authorial intentions or scholarly attempts to define them.

In the end, Hoëlle Corvest remains justifiably proud of her achievement. She hauls *Keys for Building* along with its sister books to gatherings of her fellow blind citizens, perhaps much as her precursors in the nineteenth and twentieth centuries might have done. Sighted and blind alike eagerly pick them up, some with a tentative touch, others with knowing strokes that take everything in. As the unguarded exclamations of those who engage with them make clear, the books bring pleasure and wonder. Although she is happy to sell copies, the creator of *Keys for Building* seems more excited about sharing them as beautiful objects that open doors of knowing for all.

## CHAPTER 8

# Citizenship and the Family: Parents of Children with Disabilities, the Pursuit of Rights, and Paternalism

Allison C. Carey

In 2007, "Ashley X" and her parents made headlines when the press revealed that Ashley was undergoing a series of surgical interventions, including estrogen therapy, hysterectomy, breast-bud removal, and appendectomy, intended to prevent her from growing and maturing physically. Ashley was six and a half years old and had been diagnosed with significant developmental disabilities when the course of medical interventions began. Her parents attempted to justify these interventions on the basis of an alignment of interests within the family: Ashley wanted to remain in her family home, they wanted her to be at home, and these surgeries would better enable them to provide intensive at-home care as Ashley grew older but not bigger. They asserted that they, as parents, had the right to make medical decisions that would secure Ashley a particular lifestyle and particular health outcomes. The disability rights community expressed outrage that parents would be allowed to surgically deny a disabled girl the opportunity to grow into womanhood through procedures that could not be legally performed on a child in the absence of disability.[1] They argued that Ashley's parents promoted an individualized, biological solution to a macro social problem: the community's failure to provide adequate supports and rights to persons with disabilities and their families. Rights, supports, and social justice were needed, not biomedical fixes.

This case drew attention to the long-standing tensions between parents and the disability rights movement (DRM). Parents are not always in conflict with this movement. In fact, scholarship is fostering recognition of the contributions of parent activism in achieving disability rights, such as the rights to education, community services, vocational rehabilitation, and equal opportunities.[2] But parents have also fought for more paternalistic measures, such as the preservation of institutionalization and segregated services, easy guardianship procedures, and parental authority to make decisions for their children that may seem to deny basic rights. This complex history leads one to question how parents conceptualize the relationship among rights, the family, and disability. This chapter draws on a variety of sources of parent voices, including memoirs, letters to government officials, and documents of parent organizations, to examine the ways in which parents have conceptualized the relationship between rights and the family. In doing so, I analyze the tensions across these conceptualizations, as well as the criticism they garner from the DRM.

The family did not enter into T. H. Marshall's classic study of rights and citizenship. Marshall famously argued that in contrast to the historical system of rights based on ascriptive position in society (for example, race, class, and gender), the modern system of citizenship is characterized by the conferring of an identical package of rights by the state on all citizens. These rights provide citizens with the power to call on the state to protect them from and offer redress for civil and political abuses.[3] Feminist scholars criticized Marshall's narrative of universal citizenship, pointing out that many people (for example, women and African Americans) were denied rights and that the family played an important role in maintaining and justifying exclusion. Rather than an individual possession, rights are inherently relational; rights establish sets of relational expectations and obligations and enable one to influence or alter the actions of someone else.[4] The family patriarch, portrayed as independent and rational, held authority over his "dependents," including women, children, and slaves. The so-called dependents, many of whom actually performed labor vital to the household economy, received care and protection rather than rights. Extending this argument, disability scholars showed the ways in which assumptions of nonproductivity, irrationality, and dependence were also used to deny rights to people with disabilities within and outside the family.[5] Thus hierarchical patterns of social relationships justified the denial of rights, and, in turn, the denial of rights reinforced social stratification.

One form of redress is to guarantee the individual rights of all people and thereby remove the vestiges of ascribed hierarchy. This approach emphasizes that individuals with disabilities require rights to participate in society. These may be traditional "negative liberties," that is, freedoms to act according to one's interests, such as the rights to free speech and freedom from discrimination, or they may be "positive rights," in which the state or others have an obligation to provide some good or take some action, such as the right to a public education or to treatment. However, some scholars, such as Iris Young and Will Kymlicka, have argued that individualistic rights alone cannot solve a relational problem. Rather, individual rights must be supplemented with group-specific rights. Speaking of cultural minorities, Kymlicka asserts that when traditional human rights are framed as individual rights, they "are simply unable to resolve some of the most important and controversial questions related to cultural minorities. . . . The right to free speech does not tell us what an appropriate language policy is; the right to vote does not tell us how political boundaries should be drawn."[6] Such questions of policy are left to majority politics, which may disregard the interests of minorities. Group rights recognize and protect the interests of minority groups and allow multiculturalism to prosper. Disability rights activists have certainly pursued this approach as well and have secured significant rights based on disability status.

The family, though, is a particularly complex site for the enactment of rights. The family has been portrayed as "private" and outside the reach of much government regulation and civil rights law.[7] For example, the Americans with Disabilities Act (ADA) cannot effectively be used to demand that parents make their home accessible or that they provide accessible transportation to family members. However, as already noted, the law shapes relationships within the family, as well as the interaction between the family and external individuals and institutions. Laws shape, for example, legal unions, family medical leave, access to birth control, decision making regarding a fetus, the extension of health insurance to family members, child safety, and the structure and safety of one's home. Thus the family is no less constituted by the public sphere than employment settings, although rights manifest themselves differently within it.

Parents of children with disabilities have long realized that the law and public policy have a tremendous impact on their intimate family lives. In this chapter, I argue that parents have used rights rhetoric to engage the state and professionals in different but interconnected ways. First, they have drawn on traditional conceptualizations of rights to demand negative liberties and freedom from discrimination on the basis of disability. Interestingly, they argue that disability-related discrimination affects the family, and hence all members must be ensured protection from disability-related discrimination whether or not they are individually disabled. Second, they have drawn on relational conceptualizations of rights to demand universal and group-specific positive rights to ensure the well-being of disabled citizens and their families in recognition of the specific needs they may have. According to parents, the state must provide services and supports to enable individuals with disabilities and their family members to participate meaningfully in society, to fulfill their social obligations, and to act as an effective family unit. Third, parents have asserted group-level autonomy based on the family unit to pursue the interests of the family. Specifically, parents make claims to authority within the family to resist unwanted intervention in the family.

Sometimes parents' claims align with the DRM, but they may often be in conflict. The DRM actively seeks to secure rights for people with disabilities. It also recognizes the importance of familial autonomy and seeks to protect the rights of people with disabilities to parent and to wield the same authority granted to other parents. However, the rights asserted by parents for the family may be different than the rights asserted by the DRM. For example, the autonomy of the family poses a grave threat when claims to parental authority disregard disabled family members and devalue disability more generally. Parents' rights claims potentially exist not only in conflict with the DRM but also in tension with one another. Parents seek state involvement but simultaneously resist unwanted state intervention and fight to retain control over this involvement, and the balancing act can be challenging.

## The Rights to Freedom from Discrimination, Supports for the Family, and Family

Parents' claims related to individual and group-specific rights based on disability are examined first in this chapter because these claims are the most evident in collective parent activism related to disability. Claims to parent authority will then be discussed. Although I distinguish between these types of claims for conceptual clarity regarding their underlying logic and their impact, they are often interwoven in political discourse.

Parents of children with disabilities have long argued that rights need to be understood in relation to the family, not just in relation to the individual. Early in the parents' movement, leaders of the Association for the Help of Retarded Children (now named the Arc) called attention to the importance of supporting families and communities as a means to improve the well-being of individuals with disabilities, asserting "that no child stands alone; that a child is part of a family and a community; that what happens to the family affects the child and certainly affects the family."[8] These activists and the broader parents' movement recognized that rights are enacted only in specific relational contexts, and therefore, people within an individual's community, not just the individual, must be empowered to exercise rights. A weak family under siege could not produce a strong member of society, regardless of his or her individual rights.

Parents claimed that they and their children were citizens and therefore deserved the rights provided to other citizens, as well as inclusion in public services and programs. In addition to these negative liberties, parents claimed the right to services and supports that took into account the specific needs of the individual with a disability and that individual's family members. Not surprisingly, they justified individual and group-specific rights to supports and services for people with disabilities as promoting the development of and opportunities for the individual. For example, through the provision of an appropriate public education with accommodations, the disabled child would more likely grow into a well-socialized adult who could contribute to his or her own care and support. Parents also argued, though, that these rights and services were necessary to encourage the effective functioning of the entire family. When individuals with disabilities were denied access to education, day care, employment, and adequate medical care, family members were left with responsibilities far exceeding those of other families. Thus, when author Jane Bernstein poignantly cried, "She is mine alone, my sightless child, my problem," she was expressing condemnation not of her disabled child but of a society that offered parents too little support.[9] These disproportionate responsibilities threatened parents' ability to successfully raise their disabled child and fulfill their other responsibilities. Parents could not be all things for their child—nurse, teacher, physical therapist, friend—and still fulfill their other familial obligations, such as providing care to all family members and maintaining economic self-sufficiency. Parents could not be good parents and citizens without the recognition of rights and adequate supports for all their family members. Hence it was the parents' right too for their child to receive, for example, public education. In a 1956 speech encouraging access to public education for disabled children, Pennsylvania governor George Leader placed side by side the rights of disabled children and their parents: "The retarded child must no longer be the forgotten child of Pennsylvania. The parents of a mentally defective child must no longer be counted among the neglected citizens of our state. Like other, more fortunate citizens, they too have a great stake in the future of PA—and in a very special sense. So do their children—like other children."[10]

In addition to services and rights for individuals with disabilities, parent activists argued that parents and siblings needed rights and supports, such as protection from disability discrimination and parent education to ensure their ability to create a healthy environment. Parents positioned themselves as experiencing the stigma, isolation, and discrimination society heaped on people with disabilities even if they themselves were not disabled.[11] As one sibling remembers the 1940s and 1950s: "Eugenics was popular at the time. We weren't just a family, we were a family with a disability; it defined our history, it defined our story."[12] Similarly, in 1978 a parent described, "It is a lonely feeling having a child who has been classified as a useless nuisance."[13] According to Gail Landsman, mothers of disabled children still face two persistent ideologies: that disability is a defect and that mothers have some control over their child's well-being.[14] In these ideologies, mothers are expected to work tirelessly toward the "normalization" of their children and are held responsible if their children do not successfully showcase their skills and adapt to society's expectations.[15] Therefore, devaluation and discrimination affect the family, both when disabled members are denied opportunities in a way that affects the family (for example, when exclusion from education requires a parent to engage in full-time care) and when family members are denied opportunities to feel valued and respected because of their association with disability. Parents also may feel discriminated against by policies and practices that assume "typical" parenting. For example, parent programs may fail to address the challenges parents of disabled children face in locating competent babysitters, learning and following complex medical regimes, using different methods of teaching and disciplining their children, and engaging in effective techniques of advocacy. To counter these problems, parents have asked the state to offer protection from disability discrimination, support disability awareness campaigns, provide family supports and services, and encourage the creation of inclusive public services that accommodate disabled individuals and their family members.

More recent discourse has conceptualized the right to supports as an essential component of the human right to family. The United Nations Convention on the Rights of Children declares that all children, including disabled children, have a human right to live with their parents unless doing so is not in their best interests. Reflecting earlier rights advocacy, this right requires that family members have the right to the services necessary for a life in the family home.[16] Hence the individual and family members receive rights because of the recognition that the family provides a network of relationships that fundamentally shapes an individual's life, interaction with society, and one's experience of individual rights. Rather than a body composed of several individuals, the family is recognized as a unit, and rights are provided to support the maintenance and effective functioning of the unit. In keeping with this line of argument, in 2007 the former executive director of the Arc (2005–7), Sue Swenson, explained that a model of individual rights was insufficient to ensure the rights of disabled individuals. It must be complemented with the assurance "that all families that include persons with disabilities can enjoy the support they need" to take care of their disabled members and incorporate them meaningfully into family and community life.[17]

Much of the activism for rights that support the maintenance of disabled children in their families and communities fits well with the goals of the DRM. Disability rights scholars and activists typically applaud parent activism about issues like the right to education, community supports, and equal access to accessible public services. However, the right to family supports has had a more problematic side because parents have different ideas of what constitutes "appropriate supports" and for whom these supports are appropriate. Few issues reveal this problem more vividly than activism related to institutionalization and segregated services.

Parents have always been divided on the issue of institutionalization. Some parents fought against institutionalization, and this work is typically seen as part of the DRM. Others fought to expand and preserve institutions, and it is on these parents that I will focus in this section in order to show how the rhetoric of rights at times justified policies now considered oppressive. Many of those who fought for institutional "care" argued that such services were within the appropriate range of services and supports for people with disabilities, and that the provision of institutional care benefited both the person with a disability and the family members. These parents positioned their disabled children as an integral part of the family and claimed that ensuring their care was essential to their parental obligations. Especially in the 1950s and 1960s, when physicians recommended institutional placement and other community options were not yet available, many parents believed that institutional placement would provide medically recommended care and treatment that they could not provide. These parents assumed an alignment of interests across family members: institutionalization would ensure that the needs of their child were met and would enable parents to fulfill their parental obligations to access appropriate resources for the care of their child. This presumed alignment of interests, needs, and rights is evident in the following quotes. The 1952 letter that follows requests institutional expansion because of both the needs of "retarded" children for a safe, productive environment and parents' duty to provide appropriate lifelong care for their child:

> We, the parents of mentally retarded children need your help as Governor of the Commonwealth of Pennsylvania. . . . Our children are all future patients for Pennsylvania State Schools, but there is no room for them now or for years to come. They have been barred from Special Classes in public schools so they are kept at home alone and friendless. . . . It is within your power, as Governor of this State, to change this unhealthy situation. . . . He [the retarded child] must be given the opportunity to live in his own world, with friends of his own kind—not made to bear the abuse of normal children who never realize how cruel they can be. . . . We have been visitors at Polk State School and have found it to be a beautiful haven for these innocent children who cannot live in normal society. They are happy and clean and busy children. Even their parents look happy and at peace with the world. Their children are happy and safe for the rest of their lives. These parents can die knowing their child will still be happy and taken care of. We, who must wait and wait for years do not have that peace—ours is a 24 hour a day worry.[18]

In 1957, Mrs. Philip Elkin, president of the Pennsylvania Association of Retarded Children, similarly advocated for the increased enrollment of individuals diagnosed with mental retardation in institutions (despite overcrowding and documented substandard care) by arguing that the denial of admission led to the suffering of both the child and the family:

The Commonwealth has the obligation of caring for the mentally retarded who require institutionalization. I question whether it has the
right to "close down" admissions (which may be denied) or postpone
them indefinitely as is now being done. The question of adequacy of
funds cannot be solved by postponing for one day the admission of a
mentally retarded child, by adding one day to the personal tragedy of
the parents and family of that child. As I see it, it is the child and the
family who suffer today. . . . Surely the only possible solution to the
problem of admissions is to reopen them![19]

Government officials also typically assumed that the interests and rights
of parents and individuals with disabilities were complementary. In a speech
to the newly formed National Association of Parents and Friends of Mentally Retarded Children in 1950, Minnesota governor Luther Youndahl
explicitly made the connection among institutionalization, the right to
treatment for the individual with a disability, and parents' rights: "The retarded child has the right to social assistance in a world in which he cannot
possibly compete on equal footing. He has the right to special education and
to special institutions for the retarded child who cannot be taken care of at
home. . . . He has a right to these things, and his parents have a right to know
that he has these rights. For they too are entitled to peace of mind about
what is happening to a retarded child separated from them."[20] Thus, these
parents and government officials portrayed institutionalization as an appropriate support for disabled children and their families.

Although institutions are far less common today, some parents still believe that segregated services and supports are in the best interests of both
their child and their family. Advocating for the preservation of institutions
in 2006, Voice of the Retarded activist Sam Golden argued that only a large
facility could meet the complex needs of his severely disabled daughter and
enable her to be happy and active: "With her limitations, she would not have
a good life in a small group home—the limited staff could not care for her or
involve her in the kinds of activities she now engages in."[21] Valerie Leiter's
research shows that some parents use the Individuals with Disabilities Education Act (IDEA) to pursue more rather than less restrictive settings because they believe that these are most appropriate educationally and socially
for their children.[22] And although the national organization Self-Advocates
Becoming Empowered has called for the closure of group homes, sheltered
workshops, and other segregated service settings, parent organizations

often continue to run these services and position them as an essential part of the continuum of services.

Although interpretation of a child's best interests may vary, it is far more problematic when the interests of a disabled child are discarded altogether. Rather than an alignment of interests, some parents asserted that, regardless of the interests of the child, institutionalization was necessary to support the family. As Katherine Castles has shown, the institution served as a potential resource to transform a "disabled family" into a "normal family" by visibly removing disability from the family.[23] These interests were rhetorically promoted to the status of rights by parents through the justification that institutionalization was required for parents to fulfill their perceived primary familial obligations: to care for "normal" children, to maintain economic self-sufficiency, and to ensure that their family promoted the safety, well-being, and normality of the community. A parent of a son at Polk State School stated, "I believe there are many who do not fully appreciate the importance of removing from society children of this kind because of the effect they have on family life and on the training of normal brothers and sisters." Institutionalization "would . . . permit the resumption of a normal family home with attention to the proper rearing of two normal children."[24] In these instances, the matter is not merely an interpretation of the appropriate rights and support for all family members but the even more serious problem that the rights of the disabled family member are overridden in favor of protecting the rights and well-being of the family and society.

Although both logics were used to support institutionalization, there is an important difference. The first argument assumes that the disabled individual is a vital member of the family and seeks supports for the individual and family through institutional care. This may be misguided, but the second argument discards the rights of the disabled family member in defense and support of "the family," a unit here defined as in need of protection from disability. The group basis of the rights claim shifts from a claim based on disability, where the claim to institutional care makes sense only to the extent that it both supports the care of the person with the disability and the ability of the family to support the family member with a disability, to a rights claim based on the family and the well-being of the family that may allow for the exclusion of the person with a disability if the disability is seen as harmful to the family unit. In the former, the actual care of the person with the disability and inclusion within the family matter, whereas in the latter, these issues may not matter. When parents are making claims based on the family rather than on disability, they often assert the right to parental authority and family autonomy from the state, and it is to these claims that I will now turn.

## Parental Authority, the Private Sphere, and Conflict of Rights

The family sought state support to counter social isolation and discrimination, but ironically the expansion of the service system threatened parental authority. Disability history shows that there are good reasons to be wary of state intervention in the family when disability is concerned. The intertwining of eugenics into state policies regarding the family is one of the most blatant examples of the ways in which the state intervened in and harmed particular families, in this instance primarily single-parent families, poor families, nonwhite families, and families with disabled family members who were labeled "unfit" and targeted for professional intervention.[25] By developing a causal model that explained perceived deficiencies in terms of biological maladaptation rather than social stratification or unjust social structures, professionals justified the denial of rights and the use of constraints, including home monitoring, institutionalization, and sterilization.[26] While claiming to protect "the family" and the nation, the state upheld a very particular heteronormative, classist, racist, and ableist view of the "proper" family and penalized other family forms.

Although some parents were among those who fought for the expansion of institutions, many other families with children with disabilities viewed the growth of state-funded and enforced institutions as devastating. Institutionalization was offered as one of the few ways to attain treatment and services for one's child, but it tore apart the family, often mandating the relinquishment of parental rights and discouraging sustained family participation.[27] Many parents did not quickly relinquish their parental roles; instead, they continued to advocate for their institutionalized offspring, but with little authority to do so. Denied any legal power, they found that they needed to appeal to superintendents and public officials to address problems that arose. Thus we see a stream of letters during the 1940s, 1950s, and 1960s by parents to public officials regarding their institutionalized offspring. For example, a parent concerned about the abuse of her daughter described the parents of institutionalized children as "handicapped" by the system and unable to effectively advocate and care for their child: "Parents with this type of child are handicapped by the fact that there is no other way to care for them and if they state their belief that something is wrong with the manner in which an institution is managed, the child may not even get what attention he is receiving."[28] Even those who wanted to bring their family members home from institutions at times found this a difficult task and had to appeal to government officials to regain their parental status.[29] Thus parents found that accessing recommended medical treatment required them to forfeit their parental authority, and they were reduced to using bureaucratic and political channels to fulfill typical parental roles of ensuring the rights of their children and protecting their children from harm. Therefore, some parents fought to retain their rights as parents even while their offspring received state support, including the rights to remain a physically intact family with support and services provided in the community, to remain a legally intact family while still receiving services regardless of physical placement, and to remain an emotionally intact family with the necessary supports to enable parents to fulfill their emotional roles as nurturers, protectors, and caregivers. In other words, they sought the right to receive supports from the state while protecting their family from dissolution.

Although the role of massive public institutions has declined in public policy, the role of the state in the family has not. On the contrary, the expansion of community services and access to public education created an ironic invasion into family life, albeit in a more subtle, regulatory way.[30] Parents now find themselves in frequent negotiation with professionals concerning such issues as their child's diagnosis, proper treatment and child-rearing strategies, and the financing of care for the child. For example, although parents were thrilled to receive the right to education for their children, a right that both provided opportunities to children for development and lessened parents' responsibilities for full-time care and education, entry into the public educational system was not without problems. Parents now faced a bureaucratized system with institutionalized values and goals, formal policies and procedures, categorical eligibility, and particular funding streams. On the basis of educational labels, children were assigned academic tasks, as well as peer groups, daily routines, and other hidden curricula that anticipated their future place in society. These decisions too often seemed guided more by institutional efficiency than by children's real needs and interests. Although the IDEA rhetorically positioned parents as "partners" alongside educational professionals, parents often experienced these relationships as battles regarding labels, programs, and accommodations in which they had too little power to determine the fate of their children.[31]

The rise of medical and educational therapies based in the community further led to an infiltration of the home as parents were made responsible to identify therapies, manage them, and perform them at home. Parents rejoiced over the availability of new therapies and services to improve the skills and adaptation of their children but increasingly felt monitored by professionals who placed expectations for compliance and normalization on their families. Parents like Jane Bernstein and Josh Greenfeld noted that they felt compelled to "work" rather than play with their children.[32] Not only were parents expected to take on the roles of doctor and therapist, they were supposed to do so selflessly and endlessly, regardless of their other responsibilities.[33] Parents found that their failure to comply could jeopardize their child's access to services. Thus the expansion of services, which was supposed to offer more options for parents, came with a concomitant invasion of their private lives by public rules, values, and expectations.[34] The very services and supports parents sought became potential tools of surveillance, regulation, and discrimination that threatened the family. Parents therefore continued to fight to retain their authority in such matters as medical treatments, educational placements and programs, and housing or residential options.

As seen in the preceding discussion, there are pressing reasons that parents seek protection from the state in the interests of their families, but in a society that devalues disability, parental authority can be a very real and frightening source of oppression and can be challenging to confront because of notions of the "private" family. The family is imagined as a harmonious unit with shared interests, but it can quickly be revealed as a collection of individuals with competing interests, needs, and rights. As I noted earlier, scholarship on the family and citizenship emerged first among feminist scholars who examined the deeply problematic treatment of the family as a cohesive unit, a treatment that served to legitimize patterns of domination, involving the ways in which public institutions structure our private relationships and the ways in which private relationships become constitutive of our public roles and capacities.[35] Building on this legacy, scholars tend to focus on two key ways in which domination plays out in the family: examining the oppression of the person with a disability (assumed to be the recipient of care) and examining the oppression of the caregiver (typically assumed to be nondisabled and female).

To look first at the oppression of the person with a disability, disabled family members are often portrayed as care recipients, and on this basis they may experience devaluation. The presumed dichotomous relationship in which the able-bodied person is assigned the role of the caregiver and the person with the disability the role of the care recipient disregards the potential for reciprocity, relationality, and complex role taking within a family.[36] This dichotomy also presumes that disability poses a burden disproportionate to other reasons for or types of care. Given that a report of the Centers for Disease Control defines care work as work performed to assist someone incapacitated, it is not surprising that older Americans and people with disabilities are far more likely to be defined as the recipients of care work than are, for example, spouses who are the recipients of cooking and cleaning or nondisabled children who receive transportation and assistance with self-care and homework.[37] The master status of "care recipient" may lead to the devaluation of people with disabilities and the denial of their rights manifested through the family.

The disregard of the rights and well-being of the family member with a disability is not merely a product of overwhelming care demands. Rather, "care" becomes a cultural trope by which to disregard individuals as rights-bearing citizens within the family. Broad cultural disregard, stereotypes that assume that people with disabilities are not rights-bearing citizens, and the socially enforced absence of meaningful ways to contribute all threaten the position of the person with a disability within the family.[38] Indeed, family members often hold some of the same stereotypes concerning disability perpetuated by the wider society. The lack of alternative accessible living arrangements further precludes the exercise of self-determination. If adults are not satisfied with the private arrangements offered in their family residence, it is assumed that they can leave. But extensive waiting lists for services, inaccessible housing and transportation, low-paying jobs, and high unemployment of people with disabilities all reduce the likelihood that people with disabilities can leave their family home. Moreover, supported living does not necessarily offer more choices and indeed might instead offer more rules, supervision, and bureaucratic administration than rights and choices.

It is important to note, though, that caregivers may also feel oppressed within the family context. The scholarship on care indicates that women perform the great bulk of America's household unpaid and underpaid work, which disadvantages them in the accrual of economic and political capital.[39]

A child's disability can lead to an intensification of these unbalanced demands and exacerbate the feeling among mothers that their intensive care work goes largely unrewarded and thwarts their opportunities for remunerative labor. In this situation, the potential for a conflict of rights, interests, and needs is heightened because parents' sense of equality is challenged and their sense of personal rights may be placed in competition with their child's rights and welfare.

This sense of a conflict of rights among family members is clear in writings by parents and is most easily seen in decisions regarding institutionalization. For example, Josh Greenfeld raised his son Noah in the 1970s, after the many institutional scandals had erased any illusion of the beneficence of institutions. Describing his visit to Letchworth Village, an institution in New York previously made famous in Albert Deutsch's 1948 exposé *The Shame of the States*, he stated that "the place reeked institution—the smell of urine and lye, the harsh green painted walls; the dirty windows . . . worse than my memory of a visit to Dachau. I vowed I would have to send Noah to a better place."[40] But in the early 1970s, Greenfeld could not find a small facility that served people with severe disabilities and behavioral challenges. As Greenfeld and his son Noah grew older and as Noah's behavioral outbursts and violence became less controllable, Greenfeld felt that he had to live apart from Noah. He did not believe that institutionalization would benefit Noah, but he argued that he and his wife needed time to sleep, to restore their own health and safety, and to pursue their careers and relationships. They placed Noah in an institution (and brought him back home after Noah experienced "excessive aversive therapy").

The dilemma of conflicting rights is more conspicuous in Fern Kupfer's memoir. According to Kupfer, her family could not handle the demands of caring for her son, Zachariah, but she faced a service system that mandated that Zach had rights as a child with a disability to participate in family life, reside at home, and experience "normal" life routines and opportunities. Kupfer railed against the system's adherence to these values regardless of their practicality for her and the lack of intensive social supports. She advocated for state-supported services, but in lieu of them she believed that she at least should have the authority to make private decisions in the best interests of her family. Kupfer clearly believed that the rights articulated for children with disabilities stood in violation of her rights because of the intensive, twenty-four-hour demands they placed on her; she considered that the fulfillment of Zach's rights required her own imprisonment.[41] Despite the concerns of public officials, Kupfer secured a placement for Zachary at a private facility. She argued that parents know best what is in the interests of their families and should be allowed to pursue those interests.

Institutional placement, however, is not the only source of conflict between parental autonomy and the well-being of family members with disabilities. Given the devaluation of people with disabilities and the ideology of eternal childhood, natural signs of adulthood, such as menstruation and sexuality, may become framed as problems to be resolved through techniques of prevention, segregation, and medical intervention that are largely unregulated because of the pretense of the private family. Historically, the medical profession served as both a resource for parents seeking to "remedy" the perceived problem of sexuality and a constraint on families by expecting and at times enforcing segregation and sterilization of the disabled for the protection of the nation. Parents now are more likely than a century ago to express positive views regarding their children's sexuality, but parents still hold many negative views regarding the sexuality of their disabled offspring, shelter them from typical sexuality-related experiences, discourage the development of typical sexual self-expression, and shield them from sexual knowledge and encounters.[42]

Even growth and physical development can be perceived as a dilemma when parents imagine their offspring as enduring an endless state of childhood and when they have too few supports to provide care or support self-determination and independent living. The Ashley X case shocked the nation, but the dread of growth is not unique to this case. Indeed, it is a relatively common theme in the memoirs of parents with severely disabled children. Josh Greenfeld feared Noah's growth as they moved closer to a time when he would no longer be able to restrain Noah from engaging in self-destructive behavior or withstand the physical abuse Noah sometimes inflicted, especially given the lack of community-based options for services. Nicola Schaefer worried that each additional pound gained by her daughter Catherine represented a time when she would no longer be able to care for Catherine and would have to resort to the impersonal and inadequate service system.[43] The parents of Ashley X believed that growth-attenuation surgery would keep Ashley small and thereby better enable them to provide Ashley with care, inclusion in family activities, and "normal" life experiences. From her parents' perspective, surgery became a tool to meet complementary needs and interests among family members. They believed that they, as parents, had the authority to make medical decisions to meet the perceived needs of their family. However, as with Greenfeld's and Schaefer's stories, we see the paucity of services and supports driving them toward solutions that are profoundly problematic. Rather than strive for integrated services, rights, and social justice, Ashley's parents promoted growth attenuation as an individualized, biological solution to the perceived problem of growth and asserted that they, as parents, had the right to make medical decisions to access treatments that would secure Ashley a particular lifestyle and health. They dismissed concerns regarding the conflict of interests, although these conflicts appalled disability rights activists, and thereby they dismissed Ashley's rights to bodily integrity and to a wide array of choices and opportunities associated with physical and sexual maturation.[44]

Even less attention is given to the family's role in discouraging other types of adult freedoms, such as drinking, smoking, voting, socializing with friends, and making economic and purchasing decisions. We know very little about the extent to which individuals with disabilities are allowed to make everyday choices in the context of their family homes. It seems likely that parental authority is informally used in everyday contexts to deny adults with disabilities the opportunity to engage in a host of typical adult behaviors.

## Alignment with the Disability Rights Movement

As seen in the previous sections, parents assert a host of rights. They root these claims in individual rights, group rights of people with disabilities and their families, and group rights of the family. Much of the activism by parents for rights that provide supports and services to individuals with disabilities and to their families has been in alignment with the goals of the DRM. The DRM certainly shares the goals of equal opportunity, freedom from discrimination, and the rights, among others, to family, to live in the community, and to an appropriate education. It also is not dismissive of the rights of families to be protected from state intervention. The DRM demands equal access to the rights to marriage, parenting, and sexuality for people with disabilities and supports the parental authority of parents with disabilities. Issues of parental authority are particularly important because of controversial disability-specific issues, such as the right to make choices to resist biomedical procedures intended to eradicate disability in the family and the right of deaf parents to have deaf children without pursuing treatment or cure for their children.[45] Although much of the activism for rights that provide supports and services to the family has been in alignment with the goals of the DRM, certainly some activism conflicts with it. The DRM tends to criticize rights claims that justify segregation, the denial of rights, social control, and medicalized "fixes" in lieu of social change because these are seen as devaluing disability and undermining inclusion. The DRM is also highly critical of claims to parental authority that are seen as devaluing disability and the interests of family members with disabilities.

The disability rights community has responded to these rights claims with alternative rights formulations that seek to retain the obligation of the state to provide individual and group-specific rights based on disability in order to support individuals with a disability and their families while discouraging the marginalization and devaluation of people with disabilities. First, establishing a human right of children to family is in part a way to address this dilemma. This right is fundamentally a right of children to be included and constrains the options available to parents. It argues that families have a right to supports that include all members, but not rights to supports that exclude a member. Second, the right to community has been gaining legal standing, especially since the passage of the ADA and the 1999 Supreme Court decision *Olmstead v. L. C.*[46] Steven Taylor argues that parents may have considerable authority to determine the best interests of their child, but that the state has no responsibility to financially support choices that promote segregation and deny individuals the right to community.[47] For example, parents might desire to send their child to a segregated residential program, but the state has no obligation to provide and pay for such a program. Moreover, adults with disabilities, especially those who are deemed competent, should not be held hostage by their parents' wishes for their entire lives. Decision making regarding adults legally adjudicated incompetent should follow a model of substitute decision making, gauging as best as possible what the person would choose and supporting him or her in pursuing his or her interests as imagined. For this to be feasible, adults must have available to them accessible and supported community living arrangements that do not rely on their families.

Kymlicka's formulation of group rights is in agreement with this line of reasoning. According to Kymlicka, group rights should be used as "external protections" "to limit the economic or political power exercised by the larger society over the group, to ensure that the resources and institutions on which the minority depends are not vulnerable to majority decisions."[48]

They are not intended as "internal restrictions" to limit the liberty of those within the minority group in order to attain group purity, solidarity, or a particular identity. Thus rights based on disability or family should be used to best allow members of these groups to flourish by supporting their group-specific needs and protecting them from the tyranny of the majority, not to justify segregation or social control in the name of preserving the family.

Nancy Hirschmann argues that although rights conflicts often appear as yielding zero-sum outcomes where the rights of family members are pitted against one another, they can instead be addressed through a recognition of the ethics of care, equal respect, and mutual responsibility and a commitment to a dialogue about how to meet various people's needs and interests.[49] In this light, we must take seriously the concerns of parents and disabled family members alike. This model might encourage initiatives to promote education and empowerment training for parents and individuals with disabilities, enabling both parents and their children to see the range of choices, develop informed preferences, articulate them, and fight for just solutions together rather than settling for the best choice among bad options. The right to live and participate in the community could also be incorporated into this approach. Parents often choose segregated services and paternalistic policies because they believe that integration into the community is dangerous and without meaningful supports (that is, people with disabilities are physically placed in communities but lack social roles and relationships there). These are real concerns that the disability community shares. Creating inclusive, supportive communities addresses these fears while also enabling people with disabilities to have choices that may or may not include a reliance on their families. Inclusion is not only a matter of physical access and services for people with disabilities; it also involves access to safety, economic self-support, and recreational social opportunities for all community members. The measures that support individuals with disabilities also support family and community members.

Not everyone's needs and interests, though, can be aligned or met. The exercise of rights as guided by an ethic of mutual respect and care brings people into conversation and into a process of social negotiation about how best to meet varied needs and interests, and the outcome is not set in stone. Engaging in open-ended conversations that take into account the specifics of context and relationality is challenging for large-scale political movements, and its outcomes are difficult to translate into policy and law.

Moreover, such negotiations are so fraught with power and inequality that the possibility of mutual respect and care is often abandoned. Activism based on a conflictual model in often seen as more effective and clear, especially if one "wins." Thus, although the right to community and advocacy education could be points of alliance, they are not always. When alliances fail, the right to community is argued to trump a parent's right to authority and vice versa as people head into their different camps.

## Considering Rights and the Family

Since the civil rights movements of the 1970s, rights have emerged as a key strategy for addressing social disadvantage. Thus it should not be surprising that parents of children with disabilities turned to rights activism. In so doing, parents reworked individualistic notions of rights to recognize relationality and to claim rights as individuals, as members of the disability community, and as families. Rights also served their traditional function of protecting individuals and the family from the tyranny of the state; in this case, families called on rights to protect them from harmful state interventions made possible largely through the state's role in the provision of social supports, such as welfare, education, and medical treatment. However, we have also seen that the practice of rights within the family is deeply problematic. Rather than a harmonious unit, the family can quickly disaggregate into individuals with various interests and rights. Rights can support the development of healthy relationships, but they can just as easily contribute to shaping the power dynamics within family relationships.

These issues are by no means unique to parents of children with disabilities. Rather, their experiences and advocacy draw attention to key tensions within our system of rights itself. The traditional liberal framework for civil rights in America is individualistic, but people often experience the acts of claiming and exercising rights as relational, embedded within a social context in which they are typically trying to exert power or defend themselves from the exercise of power on them. Rights structure our relationships in complex ways, at times serving as a resource to create or maintain equality, at other times to enforce freedom from oppression, and at still other times to reinforce one person's "right" to influence or oppress another. These narratives also draw attention to the tension between negative and positive rights. Negative rights in the absence of positive rights risk perpetuating the system of stratification; individuals are simply left "free" to act, but in a system of great inequality, some are much more "free" than others to act as they wish. Positive rights offer a necessary scaffold for the support of equality, meaningful participation in society, and the ability to pursue individual self-interests; however, they also bring the state into one's home and provide a potential mechanism by which the state can monitor and regulate its citizens, especially those who are most dependent on state supports for their well-being and therefore cannot opt out of them. Thus the very "supports" ideologically offered to provide positive rights to citizens can become effective mechanisms of social control.

Rights ultimately serve as a political resource across different groups attempting to shape the exercise of power across relationships. Parents seek rights for their children and themselves, and much of their activism fits well with the goals of the DRM; however, the family is also a potential site of conflict and oppression where parental authority and the right to privacy can be used to perpetuate rather than resolve inequality. Even parents who have their children's best interests at heart will often choose individualistic, medicalized, or pragmatic solutions to address their concerns, pitting the DRM and parents against each other. Many parents have never even heard of the DRM nor imagined macro social change as feasible. Parents therefore tend to be unpredictable and inconsistent in their support of the DRM, wanting rights for their children to participate in society as they wish, but also wanting to retain parental authority to make the choices they feel best meet the interests of their children and their family in their specific social context.

Although they are neither simply allies nor enemies of the DRM, parents and family members are a part of the community. In the DRM's quest for inclusive community, there seems to be an obligation to address parents' needs and interests, although not necessarily to satisfy them. Alliance with parents encourages them to gain a broader perspective of disability rights and justice and join a community committed to social change. At the same time, though, the DRM must continue to develop tools to reduce paternalism, address the denial of rights as it exists in families, and create supports that allow adults to live independently from their families if and to the extent that they wish to do so. Thus the alliance between parents and the DRM, while quite effective at times, is likely to remain an uneasy one.

## CHAPTER 9

# Cognitive Disability, Capability Equality, and Citizenship

### Lorella Terzi

The status of people with disabilities as valued citizens and equal members of the community poses significant problems for political and moral philosophy, and in particular for liberal egalitarian theories of justice. In this chapter, I discuss how an innovative egalitarian perspective, the capability approach, provides important insights into the demands of disability on justice. In so doing, my contribution aims to situate issues of philosophical theory at the core of the debate on "citizenship," "disability," and "the individual."

Underpinned by the ideals of liberty and equality, liberal egalitarian theories of justice are primarily concerned with the just design of social and institutional arrangements and the consequent distribution of benefits and burdens among individuals.[1] Egalitarian theories analyze this central concern first at an ideal level, which presupposes a highly abstract specification of principles, and then at the level of enactment in social policy.[2] According to these theories, in a society of equals, social and institutional arrangements should ideally be designed to show equal consideration and respect for all. Although they differ on the precise meaning of equality, egalitarian theories understand it as a fundamental principle of justice and as the guiding ideal for the distribution of whatever goods are deemed to be valuable for citizens in order to lead a good life. Furthermore, just social schemes, absent many important details, are usually broadly theorized as mutually advantageous systems characterized by fair terms of cooperation. In line with John Rawls's notable formulation in his foundational theory of justice, participation in these systems presupposes citizens who are fully cooperating members of society over a lifetime and are capable of exercising rational deliberation.[3] Liberal theories generally consider these two capacities the fundamental features of citizenship and hence as determining the conditions for inclusion in social schemes.

It is against this rather "rigid framework"[4] that political and moral philosophers, and among them liberal egalitarians, have recently focused attention on issues of disability and on the experience of people with physical and cognitive impairments. Indeed, political and moral philosophers consider disability, and specifically cognitive disability, a "challenge," if not a "nightmare."[5] This is because, as noted at the outset, disability raises fundamental and very difficult questions that probe not only the theoretical foundations of philosophical theories but also the moral intuitions underpinning them. In particular, disability raises two main interrelated questions for liberal egalitarian theories of justice. The first concerns how to evaluate it as a specific difference in interpersonal comparisons of relative advantage and disadvantage, and how to consider it in relation to the distribution of scarce resources among individuals. As will become clearer further on, the assessment of relative disadvantage is crucial for the discussion of issues of disability. Subsumed in this first broad question are more specific ones, such as whether people with disabilities should receive more resources than nondisabled people as a matter of justice or as a result of humanitarian duties; or whether disability is an inherent disadvantageous feature for which one should receive compensation or instead the result of specific social and institutional designs, which should therefore be modified or even radically changed.[6] The second broad question that disability raises for liberal egalitarian theories pertains to the ideal of equal citizenship. The ideal of "equal standing" in society for all citizens[7] becomes contentious for liberal theories when personal differences in physical and particularly in cognitive characteristics affect individuals' abilities to be fully cooperating members of society and, more crucially, to exercise rational deliberation and, therefore, moral agency, defined as the autonomous actions of individuals in leading their lives. Subsumed under this second broad theme are questions that address whether "those with cognitive disabilities [are] due the same respect and justice due to those who have no significant cognitive impairments"[8] and further dispute the ability to be fully cooperating members of society as essentially constitutive of equal citizenship.

In this chapter, I present a specific perspective on disability based on the capability approach as pioneered by Nobel laureate Amartya Sen and philosopher Martha Nussbaum, and I discuss how this philosophical approach provides an important, innovative normative framework—thus one that is concerned with how things ought to be—for considering equal citizenship for people with disabilities. I argue that adopting a capability perspective on disability advances the philosophical debate in two significant ways. First, such a perspective supports the important view that duties toward people with disabilities are duties of justice, and thus it accords important entitlements to these individuals. Second, conceptualizing equality in terms of capability equality, specified as equal opportunities for effective participation in society, provides a rich notion of citizenship that is sensitive to the position of individuals with disabilities, including cognitive ones. Such a notion therefore promotes a more inclusive and more just design of social arrangements than other schemes.

The chapter is organized into two sections. The first section introduces some core ideas of the capability approach; it provides a reconceptualization of disability in terms of functionings and capabilities—the main concepts of the approach—and aims to show how such a perspective leads to significant considerations of justice for people with disabilities. The second section addresses the question of equal citizenship with a particular focus on individuals with cognitive impairments in the light of innovative ideas of guardianship and surrogacy as currently discussed in some political and moral theories. Finally, I present a brief summary of my argument in the concluding comments.

## Capability and Disability

Amartya Sen originally developed the capability approach within the domains of political philosophy and welfare economics as an innovative normative framework for the evaluation of individuals' well-being and the justice of social and institutional arrangements.[9] Further articulated by Martha Nussbaum[10] and other scholars,[11] during the past twenty-five years the approach has increasingly influenced academic research and policy making and has also informed the work of many international and national agencies.

Sen's capability approach shares two fundamental ideas with other theories of justice, and in particular with John Rawls's: the idea of fairness and the priority of liberty. In line with Rawls's position, according to Sen, while fairness is "the underlying concept that helps us to understand the demands of justice,"[12] the idea of liberty has to be accorded a general preeminence, and this implies a more important place than simply acknowledging it as "one of the many influences on a person's overall advantage."[13] Sen therefore endorses the idea that in evaluating the justice of social and institutional designs, fairness should broadly guide the distribution of benefits and burdens, and freedom should be given "some kind of priority."[14] However, beyond this fundamental agreement, Sen's approach departs rather importantly from other accounts of justice, and more specifically in two of its constitutive elements. First, the approach adopts a different metric for the evaluation of advantage and hence for the comparison of people's relative positions in social schemes; second, it introduces the concept of human diversity as central to the evaluative process. These two features require a closer examination, and I begin by analyzing the first one.

Many theories of justice assess advantage mainly in terms of individuals' holdings of resources, broadly understood as income and wealth or some specifications of them, but Sen maintains that this basis of assessment is inadequate for a proper evaluative process.[15] In his view, since "the means of satisfactory human living are not themselves the ends of good living,"[16] rather than evaluating resources, "in judging the advantages that the different people have compared with each other, we have to look at the overall capabilities they manage to enjoy."[17] According to Sen, therefore, what matters for justice is people's capability sets, that is, their effective and genuine opportunities, or their substantive freedom to lead a good life. More precisely, capabilities are opportunities for functionings, that is, opportunities to be and to do what one values being and doing. Basic, essential functionings (and related basic capabilities) include being nourished and sheltered, being educated and healthy, and appearing in public without shame, while more complex ones include, for example, engaging in forms of social and political participation, or indeed in any valued occupations and pursuits.[18] In short, the distinctive metric proposed by the approach suggests that instead of evaluating the relative positions of individuals in terms of the amount of resources they hold, we need to assess what people can do with the goods they have, and hence we need to assess their capability sets. Two points are worth noting at this stage. First, Sen establishes a close link between the ideas of capability and freedom: "Since the idea of capability is linked with substantive freedom, it gives a central role to a person's actual ability to do the different things that she values doing."[19] Second, valued lives are those that people have reason to value, and hence the idea of reasoning is itself constitutive of a good life.

In addition to the introduction of the idea of capability as the currency of justice, Sen brings to the fore a second innovative element of the evaluative process, hitherto neglected or intentionally unaccounted for by other perspectives of justice, namely, the "fact" of human diversity. According to Sen, interpersonal comparisons of advantage should consider the fundamental fact of human diversity as crucial and should therefore include it in any assessment. In Sen's account, there are four important sources of diversity. These include: personal heterogeneities, such as age, gender, disability, and mental and physical abilities; environmental differences, such as climatic conditions; differences in social and cultural conditions, and heterogeneities in relational patterns and social perspectives.[20] Underpinning this concept of human diversity is a consideration of individuals' different abilities to convert resources into good living. This difference is notably illustrated by the example of a pregnant woman, who needs a higher level of resources for functioning than a nonpregnant woman, other things being equal.[20] Ultimately, Sen maintains that since people vary substantially in what they can do and be with the resources at their disposal, and since such variation in converting resources determines very different possibilities to lead good lives, these differences should be accounted for in any evaluation of justice. Finally, as we shall see in the next section, capability identifies the relevant variable for evaluating disadvantage, but it also represents what social and institutional arrangements should seek to equalize. The approach therefore supports a conception of equality in terms of equalizing a person's capability set, or one's range of opportunities "to enjoy valuable activities and states of being"[21] and thus to achieve well-being. In short, in capability terms, the fundamental liberal egalitarian value of equal consideration and respect is expressed by providing people with equal, effective opportunities to lead lives they have reason to value.

As I stated at the outset, it is within this framework of justice that disability can be reconceptualized and reevaluated in order to determine a more appropriate understanding of equal respect and equal citizenship for individuals with disabilities.[22] I now turn my attention to this point.

Considerations of disability have always been central to the capability approach. Indeed, Sen developed his approach to justice and equality as a response to some of the limitations of other theories in assessing the relative advantage of all individuals, and individuals with disabilities in particular.

Sen argues that "the relevance of disability in the understanding of deprivation in the world is often underestimated" and emphasizes that "people with physical or mental disability are not only among the most deprived human beings in the world, they are also, frequently enough, the most neglected."[23] Throughout his work, Sen provides numerous examples of disability and its demands on justice, in particular with reference to the different conversion of resources into valued functionings experienced by people with disabilities. He further contends that the "difficulty in converting incomes and resources into good living, precisely because of disability" (a difficulty that he names "conversion handicap"),[24] is often compounded by an income-conversion disadvantage and therefore results in pervasive inequalities and significant reductions in people's well-being. No other account highlights so clearly the demands of justice for disability, Sen maintains, and for this reason alone the capability approach should therefore be preferred over other perspectives.[25]

Despite his important attention to the position of people with disabilities, Sen has not elaborated a specific understanding of disability, nor has he extensively participated in the growing debate on disability issues (unlike Nussbaum's more explicit and sustained engagement, particularly in her more recent work).[26] Nevertheless, some important considerations, both conceptual and normative, can be developed from understanding disability in terms of functionings and capability and from referring to the concept of human heterogeneity central to Sen's approach.[27] A first consideration is that the concepts of functionings and capability can significantly account for the distinction between impairment and disability while importantly expressing their related inequalities.[28] More precisely, impairment can be seen as relating to possible restrictions in functionings, and disability to the consequent limitations in capability. A visual impairment, for instance, is appropriately expressed in terms of limitations on the functionings associated with sight. This restriction on functionings can result in a disability, in terms of a functional inability, when or if no alternative or atypical functionings can be achieved. This functional inability is a result of the interaction of the features of an individual with a specific external environment or institutional design. Environmental factors, such as the availability of Braille resources or appropriate auditory signals in public structures, play a fundamental role in determining whether the restriction of functionings of a visual impairment results in a disability and thus in limitations of capabilities (that is, in real opportunities for functionings). Likewise, impairments in communication, for example, those characterizing some forms of autism spectrum disorder, are appropriately expressed in terms of limitations on functionings pertaining to verbal and nonverbal language. This restriction on functionings can lead to disability when no alternative forms of communication can be developed and established. Here again, both the presence of alternative systems of communication and the use of language developmental schemes such as Alternative-Augmentative Communication Methods (for example, Picture Exchange Communication System, or PECS, for children)[29] and the presence of appropriate forms of facilitation of communication play crucial roles in the extent to which the cognitive impairment of some forms of autism results in a disability and affects the individual's opportunities to lead a good life. In short, and to reemphasize what has just been expressed, the focus here is both on the functionings enjoyed by disabled people and on their opportunities to achieve these functionings, and thus to achieve well-being, while considering the interactions of personal and circumstantial characteristics. This leads to a second, interrelated consideration entailed by my approach, namely, the important recognition that disability can be seen simultaneously as one of the many aspects of human heterogeneity and as inherently relational, or as emerging from the interaction of certain features of an individual (her impairment) with the social, institutional, and environmental structures she inhabits. Here the relational nature of disability implies the feminist understanding of relational as referring to the relationship with other individuals, but it extends beyond this understanding to include a relation with the social, cultural, and physical environment inhabited. Although considering disability as one of the many features of human diversity might help avoid the negative stigmatization that still hinders the position of people with disabilities, the relational nature of disability highlighted by my approach avoids situating the disadvantage uniquely within the individual. At the same time, this reconceptualization goes beyond the dichotomy between natural and social causes of disability that has long polarized the debate on disability and justice and, to a great extent, hindered progress in it.[30] Finally, a capability view of disability includes both physical and, importantly, cognitive disabilities, as well as different degrees of severity of disability, and thus encompasses the case of people with multiple and complex disabilities within a unified understanding and evaluation.

On the basis of these considerations, it is now important to address how this reconceptualization and reevaluation of disability leads to an understanding of duties toward people with disabilities as duties of justice. First, as outlined in the examples provided earlier, in order to legitimately acknowledge the specific needs of a visually impaired person or a person with autism and thus to provide appropriately for them, recourse to concepts of functionings is necessary. To emphasize the idea at play here, a just, differential, and appropriate provision for these individuals is legitimate only in relation to the absence of certain important functionings and thus to the consequent failure in capability that this implies. A further important element of this perspective resides in its sensitivity to the actual conversion of resources into functionings and thus in its attention to the interrelation between impairment and circumstantial factors. More specifically, the capability metric evaluates the actual functionings that a person with a visual or a communicative impairment can achieve, given that person's personal and contextual circumstances. Hence the normative question that a capability theorist addresses, as Sen says, is "whether a person is really able to do the things that she would choose to do and has reason to choose to do,"[31] and this is extremely important for justice. Furthermore, the capability approach addresses cultural and attitudinal factors, as well as societal norms, as specific elements that may result in disadvantage and thus compromise the equal position in society of people with disabilities. The approach seems therefore to recognize and account for the unusual and atypical beings and doings that disability might entail, and this seems particularly relevant for cognitive disabilities. In this case, campaigns to change commonly assumed views about cognitive disability and to modify norms and perceptions can be considered part of the equalization of the capability of people with disabilities suggested by the approach.

In short, in placing human heterogeneity at the core of the evaluative comparison of advantage, and in considering disability as a specific human variation resulting from interaction with the environment while accounting also for the complex nature and the severity of degrees of some disabilities, the capability approach provides a perspective that evaluates the demands of disability as fundamental demands of justice. According to the capability approach, duties toward people with disabilities are duties of justice. This position entails the equalization of the opportunities for valued functionings of these individuals, with due consideration to the different and atypical ways in which people can indeed function and ultimately lead valuable lives. The capability approach therefore provides a broad and comprehensive evaluation of the elements that hinder the equal position of people with disabilities in social and institutional arrangements. Further, in supporting the view that duties toward people with disabilities are duties of justice, the approach seems to respond to the main questions raised by issues of disability for liberal egalitarian justice. The latter point, however, needs further discussion with reference to issues of citizenship. I now turn my attention to the concept of equal capability and its related understanding of effective opportunities to participate in society as important elements of a conception of citizenship that is sensitive to the demands of disability.

## Capability Equality and Equal Citizenship

The importance of Sen's capability approach in responding to the demands of disability for theories of justice resides not only in its reconceptualization of disability in terms of capability limitation or deprivation but also in the idea of capability equality, or, as Sen says, in the general concern "for fairness in the distribution of freedoms and capabilities."[32] As I have argued in the previous section, the approach expresses the liberal egalitarian ideal of equal consideration and respect for all through the concept of capability equality, that is, through the idea of providing people with equal, effective, and genuine alternatives to lead valued lives. In this section, I address the idea of capability equality in relation to the demands of citizenship, with a particular, but not exclusive, focus on cognitive disability. I maintain that the specific view of citizenship as "equal standing in society" theorized by Elizabeth Anderson in relation to notions of democratic equality[33] entails the conditions of equal citizenship for people with disabilities and, moreover, offers the potential to broaden the scope of citizenship to individuals with cognitive disability. To this end, I consider the concepts of guardianship and surrogacy as articulated by some moral and political philosophers[34] in relation to the moral status of people with cognitive impairment, and I maintain that although these concepts appear promising for the inclusion of individuals whose intellectual features differ from the standard capacities hitherto associated with citizenship, further debate on these positions is needed. I will begin my discussion by briefly addressing the main points of Sen's perspective on equality and then will analyze equal citizenship in light of Anderson's conception of democratic equality and of notions of guardianship and surrogacy.

As we have seen, Sen introduces a conception of equality in terms of capability equality and maintains that individuals should have equal, genuine opportunities to achieve valued functionings and thus to choose among valuable, alternative kinds of lives. It is important to emphasize that the idea of capability equality is situated within the broader idea of equality of opportunity: capabilities, in Sen's view, are genuine opportunities to choose among valuable functionings.[35] Hence, as Anderson notes, "Capabilities measure not actually achieved functionings, but a person's freedom to achieve valued functionings. A person enjoys more freedom the greater the range of effectively accessible, significantly different opportunities she has for functioning or leading her life in ways she values most."[36]

Although Sen articulates a complex conception of equality, his perspective does not specify what capabilities are constitutive of a good life and should therefore be equalized among individuals, nor at what level, if any, they should be secured. However, as we have seen in the previous section, Sen indicatively selects a small number of "basic capabilities" essential for well-being, which include being nourished, sheltered, educated, and healthy and being able to appear in public without shame. Although he maintains that equality should be sought primarily in these basic capabilities or freedoms, he does not provide any further specification or any list of relevant capabilities. In this respect, his position differs significantly from Nussbaum's version of the capabilities approach. Nussbaum provides a universal dimension to the approach by stipulating a list of ten Central Human Capabilities that are essential to human dignity and to lead a human life. Nussbaum's list of capabilities includes "life," "bodily health," "bodily integrity," "sense, imagination, and thought," "emotions," "practical reason," and "affiliation," as well as "play," "other species," and "control over the environment."[37] In her view, these central human capabilities can be seen as the result of a process of overlapping consensus; moreover, they form the basis of fundamental constitutional guarantees that should be secured as a matter of justice to all citizens at an adequate level. As we have seen, Sen maintains instead that valued capabilities should be the result of processes of democratic participation, since it is only through these processes (involving all those who will be affected by the decisions) that we can arrive at a shared selection of capabilities applicable to specific situations. This explicit endorsement of democratic decision-making processes in selecting relevant capabilities and the intentional rejection of any specific a priori list have prompted various critiques of Sen's approach, in particular the view that it is both incomplete and unworkable. These claims relate not only to the absence of a list of relevant capabilities but also to the lack of relative weightings of different capabilities, which in turn is seen as leading to an indeterminate evaluation of functionings and capabilities that have different imports (for example, playing golf compared with expressing one's political opinions). Although addressing these limitations is not central to the issues analyzed in this chapter, it should suffice to note that Sen has extensively responded to these critiques by reaffirming the value of the "reach of democracy" and public reasoning, by highlighting the possible limitations of any theory that would "freeze" a list of capabilities in the abstract, and by pointing to the actual importance he assigns to the basic capabilities in guiding our concern for equality.[38]

Among the various developments of the capability approach, Elizabeth Anderson's conception of democratic equality provides an important specification of the idea of capability equality. Anderson maintains that liberal egalitarianism should have two distinctive political aims: "to end social oppression" and "to create a community in which everyone stands in relations of equality to others."[39] These aims form the bases of her conception of "democratic equality," which "guarantees all law-abiding citizens effective access to the social conditions of their freedom at all times."[40] Anderson endorses Sen's view that "egalitarians should seek equality in the space of capabilities"[41] and develops her conception of equal citizenship accordingly. As she specifies, although democratic equality aims for equality across a wide range of capabilities, in keeping with the two main aims of egalitarianism it also legitimately defends a structure of egalitarian guarantees that supports individual functionings in three fundamental areas: functionings as human beings, as participants in a system of cooperative production, and as citizens in a democratic state. Democratic equality, therefore, is achieved when people have equal effective capabilities to function in those three fundamental spaces. According to Anderson, ultimately, "The fundamental requirement of democracy is that citizens stand in relation of equality to one another. Citizens have a claim to a capability set sufficient to enable them to function as equals in society (assuming they have the potential to do so)."[42]

The notion of democratic equality defended by Anderson is in line with Sen's emphasis on the importance of assessing inequalities in the space of capabilities, but it also responds directly to some of the critiques of indeterminacy leveled at the capability approach. Furthermore, the notion of democratic equality entails a conception of citizenship as equal, effective participation in one's dominant social framework and allows for processes of democratic decision making that produce a shared list of valued capabilities to be secured to all at the level adequate for equal participation. Here the idea of equal and effective participation in one's dominant social framework entails the view of an individual who has genuine, effective opportunities to lead a valuable life, free from the limitations of deep inequalities of freedoms and well-being, and is able to choose those capabilities that she has reason to value. Moreover, effectiveness in participating in society entails exercising autonomy and agency in bringing about those changes, both in one's life and in society, that one has reason to value. By having effective and genuine opportunities to function in those dimensions, people are enabled to stand as equals in society, and this in turn warrants the removal of relations of subordination and oppression.[43] Democratic equality therefore secures the conditions for equal consideration and respect for all and offers a justified perspective on which capabilities should be equalized.

It is this idea of equal citizenship as "equal standing" in society that, in my view, provides a rich and fruitful notion of citizenship for people with disabilities. However, although people with sensory or physical impairments are easily part of such a notion, since appropriate assistive devices, as well as modifications in environmental designs, are part of the equalization of their capabilities and provide opportunities to lead valuable lives (as argued earlier), the position of people with cognitive disabilities appears more complex, and it is on this latter aspect that I shall now focus my attention.

The difficulty of an equal standing for people with cognitive disabilities relates to the fact that such disabilities may entail "significant limitations both in intellectual functioning and in adaptive behaviour as expressed in conceptual, social and practical adaptive skills."[44] Since intellectual, conceptual, and practical reasoning functionings are essentially part of active citizenship, and since cognitive disability may entail a limitation of these functionings, a fundamental question then arises: how can people with cognitive disabilities be included in a notion of citizenship based on the exercise of choices with reference to one's valuable life, particularly when a valuable life is justified as that which one has reason to value, and on acting autonomously in bringing about the realization of one's choices? Although I cannot offer here a fully justified answer to this question, in my view the conceptions of disability as capability deprivation and as relational, on the one hand, and that of capability equality as securing the condition of full participation to all, on the other, are promising insights toward such a justified answer. Moreover, a view of autonomous agency as relational, entailing concepts of guardianship and surrogacy in the enactment of full citizenship for individuals with severe cognitive impairments, advances the debate on citizenship and cognitive disability. I shall now attempt to address these points in more detail.

As we have seen in the previous section, the capability approach highlights not only the relational nature of disability but also its consequent limitations of capability as inequalities that have to be addressed as matters of justice (an element that is absent from other theories of justice and is not entirely addressed or justified by positions within the social model of disability).[45] Although commonly assumed views of cognitive disability tend to identify it with a specific, fixed feature of the individual, the capability approach endorses instead a view of cognitive disability as relational and thus as emerging from the interaction of cognitive impairment with circumstantial factors. In short, like physical disability, cognitive disability too can be considered relational. Recall, for example, the communicative limitations in the case of autism spectrum disorder mentioned in the previous section. Although the approach recognizes that there are specific personal features of the disorder that may limit communicative, social, and deliberative functionings, it is sensitive to the importance of the external environment of the individual and its direct influence on his or her actual functionings. Likewise, the approach considers Down syndrome as entailing limitations on functionings related to complex reasoning and judgment but emphasizes at the same time how these can be amplified or minimized by the design of societal arrangements. When arrangements are supportive and appropriately devised, for example, with educational and mentoring schemes in place, people with Down syndrome can and do function effectively in society. In this regard, however, the relational nature of cognitive disability needs to be seriously considered, in particular in evaluating how complex postindustrial societies, with their taxing demands for high conceptual skills and levels of knowledge and expertise, can be very disadvantageous for individuals with cognitive disabilities and for the promotion of their full participation. And although there may be fundamental reasons for not lowering the extent of the demands of highly developed societies on their citizens' functionings,[46] the disadvantages that these demands place on some citizens should be acknowledged and addressed. A further aspect pertaining to cognitive disability refers both to the extent to which individuals with cognitive disabilities can develop many intellectual functionings and to the numerous changes over time in society's understanding and knowledge of such disabilities (all part of an epistemic claim on this matter). As many scholars remind us,[47] although almost all individuals with cognitive disability have the potential to develop at least some forms of basic reasoning, much is still unknown about the extent of this potential development and the acquisition of knowledge and about skills of reasoning and deliberation in certain cognitive disabilities (for example, Down syndrome). Indeed, Michael Bérubé has effectively described how his son Jamie, who has Down syndrome, can speak French better than he can, is able to express reasoned preferences on many aspects of his own everyday life, and certainly shows forms of choices of functionings that constitute a valuable life.[48] In line with the argument for justice suggested in the previous section, it therefore seems that the relational nature of cognitive disability and the fact that many individuals with cognitive disabilities have the potential to be able to participate in society (one of the conditions of citizenship set by Anderson) lead to a duty to equalize such participation for these persons and to consider them as equal citizens.[49] This can be achieved both through supporting the development of individuals' cognitive functionings and by providing appropriate external institutional arrangements.

A further important element in the discussion of equal citizenship in relation to cognitive disability concerns autonomy and agency. Notions of autonomous choice and agency and the importance accorded to autonomous choices in the exercise of citizens' duties and responsibilities, as well as in leading one's life, are central to equal citizenship. Recall here that a valuable life in capability terms is defined as a life that one has reason to value and is characterized by autonomous agency and thus by actions aimed at realizing one's worthwhile life plans. Furthermore, the possibility to lead a valuable life is fundamental to human dignity. Two points are worth noting in this respect. First, forms of choice and autonomous actions are part of the set of functionings of many individuals with cognitive disabilities, and these lead to these individuals being able to find their worthwhile place in society. Particularly innovative social policies for people with cognitive disabilities, recently introduced in parts of the United Kingdom, have demonstrated how such forms of choice as managing one's predetermined budget have enriched the effective participation and the overall well-being of these people, as well as their families.[50] These policies and their results provide an interesting endorsement of the many claims of actual and potential possibility of citizenship for people with cognitive disabilities, as mentioned earlier. Second, although autonomous agency is certainly central to an individual's position as an equal in society, some political and moral philosophers argue that autonomous agency should not be considered uniquely individually based.[51] Instead, some conceptions of agency support a relational model, one that is not confined within an individual—and hence "conceived and executed by a singular individual"[52]—but is rather more relational and social in nature. These relational modes of agency include forms of trusteeship, guardianship, and surrogacy and are particularly relevant in expressing full citizenship for individuals with severe and profound levels of cognitive impairment, and for the enactment of their dignity.

Scholars Martha Nussbaum, Eva Kittay, and Michel Bérubé,[53] among others, endorse the idea that people with cognitive disabilities ought to be accorded full citizenship, and that this should include participation in political and civic duties, such as voting or participating in jury service.[54] Before analyzing the case of civic duties, however, it is important to highlight that forms of guardianship and trusteeship can be considered as facilitating and supporting the enactment of autonomous choices of individuals with cognitive disabilities, and particularly with severe degrees of impairment, and therefore as supporting their range of opportunities for functionings and leading valuable lives. As Kittay reminds us, for example, by virtue of the particular relationship established, a guardian can support an individual with cognitive disabilities in leading his or her worthwhile life, and the position of the guardian can therefore be seen simultaneously as one of care and of enablement.[55] However, the full enactment of citizenship in terms of participation in civic duties appears more complex. Nussbaum has developed a view in support of the full civic participation of individuals with cognitive disabilities. She argues that equal respect for these persons entails the equalization of those capabilities necessary to exercise civil and political rights, and that these functionings can be enacted through appropriate forms of guardianship and surrogacy. For some individuals with cognitive disabilities, this prospect is achievable through different kinds of support and facilitation (for example, reader-friendly political material), but for individuals with more severe disabilities, this might entail the exercise of these functionings through a guardian. Indeed, judiciary and social policy have long applied forms of guardianship and surrogacy to areas such as health and property rights for individuals with disabilities. On those bases, Nussbaum contends, guardianship and surrogacy should be applied to other areas of democratic participation. For example, Nussbaum defends the position that if a person can form a political view but is unable to express it, a guardian "ought to be entitled to exercise that function on that person's behalf."[56] But even further, she maintains that a guardian ought also to be able to enact civil and political duties on behalf of individuals with severe cognitive disabilities who are unable to form a specific political view. In this case, the guardian's act would be a surrogate act on behalf of the person with the disability but would still reflect the exercise of full citizenship on the part of the person. Furthermore, the guardian in this case should be given the kinds of support and facilitation necessary to act in the best interest of the individual. Although more critical in relation to some civic duties, for example, taking part in jury service, Bérubé also endorses the importance of guardianship and surrogacy. He states, "The idea that the interests of cognitively disabled adults should be expressed by the votes of guardians and surrogates seems unassailable to me, and an important means of combating everyone and everything that would seek to deny people with cognitive disabilities the full status of political personhood."[57] In short, these positions endorse the view that guardianship and surrogacy would enact full citizenship for individuals with cognitive disabilities, even in areas, such as political expression, that have hitherto been precluded to these individuals. Moreover, forms of guardianship and surrogacy would allow full participation in society much as assistive technological devices help in achieving full participation for individuals with physical and sensory disabilities by providing alternative functionings. The parallel with the alternative functionings of persons with physical or sensory impairments opens the possibility of civic functionings for persons with severe cognitive impairments in terms of "surrogate civic functionings" and further allows for the full recognition of the person with disabilities as a citizen.

Ultimately, a robust concept of surrogacy aimed at enacting full and equal citizenship for persons with cognitive disabilities entails not only acting in the person's best interest, when necessary, but also acting on behalf of the person in specific areas of entitlement. If we inscribe this position within the conception of citizenship as "equal standing in society," we might also recognize the importance of providing surrogacy and guardianship as matters of justice for people with cognitive disabilities, or indeed as part of the equalization of their capabilities to participate in society.

Although this position is certainly important, it seems to provide only a partially justified answer to the question of equal citizenship for individuals with severe cognitive disability. In particular, it remains open to the main objection of paternalism, and more specifically to the problem of whether guardianship and surrogacy can truly respect the autonomy of the individual who is "protected" and thus really enact a notion of equal citizenship.[58] Furthermore, such a notion may be seen as painting a rather too optimistic and ahistorical view. After all, guardianship has long been the accepted rationale for institutionalizing people with disabilities, particularly those with cognitive ones, and has been fiercely opposed by political movements of people with disabilities. This is a complex question, and any claim at present is necessarily very tentative, but two considerations are worth addressing in this respect. The first concerns the due recognition of the equal dignity of people with cognitive disabilities as constitutive of their full citizenship. As Bérubé reminds us, "With regard to people with cognitive disabilities, the surest way of recognizing their dignity is to recognize their guardians as people with the right and the responsibility of speaking for others."[59] Furthermore, Nussbaum highlights that the only alternative to the possibility of surrogacy at present is that "a large group of citizens are simply disqualified from the most essential functions of citizenship."[60] Although both these points certainly do not directly address or respond to the core of the paternalistic objection, they perhaps suggest the need to relate the exercise of autonomy and the enactment of dignity in ways that allow guardianship to be part of the equation, at least for some individuals and in forms that truly safeguard their full participation. Thus the very presence of the guardianship or surrogacy may be seen as representing autonomous action of the individual with severe cognitive disabilities. Furthermore, the central role given by the capability approach to processes of political activism and participation can assist in, and perhaps facilitate, the enactment of appropriate forms of guardianship and surrogacy while safeguarding against discriminatory and oppressive forms. Here the role of political participation is considered both in relation to its enhancement of freedom of other kinds and to the "protective role" it may exercise in defense of the equal citizenship of people with disabilities.[61] Admittedly, however, much more discussion is needed in order to fully articulate and justify the role of guardianship and surrogacy for people with severe cognitive impairments.

The second consideration relates to the crucial need to avoid forms of paternalistic policies that have long hindered the equal participation of people with disabilities (for example, forms of mandatory institutionalized living, as mentioned earlier). This is recognized by all the scholars defending forms of guardianship and surrogacy, who argue for fully inclusive policies across a broad range of areas of entitlement, such as health care, education, property law, and employment, to mention but a few current pressing concerns. In this respect, furthermore, the policies in the United Kingdom mentioned earlier are representative of a different way of enacting support for people with cognitive disabilities while respecting their agency and autonomous choices in light of a recognition of the capability limitations experienced by those individuals. Such policies have provided schemes based not only on the transfer of resources from central agencies to the individuals using the services but also on organized ways of support (via support plans available on demand or on encountering difficulties) that have enhanced personal choices and decreased more centralized services, thus somewhat decreasing the level of paternalism of the overall scheme. Although these are only initial steps toward a different provision of support for people with cognitive disabilities, they appear promising for the recognition of their full citizenship.

In conclusion, although much remains to be addressed, it seems legitimate to argue that, in line with a capability view of democratic citizenship, people with disabilities, including those with cognitive disabilities, are entitled to the equalizations of those capabilities that enable their full citizenship, and hence they are entitled to the conditions of their "equal standing" in society. This might entail conditions of guardianship and surrogacy for some persons whose cognitive disabilities are particularly severe.[62]

I have argued that a capability perspective on disability advances our understanding of the demands of disability on justice and provides an appropriate framework for the enactment of the fundamental liberal egalitarian value of equal respect and consideration for all. I have provided some reasons for reconsidering disability within the capability approach and have highlighted how the notions of capability equality and democratic equality offer an important ground for the enactment of equal citizenship for people with disabilities, including the more difficult case of individuals with cognitive disabilities. Although the notions of surrogacy and guardianship presented in support of the equal standing of people with severe cognitive disability appear promising, more sustained analysis is needed to fully justify this position, in particular against the objection of paternalism. Notwithstanding this aspect, the results of this investigation show that a just society is indeed one in which individuals with disabilities are able to stand as equals and are therefore provided with genuine opportunities to choose the life they have reason to value, even in cases in which such choice might be expressed through surrogate functionings.

CHAPTER 10

# Invisible Disability: Seeing, Being, Power

Nancy J. Hirschmann

When many people, particularly "able-bodied" ones, think of the word "disability," they think of someone sitting in a wheelchair, or perhaps a blind person with a guide dog or white cane.[1] Perhaps they think of a poster child from the March of Dimes sporting metal leg braces and crutches, or an adult with cognitive impairment severe enough to be led around in a store by an aging parent or other supervisory adult. Disability is conceived as clearly demarcated from the "normal," decidedly "other," and highly visible.

But many disabilities are those we cannot or do not see. I focus here on invisible disability to help us understand the ways in which we do not see the exclusion and production of disability, in part because disabled persons have been effectively banished from public life—including the academy. Susan Schweik's work on "the ugly laws" in the nineteenth century documented that disabled people were literally banned from appearing on the streets.[2] But in what we think of as the enlightened, post-ADA (Americans with Disabilities Act) twenty-first century, such banning also takes many subtler forms of exclusion, enacted through language, epistemology, and social meaning.

As disability activism and scholarship proliferate throughout the West, it becomes even more imperative to understand the variety of ways in which disabled people are still excluded from society and politics, dehumanized and discriminated against, and denied recognition, citizenship, and rights. In the process, it is equally important to show the ways in which disability as a category is produced, shaped, and defined in discourse and in our frameworks for understanding the subject. Among disability scholars themselves, "the question of nonvisible disability is emerging as a highly vexed, profoundly challenging concern."[3] But such attention is generally devoted to the various problems experienced by those with hidden disabilities, such as dyslexia, and the concept of invisible disability itself has not been theorized to any great extent.[4] Moreover, generally missing from disability analysis is a complex understanding of politics and the workings of power.

In this chapter, I argue that there are different ways of being invisible that pertain as much to the specific identity of the disability as to the way in which it is arranged, structured, considered, and treated within the social frame. The typology I introduce can help enlarge our understanding of the different ways in which the subject's relationships to public space, public resources, and public power are expressed, compromised, enabled, and restricted. I hope that the typology of invisible disabilities I develop will contribute to deepening our political and theoretical understanding of the place of disability in experience, identity, culture, language, and, of course, politics. How the disabled are seen—and not seen—constructs the ontological status of disability and is structured by and through relations of power. In that regard, the invisibility of disability is intensely political.

I will first discuss the issue of invisibility and its relationship to the fundamental concepts of disability; I will then present my typology of the various forms that invisibility takes in the case of disability. The typology does not build in sequential fashion, but it does become more complex with each new category, leading to a theoretical vision of the political potential of the concept of "invisible disability." I close with a suggestion for how this theoretical framework of invisibility can contribute to changing the way in which we think about disability, whether visible or not.

## Disability and the Power of the Seen

The idea of "invisibility" may seem self-evident: that which we cannot see. But there are different configurations of invisibility, ranging from what one literally cannot see no matter how hard one tries to what is difficult to see but can be seen with some effort or knowledge of where to look or what to look for and still further to what is actively hidden from view or camouflaged. The first may seem "naturally" invisible and the second and third "socially constructed" to be unseen, but it is important to note that all forms of invisibility I discuss are political and are manifestations of language, interpretation, and social structure.

This is true of disability itself; the dominance of the "social model" of disability over the "medical model" in disability studies makes it almost a truism that disability is a "social construction." However, the "invisibility" of many disabilities is a further way in which power is expressed in the social construction of disability; the invisibility of disability is an additional function of social structure, a logical extension of the turning of impairment into disability.

To understand how invisibility works, it is first necessary to understand how disability operates as a category of the seen. It starts with the recognition that vision structures our normative and intellectual world. "Certain assumptions about the correlation between appearance and identity have resulted in an almost exclusive focus on visibility as both the basis of community and the means of enacting social change," Ellen Samuels notes; "Identities and subjectivities are structured by how people are seen and perceived, based on body type, skin color, and physical characteristics."[5] Martin Jay points out that vision is the central organizing category for comprehending and communicating about our world.[6] Seeing is believing; a picture is worth a thousand words.

This is particularly true of disability, which Lennard Davis calls "a specular moment," by which he means that the mark of disability is the visual presentation of a difference that translates as distortion, abnormality, and disfigurement as the gaze becomes the stare.[7] The exclusion of the vision-impaired from such a schema is, of course, ironic from a disability perspective (and indeed, without visible "markers" such as a white stick or a guide dog, the visually impaired themselves may go unnoticed).[8] But what we actually "see" when we encounter other people—particularly through sight but through other senses as well—is always filtered through conceptual categories, frameworks of comprehension, and expectations of "normality." What Rosmarie Garland-Thomson calls the "normate" body—white, male, middle class, and in perfect health and biological functionality—dominates the common imagination of physical ideals even though few human beings live up to that ideal. The normate is what we "see" even if that is not a correct reflection of what stands before us. It is an ideal, or perhaps an illusion, that serves to fend off fear of weakness, illness, and death. She argues that the disabled are "the ultimate other" because the able-bodied know that they could become disabled at any time, and they fear that possibility: "Cast as one of society's ultimate 'not me' figures, the disabled other absorbs disavowed elements of this cultural self, becoming an icon of all human vulnerability and enabling the 'American Ideal' to appear as master of both destiny and self. At once familiarly human but definitively other, the disabled figure in cultural discourse assures the rest of the citizenry of who they are not while arousing their suspicions about who they could become."[9] Or, as Tobin Seibers puts it, "Disability is the other other that helps make otherness imaginable."[10] Visibility is key to this; Harlan Hahn maintains that the appearance of disabled people is the primary genesis of their discriminatory treatment because the nondisabled "project fears about their own vulnerability onto the appearance of a disabled person."[11] Such theorists identify a psychic and social investment in the denial of the humanity of disabled people: if their humanity is recognized, then the recognition of the possibility of becoming disabled oneself becomes more immediate, more real. "Disability's indisputably random and unpredictable character translates as appalling disorder and persistent menace. . . . the self gone out of control."[12] The visibly disabled are often looked at with repulsion, emblematizing "the rejected body," as Susan Wendell puts it; the disabled body serves as a material reminder of human weakness, of the inevitability of the decay of the flesh.[13] As Martha Nussbaum notes, "Normals know that their bodies are frail and vulnerable, but when they can stigmatize the physically disabled, they feel a lot better about their own human weakness."[14] Accordingly, Nicholas Watson notes that "disabled people face a daily barrage of images of themselves as other, as unworthy, as something to be feared."[15]

This fear is threefold. The first is a fear of fraud. The history of disability claims is marked by accusations that such people are simply lazy and do not want to work; they are asking for something for nothing. Such fears of disability fraud go back to the early modern era, at least, when English philosopher John Locke advocated permits for begging for the "truly" disabled and forced labor for everybody else. Such views carried through to the nineteenth-century "ugly laws," where anxiety about fraudulent beggars was prominent to the point of banning disabled persons from public space, and to twentieth-century anxieties about "goldbrickers" who faked injuries to claim workers' compensation or, more recently, ADA accommodation as "special privilege."[16] But I believe that this anxiety about fraud and the resulting hostility to disability masks a more fundamental fear of becoming ill or disabled oneself.[17] Tomorrow, any given "healthy" individual could succumb to an autoimmune virus. Genetic predispositions to certain conditions could be triggered by the pollutants in the air accumulating in our bodies over a lifetime or by the stressors of one's job. Driving home from work, one could be in an automobile accident that results in serious permanent injury. And if one is supremely lucky, one may live into old age, which will very likely bring loss of mobility, hearing impairment, cognitive difficulties, and a range of other bodily changes; Davis notes that "people over sixty-five make up one-third of those with disabilities."[18]

But this immediate fear signals a much deeper fear of the undecidability of the body: the notion that our bodies are not essentially given to us nor static and unchanging, but rather are in states of flux and uncertainty. Judith Butler upended feminist theory when she challenged the accepted wisdom that "sex" constituted the biological reality of female bodies (reproductive organs and so on), whereas "gender" constituted human-made social roles (for example, women as mothers). She argued instead, following Michel Foucault, that sex and the sexed body itself are socially constructed and constituted by language and discursive practices. This way of understanding the sex/gender divide cast theorists' understanding of the body into a state of flux and uncertainty: undecidability.[19] Disability brings that flux into view in a particularly sharp manner; although my understanding of my gender and sexual identity may suddenly shift, I am confident that I will not wake up tomorrow with a penis. By contrast, I could wake up tomorrow in immobilizing pain or become blinded or paralyzed in an accident. Such things happen to people every day; a minority of people with disabilities, about 15 percent, were born with them.[20] The apprehension of disability forces individuals to come to grips with the way the body changes and can change further without warning, betraying the self's conception of who and what one is.

Keeping the disabled invisible, or hidden from view, modulates such fear through the averted gaze. Feminists have identified "the gaze" as a powerful tool of patriarchal subordination. But the aversion of the gaze, the refusal to see, is also powerful because of its withholding of recognition. Davis insists that "the disabled body must be explained";[21] but if the nondisabled cannot see disabled persons, they do not need to imagine, much less confront, the physical pain and suffering that some sick and disabled individuals experience, nor the social pain of exclusion and ostracism that many disabled persons endure, nor can they see any value that disability adds to human life, all of which are necessary for seeing disabled persons as equal human beings. Hence, despite the advances in disability access achieved over the past few decades, disabled people commonly describe the ways in which the able-bodied view them only as objects of pity rather than as equal human beings. And even this pity is often couched in terms of repulsion rather than willingness to give aid.[22] But it is important to acknowledge that the failure to see is often produced by choice, whether conscious or unconscious, in the averted gaze.

As may be inferred from my examples in the previous paragraphs, I treat illness and disability together, although I recognize that there is considerable controversy over doing so. Clearly, the two categories are conceptually distinct, and it is appropriate and useful to make accurate distinctions between people with disabilities who are also ill and those who are in good health, and between people with illnesses who are thereby disabled and those who are not. The misconception that all disability is an illness, that disabled people are sick, is one that has hurt disabled people and has contributed to making them "disabled" in the social model.

But the empirical manifestations of this distinction are often arbitrary, and its strict enforcement sacrifices accuracy for a false sense of clarity. Many disabilities do stem from illness. Multiple sclerosis, for instance, almost always eventually results in mobility impairment; indeed, it is the eventuality of such impairment that makes early diagnosis and treatment of the disease so important. Furthermore, some illnesses by their very nature are disabling, such as myalgic encephalomyelitis, better known in the United States as chronic fatigue syndrome, the primary identifier of which is that the sufferer is so weak and exhausted that she or he is unable to perform many "basic life functions" or is able to do so only with difficulty, which is a not-uncommon definition of disability.[23] Conditions such as cystic fibrosis could be said to fall into both categories simultaneously. Finally, dealing with illness—the constraints that people with certain illnesses must impose on their activity or the demands of time and energy required to manage the disease so as to be able to continue to participate in daily life—can itself constitute a disability. A person with multiple sclerosis may be perfectly able to exert herself physically, for instance, but doing so may hasten the onset of physical disabilities that will eventually manifest themselves. However, the most important point is that I focus in this chapter on the concept of invisibility, and such invisibility often works in similar ways for sick and disabled persons, as examples I draw on will show.[24]

## Ways of Invisibility

By ways of being invisible, I mean that the reasons for invisibility and the forms in which invisibility is deployed and constructed can vary widely across disabilities. A given disabled person can experience multiple forms of invisibility serially or simultaneously; these forms of invisibility may complement and interact with one another, and some may give rise to other forms. To different degrees of consciousness, agency, and intentionality, the ways in which people who have disabilities are understood and imagined, the assumptions and beliefs that others impose on the disabled experience, the ways in which the disabled imagine, understand, and present themselves, how cultural meaning and language set the parameters for talking about, describing, and identifying disability, and the material treatment that disabled persons receive from other people, institutions, states, and laws all contribute to various forms of invisibility.

The first and most literal kind of invisibility is *endemic invisibility*, that is, invisibility that is not just unseen but unseeable, structured by the character of the impairment or illness per se. This is the usual meaning of "invisible" or "hidden disability," and the term is most commonly used to refer to learning disabilities because the impairment occurs inside the person's brain and hence is not something that others can actually see.[25] They can see only particular behaviors that the condition might generate, but not the condition itself. Indeed, even the disabled person herself may be unable to see it; for instance, the dyslexic can see inverted letters, but she may not recognize that they are inverted. Even when behavioral symptoms are seen by others, they may be interpreted as something else, such as disrespect. Hearing impairment is often not seen, particularly given the increasingly small size of hearing aids, if one is worn at all. Many disabling chronic illnesses are not evident as well, such as fibromyalgia.

I call this kind of invisibility endemic invisibility because the invisibility is part of the impairment, and the person with the impairment must make a positive effort to reveal it, usually by telling others. But some of these examples also overlap with *conditional invisibility*, in which the physical dimensions of the disabling condition are difficult but not impossible to see. Perhaps visibility is sporadic, as with epilepsy, which can be seen only when a seizure is in progress, or repetitive stress injuries, which are apparent to others only when one wears a corrective brace.[26] Or perhaps the signs are subtle. Others need to know what to look for, and they need to remember in the stretches of time between visible episodes. This is not to say that one could not see such disabilities if one looked, but seeing them requires that one knows what to look for and looks very carefully. For instance, you will probably not notice another person's diabetes unless he pulls out his blood glucose meter or insulin syringe in front of you or places his insulin pump in an obvious location; once he does that, the condition is normally visible, though frequently not, depending on the circumstances. The signs of hypoglycemia are often difficult to detect unless one knows what to look for; symptoms such as profuse sweating and disoriented behavior are visible symptoms, but one would not know that they were caused by low blood sugar, or even related to diabetes, without having more detailed knowledge about the disease and about the individual exhibiting the symptoms. This kind of invisibility is conditional because it will be visible only in specific circumstances, some of which are endemic to the disability (when an epileptic seizure is in progress), while others are dependent on the disabled person making them visible, whether by accident or by choice (whether a diabetic retreats to the privacy of a bathroom stall to inject insulin or does so at a restaurant table).

These two forms of invisibility have a problematic relation to the social model of disability because they are caused at least as much by the physical nature of the condition as by social context. But invisibility more clearly enters the realm of the social when it takes the form of *voluntary invisibility*, in which a sick or disabled person makes a choice to hide or dissemble a disability that is otherwise endemically or conditionally invisible. Perhaps a person does not actively hide or deny his disability but does not take positive action to make the disability seen, either. He seeks invisibility as a good in his life.

There are many reasons that someone might not wish to reveal a disability, ranging from anxiety about social rejection to fear of professional repercussions. Employers may be skeptical that disability claims are legitimate and may also be afraid that if they are, disabled employees will cost them more money than nondisabled workers, despite the available evidence.[27] Additionally, fellow employees may resent what they perceive as special treatment that a disabled coworker receives in accommodation. Disabled women who are caring for others, particularly small children, may hide their disabilities because of the deeply held prejudice that they will not be able to cope with their responsibilities and their resulting fear of losing their children.[28] A disabled person may have privacy concerns, although this might be coupled with, or even motivated by, shame at his condition. A disabled person may not wish to incorporate the disability into her sense of who she is, for "accepting [one's own] disability means making a deep change of identity."[29] As Erving Goffman argues, the stigma of disability is significant, and he notes that "it is through our sense of sight that the stigma of others most frequently becomes evident."[30]

In other words, it is important to understand that invisibility is not necessarily a bad thing, not necessarily a function of power in the sense of domination and oppression. Indeed, later in this chapter I will suggest that voluntary invisibility has a significant political potential. The reason that it is important to recognize this is that the following forms of invisibility may seem much less benign. For instance, in *situational invisibility*, a disability is literally visible, often highly so, but is actively hidden or obscured by particular material conditions and policy choices that situate the disabled person in a particular setting. The most obvious case is persons who are institutionalized in hospitals or special care facilities or are restricted to their own homes. Some may have endemically invisible disabilities, but most do not. Indeed, the most visibly disabled people may be trapped in such settings and hence hidden from public view. Such sequestration and its attendant invisibility may be to some degree unavoidable and perhaps even desirable from the perspective of the person in question. For example, an Alzheimer's patient might have an easier life in an institution than at home, where the familiar and remembered mingle with the strange and forgotten in upsetting ways. She may also have special labor-intensive needs that, given the current structure of society, are best met, and thereby produce the best quality of life for her, in such a setting.

At the same time, it is important to recognize that institutionalization is a way in which society can shunt the disabled aside and not implement changes in the structure of the social and political landscape that would be required for their participation in the public sphere. Indeed, many situations in which the disabled are made invisible, particularly institutionalizations, are clearly the result of the ways in which social resources are allocated and social relations are organized. The history of disability is one in which people with all sorts of impairments were institutionalized, ranging from "the great confinement" that began in eighteenth-century Europe[31] to "ugly laws" that prohibited disabled individuals from appearing in public and to twentieth-century horror stories like Willowbrook, the New York institution mentioned in the present volume's introduction.[32] Again, this "invisibility" is not literal, because one could see if one looked; indeed, it is because of their visibility that such people are removed from public view. Rather, invisibility is a function of the ways in which treatment of the disabled is structured.

Situational invisibility occurs within these institutions as well. Although there are some high-quality institutions, people who make their living caring for the sick, disabled, and frail often fail to see their charges as fully human, as ends-in-themselves, as Kant put it,[33] but only as means to the end of a paycheck or worse; consider, for instance, the relatively high rates of theft and of sexual and physical abuse in nursing homes. A 2011 *New York Times* exposé of the Oswald D. Heck Developmental Center revealed that attendants regularly abused its residents, all of whom were developmentally disabled, and eventually killed a thirteen-year-old boy.[34] But even when treatment is competent, Anita Silvers argues that "in these institutionalized relationships, the devalued find themselves perceived merely as means for furthering other people's self-regard, not as the valued ends of other people's actions."[35] Of course, the fact that such work is often paid very poorly makes a dramatic statement about the low value our society places on such work, and hence on the people for whom the work must be done: Are they really people? Are they really "there"?

These examples suggest that in various ways and to different degrees, sick and disabled persons experience a particular kind of invisibility within these situational settings: a there/not-there semipresence that must periodically be acknowledged but for the most part is ignored. Situational invisibility is thus constituted by a refusal to see the subjectivity and humanity of the sick and disabled. It is precisely the fact that what is being ignored can be seen if one makes the effort to look that makes this sort of invisibility so morally problematic.

It reaches its most extreme form in *obliterative invisibility*, where the reluctance or refusal to see the sick or disabled produces the figural or even literal obliteration (through death) of the individual. Aside from the institutional atrocities just mentioned, the eugenics movement of the nineteenth century sought to solidify a standard of normality that made the disabled "disappear" from the population, primarily through forced sterilization, institutionalization that would severely limit reproductive freedom, and other forms of surveillance that continued into the first half of the twentieth century.[36] Sterilization was practiced routinely in parts of both the United States and Sweden until the 1980s and still happens in some cases. Further, some disability scholars maintain that the current focus on genetic screening, counseling, and enhancement is a new form of eugenics.[37] More generally, the able-bodied and healthy often wish that the sick and disabled would "just go away"; this is rarely expressed consciously or verbally, but it is

clearly expressed by actions, such as resistance to disability accommodation.[38] When people say "I'd rather be dead" than blind, or paralyzed, or have
to inject themselves several times daily, they are at least in part suggesting
that anyone who is blind, or paralyzed, or has to inject himself should be
dead, that there is something wrong or weak about them that they are still
alive. Whether or not one supports the right to commit suicide, we have reason to be skeptical that such statements constitute an innocent preference; as
Silvers points out, when the ADA was first passed in 1990, the original version of the Oregon Health Plan denied disabled people access to many kinds
of health-care treatments, in large part on the basis of a telephone survey of
able-bodied Oregonians in which large numbers said that "they would
rather be dead than confined to a wheelchair." Yet multiple studies show
that even though disabled people report levels of well-being and happiness
roughly equivalent to those of nondisabled people, the latter routinely report that were they disabled, they would anticipate much lower levels of welfare and happiness.[39]

Hence Susan Wendell maintains that the "first commandment of sickness
is . . . get well or die."[40] At the same time, the deep fear of death lies behind
such shunning: we do not wish to be reminded of our own mortality. This
deep fear of and repulsion toward sickness and disability plugs into the "otherness" of the sick and disabled, who serve as a material reminder of human
weakness. Thus withholding treatment and "euthanasia" are often justified as
being in a disabled person's best interest, regardless of that person's wishes.

Obliterative invisibility takes a different form in abortion. Though a woman's right to abortion is somewhat controversial among disability scholars, it
is vital to recognize that cultural pressure to adhere to the "normate" ideal
exaggerates the challenges of raising a disabled infant and encourages the
elimination of fetuses shown through prenatal screening to be impaired.[41]
The frequent failure of society to provide resources to parents enabling them
to raise impaired infants, is both facilitated and justified by the continued
pressures to abort such fetuses.[42] For abortion to be a "choice" for pregnant
women, such resources must be available. The flip side of this is the obstacles,
censure, and state interference with disabled women's reproduction, ranging
from sterilization to the state's removal of children to foster or institutional
care and to dissuasion, disapproval, and censure by medical personnel and
family members.[43]

Other forms of invisibility that arguably reflect power as domination are
somewhat less obvious. *Epistemic invisibility* occurs when a disability is,

once again, fairly visible, even in the public realm, but is nevertheless "unseen." It takes two distinct but related forms. The first is *denial* and involves the reluctance or even refusal of the able-bodied to see, acknowledge, or accept disability. Like Ralph Ellison's invisible man, "a man of substance, of flesh and bone" whom "people refuse to see,"[44] although one may be looking directly at an impaired body, one denies what one sees. Does one then really see it? Is it actually visible? Wendell's experience of chronic fatigue syndrome recounts people simply not believing that she was ill because she did not "look sick." Her "appearance" was defined by what seemed important to the able-bodied (for example, mobility) rather than what was important to her (fatigue after mild exertion). Although others may know or see the disability condition, they refuse to categorize it as disability; "disability" must be a totalized condition, so if one is not completely incapacitated, thus eliminated from the workplace or shopping mall or classroom, and thereby literally excluded from the line of sight, the person becomes virtually invisible because of the refusal of others to see her as "disabled."[45]

The cognitive dissonance created by such denial can sometimes be experienced by the disabled person herself, particularly when a person denies that she has an illness and refuses treatment, or when the person continues to act as if "nothing has changed." Such self-denial can sometimes be sustained for a long time, although failure to respond to one's own illness or disability often results in significant consequences for the affected person; a diabetic who denies his condition is likely to damage his kidneys, lose his eyesight, or suffer an amputation. Additionally, such denial takes a variety of forms, ranging from the personal (when a family member does not want to acknowledge it because he perceives it as a threat to his current lifestyle) to the social (purposely ignoring a colleague's condition under the guise of privacy). But it is also a matter of language and knowledge categories, namely, fitting a particular observed person—or oneself—into the category "disabled."

The other form of epistemic invisibility borrows from Wendell's "epistemic invalidation," a situation caused by the failure of the medical community to diagnose a disability. I call this *epistemological invisibility*, and the two forms of epistemic invisibility are closely related, though subtly distinct. Whereas denial-based invisibility is premised on an identifiable and identified illness or disability that certain others ignore or do not accept or believe because of phenomenal misperception, epistemological invisibility pertains to the existential character of one's physical situation, for nobody can recognize it; it lies outside the realm of the knowable. This stems primarily from the fact that "modern medical science . . . has a tendency to ignore, minimize the importance of, or deny outright any . . . bodily experiences that it cannot explain." Before chronic fatigue was recognized as a real medical syndrome, for instance, sufferers were accused of faking illness or dismissed as having a psychological and psychosomatic disorder. Reactions such as these create an epistemologically uncertain state for the disabled person because "subjective descriptions of . . . bodily experience need the confirmation of medical descriptions to be regarded as accurate and truthful."[46] If medical science must declare that a condition exists in order for it to actually exist, then the patient cannot have that condition despite empirical sensations felt in the body; it is epistemologically invisible; we cannot "know" our own experience, or what we "know" through felt sensation and bodily experience is negated. The surreality of this situation, to have physical experience negated by another who sits in an authoritative position to define one's own experience, produces a level of self-doubt about one's own existence that makes one question one's own visibility in the empirical world.

## The Politics of Invisibility

The various forms of invisibility I have articulated interact and compound one another. Consider pain, for example. Nobody else can see or feel my pain, so it is endemically invisible. Others can see me react to pain, and of course this formed the basis for David Hume's theory of sympathetic reaction: I observe another in pain, and I form an inference of her state of mind, namely, an idea of her pain. This idea is "enlivened" by the imagination, "converted into an impression, and acquires such a degree of force and vivacity, as to become the very passion itself, and produce an equal emotion, as any original infection."[47] But clearly Hume was wrong; even intense empathy, such as that a parent feels for her child, produces a kind of pain that is quite different in quality and kind. I cannot feel the pain my child feels from the tumor pressing on her brain; I can feel only my own pain at knowing that she suffers and that I might lose her. Even attempts to measure pain objectively, usually by asking patients to assess their pain on a scale of one to ten, necessarily entail that person's subjective experience: how can I know that my "five" is the same as yours? Indeed, because of this uncertainty, a much more common reaction to observing another in pain is (at least a measure of) disbelief.

Consider how undertreated pain generally is, particularly if it is chronic. As Elaine Scarry argues, pain is the sensation most difficult for others to imagine and identify with, the most difficult to "see."[48] Pain is therefore ignored and denied, and endemic invisibility yields epistemic invisibility because what is not obvious to view is claimed not to exist. This denial will result in a worsening of the condition itself, thus heightening the endemic invisibility of the condition, resulting in situational invisibility as the individual is forced to withdraw more and more from social contact.

This interactive quality of invisibility demonstrates the links between the social and the biological and suggests that neither the social model nor the medical model alone is adequate to encompass disability. But it also leads to my last category, *political invisibility*, which subsumes all the foregoing categories and is more conceptual than descriptive. Political invisibility most obviously includes literal exclusion, such as being unable to run for office or vote, as well as the lack of disability issues on public policy agendas. But it also includes aspects of social life, especially the exclusion of the disabled from public facilities, such as parks, buildings, and transportation, as well as from employment. Finally, political invisibility includes figurative forms, especially the "representation" of disability perspectives by the able-bodied, social workers, health-care providers, and social scientists, which is often filtered through inaccurate negative assessments of disability conditions that misconstrue what disabled people want and need and usurp their ability to speak for themselves.

The first two categories of political and social exclusion may seem more concrete, but the third kind of political invisibility fuels the other two. For instance, the ADA Amendments Act was passed in part because courts interpreted the ADA on the basis of problematic figurations of what "disability" is.[49] Similarly, as Nancy Weinberg shows, able-bodied people simply disbelieve empirical evidence that disabled persons are happy, and are even more incredulous that they would not prefer to be able-bodied. Studies also show that disability poses no greater obstacle to happiness than other problems, such as divorce, losing one's job, or death of a loved one. Beatrice Wright further shows that investigators' interpretation of results in attitudinal studies is itself influenced by this "fundamental negative bias," such that studies maintain a more negative attitude toward disability than is expressed by test subjects.[50] Such misrepresentations, a form of epistemic invisibility, are often the political foundation for public policies and interpretations of antidiscrimination law.

Political invisibility particularly creates situational invisibility, which is often a function of the lack of services and accommodations that would allow disabled people to occupy the public realm. At the same time, we take for granted the enormous number of services and accommodations that are made to nondisabled people every day, such as "education, training . . . public communication and transportation facilities, public recreation."[51] We systematically provide privileges to some kinds of bodies and deny them to others, even to the extent that those others' very existence is called into question, catalyzing obliterative invisibility. Social relations, epistemological frameworks, and ethical systems are all arranged so that certain bodies are visible and others are not. These are political choices that are made within a political framework that is itself made epistemically invisible by the rubric of "normality."

Political invisibility thus in many ways captures the essence of what is problematic about all the forms of invisibility I have articulated, namely, the power relations that adhere in the relationship between the sick and the healthy, the disabled and the able-bodied. What gives the critique of Thomson's "normate" ideal such force is that it is a political analysis of disability, not just a normative or ethical one. It is not just morally wrong that the disabled are treated badly, nor is it just existentially problematic in the creation of a class of "others" to whom most people deny subjectivity and the "reality" of their experience. It is also a political matter of power, oppression, and freedom.

But power in what sense? Insofar as invisibility often appears as something that the able-bodied impose on the disabled for various morally problematic and empirically inaccurate reasons, it would seem to illustrate power in its crudest form of oppression and domination: the able-bodied do not wish to see disability, and so they shut it away, or hide it, or deny it. In the case of endemic invisibility, it may be nobody's "fault" that the disability cannot be seen, but even here, the process of making such disabilities visible, often by telling others about one's disability, can lead to other forms of invisibility, particularly situational, such as when one is denied unemployment benefits, and epistemic, such as when accommodation is denied because one is assumed to be faking. These modes of invisibility are a function of that same mode of power as oppression and domination.

Understanding the politics of invisibility opens up a different way of seeing power in disability, however, and it is expressed particularly in voluntary invisibility. Here the vectors of power arguably take on a more complicated dimension because the invisibility is a function of the disabled person's choice. Disability scholars most often treat such invisibility as "passing," a term with pejorative connotations. Borrowing from queer theory, scholars such as Carole-Anne Tyler and Ellen Samuels suggest that passing is often seen as a "sign of the victim, the practice of one already complicit with the order of things, prey to its oppressive hierarchies," or "a sign of assimilationist longing."[52] Choosing invisibility is accordingly assumed to be a sign of shame and fear of discrimination.

This negative reaction to passing operates out of an understandable desire on the part of disability scholars and activists for acceptance of the bodily difference that disability entails. But the reason for this reaction has to do with politics. I previously offered a number of reasons that disabled individuals would choose not to reveal impaired conditions, and many of these reasons fit the social model of disability very well: if I will be discriminated against and stigmatized, if my rights, my livelihood, or my children will be taken away, then my "choice" to be invisible is as much a function of domination as is the case for someone who is placed in an institution against her will. Disability activists in particular believe that the way to fight such discrimination is not to hide but to reveal yourself, join with others, and fight discriminatory treatment. Those who claim privacy, the presentation of the self, or the desire to control others' perception of the self as reasons for hiding one's disability are seen as victims of false consciousness.

From the perspective of a more sophisticated understanding of power, however, this reaction is extremely problematic, not to mention simplistic. In the first place, the negative view of voluntary invisibility ironically buys into the nondisabled view of disability: if disability really is "just a difference," as disability scholars want to argue, not intrinsically a disadvantage, then I should be able to live my difference however I wish. The demand that a disabled person "out" herself is a tacit claim that the "difference" she or he embodies is of a certain kind; and that kind has already been established by the dominant discourse as inferior and disadvantaged.

Furthermore, becoming visible may involve a lot of effort and work that the disabled person, already burdened by dealing with her condition in hostile circumstances, cannot afford to make. It may subject the person to accusations of fraud because she does not fit the stereotype of disability, as when a person in a wheelchair stands up briefly to reach for something on a shelf. Such individuals' disability status is disbelieved unless they heighten and exaggerate the disability's visibility.[53] But by doing so, one reinforces one's status as the other, who can then be categorized, controlled, and excluded—that is, made invisible in other ways. Overcoming one kind of invisibility (say, endemic) engenders another form of invisibility (epistemic, situational).

A truly resistant political strategy, I suggest, would recognize the power in self-construction. Historian Darlene Clark Hine notes that African American women in the late nineteenth century engaged in "a culture of dissemblance" that "shielded the truth of their inner lives and selves from their oppressors." Hine claims that these women's "self-imposed invisibility" enabled them to "accrue the psychic space and harness the resources needed to hold their own in the often one-sided and mismatched resistance struggle."[54] Hine shows that voluntary invisibility is not simply a defensive survival strategy. There is epistemological power in invisibility: because you deny the other the ability to construct you as she wishes, she must see you as you present and construct yourself. The choice to be invisible involves a retention of knowledge denied to the other; what Eve Sedgwick calls "the epistemology of the closet" involves the duality of knowledge retained and expression suppressed.[55] Even the denial of diagnosis has liberatory potential, since diagnosis begins the process of categorization and otherization. Insofar as a lack of diagnosis causes existential crisis, it may because we are already caught up in the medical model and think of disability as a disorder of the body that must be cured rather than a social condition created by a hostile built environment.

I recognize that what I am advocating is somewhat paradoxical: how can someone with a hidden disability change anything unless she reveals what is hidden? This is the crux of the disability movement's position. I also do not wish to appear sanguine about constitutive power, for it always already presupposes the power of oppression as well. The UPS driver who does not reveal his very well-controlled diabetes for fear he will lose his job, the HIV-positive colleague who fears ostracism, and the dyslexic student who does not ask her professor for more time on an exam for fear she will be disbelieved and penalized all operate within parameters defined by the able-bodied. They also cannot access resources they may need to deal with their condition.

But voluntary invisibility also offers a political strategy of ambiguity and uncertainty as a way to unsettle the ability of the nondisabled to police the boundaries of their community. There are various kinds of power that play important roles in the collective struggle to change the perception of disability, and I am suggesting that voluntary invisibility has a particular contribution to make. As Lisa Walker notes about lesbianism, "The passer, as a figure of indeterminacy, destabilizes identities predicated on the visible to reveal how they are constructed."[56] Similarly, although the visibly disabled are often looked at with repulsion because disability serves as a material reminder of human weakness, invisibility is a potentially greater threat because it prevents the externalization and projection of that fear. As Schweik shows, the nondisabled in the nineteenth century were as afraid of disabled "passers" mingling in their midst as they were of "frauds" who would exploit disgust and pity to receive undeserved compensation.[57]

Although all the kinds of invisibility I have described have important ethical and political implications, voluntary invisibility is the most complicated because power plays a much more ambiguous role. It is not the reductive, even caricatured notion of power as oppression that is exercised by the able-bodied over and against the disabled and that must be unequivocally resisted. Neither is it the equally caricatured post-Nietzschean *ressentiment* that the able-bodied complain is expressed by disabled persons in their supposedly narcissistic claim for attention and resources at the cost of social welfare for the majority. Rather, voluntary invisibility suggests and deploys a constituting power, a mode by which the disabled person is able to construct and control, to some degree, her identity, her relationship to work, and her social relationships. This ability is, in a Foucaultian framework, exerted by all disabled people to various degrees, including those who have no choice about their visibility; but the phenomenon of voluntary invisibility is the mode through which such power is most strongly developed and expressed. Voluntary invisibility has the potential to destabilize the normate ideal. As Ellison's invisible man tells us, and as Foucault suggested, invisibility creates abilities denied to the seen, abilities of movement and maneuvering that the dominant group not only cannot see but fails to recognize until it is too late. Those who choose to make their disabilities invisible can operate in the nondisabled world of privilege to destabilize common narratives of disability, social policies, and practices and thereby can contribute to a collective unease about what we, as human beings, "truly are." For in the end, if the body is as undecidable as Butler claims, then who are we, truly? If anyone can be disabled, then where can the "normate" go?

What does this mean, though, in a practical sense? At a minimum, the political implications of what I have just argued lead to the suggestion that theorists of all disciplines and persuasions should start writing and thinking about disability in order to reorient our conception of who "the citizen" is, and how ethics and politics ought to operate. But more specifically, I suggest that the concept of invisible disability can help us reorient our thinking about the political subject. Zillah Eisenstein argued that feminists should take the pregnant body as the norm and starting point for thinking about law, rights, and citizenship.[58] One might suggest a similar argument for the disabled body; indeed, arguments for universal access tacitly employ such an idea, arguing that access should accommodate a wide variety of bodies rather than thinking in terms of creating "special" accommodation for "abnormal" bodies. Ramps, to take the most common example, are not just important for people in wheelchairs but are also easier for people with canes and crutches and the elderly; indeed, they can be negotiated by all able-bodied individuals as easily as stairs can. Thus a ramp is not "special accommodation" but rather provides universal access.

If we considered the invisibly disabled body as the norm, this would take us further because we cannot know what that body can and cannot do. That is, when nondisabled people conjure up an image of a person in a wheelchair, or a blind person, or a deaf person, they think that they know what the disabled person can and cannot do; and often they are wrong.[59] Such mistaken assumptions, however, are what end up forming the basis for laws, policies, and practices. In contrast, taking invisible disability as the norm could forestall that; assuming that a body is disabled without knowing what impairment(s) that body has would yield a different way of thinking that addresses disability concerns of universal access while at the same time reminding the nondisabled that they, too, could become disabled, that we do not know the form that their disability might take, and that the difference between disabled and nondisabled is not very great—and that maybe it is not so bad, not so alien, not so "other." Recognition of the temporality of ability, the uncertainty of disability, and the undecidability of the body is vital to the full inclusion of disabled individuals in the body politic. The concept of invisible disability offers a useful theoretical tool to help realize this.

# CHAPTER 11

# Disability Trouble

## Tobin Siebers

My title is "Disability Trouble," but my word choice is ironic because I intend to argue in support of disability identity in particular and identity politics in general, not against them. "Trouble" is the term of choice used to mark incoherent, dysfunctional, or imaginary identities, be they the fluid gender identities discussed by Judith Butler or the other troublesome identities collected under the rubric of diversity.[1] For example, thanks to new work in genetics, we now know, or think we do, apparently, that race no longer exists and that identity politics based on race has no real object. On both the right and the left, minority identity is pictured increasingly as a troubling and imaginary construct that appeals to weak or uniformed personalities. In fact, critics of diversity have begun to argue, with the help of disability identity, that minority identity is itself pathological and that identity politics should cease to exist.

My purpose is to dispute the use of disability as a weapon to attack the politics of identity. I offer a counterargument to claims on the right and the left that identity politics is based on pathological identities and should be rejected as a result. Rather, I believe that identity politics is a valuable tool for contributing the experience of minority groups to progressive, democratic reform, as well as to the knowledge base of our society. Given the broad attacks on minority identity in our nation and the crisis of racial discrimination and poverty, identity politics is more important, I believe, than ever before.

I use disability studies as a crutch in making my counterargument. If this expression seems negative or infelicitous, please think again. A crutch is a valued support, and the capacity of disability to raise critical awareness about attacks on diversity offers valuable support as well.

Disability studies defines disability not as an individual defect lodged in a person but as a product of social injustice that requires not the cure or elimination of the defective person but significant changes in the social and built environment. At the same time, it is necessary to recall that disability does not resolve only and automatically into problems in the environment. In addition to conditions caused by the environment, disability includes chronic pain, aging, and change of disability status, to name only a few instances, as well as the deeply human work of adjusting to them. Although disability identity itself is never negative, disability as a condition of minds and bodies has both positive and negative values—and necessarily so. Disability embodiment is always complex and often contradictory. The theory of "complex embodiment" supplements the social model of disability and accounts for the fact that the body is a chaotic, vital, and living entity whose appearance draws on various and sometimes opposing sources.[2] First, embodiment is the site of human variation, conceived as both differences among individuals and as differences in one individual experienced over the human life span, and this variation exercises power equal to the social forces that change bodies. Second, complex embodiment considers the body and its representations as mutually transformative. Social representations affect the body, but the body also possesses the ability to determine its social representation. Third, the idea of complex embodiment gives people with disabilities greater knowledge of and control over their body in situations where increased knowledge and control are possible.

Disability studies does not treat disease or disability, hoping to cure or avoid them; it studies the social meanings, symbols, and stigmas attached to disability identity and asks how they relate to enforced systems of exclusion and oppression, attacking the widespread belief that having an able body and mind determines whether one is a quality human being. More specifically, disability studies names the states of social oppression unique to people with disabilities while asserting at the same time the positive values and knowledge that they may contribute to society. The result is the possibility of new political coalitions, energized by the epistemology of disability identity, by which disabled people may offer motives for social change, as well as determined opposition to discrimination and oppression.

From a disability studies perspective, then, the use of disability as a device to pathologize the arguments of certain people derives from a prejudice unrelated to any verifiable hypothesis. I will be tracking the use of disability to disqualify minority groups and their identity politics on the American scene over the past twenty or so years. I purposely refer to commentators from opposing political camps because one of the leitmotifs of this essay is that there is little difference between the academic Right and the academic Left in the use of disability to pathologize identity. The conceptual bookends for my discussion will be the 1987 *Closing of the American Mind* by Allan Bloom and the 2006 *The Trouble with Diversity* by Walter Benn Michaels, although my readings, as in all good bookshelves, will spill out on either end.

Allan Bloom did not originate the brouhaha over political correctness in the 1980s, but his book did bring to the forefront everything that the Right found troublesome about identity politics in the United States. The accusation of political incorrectness supposedly served to dampen open debate and the advancement of knowledge by giving preference to political values over scientific truths. The Right attacked the identity politics of the multicultural movement as excessively sensitive and claimed that giving into this oversensitivity endangered education and the quest for knowledge. It also had dire consequences for morality because multiculturalism was supposedly based on moral relativism. However, the argument that multiculturalism had a negative impact on the state of knowledge soon fell away in favor of the idea that the so-called oversensitivity of minority groups derived from a pathological condition that made their claims illegitimate. This shift from epistemology to pathology is of signal importance because it allowed the rejection of diversity as a form of disability without having to consider the arguments made by women, people of color and diverse sexualities, and the disabled.

Bloom begins *The Closing of the American Mind* by attacking the idea, supposedly embraced by all American students, that truth is relative, but his complaint soon turns to the pathological causes of relativism. He diagnoses a society in love with separateness and self-centeredness. The most famous example is perhaps the passage in which he updates Socrates's complaint about self-absorbed Athenian youths who laze about playing the lyre with this snapshot of American culture:

> Picture a thirteen-year-old American boy sitting in the living room of his family home doing his math assignment while wearing his Walkman headphones or watching MTV. He enjoys the liberties hard won over centuries by the alliance of philosophic genius and

political heroism, consecrated by the blood of martyrs; he is provided with comfort and leisure by the most productive economy ever
known to mankind; science has penetrated the secrets of nature in
order to provide him with the marvelous, lifelike electronic sound
and image reproduction he is enjoying. And in what does progress
culminate? A pubescent child whose body throbs with orgasmic
rhythms . . . whose ambition is to win fame and wealth in imitating
the drag-queen who makes the music. In short, life is made into a
nonstop, commercially prepackaged masturbational fantasy.[3]

Tocqueville warned us, Bloom recalls that "in democratic societies, each
citizen is habitually busy with the contemplation of a very petty object,
which is himself."[4] Because relationships are based on narcissism and self-
centeredness, the family declines, divorce rises, and "there is no good reason for anything but self-indulgence."[5] Democracy also makes an assault on
the love of learning by infiltrating the university with moral relativism and
commercialism. Bloom finds the greatest proof of this infiltration in university identity politics. Black studies programs offer opportunities for blacks
to "stick together," "to live and study the black experience, to be comfortable, rather than be constrained by the learning accessible to man as man."[6]
He offers similar critiques of women's studies programs. The trouble with
diversity, then, is not demonstrated on epistemological grounds; the argument is that proponents of diversity are engaged in a selfish preoccupation
with their own interests, and that their will to separatism derives from self-
indulgence and self-centeredness. Moreover, when these selfish interests are
threatened, minority groups respond with aggression and violence, Bloom's
infamous example being the black student takeover at Cornell University in
1969.

Bloom never mentions the word "narcissism," but its psychology is central to his critique, as his repeated references to self-centeredness and self-
indulgence demonstrate. In this sense, *The Closing of the American Mind*
follows closely on the heels of *The Culture of Narcissism* by Christopher
Lasch. For Lasch, the problem is capitalism, while for Bloom it is democracy, but both men use minority identities as examples of pathological narcissism, and their critiques of American society mirror each other. The logic
of individualism, according to Lasch, has carried our society to the extreme
of a war of all against all and to a pursuit of happiness defined as the dead
end of narcissistic self-absorption. The failure of culture is the failure of the

narcissistic personality: the poverty of the narcissist's inner life reflects a willingness to devalue the past, to live for oneself, and to disregard achievement.[7] University identity politics is a major part of Lasch's analysis. The rise of what Lasch calls the "multiversity" is responsible for the general decline of education.[8] Feminism only intensifies sexual warfare between men and women. "Black studies, women's studies, and other forms of consciousness raising," Lasch claims, lower the "value of a university education" and balkanize society.[9]

In the worst moments of the analysis pursued by Bloom and Lasch, the social conditions in which the individual develops cause narcissistic identity. Supposedly, minorities suffering from discrimination are thrown back on themselves and their limited knowledge because their education and environment are so poor, but if they gain entrance to the university, they demand new disciplines, such as black studies and women's studies, that merely reproduce their inferiority. More worrisome, according to Bloom and Lasch, is that minority demands actively transform educational goals from broad learning to narrow self-gratification, ending in, among other things, the reign of universal ignorance, the culture of narcissism, and the closing of the American mind. Notice, I repeat, that no one needed to verify the knowledge claims made by minorities because minority identity was rejected out of hand as pathological. Minority identity became disabled identity—essentially worthless, an identity to be discarded—and if anyone showed the desire to claim this identity, it only confirmed that this individual was already sick or damaged.

The academic Left soon joined the attack on identity politics by the Right under the banner of either antivictimology or antiessentialism, although this either/or is ultimately not important because the end product of both charges is the same: acknowledging the victim leads to self-victimization and violence against others, while essentialist thinking leads to exclusionary and oppressive behavior. The academic Left not only strengthened the argument against injured or disabled identity but also placed in doubt the status of knowledge associated with minority experience. I think here, for example, of Joan Scott's 1991 attack on the use of minority experience as evidence for both political and epistemological claims.[10] In fact, there are few poststructuralists of this period who do not represent identity politics as a failure because identity politics is based on injured or disabled identity. Repeatedly, we are told that identity politics should be rejected because it relies on the pathology of the suffering subject.

Consider briefly two well-known figures who should have known better, considering that their politics appear to be progressive: Wendy Brown and Judith Butler. Wendy Brown argued in 1995 that identity politics becomes "invested in its own subjection," feasts on "political impotence," and descends into a melancholy based on a "narcissistic wound."[11] "Politicized identity thus enunciates itself, makes claims for itself, only by entrenching, restating, dramatizing, and inscribing its pain in politics; it can hold out no future—for itself or others—that triumphs over this pain."[12] Judith Butler came to the same conclusion in 1997: identity tied to injury—her formulation for identity politics—has little chance of freeing itself from oppression because once one is "called by an injurious name," "a certain narcissism takes hold of any term that confers existence, I am led to embrace the terms that injure me because they constitute me socially."[13] Both commentators assume the same tired psychological scenario in which the members of a group suffering from injustice try to turn their experiences into a positive basis for political action, but because their identity is born from suffering, they are unable to escape their pain and end by using it as a justification for oppressing others.

Even if this psychological scenario were credible—and it is not, because it derives from false ideas about disability—it is amazing that so-called politically minded people are worried that a few minority groups might somehow, someday, gain the power to retaliate for injustice when the wealthy, powerful, and wicked are actively plundering the globe in every conceivable manner: the decimation of nonindustrial countries by the industrial nations, arms trafficking, enforcement of poverty to maintain the circuit between cheap labor and robust consumerism, global warming, sexual trafficking of women, industrial pollution by the chemical and oil companies, inflation of the costs of drugs necessary to fight epidemics, and the cynical failure by the wealthiest nations to feed their own poor, not to mention starving people outside their borders.

The use of narcissism to condemn identity is not a coincidence but involves the very origin of the psychological scenario that uses disability to pathologize identity. The "study of organic disease," Freud argues in "On Narcissism: An Introduction," may help launch a "better knowledge of narcissism."[14] Disability and the state of sleep are the two analogies used by Freud to introduce the idea of narcissism, and disability is more primary and enduring. "It is universally known," he explains, "and we take it as a matter of course, that a person who is tormented by organic pain and discomfort gives up his interest in the things of the external world, in so far as they do not concern his suffering. Closer observation teaches us that he also withdraws *libidinal* interest from his love-objects: so long as he suffers, he ceases to love."[15] Freud's *Beyond the Pleasure Principle* expands this theory, but the signal description of identity disabled by suffering occurs in "Some Character-Types Met with in Psychoanalysis," where Freud illustrates the character type called the "exceptions" with the opening soliloquy of Shakespeare's disabled Richard III. Freud argues that "the claim to be an exception is closely bound up with and is motivated by the circumstance of congenital disadvantage," examples of which include painful organic trouble, protracted sickness, femininity, and Richard's physical disabilities:

> Richard's soliloquy does not say everything; it merely gives a hint, and leaves us to fill in what it hints at. . . . The bitterness and minuteness with which Richard has depicted his deformity make their full effect, and we clearly perceive the fellow-feeling which compels our sympathy even with a villain like him. What the soliloquy thus means is: "Nature has done me a grievous wrong in denying me the beauty of form which wins human love. Life owes me reparation for this, and I will see that I get it. I have a right to an exception to disregard the scruples by which others let themselves be held back. I may do wrong myself, since wrong has been done to me." And now we feel that we ourselves might become like Richard, that on a small scale, indeed, we are already like him. Richard is an enormous magnification of something we find in ourselves as well. We all think we have reason to reproach Nature and our destiny for congenital and infantile disadvantages; we all demand reparation for early wounds to our narcissism, our self-love.[16]

Freud's psychology of injured identity forms the unquestioned foundation of all twentieth-century attacks on identity politics. I do not know of a single argument against identity politics that does not suggest or repeat it, but there is no shred of evidence supporting these claims outside the narrow sphere of psychoanalysis.[17] Indeed, the most recent work in the social sciences on face-to-face encounters between nondisabled and disabled individuals demonstrates none of the emotions or behaviors described by Freud. People experiencing discrimination or physical injuries are no more likely to be self-absorbed, self-interested, and violent than anyone else. The idea that people justify discrimination against others on the basis of past discriminations against themselves has no basis in fact.

By the year 2006 the term "political correctness" was not much used, but the basic idea was still alive and well, still being used to complain about the oversensitivity of minority peoples. Here is Katha Pollitt writing in the *Nation* about Walter Benn Michaels's book:

> I wanted to admire *The Trouble With Diversity*, Walter Benn Michaels's much-discussed polemic against identity politics and economic inequality. Like him, I'm bothered by the extent to which symbolic politics has replaced class grievances on campus, and off it too: the obsessive cultivation of one's roots, the fetishizing of difference, the nitpicky moral one-upmanship over language. Call an argument "lame" on one academic-feminist list I'm on and you'll get—still!—an electronic earful about your insensitivity to the disabled.[18]

Despite all the evidence against it, the psychology of injured identity is still irresistible, making disability the secret paradigm for condemning identity politics. Pollitt cannot avoid it when she raises the problem of symbolic politics, and Michaels, we will see, repeats the tired scenario as well. The major difference between 1987 and 2006 is that now both the Right and the Left are trying to outflank diversity initiatives by recourse to an argument about economic inequality, the Right because it wants affirmative action for white people, the academic Left because it wants to avoid the twin evils of identity politics and essentialism (apparently since both lead to oppression, the first because injured identities seek revenge, the second because essentialist classifications of people restrict freedom of opportunity in the social order). For both sides, however, race does not exist.

*The Trouble with Diversity*, subtitled *How We Learned to Love Identity and Ignore Inequality*, is Michaels's particular spin on why we keep talking about racial identity even though it does not exist, and on how the promotion of diversity both weakens American higher education and preserves economic disparities between the rich and the poor. For Michaels, universities are rich people's shopping malls where diversity of thought is for sale, but the university brand of diversity has two problems.[19] First, diversity of thought holds that all thoughts are of equal value, with the consequence that genuine disagreements turn into "mere differences in perspective."[20] In short, relativism, à la Allan Bloom, still reigns at the university. Second, the paradigm of diversity conceives of difference not on the model of economic inequality but on the model of cultural identity—an effect that actively masks the problem of economic difference by absorbing people into the pathological attractions of identity formations.[21] In short, narcissism, à la Christopher Lasch, still troubles minority identity. Michaels reads the emphasis given to race and gender identities as a plot used by the rich to draw attention away from the crisis of economic inequality in the United States, but the plot would fail if it were not for the psychopathological appeal of minority identity. Here is Michaels's microhistory of the rise of minority identity as the American addiction:

> The commitment to diversity became deeply associated with the struggle against racism. Indeed, the goal of overcoming racism, which had sometimes been identified as the goal of creating a "color-blind" society, was not reconceived as the goal of creating a diverse, that is, a color-conscious society. Instead of trying to treat people as if their race didn't matter, we would not only recognize but celebrate racial identity. Indeed, race has turned out to be a gateway drug for all kinds of identities, cultural, religious, sexual, even medical. To take what may seem like an extreme use, advocates for the disabled now urge us to stop thinking of disability as a condition to be "cured" or "eliminated" and to start thinking of it instead on the model of race: we don't think that black people should want to stop being black; why do we assume the deaf want to hear?[22]

Although there exists no chemical craving for identity, Michaels uses the metaphor of drug use without providing an explanation, but there is no need for an explanation because no one questions the underlying diagnosis that minority identity is pathologically addictive. Racial identity is the "gateway drug" that leads to other addictions, some of them supposedly extreme, such as the dependence on disability identity. I want to focus briefly on Michaels's statements about disability because they reveal a great deal about the use of cultural identity in his argument about economic inequality. First, I need to say that I do not question the necessity of ending economic disparities in the United States and worldwide. For me, the issue is whether turning away from the struggle for racial and gender equality is the best way to pursue economic equality. I am committed as well to eliminating discrimination based on disability. But I will say more on what we should be doing shortly.

Michaels's treatment of disability, especially deafness, underlies the logic of his entire argument because his explanation about why we should not value certain cultural identities turns on the example of disability. Michaels's premise is that we are being taught to appreciate cultural identities as if they were aesthetic objects. Different identities bring with them unique cultural meanings supposedly worth preserving. This is the way, according to Michaels, in which we think about diversity. But Michaels does not agree that identities are like works of art, because there are better and worse art objects, whereas people are now reluctant, thanks to the diversity industry, to conclude that there are better and worse cultural identities. To buck the diversity trend, Michaels would need to make the case that a given identity does not have cultural values worth preserving, that black identity, for example, is inferior to other cultural identities.

Michaels is not about to repeat Lasch's or Bloom's direct assault on black studies or women's studies—think where that would put him—but disability studies is another story. Michaels eases into the assault on minority identity with the example of American Sign Language and eventually ties it to his central argument that identity issues prohibit the advance of economic equality by putting in place a fantasy of equality.

> In a world where economic opportunity depends on the ability to speak Hindi, why would I want to keep speaking English? . . . And if I want what's best for my kids, don't I want them to speak the language that will get them the best job? . . . But we can get a sense of how attractive the idea of cultural equality has become and of how successfully it can function to obscure more consequential forms of inequality by recognizing that even in situations where the disappearance of the language would seem to be an unequivocally good thing, some people refuse to let go. Suppose the language you speak is not English but ASL, American Sign Language. . . . The hope for ASL is that inadequate health care and some really catastrophic new diseases could keep it alive for a while longer; the fear is that the cochlear implant and genetic testing will eventually kill it. . . . To those who think of deafness as essentially a culture, the cochlear implant and genetic testing look like versions of the deaf-no-more procedure, more a symptom of the problem than a solution to it.

The alternatives here are a version of the ones we already encountered in thinking about the difference between belonging to an
identity group and belonging to an economically defined class. If
you think the bad thing about being poor is not that you haven't got
any money but the way people treat you because you haven't got any
money, you're a victim of classism. If you think the bad thing about
being deaf is not that you can't hear but the way that people treat
you because you can't hear, you're a victim of what gets called "aud-
ism." . . . We're being encouraged to think that the problem is the
"stigma" placed on disability, not the disability itself. And that the
solution is to celebrate diversity instead of stigmatizing it.

But do deaf parents want their children to be deaf like them? Do
poor parents want their children to preserve the culture of poverty?
The reason the answer to both of these questions is no is that when
push comes to shove, all parents understand that hearing and money
are not diversity issues, and to think of them as if they were is to substitute a fantasy of equality for the real thing.[23]

This passage is crucial because it does two things required if Michaels's
argument is to advance. First, it shows how the attractions of minority
identity distract people from "the real thing," or Michaels's assumption that
making money is the measure of a person's value. Second, it demonstrates
that some minority identities are in fact inferior to others—a signal gesture
because it is on the basis of the inferiority of deafness that Michaels claims
that the inferiority of the poor should not be addressed by the rallying cry of
identity politics.

I want to stress how new, paradoxical, and disturbing is Michaels's introduction of the category of inferiority as a device to end discrimination.
Inferiority has always been used, of course, to justify discrimination. Old-
style racists claim that some human beings are biologically inferior and deserve to be treated differently under the law. New-style racists argue that
some human beings are culturally inferior and deserve to be treated differently under the law. The idea that minority identities are socially constructed
was designed to attack both types of discrimination by asserting that human inferiority does not exist in reality, only in language, and that we can
change people's languages and rid the world of discrimination as a result.
The new idea that race is not a biological given is supposed to work in a
similar way to disqualify racial discrimination. Neither idea does much to

deal with race as a social meaning, and the new emphasis on biology actually makes matters worse in the case of disability because it serves to justify in most people's minds the inferiority of disabled people. Thus Michaels argues that deafness cannot be a condition that any parent would really want for a child, and that ASL has no hope of survival unless inadequate health care keeps deafness around. Of course, Michaels has not bothered to look at the facts. Screening for deafness is an ongoing practice in the Deaf community, and ASL is the fastest-growing language taught on college campuses. ASL experienced a 432 percent growth between 1996 and 2002. Apparently, only Spanish has been unaffected by ASL's classification as a language that fulfills foreign-language requirements.[24]

The real point here, however, is that Michaels uses disability to reestablish the language of inferiority necessary to his argument about the poor. "The left and right," he complains, "collaborate in what has become a new commitment not only to making people comfortable with their difference but to making them feel better about their inferiority."[25] The reason, then, that I am stressing Michaels's focus on disability is not that it is my area of study but that this focus undergirds his entire characterization of identity politics— that identity politics redeems inferiority by emphasizing relativism and appreciation. But Michaels is wrong about identity politics. If identity politics were about appreciation and not politics, we would call it identity aesthetics. Michaels claims that identity politics is about appreciating diversity when it is really about changing laws, economic distribution, rules of political engagement, public policy, and the material and social conditions of the built environment. He is right that we do not need to appreciate the poor if it means ignoring their situation. But neither do we need to conclude that the poor are inferior, as Michaels repeatedly suggests. Rather, an identity politics of the poor should be about mobilizing the poor politically to end economic inequality. In this goal, disability studies can be of assistance because disabled people build communities through a more transparently political process than other minority groups. Because they cannot rely on seemingly more "natural" associations, such as family history, race, age, gender, or geographic origin, they tend to organize themselves according to health-care needs, information sharing, and political advocacy. In short, the disabled rely heavily in their coalition building on the epistemological basis of identity. The poor might organize along similar lines.

The idea that we should stop talking about race, gender, or disability if we want to end discrimination is a bad idea. Less talk about racism will produce more racism, not less, and the same applies to other areas of discrimination. We need to talk about how economic disparity arises from systems of exploitation that stigmatize race, gender, sexuality, disability, and other minority identities. We need to pursue an analysis of economic disparity in concert with other forms of discrimination. Most important, we need to set aside the tired psychological scenario of injured identity used to attack minority groups, not only because it uses disability to justify accusations of inferiority and inequality but also because there is no evidence for its claims.

If there is going to be an argument for or against identity politics, it needs to be made epistemologically by asking whether minority identity and experience make a genuine contribution to society and its knowledge base. But, of course, there are reasons why the opponents of identity politics have refused to engage on epistemological grounds. The impact of women's studies on almost all academic disciplines and university policies, the critical advances made in philosophy by feminist standpoint theory, the research on the superiority of racially diverse classrooms, juries, and lawmaking bodies, the radical transformation of canonical sources in the humanities and social sciences, the liberation of sexuality by queer theorists, and the emerging critique of the built environment by disability activists—these and the many discoveries made by the social and political movements of the past thirty years lead to the conclusion that minority people not only know something about our society that other members do not but also that their knowledge has a real and transformative influence necessary to the future. None of these advances would have taken place without identity politics, but there is more work to be done. We need identity politics now.

# NOTES

## Introduction

1. Some other books in the University of Pennsylvania Press series Democracy, Citizenship, and Constitutionalism that examine citizenship are Patrick Weil, *The Sovereign Citizen: Denaturalization and the Origins of the American Republic* (2012); Teresa Anne Murphy, *Citizenship and the Origins of Women's History in the United States* (2013); Sigal Ben-Porath and Rogers M. Smith, eds., *Varieties of Sovereignty and Citizenship* (2012); and Willem Maas, ed., *Multilevel Citizenship* (2013). Series editor Rogers Smith is noted for his work on citizenship and political membership, including *Civic Ideals* (New Haven, Conn.: Yale University Press, 1997) and *Stories of Peoplehood* (Cambridge: Cambridge University Press, 2003). Many other texts are cited throughout this introduction.

2. There are some notable exceptions. Michael Bérubé gives a brief overview in "Citizenship and Disability," *Dissent* (Spring 2003): 52–57. Sociologists Allison Carey and Richard Scotch discuss the history and sociology of civil rights but do not develop a theory of citizenship per se. See Carey, *On the Margins of Citizenship: Intellectual Disability and Civil Rights in Twentieth-Century America* (Philadelphia: Temple University Press, 2009); and Scotch, *From Good Will to Civil Rights: Transforming Federal Disability Policy*, 2nd ed. (Philadelphia: Temple University Press, 2001). Historians Douglas Baynton and Kim Nielsen also address the history of citizenship for particular disability groups. See Baynton, "Disability and the Justification of Inequality in American History," in *The New Disability History: American Perspectives*, ed. Paul K. Longmore and Lauri Umansky (New York: New York University Press, 2001), 33–57, 52; and Nielsen, *The Radical Lives of Helen Keller* (New York: New York University Press, 2004). The most robust attempts to theorize disability citizenship can be found among Canadian disability scholars. See Michael Prince, *Absent Citizens: Disability Politics and Policy in Canada* (Toronto: University of Toronto Press, 2009); and Diane Pothier and Richard Devlin, *Critical Disability Theory: Essays in Philosophy, Politics, Policy, and Law* (Vancouver: UBC Press, 2006).

3. Political scientist Harlan Hahn notes the disincentives to work built into federal policy: "Many disabled persons, with physical conditions which may make

them especially susceptible to catastrophic medical costs, prefer to continue to accept relatively meager SSI or SSDI support rather than to risk the loss of government health care protection provided by those programs." Harlan Hahn, "Toward a Politics of Disability: Definitions, Disciplines, and Policies," Independent Living Institute, accessed January 8, 2014, http://www.independentliving.org/docs4/hahn2.html. In 1988, historian Paul Longmore took action against such perverse work disincentives and burned his own book in front of the Federal Building in downtown Los Angeles in protest against Social Security policies that essentially preclude disabled professionals from working and receiving assistive care and devices that are essential to their productivity. See Paul Longmore, *Why I Burned My Book, and Other Essays on Disability* (Philadelphia: Temple University Press, 2003).

4. Harold Lasswell, *Politics: Who Gets What, When, and How* (New York: McGraw-Hill, 1936); John Rawls, *A Theory of Justice* (Cambridge, Mass.: Belknap Press of Harvard University Press, 1971); Lauren Berlant, *The Queen of America Goes to Washington City: Essays on Sex and Citizenship* (Durham, N.C.: Duke University Press, 1997).

5. Bérubé, "Citizenship and Disability," 54.

6. Historian Linda Gordon has demonstrated the gender inequity of the U.S. welfare state, showing how unemployment insurance and old-age pension provisions of the 1935 Social Security Act were intended for men and thus were construed as entitlements that had been earned by virtue of their gender and employment status. On the other hand, assistance for poor mothers (through Aid to Dependent Children) was seen as discretionary and stigmatized "aid," given out only to those applicants who were worthy of such "handouts." The history of disability welfare policy follows a trajectory similar to that of the history of federal aid made available to women. Linda Gordon, *Pitied but Not Entitled: Single Mothers and the History of Welfare, 1890–1935* (New York: Free Press, 1994).

7. Richard Devlin and Dianne Pothier, "Introduction: Toward a Critical Theory of Dis-citizenship," in Pothier and Devlin, *Critical Disability Theory*, 2.

8. Carey, *On the Margins of Citizenship*.

9. We should note that virtually all the essays in this volume focus on disability in the United States. A few take up theoretical conceptions that could in principle apply to any locality, although they are generally situated within Western theoretical frameworks (Terzi, for instance, draws on the capabilities approach that was developed by Amartya Sen to provide a way of assessing well-being in India and other Asian sites of poverty that did not rely on gross national product). This may be unavoidable when one is dealing with the concept of citizenship, which relies on "civic myths" that guide our ideal conceptualizations. As Rogers Smith argues, these myths both distort the reality of unequal distribution of the privileges and duties of citizenship and guide struggles for greater equalization (Smith, *Civic Ideals*). But we acknowledge that there is a need to look at disability and citizenship in non-Western contexts, and we hope that the present volume will inspire other scholars to undertake such a project.

10. Cited by Stephen Knadler, "Dis-abled Citizenship: Narrating the Extraordinary Body in Racial Uplift," *Arizona Quarterly* 69, no. 3 (Autumn 2013): 98.

11. The terms "medical" and "social" models of disability are so widely used in disability studies that it would be impossible to identify their source of origin, but two good introductory readers in disability studies, in which various aspects of these models are explored and articulated, are Tom Shakespeare, ed., *The Disability Reader: Social Science Perspectives* (London: Cassell, 1998); and Lennard J. Davis, ed., *The Disability Studies Reader*, 2nd ed. (New York: Routledge, 2006).

12. Devlin and Pothier, "Introduction," 14.

13. Rosemarie Garland Thomson, *Extraordinary Bodies* (New York: Columbia University Press, 1997). See also Nancy J. Hirschmann, "Invisibility, Power, and Women's Lives: A Critical Introduction," in "Disability and Disclosure," ed. Allison Parker, special issue, *Journal of Historical Biography* 13 (Spring 2013): 1–26.

14. Michel Foucault, *Madness and Civilization: A History of Insanity in the Age of Reason*, trans. Richard Howard (New York: Pantheon Books, 1965); but see also Roy Porter, "Foucault's Great Confinement," *History of the Human Sciences* 3, no. 1 (1990): 47–54, who maintains that in England the mentally disabled were not institutionalized in great numbers until the late eighteenth century and more likely the nineteenth.

15. Susan M. Schweik, *The Ugly Laws: Disability in Public* (New York: New York University Press, 2009).

16. Peter L. Tyor and Leland V. Bell, *Caring for the Retarded in America: A History* (Westport, Conn.: Greenwood Press, 1984); and "Excerpts from Statement by Kennedy," *New York Times*, September 10, 1965. See also David J. Rothman and Sheila M. Rothman, *The Willowbrook Wars: Bringing the Mentally Disabled into the Community* (New York: Transaction Books, 2005).

17. Danny Hakim, "A Disabled Boy's Death, and a System in Disarray," *New York Times*, June 5, 2011.

18. See Susan Wendell, "The Unhealthy Disabled: Treating Chronic Illnesses as Disabilities," *Hypatia* 16, no. 4 (2001): 17–33; and Tobin Siebers, *Disability Theory* (Ann Arbor: University of Michigan Press, 1995).

19. Michael Sokolove, "The Fast Life of Oscar Pistorius," *New York Times*, January 18, 2012.

20. T. H. Marshall, "Citizenship and Social Class," in *Class, Citizenship, and Social Development* (Garden City, N.Y.: Doubleday, 1964), 71.

21. Will Kymlicka and and Wayne Norman, "Return of the Citizen: A Survey of Recent Work on Citizenship Theory," *Ethics* 104, no. 2 (1994): 352–81.

22. Maas, *Multilevel Citizenship*, 3.

23. Linda Bosniak, *The Citizen and the Alien: Dilemmas of Contemporary Membership* (Princeton, N.J.: Princeton University Press, 2006), 1, 35.

24. Berlant, *Queen of America*, 20.

25. Joanna Grossman and Linda McClain, introduction to *Gender Equality: Dimensions of Women's Equal Citizenship*, ed. Linda McClain and Joanna Grossman (New York: Cambridge University Press, 2009), 9.

26. Marcia H. Rioux and Fraser Valentine, "Does Theory Matter? Exploring the Nexus Between Disability, Human Rights and Public Policy," in Devlin and Pothier, *Critical Disability Theory*, 55.

27. Marilyn Friedman, introduction to *Women and Citizenship*, ed. Marilyn Friedman (New York: Oxford University Press, 2005), 3.

28. *United States v. Virginia*, 518 U.S. 515, 532 (1996).

29. Prince, *Absent Citizens*, 179.

30. Marshall, "Citizenship and Social Class," 70, 84, 92.

31. Consider, for example, the homelessness rate among U.S. veterans—almost 60,000 were reported in May 2012. Leo Shane, "VA Figures Show Steep Decline in Number of Homeless Veterans," *Stars and Stripes*, May 30, 2013. See also Beth Linker, *War's Waste: Rehabilitation in World War I America* (Chicago: University of Chicago Press, 2011); and Susan Schweik's essay in this volume.

32. Title 8 of the U.S. Code elaborates on this basic definition to include children born outside the United States whose parents who are U.S. citizens, as well as foundlings for whom there is no proof that they were not born in the United States. If only one parent is a U.S. citizen, that parent must meet certain residency requirements. See Cornell Law School, U.S. Code, Title 8: Aliens and Nationality, accessed April 11, 2014, http://www.law.cornell.edu/uscode. We should note that the "naturalization" category is less ambiguous than birth because disabled immigrants have been denied the right even to enter the United States, much less naturalize, as Douglas Baynton's essay in this volume shows. On citizenship and immigration, see also Joseph Carens, *The Ethics of Immigration* (New York: Oxford University Press, 2013), esp. chap. 2. He notes that at least on the matter of "birthright," the United States has historically been more liberal than many other states, granting citizenship to all infants born to parents who resided in the United States, regardless of the legality of their immigration status.

33. Gretchen Ritter, *The Constitution as Social Design: Gender and Civic Membership in the American Constitutional Order* (Stanford, Calif.: Stanford University Press, 2006).

34. *Plessy v. Ferguson*, 163 U.S. 537 (1896). See Phillip Klinkner and Rogers M. Smith, *The Unsteady March: The Rise and Decline of Racial Equality in America* (Chicago: University of Chicago Press, 2002). The 2013 U.S. Supreme Court decision striking down key components of the Voting Rights Act of 1965 stirred considerable outrage, showing that voting as a mark of citizenship is still vitally important to African Americans. Adam Liptak, "Supreme Court Invalidates Key Part of Voting Rights Act," *New York Times*, June 25, 2013.

35. According to Marshall's view, social rights, previously "the monopoly of the few," have progressively been brought within the "reach of the many." Marshall, "Citizenship and Social Class," 70, 84, 92. See also Ronald Beiner and Anthony Rees, eds.,

*Citizenship Today: The Contemporary Relevance of T. H. Marshall* (London: University College London Press, 1996).

36. Helen Meekosha and Leanne Dowse, "Enabling Citizenship: Gender, Disability and Citizenship in Australia," *Feminist Review* 57, no. 1 (1997): 50; Baynton, "Disability and the Justification of Inequality," 33.

37. Richard Hernstein and Charles Murray, *The Bell Curve: Intelligence and Class Structure in American Life* (New York: Free Press, 1996).

38. Baynton, "Disability and the Justification of Inequality," 43.

39. Bérubé, "Citizenship and Disability," 54.

40. Anita Silvers, "People with Disabilities," in *The Oxford Handbook of Practical Ethics*, ed. Hugh LaFollette (New York: Oxford University Press, 2003), 301.

41. Domenico Losurdo, *Liberalism: A Counter-history* (Brooklyn, N.Y.: Verso, 2011), chap. 5. See also Smith, *Civic Ideals*.

42. Anita Silvers, David T. Wasserman, and Mary Briody Mahowald, *Disability, Difference, Discrimination: Perspectives on Justice in Bioethics and Public Policy*, (New York: Rowman and Littlefield, 1998).

43. Martin Luther King, Jr., "Letter from Birmingham City Jail," in *Civil Disobedience: Theory and Practice*, ed. Hugo Adam Bedau (New York: Pegasus Press, 1969), 74.

44. Ibid., 78–79.

45. Ibid., 73, 88.

46. Jacobus tenBroek, "The Right to Live in the World: The Disabled in the Law of Torts," *California Law Review* 54, no. 2 (May 1966): 841–919. See also Jacobus tenBroek, "The Disabled in the Law of Welfare," *California Law Review* 54, no. 2 (May 1966): 809–40.

47. tenBroek, "Right to Live in the World," 849, 844.

48. Ibid., 847, 849, 851.

49. There is a large literature on the history of the U.S. welfare state, including the inception of Social Security. For some examples, see Linda Gordon, *Pitied but Not Entitled*; and Michael B. Katz, *The Price of Citizenship: Redefining America's Welfare State* (New York: Metropolitan Books, 2001). For disability and welfare history, see Scotch, *From Good Will to Civil Rights*; Carey, *On the Margins of Citizenship*; and Longmore, *Why I Burned My Book*.

50. Jacobus tenBroek, "Have Our Blind Social Security?," radio speech, National Federation of the Blind national convention, Wilkes-Barre, PA, November 15, 1945; reprinted in Floyd W. Matson, *Walking Alone and Marching Together: A History of the Organized Blind Movement in the United States, 1940–1990* (Baltimore: National Federation of the Blind, 1990), 13–15.

51. Berlant, *Queen of America*, 5.

52. On the burdens imposed on disabled persons by U.S. policy, see Longmore, *Why I Burned My Book*, and Samuel Bagenstos, "Disability and the Tension Between Citizenship and Social Rights" (paper presented at the Program on Democracy,

Citizenship and Constitutionalism, University of Pennsylvania, October 15, 2014). On the comparative superiority of Scandanavian countries regarding disability policy, see Kjersti Skarstad and Malcolm Langford, "Measuring Compliance: The Promise and Perils of Quantitative Methods," in Disability Social Rights, ed. Michael Stein and Malcolm Langford (New York: Cambridge University Press, forthcoming).

53. Marshall, "Citizenship and Social Class," 80.

54. Iris Marion Young, "The Logic of Masculinist Protection: Reflections on the Current Security State," *Signs: Journal of Women in Culture and Society* 29, no. 1 (2003): 21.

55. Grossman and McClain, introduction.

56. Marshall, "Citizenship and Social Class," 72; tenBroek, "Law of Torts."

57. We now realize that social status includes such identity categories as race, ethnicity, gender, and disability, although Marshall himself recognized only class as a relevant social marker.

58. Prince, *Absent Citizens*, 21.

59. It is not insignificant that, when both the ADA and the ADAAA were passed into law, a number of members of the House and Senate either themselves had disabilities or had close family members with one; presumably that made it more difficult to deny the humanity of disabled persons or to deny their connection to citizenship.

60. Iris Marion Young, *Intersecting Voices: Dilemmas of Gender, Political Philosophy, and Policy* (Princeton, N.J.: Princeton University Press, 1997), 126.

61. Jenny Morris, "Impairment and Disability: Constructing an Ethics of Care That Promotes Human Rights," *Hypatia* 16, no. 4 (Fall 2001): 12.


Chapter 1. Homer's Odyssey

1. On the concept and material culture of prosthesis, see Donna J. Haraway, "A Cyborg Manifesto: Science, Technology, and Socialist-Feminism in the Late Twentieth Century," in *Simians, Cyborgs, and Women: The Reinvention of Nature* (New York: Routledge, 1991), 183–201; Steven Kurzman, "Presence and Prosthesis: A Response to Nelson and Wright," *Cultural Anthropology* 16, no. 3 (2001): 374–87; Katherine Ott, David Serlin, and Stephen Mihm, eds., *Artificial Parts, Practical Lives: Modern Histories of Prosthesis* (New York: New York University Press, 2002); and, most important in this context of narrative, David Mitchell and Sharon Snyder, *Narrative Prosthesis: Disability and the Dependencies of Discourse* (Ann Arbor: University of Michigan Press, 2001).

2. On the multiplication (usually by three) of returning servicemen in World War II homecoming films, see Charles Affron and Mirella Jona Affron, *Best Years: Going to the Movies, 1945–1946* (New Brunswick, N.J.: Rutgers University Press, 2009), 231. Martin Norden provides the definitive summary of disabled-veteran films in *The Cinema of Isolation: A History of Physical Disability in the Movies* (New Brunswick, N.J.: Rutgers University Press, 1994), 156–68, 176–83.

3. Sarah Kozloff, *The Best Years of Our Lives* (London: Palgrave Macmillan/British Film Institute, 2011), 92–93. William Wyler wrote of the three veteran characters at the center of *The Best Years of Our Lives* that "Homer, in spite of his physical disability, makes a better adjustment than the other two veterans . . . who both had emotional disturbances caused by the war but no physical injuries." Here is the characteristic move: the two other veterans are both placed in tenuous relation to disability (as "disturbance," as invisible scarring "caused by the war") and sharply differentiated from the positively disabled Homer. Wyler, introduction to *The Best Years of My Life*, by Harold Russell with Dan Ferullo (Middlebury, Vt.: Paul S. Eriksson, 1981), x.

4. "By the war's end, approximately 671,000 Americans had been wounded, 300,000 seriously enough to require long-term hospitalization and often systematic rehabilitation. No less pressing were the neuropsychiatric casualties, whose numbers mounted steadily in the last two years of the war, as large numbers of men from every condition of life were called up to fill draft quotas. As many as 500,000 men were said to have been hospitalized for neuropsychiatric causes in the last year of the war alone. Contemplating such data, the Veterans Administration Director of Social Work predicted that the release of men from the military would occasion 'a psychiatric problem of a dimension never before experienced in any country.'" David Gerber, "Heroes and Misfits: The Troubled Social Reintegration of Disabled Veterans in *The Best Years of Our Lives*," *American Quarterly* 46, no. 4 (1994): 551.

5. Kozloff, *Best Years of Our Lives*, 16; see also Gerber, "Heroes and Misfits," 547–48.

6. Kozloff, *Best Years of Our Lives*, 16.

7. Gerber, "Heroes and Misfits," 552.

8. Kaja Silverman, *Male Subjectivity at the Margins* (New York: Routledge, 1992), 53.

9. Michael Anderegg, *William Wyler* (Boston: Twayne, 1979), 128–29.

10. Jan Herman, *A Talent for Trouble: The Life of Hollywood's Most Acclaimed Director, William Wyler* (New York: Da Capo, 1997), 228; Russell, *Best Years of My Life*, 44.

11. Beth Linker, *War's Waste: Rehabilitation in World War I America* (Chicago: University of Chicago Press, 2011), 7.

12. David Gerber, "Anger and Affability: The Rise and Representation of a Repertory of Self-Presentation Skills in a World War II Disabled Veteran," *Journal of Social History* 27 (Fall 1993): 14; Harold Russell (with Victor Rosen), *Victory in My Hands* (New York: Creative Age Press, 1949), 187–88, 197.

13. Gerber, "Heroes and Misfits," 567.

14. MacKinlay Kantor, "Kantor Says Ex-G.I.'s Transmute His War Novel to Film Perfectly," *New York Herald Tribune*, November 14, 1946.

15. Thomas Pryor, "William Wyler and His Screen Philosophy," *New York Times*, November 17, 1946.

16. Paul Karney, "Kantor Scores Goldwyn for 'Best Years' Snub," *Screen Publicists Guild News* 7, no. 2 (March 1947).

17. Pryor, "William Wyler."

18. MacKinlay Kantor, *Glory for Me: A Novel in Verse* (New York: Coward-McCann, 1945).

19. Anderegg, *William Wyler*, 123; Herman, *Talent for Trouble*, 250–57; Kozloff, *Best Years of Our Lives*, 3, 7; Norden, *Cinema of Isolation*, 164; Gerber, "Heroes and Misfits," 553; Wyler, introduction to *The Best Years of My Life*, xi.

20. Herman, *Talent for Trouble*, 275.

21. Ibid., 277.

22. Russell, *Victory in My Hands*, 187.

23. Arthur Marx, *Goldwyn: A Biography of the Man Behind the Myth* (New York: Ballantine, 1977), 308.

24. I do not have space here to address fully how openly (and how uncritically) Kantor explores or exploits disability demasculinizations in the representation of Homer; the feminization of the disabled man is clearly very much at play at moments like the metaphor of the girlie lingerie. Sonya Michel offers a rich exploration of gender in *Best Years* that is illuminating here: "Danger on the Home Front: Motherhood, Sexuality, and Disabled Veterans in American Postwar Films," *Journal of the History of Sexuality* 3 (July 1992): 109–28.

25. The rhetoric of "signature injury" is ubiquitous in both popular media coverage and analysis in medical journals of traumatic brain injury in the war zones of Iraq and Afghanistan. For a general discussion of the intensity of the problem of war-related brain injury today, see Jonathan Silver, Thomas W. McAllister, and Stuart C. Yudofsky, *Textbook of Traumatic Brain Injury* (Arlington, Va.: American Psychiatric Publishing, 2011).

26. Kantor, *Glory for Me*, 40.

27. Ibid., 95.

28. Pryor, "William Wyler." The complicated way in which Homer's "spasticity" is introduced in Kantor's description of Homer—diagnosed "a dozen times," "but jerking nonetheless"—hints at some of the slipperiness in what the word meant in the 1940s. On the one hand, any generalized spasmodic or uncoordinated movement might be styled "spastic"; on the other, the word referred technically to specific conditions like "spastic paralysis" or an effect of what had earlier been known as "Little's disease" and was by then called "cerebral palsy."

29. Norden, *Cinema of Isolation*, 164, notes that Wyler had worked as a young man in the crew for Chaney's *Hunchback of Notre Dame* and writes that Wyler drew the conclusion that, in Wyler's words, "no matter how good a performance an actor can give of a man without hands, an audience could reassure itself by saying, 'It's only a movie.' With Russell playing Homer, no such reassurance was possible." This was a strong principle, but the quotation from Wyler in fact emphasizes that a nondisabled actor's performance may be very good indeed.

30. Russell, *Victory in My Hands*, 172.

31. Herman, *Talent for Trouble*, 281.

32. Anderegg, *William Wyler*, 127.

33. Quoted in Herman, *Talent for Trouble*, 281. On disability and disgust, see Susan M. Schweik, *The Ugly Laws: Disability in Public* (New York: New York University Press, 2009), 94–97; and, in the pertinent context of filmic representation, Susan Lederer, "Repellent Subjects: Hollywood Censorship and Surgical Images in the 1930s," *Literature and Medicine* 17, no. 1 (1998): 91–113.

34. Russell, *Victory in My Hands*, 187.

35. Harold Russell puts it like this: "The young sailor of [Kantor's] story . . . was a spastic. That very nearly made a spastic out of Goldwyn." Ibid., 171.

36. Anderegg, *William Wyler*, 128.

37. David Church, "Fantastic Films, Fantastic Bodies: Speculations on the Fantastic and Disability Representation," *Offscreen* 10, no. 10 (October 31, 2006), 1–3.

38. Beth Linker, personal communication to the author, May 14, 2012.

39. Russell, *Best Years of My Life*, 39.

40. Russell, *Victory in My Hands*, 193–94.

41. I thank Beth Linker for this formulation. Beth Linker, personal communication to the author, May 14, 2012.

42. Kantor, *Glory for Me*, 250.

43. David Serlin, "The Architecture of Empathy" (Arcus Lecture, University of California–Berkeley, March 16, 2011).

44. Earl Carlson, *Born That Way* (New York: John Day Co., 1941), 95. Linker, *War's Waste*, 53, notes that many orthopedists who created rehabilitation regimes were disabled themselves.

45. Robert McRuer has used this phrase in a number of contexts, including "Crip Citizenship: Neoliberalism, Affect, Intensity" (presentation at the conference "Civil Disabilities: Theory, Citizenship, and the Body," University of Pennsylvania, March 31, 2011).

46. Carlson, *Born That Way*, 84.

47. "Medicine: Tilney Memorial," *Time*, May 6, 1940.

48. On "dead citizenship," the foundational source is Lauren Berlant, *The Queen of America Goes to Washington City: Essays on Sex and Citizenship* (Durham, N.C.: Duke University Press, 1997).

49. James Agee, "The Best Years of Our Lives," *Nation*, December 14, 1946.

50. MacKinlay Kantor, "A Manuscript of a War Narrative," n.d., MacKinlay Kantor Collection, Library of Congress.

51. Ibid., n.p.

52. Margot Canaday, *The Straight State: Sexuality and Citizenship in Twentieth-Century America* (Princeton, N.J.: Princeton University Press, 2011); Serlin, "Architecture of Empathy"; David Matless, "Moral Geographies of English Landscape," *Landscape Research* 22, no. 2 (1997): 141–55.

53. Gerber, "Heroes and Misfits," 12; Kozloff, *Best Years of Our Lives*, 34.

54. Gerber, "Anger and Affability," 13; Marx, *Goldwyn*, 308, 311.

55. Kozloff, *Best Years of Our Lives*, 13, notes that "Sherwood was writing the script and debating each scene with Goldwyn and Wyler through the autumn of 1945 and winter months of 1946. The generals' decisions to keep troops [waiting for demobilization] in unstable areas, the War Department's bureaucracy, a severe shortage of ships and railway snafus led to great frustration. Servicemen waiting in overseas outposts took to the streets in angry protests; the near 'mutiny' in Manila of 20,000 servicemen in January 1946 demonstrated their sharp discontent."

By election day in August 1946, veterans in one town in Tennessee had opposed vote fixing by taking up arms in a shoot-out against a long-entrenched political ring, making use of the combat tactics they had learned overseas, in what came to be called "the Battle of Athens." "Will the vets of World War II turn into the Storm Troopers who will destroy democracy?" Columbia University social work professor Willard Waller had asked two years earlier. David Gerber, "Heroes and Misfits," 548, notes that Waller was particularly concerned that disabled veterans would be especially prone to antisocial violence.

56. Norden, *Cinema of Isolation*, 162.

57. Ibid.

58. "*Till the End of Time*," writes Norden, "was seriously hampered by a low budget and mediocre acting" on the part of Guy Madison (*Cinema of Isolation*, 163). Kozloff describes the film as "heavy on cloying patriotic sentiment" (*Best Years of Our Lives*, 26).

59. Niven Busch, *They Dream of Home* (New York: Grosset and Dunlap, 1944), 7.

60. Ibid., 11.

61. Aaron Belkin, *Bring Me Men: Military Masculinity and the Benign Facade of American Empire, 1898–2001* (New York: Columbia University Press, 2012), 127.

62. Busch, *They Dream of Home*, 258.

63. Gerber, "Heroes and Misfits," 552.

64. Busch, *They Dream of Home*, 283.

65. Not that the scene is not filled with anxious undercurrents—particularly on the question of what kind of sex, and with what pleasures for whom, the bride and groom are about to engage in; see Michel, "Danger on the Home Front." I thank Nancy J. Hirschmann for reminding me of this ongoing conflict.

66. The echo of the signature title of the World Institute on Disability's annual keynote events, "Ever Widening Circle," is deliberate. See World Institute on Disability, accessed April 4 2014, http://www.wid.org.

67. Russell, *Victory in My Hands*, 232–34.

68. Russell, *Best Years of My Life*, 157.

69. Robert Warshow, "The Anatomy of Falsehood," 1947; reprinted in *The Immediate Experience: Movies, Comics, Theatre and Other Aspects of Popular Culture* (Cambridge, Mass.: Harvard University Press, 2001), 128.

70. Ibid., 130.

71. Douglas Baynton, "Disability and the Justification of Inequality in Amjerican History," in *The New Disability History: American Perspectives*, ed. Paul K. Longmore and Lauri Umansky (New York: New York University Press, 2001), 52.

72. Erich Auerbach, *Mimesis: The Representation of Reality in Western Literature*, trans. Willard Trask (Princeton, N.J.: Princeton University Press, 1953; originally published in German in 1946), 3.

## Chapter 2. Defect

1. Simo Vehmas, "Live and Let Die? Disability in Bioethics," *New Review of Bioethics* 1, no. 1 (November 2003): 145–57; Ayo Wahlberg, "Reproductive Medicine and the Concept of 'Quality,'" *Clinical Ethics* 3, no. 4 (December 2008): 160–63; Jackie Leach Scully, "Disability and Genetics in the Era of Genomic Medicine," *Nature* 9 (October 2008): 797–802.

2. Charles Darwin, *Variation of Animals and Plants Under Domestication*, vol. 1 (New York: D. Appleton and Co., 1915), 6.

3. Charles Darwin, *The Descent of Man, and Selection in Relation to Sex* (New York: D. Appleton and Co., 1871), 161–62.

4. Martin S. Pernick found that although most eugenicists took a public position against euthanasia, few openly spoke against the physician Harry Haiselden when he advocated and practiced euthanasia of "defective" infants; *The Black Stork: Eugenics and the Death of "Defective" Babies in American Medicine and Motion Pictures Since 1915* (New York: Oxford University Press, 1996), 84–85.

5. Robert DeCourcy Ward, *Crisis in Our Immigration Policy*, Publications of the Immigration Restriction League, no. 61 (Boston: Immigration Restriction League, 1913), 7.

6. James W. Trent, Jr., *Inventing the Feeble Mind: A History of Mental Retardation in the United States* (Berkeley: University of California Press, 1994), 131–83; Philip R. Reilly, *The Surgical Solution: A History of Involuntary Sterilization in the United States* (Baltimore: Johns Hopkins University Press, 1991).

7. Harry H. Laughlin, "Eugenical Sterilization in the United States," *Social Hygiene* 6, no. 4 (October 1920): 530.

8. Albert Edward Wiggam, *The New Decalogue of Science* (Garden City, N.Y.: Garden City Pub. Co., 1925), 110–11.

9. American Eugenics Society, *A Eugenics Catechism* (New Haven, Conn.: The Society, 1926), 10.

10. Pernick, *Black Stork*, 95–96.

11. Laws restricting Asian immigration have usually been treated as a separate body of legislation. See Mae M. Ngai, *Impossible Subjects: Illegal Aliens and the Making*

*of Modern America* (Princeton, N.J.: Princeton University Press, 2004), 18; Lucy Salyer, *Laws Harsh as Tigers: Chinese Immigrants and the Shaping of Modern Immigration Law* (Chapel Hill: University of North Carolina Press, 1995), viii, 32; and Roger Daniels, *Guarding the Golden Door: American Immigration Policy and Immigrants Since 1882* (New York: Hill and Wang, 2004), 3, 19–26.

12. On disability and the construction of race, see Douglas C. Baynton, "Disability and the Justification of Inequality in American History," in *The New Disability History: American Perspectives*, ed. Paul K. Longmore and Lauri Umansky (New York: New York University Press, 2001), 33–57.

13. John B. Weber and Charles Stewart Smith, "Our National Dumping-Ground: A Study of Immigration," *North American Review* 154 (April 1892): 425.

14. George Lydston, *The Diseases of Society and Degeneracy* (Philadelphia: J. B. Lippincott Co., 1908 [1904]), 93.

15. Francis Galton, "Studies in Eugenics," *American Journal of Sociology* 11, no. 1 (July 1905): 23.

16. Letter from Victor Safford to the Commissioner, May 16, 1906, Immigration Restriction League Records, US 10583.9.8–US 10587.43, box 4, folder Safford, M. Victor, "Definitions of Various Medical Terms Used in Medical Certificates, 1906," Houghton Library, Harvard University.

17. Martin W. Barr, *Mental Defectives: Their History, Treatment, and Training* (Philadelphia: P. Blakiston's Co., 1904), 100–101.

18. "The Study of the Criminal," *Boston Medical and Surgical Journal* 125 (July–December 1891): 579.

19. United States Public Health Service (USPHS), *Regulations Governing the Medical Inspection of Aliens* (Washington, D.C.: Government Printing Office, 1917), 16–19; Douglas C. Baynton, "Defectives in the Land: Disability and American Immigration Policy, 1882–1924," *Journal of American Ethnic History* 24 (Spring 2005): 31–44.

20. Philip Taylor, *The Distant Magnet: European Immigration to the U.S.A.* (New York: Harper and Row, 1971), 241–42.

21. Alan M. Kraut, *Silent Travelers: Germs, Genes, and the "Immigrant Menace"* (New York: Basic Books, 1994), 54–57.

22. Similar critiques have been made in other fields of history. See Beth Linker, *War's Waste: Rehabilitation in World War I America* (Chicago: University of Chicago Press, 2011); David Gerber, *Disabled Veterans in History* (Ann Arbor: University of Michigan Press, 2000); David Serlin, *Replaceable You: Engineering the Body in Postwar America* (Chicago: University of Chicago Press, 2004); and Henry Friedlander, *The Origins of Nazi Genocide: From Euthanasia to the Final Solution* (Chapel Hill: North Carolina University Press, 1995).

23. Claudia Goldin, "The Political Economy of Immigration Restriction in the United States, 1890 to 1921," in *The Regulated Economy: A Historical Approach to Political Economy*, ed. Claudia Goldin and Gary D. Libecap (Chicago: University of Chicago Press, 1994), 223.

24. Hasia R. Diner, *The Jews of the United States, 1654 to 2000* (Berkeley: University of California Press, 2004), 75.

25. Randall Hansen and Desmond King, "Eugenic Ideas, Political Interests, and Policy Variance: Immigration and Sterilization Policy in Britain and the U.S.," *World Politics* 53, no. 2 (January 2001): 242.

26. Ngai, *Impossible Subjects*, 17.

27. Michael Lemay and Elliott Robert Barkan, eds., *U.S. Immigration and Naturalization Laws and Issues: A Documentary History* (Westport, Conn.: Greenwood Press, 1999), 41.

28. *United States Statutes at Large*, vol. 22 (Washington, D.C.: Government Printing Office, 1883), 214 (hereafter, abbreviated as *U.S. Statutes*); *U.S. Statutes*, vol. 26 (1891), 1084; *U.S. Statutes*, vol. 34 (1907), 898–99; emphases added.

29. United States, *Annual Report of the Commissioner-General of Immigration* (Washington, D.C.: Government Printing Office, 1907), 62. Hereafter, the *Annual Report* is cited by title and year alone.

30. *U.S. Statutes*, vol. 32 (1903), 1213; *U.S. Statutes*, vol. 34 (1907), 898; USPHS, *Regulations*, 25–26, 28–29, 30–31.

31. Victor Safford, *Immigration Problems: Personal Experiences of an Official* (New York: Dodd, Mead, 1925), 244–46.

32. Quoted in Elizabeth Yew, "Medical Inspection of Immigrants at Ellis Island, 1891–1924," *Bulletin of the New York Academy of Medicine* 56 (June 1980): 497–98.

33. *Physical Examination of Immigrants: Hearings Before the Committee on Immigration and Naturalization, House of Representatives*, 66th Cong., 3rd Sess. (January 11, 1921), 11.

34. Allan McLaughlin, "How Immigrants Are Inspected," *Popular Science Monthly* 66 (February 1905): 359; Amy L. Fairchild, *Science at the Borders: Immigrant Medical Inspection and the Shaping of the Modern Industrial Labor Force* (Baltimore: Johns Hopkins University Press, 2003), 90; Kraut, *Silent Travelers*, 55.

35. United States Government, *Abstracts of Reports of the Immigration Commission*, vol. 1 (Washington, D.C.: Government Printing Office, 1911), 35.

36. Ibid.; *Annual Report of the Commissioner-General of Immigration*, 1912, 125.

37. Figures until 1910 can be found in United States Government, *Abstracts*, vol. 1, 110–11. Figures for 1915 and 1920 can be found in: *Annual Report of the Commissioner-General of Immigration*, 1915, 51; *Annual Report of the Commissioner-General of Immigration*, 1920, 9.

38. *U.S. Statutes*, vol. 27 (1893), 569; *U.S. Statutes*, vol. 34 (1907), 901–2.

39. Edith Abbott, *Immigration: Select Documents and Case Records* (Chicago: University of Chicago Press, 1924), 71; *Annual Report of the Commissioner-General of Immigration*, 1907, 62, 83; United States, *Annual Report of the Superintendent of Immigration* (Washington, D.C.: Government Printing Office, 1894), 12–13 (hereafter, the *Annual Report* is cited by title and year alone); United States Government,

*Abstracts*, vol. 1, 26. Fairchild, *Science at the Borders*, 56–63, describes the multiple inspections immigrants faced.

40. John Higham, *Strangers in the Land: Patterns of American Nativism, 1860–1925* (1955; repr., New Brunswick, N.J.: Rutgers University Press, 1998), 99, 186–87.

41. *U.S. Statutes*, vol. 34 (1907), 898–99.

42. Higham, *Strangers in the Land*, 162–63, 186–87, 202–4.

43. Marion T. Bennett, *American Immigration Policies: A History* (Washington, D.C.: Public Affairs Press, 1963), 15, 29.

44. Edward Prince Hutchinson, *Legislative History of American Immigration Policy, 1798–1965* (Philadelphia: University of Pennsylvania Press, 1981), 167.

45. Roger Daniels, *Coming to America: A History of Immigration and Ethnicity in American Life* (New York: HarperCollins, 1990), 274, 278–79.

46. Kenneth M. Ludmerer, *Genetics and American Society: A Historical Appraisal* (Baltimore: Johns Hopkins University Press, 1972), 96–97.

47. See Paul Longmore and David Goldberger, "The League of the Physically Handicapped and the Great Depression: A Case Study in the New Disability History," *Journal of American History* 87 (December 2000): 888–922.

48. Deirdre M. Moloney, "Women, Sexual Morality, and Economic Dependency in Early U.S. Deportation Policy," *Journal of Women's History* 18, no. 2 (Summer 2006): 98.

49. Quoted in Brad Byrom, "A Pupil and a Patient: Hospital Schools in Progressive America," in Longmore and Umansky, *New Disability History*, 138–39.

50. Robert M. Buchanan, *Illusions of Equality: Deaf Americans in School and Factory, 1850–1950* (Washington, D.C.: Gallaudet University Press, 1999), 75–76.

51. Gertrude R. Stein, "Placement Technique in the Employment Work of the Red Cross for Crippled and Disabled Men," in *Publications of the Red Cross Institute for Crippled and Disabled Men*, series 1, ed. Douglas C. McMurtrie (New York: Red Cross Institute, 1918), 3–4.

52. Frank B. Gilbreth and Lillian Moller Gilbreth, *Motion Study for the Handicapped* (London: Routledge, 1920), 27, 135–36.

53. National Archives, Records of the Immigration and Naturalization Service (INS), RG 85, entry 7, file 48,599/4.

54. National Archives, Records of the INS, RG 85, entry 7, file 49833-2.

55. National Archives, Records of the INS, RG 85, accession no. 60A600, file 53,700/974.

56. National Archives, Records of the INS, RG 85, accession no. 60A600, file 51,806–16.

57. See, for example, Richmond Mayo-Smith, *Emigration and Immigration: A Study in Social Science* (New York: Charles Scribner's Sons, 1890), 276; *Annual Report of the Commissioner-General of Immigration*, 1897, 4–5; and Frederick A. Bushee, "Ethnic Factors in the Population of Boston," *Publications of the American Economic Association*, 3rd ser., 4, no. 2 (May 1903): 12.

58. *Annual Report of the Superintendent of Immigration*, 1893, 8, 11.

59. Ibid., 10–11.

60. *Annual Report of the Superintendent of Immigration*, 1894, 12–13.

61. *Annual Report of the Commissioner-General of Immigration*, 1895, 13.

62. *Annual Report of the Commissioner-General of Immigration*, 1897, 4–5.

63. Weber and Smith, "Our National Dumping-Ground," 437–38; William E. Chandler, "Shall Immigration Be Suspended?," *North American Review* 156, no. 434 (January 1893): 4, 6–8; Dr. Joseph H. Senner, "How We Restrict Immigration," *North American Review* 158, no. 449 (April 1894): 498.

64. Henry Sidney Everett, "Immigration and Naturalization," *Atlantic Monthly* 75 (March 1895): 352.

65. United States Government, *Abstracts*, vol. 1, 47–49.

66. United States Immigration Commission, *Reports of the Immigration Commission: Immigration Legislation*, vol. 39 (U.S. Government Printing Office, 1911), 47, 56.

67. Immigration Restriction League, *The Reading Test: Why It Should Be Adopted*, Publications of the Immigration Restriction League, no. 63 (Boston: Immigration Restriction League, 1914), 5; Immigration Restriction League, *Constitution of the Immigration Restriction League* (Boston: Immigration Restriction League, 1894 or 1895), 1.

68. Prescott Hall, "Selection of Immigration," *Annals of the American Academy of Political and Social Science* 24, no. 1 (July 1904): 179, 182. Robert DeCourcy Ward, "The Immigration Problem," *Charities* 12 (February 1904): 138, 150. See also Robert De C. Ward, "National Eugenics in Relation to Immigration," *North American Review* 192 (1910): 64; and Winfield S. Alcott, "The Modern Problem of Immigration," *New England Magazine* 34 (July 1906): 553, 560, 562.

69. See Hall, "Selection of Immigration," 179, 182.

70. Immigration Restriction League, *Brief in Favor of the Illiteracy Test*, Publications of the Immigration Restriction League, No. 56 (Boston: Immigration Restriction League, 1910), 4.

71. Prescott Hall, "Immigration and the Educational Test," *North American Review* 165, no. 491 (October 1897): 395.

72. Robert DeCourcy Ward, "Race Betterment and Our Immigration Laws," in *Official Proceedings of the National Conference on Race Betterment* (Battle Creek, Mich.: Race Betterment Foundation, 1914), 543; Ward, "Immigration Problem," 140.

73. Ward, "Immigration Problem," 147–49.

74. Charles Benedict Davenport, *Heredity in Relation to Eugenics* (New York: Henry Holt and Co., 1911), 222–24.

75. Chandler, "Shall Immigration Be Suspended?," 8.

76. Laughlin, "Eugenical Sterilization in the United States," 531.

77. Alcott, "Modern Problem of Immigration," 560.

78. *Annual Report of the Commissioner-General of Immigration*, 1898, 32.

79. "Immigration Problems Before the Nation," *New York Times*, May 24, 1903, 3; William Williams, "Ellis Island Station," in *Annual Report of the Commissioner-General of Immigration*, 1904, 105–6; William Williams, "The New Immigration:

Some Unfavorable Features and Possible Remedies," *Proceedings of the National Conference of Charities and Correction* 33 (Philadelphia, May 1906), 7–8; William Williams, "Remarks on Immigration," quoted in Kraut, *Silent Travelers*, 68, 298n57.

80. Letter from Frank P. Sargent, Commissioner-General of the Bureau of Immigration, to the Commissioner of Immigration on Ellis Island, April 17, 1905, National Archives, Records of the Public Health Service, RG 90, entry 10, file 219.

81. Robert DeCourcy Ward to Frank P. Sargent, Commissioner-General of Immigration, Washington, D.C., dated January 11, 1905, Records of the Immigration and Naturalization Service, RG 85, entry 9, file 51490/19; Robert DeCourcy Ward, "National Eugenics in Relation to Immigration," *North American Review* 192 (1910): 67; Prescott Hall, *Immigration and Its Effects upon the United States* (New York: Holt, 1906), 87, 244; *U.S. Statutes*, vol. 34 (1907), 898–99.

82. Alfred C. Reed, "The Medical Side of Immigration," *Popular Science Monthly* 80 (April 1912): 390.

83. *Annual Report of the Commissioner-General of Immigration*, 1910, 5.

84. Montaville Flowers, *The Japanese Conquest of American Opinion* (New York: George H. Doran, 1917), 261.

85. Edward M. East, "Population Pressure and Immigration," in *The Alien in Our Midst; or, Selling Our Birthright for a Mess of Industrial Pottage*, ed. Madison Grant and Charles Steward Davison (New York: Galton Publishing Co., 1930), 93, 97.

86. Letter dated June 10, 1911, letterhead: Dr. Arthur L. Fisk, NYC, Immigration Restriction League Records, US10583.9.8–US10587.43, box 2: "Correspondence: Fe–Q," folder "Fisk, Arthur L.," Houghton Library, Harvard University.

87. Irving Fisher, "Impending Problems of Eugenics," *Scientific Monthly* 13, no. 3 (September 1921): 214, 227–30.

88. *Physical Examination of Immigrants*, 11.

89. "Two Immigrants out of Five Feebleminded," *Survey*, September 15, 1917, 528–29. See also Trent, *Inventing the Feeble Mind*, 166–69.

90. Thomas Wray Grayson, "The Effect of the Modern Immigrant on Our Industrial Centers," in *Medical Problems of Immigration* (Easton, Pa.: American Academy of Medicine, 1913), 103, 107–9.

91. Bushee, "Ethnic Factors in the Population of Boston," 82–83, 150.

92. Reed, "Medical Side of Immigration," 389; "Going Through Ellis Island," *Popular Science Monthly* 82 (January 1913): 8–9; "Immigration and the Public Health," *Popular Science Monthly* 83 (October 1913): 325.

93. Edward Alsworth Ross, *The Old World and the New: The Significance of Past and Present Immigration to the American People* (New York: Century Co., 1914), 285–90.

94. James J. Davis, *Selective Immigration* (St. Paul, Minn.: Scott Mitchell Publishing Co., 1925), 33, 86.

95. See, for example, Eithne Luibhéid, *Entry Denied: Controlling Sexuality at the Border* (Minneapolis: University of Minnesota Press, 2002); and Martha Gardner, *The*

*Qualities of a Citizen: Women, Immigration, and Citizenship, 1870–1965* (Princeton, N.J.: Princeton University Press, 2005).

96. Salyer, *Laws Harsh as Tigers*, 15–16.

97. G. K. Chesterton, *Eugenics and Other Evils* (London: Cassell and Company, 1922), 178–79.

98. See Trent, *Inventing the Feeble Mind*, 131–83; Susan M. Schweik, *The Ugly Laws: Disability in Public* (New York: New York University Press, 2009), 63–84, 165–204; and Pernick, *Black Stork*, 41–80.

## Chapter 3. The Disremembered Past

1. *Meriam-Webster Dictionary*, s.v. "Remember."

2. Although the subject of formal commemoration and memorialization falls outside this essay's purview, the interested reader can find an entire historiography built around the issue. Gaines Fosters's wonderful book *Ghosts of the Confederacy: Defeat, the Lost Cause, and the Emergence of the New South* (New York: Oxford University Press, 1987) is an early example. There are many other studies that analyze both the memory of the Civil War and those of other wars and atrocities. In addition, there are also many analyses of the role of commemoration and memorialization in social history. A comprehensive bibliography can be found at http://www.indiana.edu/~cshm /books.html.

3. Glenda Gilmore, *Gender and Jim Crow: Women and the Politics of White Supremacy in North Carolina, 1896–1920* (Chapel Hill: University of North Carolina Press, 1996), xvi.

4. See, for example, W. Fitzhugh Brundage, *Lynching in the New South: Georgia and Virginia, 1880–1930* (Urbana: University of Illinois Press, 1993); Estelle B. Freedman, *Redefining Rape: Sexual Violence in the Era of Suffrage and Segregation* (Cambridge, Mass: Harvard University Press, 2013); Janice Brockley, "Martyred Mothers and Merciful Fathers: Exploring Disability and Motherhood in the Lives of Jerome Greenfield and Raymond Repouille," in *The New Disability History: American Perspectives*, ed. Paul K. Longmore and Lauri Umansky (New York: New York University Press, 2001), 293–312; Benjamin Madley, "From Africa to Auschwitz: How German South West Africa Incubated Ideas and Methods Adopted and Developed by the Nazis in Eastern Europe," *European History Quarterly* 35, no. 3 (July 2005): 429–64; and Madley, "The Genocide of California's Yana Indians," in *Centuries of Genocide: Essays and Eyewitness Accounts*, ed. Samuel Totten and William S. Parsons (New York: Routledge, 2013), 16–53.

5. Katherine Ott, David Serlin, and Stephen Mihm, eds., *Artificial Parts and Practical Lives: Modern Histories of Prosthetics* (New York: New York University Press, 2002); Paul K. Longmore, *Why I Burned My Book* (Philadelphia: Temple University Press, 2003); Kim Nielsen, *A Disability History of the United States* (Boston: Beacon Press, 2013).

6. According to a U.S. census resource, issued in 2008 and focusing on 2005, approximately 20 percent of the American population has an identifiable disability. Given the stigma attached to disability, among other factors, the actual numbers are likely much higher than this. See, for example, "Americans with Disabilities: 2005," March 15, 2014, http://www.census.gov/prod/2008pubs/p70-117.pdf.

7. Gerda Lerner, *The Creation of Patriarchy* (New York: Oxford University Press, 1986), *passim*; Gerda Lerner, *The Majority Finds Its Past: Placing Women in History* (New York: Oxford University Press, 1979), 145–46.

8. See, for example, Wendy Brown, *States of Injury: Power and Freedom in Late Modernity* (Princeton, N.J.: Princeton University Press, 1995).

9. See for example, Evelyn Brooks Higginbotham, "African American Women's History and the Metalanguage of Race," *Signs* 17, no. 2 (Winter 1992): 251–74; Vicky Ruiz, *From Out of the Shadows: Mexican Women in Twentieth-century America* (New York: Oxford University Press, 1998); Vicky Ruiz and Ellen DuBois, *Unequal Sisters: A Multicultural Reader in US Women's History* (New York: Routledge, 2000).

10. Wendy Brown, "The Impossibility of Women's Studies," *differences: A Journal of Feminist Cultural Studies* 9, no. 3 (1997): 79–101.

11. Historian Charles Joyner offers this phrase to describe microhistories. See, for example, Joyner, foreword to *Ballots and Fence Rails: Reconstruction on the Lower Cape Fear*, by William McKee Evans (Athens: University of Georgia Press, 1995), xii.

12. For a broader study of Junius Wilson's life, see Susan Burch and Hannah Joyner, *Unspeakable: The Story of Junius Wilson* (Chapel Hill: University of North Carolina Press, 2007). This work focuses especially on the ways racism, language, eugenics, institutionalization, and civil rights shaped Wilson's experiences as a black deaf man in the South.

13. David left in the early 1890s when the legislature moved the white deaf school to Morganton, but Thomas stayed on, working with the black deaf students for another decade.

14. Susan Burch, personal correspondence with Mary Herring Wright, April 2001. For more on black sign language, see James Woodward, Jr., "Black Southern Signing," *Language in Society* 5 (1975): 211–18; John Lewis, Carrie Palmer, and Leandra Williams, "Existence of and Attitudes Toward Black Variations of Sign Language," in *Communications Forum*, vol. 4, ed. Laura Byers, Jessica Chaiken, and Monica Mueller (Washington, D.C.: School of Communication, 1995), 416–28; Anthony J. Aramburo, "Sociolinguistic Aspects of the Black Deaf Community," in *The Sociolinguistics of the Deaf Community*, ed. Ceil Lucas (New York: Academic Press, 1989); and Ceil Lucas, Robert Bayley, and Clayton Valli, *Sociolinguistic Variation in American Sign Language* (Washington, D.C.: Gallaudet University Press, 2001).

15. Susan Burch, personal correspondence with Mary Herring Wright (April 2001). According to Roger Williams, a social worker hired to evaluate Wilson, "The schools being segregated, [Wilson's] school did not have access to the same quality of

teachers and as a result, the school kind of made up its own sign language, if you will. In part there is an American Sign Language vocabulary component, but there are also signs that sort of the school made up over the years. . . . There are one or two signs that are sort of unique to that school . . . But because [the school] was so segregated, that was true even more so, and so the students kind of taught themselves sign and it was kind of handed down over the years." Roger Williams, Deposition, December 11, 1995, 13.

16. This kind of cultural expression was common at virtually all-residential deaf schools during the nineteenth and twentieth centuries. Graduates of both African American and white schools offer similar anecdotes about school life: Everett Parker, interview by Susan Burch, March 21, 2002; and Jack Gannon, *Deaf Heritage* (Silver Spring, Md.: National Association of the Deaf, 1981). For more on the school Wilson attended, see Manuel Houston Crockett and Barbara Crockett Dease, *Through the Years, 1867–1977: Light out of Darkness; A History of the North Carolina School for the Negro Blind and the Deaf* (Raleigh, N.C.: Barefoot Press, 1990). For more on American deaf culture in general, see Carol Padden and Tom Humphries, *Deaf in America: Voices from a Culture* (Cambridge, Mass.: Harvard University Press, 1988); and Carol Padden and Tom Humphries, *Inside Deaf Culture* (Cambridge, Mass.: Harvard University Press, 2005).

17. A close reading of student records reveals strongly gendered patterns in combination with racial, disability, and class assumptions: "unsatisfactory conduct" for boys typically marked insolent behavior; girls received this label for "sexual immorality"; other girls who were caught having sexual relations were expelled for "feeblemindedness."

18. Student record: Junius Wilson, North Carolina School for the Deaf and Blind, Negro Department (Morganton, N.C.: State School for the Deaf Archives).

19. As scholars Steven Noll, J. David Smith, James Trent, Michael Rembis, and others have noted, the term "feebleminded" encompasses a long history. In eugenic theories, this term typically referred to individuals with heritable and incurable cognitive disabilities. In reality, "feebleminded" reflected a broad array of stigmatized identities, including, but not limited to, poverty (real or perceived), sexual deviance, and (multi) racial or ethnic-minority status. The 1927 U.S. Supreme Court decision in *Buck v. Bell*, which upheld the constitutionality of forced sterilization, drew heavily on eugenic concerns over "the menace of the feebleminded." For more on the history of feeblemindedness, see James W. Trent, Jr., *Inventing the Feeble Mind* (Berkeley: University of California Press, 1994); J. David Smith, *Minds Made Feeble: The Myth and Legacy of the Kallikaks* (Rockville, Md.: Aspen, 1985); Steven Noll, *Feeble-Minded in Our Midst: Institutions for the Mentally Retarded in the South, 1900–1940* (Chapel Hill: University of North Carolina Press, 1995); and Michael Rembis, *Defining Deviance: Sex, Science, and Delinquent Girls, 1890–1960* (Chicago: University of Illinois Press, 2011).

20. For more on deinstitutionalization, see, for example, Fuller Torrey, *Out of the Shadows: Confronting America's Mental Illness Crisis* (New York: John Wiley and Sons,

1997). Excerpts from this book can be found at "Deinstitutionalization: A Psychiatric Titanic," PBS, accessed July 3, 2013, http://www.pbs.org/wgbh/pages/frontline/shows /asylums/special/excerpt.html.

21. Physician questionnaire for Junius Wilson, December 29, 1975. Author has copy of questionnaire on file.

22. Treatment team review, October 19, 1978, Junius Wilson medical file.

23. Treatment plan notes, July 27, 1978, Junius Wilson medical file.

24. Rick Mileski, social worker, April 24, 1980, report of Community House Screening Team, Junius Wilson medical file.

25. Rachel Wright, interview by Susan Burch, August 6, 2003.

26. See, for example, John Van Cleve and Barry Crouch, *A Place of Their Own: Creating the Deaf Community in America* (Washington, D.C.: Gallaudet University Press, 1989); Harlan L. Lane, Robert Hoffmeister, and Benjamin J. Bahan, *A Journey into the Deaf-World* (San Diego: DawnSign Press, 1996); and John Vickrey Van Cleve, ed., *The Deaf History Reader* (Washington, D.C.: Gallaudet University Press, 2007).

27. Padden and Humphries, *Inside Deaf Culture*, 14.

28. See, for example, ibid., 13.

29. Chimamanda Adichie, "The Danger of a Single Story," TEDTalk, accessed March 10, 2013, http://www.ted.com/talks/chimamanda_adichie_the_danger_of_a_ single_story.html. For a transcript of this talk, see http://dotsub.com/view/63ef5d28 -6607-4fec-b906-aaae6cff7dbe/viewTranscript/eng?timed=true.

30. See, for example, Van Cleve and Crouch, *Place of Their Own*; Lane, Hoffmeister, and Bahan, *Journey into the Deaf World*; Jack Gannon, *Deaf Heritage: A Narrative History of Deaf America* (Washington, D.C.: Gallaudet University Press, 2012); John Van Cleve, ed., *Deaf History Unveiled: Interpretations from the New Scholarship* (Washington, D.C.: Gallaudet University Press, 1999); and Leila Monaghan, Constanze Schmaling, Karen Nakamura, and Graham H. Turner, eds., *Many Ways to Be Deaf: International Variation in Deaf Communities* (Washington, D.C.: Gallaudet University Press, 2003).

31. See, for example, "Three Cases," *Silent Worker* 32, no. 4 (January 1920): 108; and "The Crime of Parents," *Silent Worker* 18, no. 10 (July 1906): 153.

32. See, for example, Douglas Bayton, Jack R. Gannon, and Jean Lindquist Bergey, *Through Deaf Eyes: A Photographic History of an American Community* (Washington, D.C.: Gallaudet University Press, 2007), 29. The film *Through Deaf Eyes* also recounts multiple stories by deaf people about their initial experiences at the deaf schools. Lawrence R. Hott, dir., *Through Deaf Eyes* (Washington, D.C.: WETA and Florentine Films, 2007). See also Mary Herring Wright, *Sounds Like Home* (Washington, D.C.: Gallaudet University Press, 1999), 87.

33. Maxine Childress Brown, *On the Beat of Truth: A Hearing Daughter's Stories of Her Black Deaf Parents* (Washington, D.C.: Gallaudet University Press, 2013), 32.

34. For example, Helen Heckman, *My Life Transformed* (New York: MacMillan, 1928), 5–6; Padden and Humphries, *Deaf in America*; and National Theatre for the

Deaf, *My Third Eye* (1971). Articles in deaf newspapers echo this. See, for example, "Three Cases," 108. which describes the partings between parents and children as "heart breaking"; and "Crime of Parents," 153, which describes parents who resist efforts to place their children in residential schools because of their "great affection" and desire to have the children stay and work at home. "A Valuable Hint to Parents," *Silent Worker* 12, no. 1 (September 1899): 9, describes parents who leave their children only to return one or two days later to retrieve them because it is too painful for the parents to be apart from their offspring. The article praises parents who let their children stay at school. "Parental Wisdom," *Silent Worker* 20, no. 7 (April 1908): 130, offers an allegorical story of two families with children at deaf schools. Both children and parents struggle with separation, but the deaf children eventually recover. The different parental responses to their children's separation teaches readers that it is best to leave the children at the school. "The Change in Demeanor," *Silent Worker* 23, no. 9 (June 1911): 170, describes the evolution of children before entering school (as ignorant and in darkness) to the slow realization of cultural expectations on identities. Although the article is laudatory of this evolution, it maps the process of significant transformation, underscoring the profound impact that removal from home to school typically brought.

35. From Bragg, *My Third Eye*, as translated by Carol Padden and Tom Humphries, in *Deaf in America: Voices from a Culture* (Cambridge: Harvard University Press, 1988), 18–19.

36. See also Albert Ballin, *A Deaf Mute Howls* (Washington, D.C.: Gallaudet University Press, 1998); Harry Lang, *Edmund Booth: Deaf Pioneer* (Washington, D.C.: Gallaudet University Press, 2004); Van Cleve and Crouch, *Place of Their Own*; and Hannah Joyner, *From Pity to Pride* (Washington, D.C.: Gallaudet University Press, 2004).

37. Padden and Humphries, *Inside Deaf Culture*, 13–14.

38. Mary Herring Wright, *Sounds like Home*, 88–89.

39. Maxine Childress Brown, *On the Beat of Truth*, 48–49.

40. Described by Rachel Wright, interview by Susan Burch, June 8, 2003.

41. William Novasky, *The Racial Desegregation Study: First Interim Report* (North Carolina, 1965), 10.

42. King specifically examines American Indians in his essay, but the assessment applies in many ways to Wilson and other incarcerated people. See C. Richard King, "The Good, the Bad, and the Mad: Making Up (Abnormal) People in Indian Country, 1900–1930," *European Journal of American Culture* 22, no. 1 (March 2003): 42.

43. Ibid.


Chapter 4. Integrating Disability, Transforming Disease History


1. Selman A. Waksman, *The Conquest of Tuberculosis* (Berkeley: University of California Press, 1964); George J. Wherrett, *The Miracle of the Empty Beds: A History*

*of Tuberculosis in Canada* (Toronto: University of Toronto Press, 1977); Thomas M. Daniel, *Captain of Death: The Story of Tuberculosis* (Rochester, N.Y.: University of Rochester Press, 1997); Leonard G. Wilson, "The Historical Decline of Tuberculosis in Europe and America: Its Causes and Significance," *Journal of the History of Medicine and Allied Sciences* 45, no. 3 (1990): 366–96.

2. Henry Sigerist, *Civilization and Disease* (Ithaca, N.Y.: Cornell University Press, 1943; repr., Chicago: University of Chicago Press, 1962), 81, as quoted in *Tuberculosis Then and Now: Perspectives on the History of an Infectious Disease*, ed. Linda Bryder, Flurin Condrau, and Michael Worboys (Montreal: McGill–Queen's University Press, 2010), 5. Before McKeown, René Dubos and Jean Dubos made a similar claim about the importance of living standards and nutrition in *The White Plague: Tuberculosis, Man and Society* (Boston: Little, Brown and Company, 1952).

3. For more on the historiography of tuberculosis history, see Nancy Tomes, "The White Plague Revisited," *Bulletin of the History of Medicine* 63 (1989): 467–80; Barbara Gutmann Rosenkrantz, preface to *From Consumption to Tuberculosis: A Documentary History* (New York: Garland Publishing, 1994), xiii–xxii; and Linda Bryder, Flurin Condrau, and Michael Worboys, "Tuberculosis and Its Histories: Then and Now," in Bryder, Condrau, and Worboys, *Tuberculosis Then and Now*, 3–23.

4. For an example of the "new" tuberculosis literature, see Matthew Gandy and Alimuddin I. Zumla, eds., *The Return of the White Plague: Global Poverty and the "New" Tuberculosis* (London: Verso, 2003).

5. Dorothy Porter "The Mission of Social History of Medicine: An Historical View," *Social History of Medicine* 8, no. 3 (1995): 348, as quoted in Bryder, Condrau, and Worboys, "Tuberculosis and Its Histories," 7.

6. Susan Sontag, *Illness as Metaphor* (New York: Farrar, Straus and Giroux, 1978), 11.

7. Bryder, Condrau, and Worboys, "Tuberculosis and Its Histories," 3. There are a few notable exceptions. See Beth Linker, *War's Waste: Rehabilitation in World War I America* (Chicago: University of Chicago Press, 2011), especially chap. 2. See also Meghan Crnic and Cynthia Connolly, " 'They Can't Help Getting Well Here': Seaside Hospital for Children in the United States, 1872–1917," *Journal of the History of Childhood and Youth* 2 (2009): 220–33.

8. See Emily K. Abel, *The Inevitable Hour: A History of Caring for Dying Patients in America* (Baltimore: Johns Hopkins University Press, 2013); and Abel, *Hearts of Wisdom: American Women Caring for Kin, 1850–1940* (Cambridge, Mass.: Harvard University Press, 2000).

9. For more on disability as an analytic frame, especially in relation to disease history and the history of medicine, see Beth Linker, "On the Borderland of Medical and Disability History," *Bulletin of the History of Medicine* 87, no. 4 (Winter 2013): 499–535. See also Douglas C. Baynton, "Disability and the Justification of Inequality in American History," in *The New Disability History: American Perspectives*, ed. Paul K. Long-

more and Lauri Umansky (New York: New York University Press, 2001), 33–57; and Julie Livingston, "Comment: On the Borderland of Medical and Disability History," *Bulletin of the History of Medicine* 87, no. 4 (Winter 2013): 560–64.

10. Just as Rosemary Garland-Thomson reappropriated feminist theory for the purpose of advancing work in feminist disability theory, we think that the same method of recruitment should be employed in medical history in order to transform traditional disease history narratives into disability history. Thomson, "Integrating Disability, Transforming Feminist Theory," *NWSA Journal* 14, No. 3 (Autumn 2002): 1–32.

11. The literature on tuberculosis history is quite extensive. For some examples of discussion of stigma and tuberculosis, see Barbara Bates, *Bargaining for Life: A Social History of Tuberculosis, 1876–1938* (Philadelphia: University of Pennsylvania Press, 1992); David S. Barnes, *The Making of a Social Disease: Tuberculosis in Nineteenth-Century France* (Berkeley: University of California Press, 1995); Linda Bryder, *Below the Magic Mountain: A Social History of Tuberculosis in Twentieth-Century Britain* (Oxford: Clarendon Press, 1988); Barron Lerner, *Contagion and Confinement: Controlling Tuberculosis Along the Skid Road* (Baltimore: Johns Hopkins University Press, 1998); Katherine Ott, *Fevered Lives: Tuberculosis in American Culture Since 1870* (Cambridge, Mass.: Harvard University Press, 1996); Randall M. Packard, *White Plague, Black Labor: Tuberculosis and the Political Economy of Health and Disease in South Africa* (Berkeley: University of California Press, 1989); and Sheila Rothman, *Living in the Shadow of Death: Tuberculosis and the Social Experience of Illness in American History* (New York: Basic Books, 1994).

12. Bryder, *Below the Magic Mountain*, 236–37.

13. Allison C. Carey, *On the Margins of Citizenship: Intellectual Disability and Civil Rights in Twentieth-Century America* (Philadelphia: Temple University Press, 2009), 1.

14. Nancy Fraser and Linda Gordon. "A Genealogy of Dependency: Tracing a Keyword of the U.S. Welfare State," *Signs* 19, no. 2 (January 1, 1994): 309–36. See also Emily K. Abel, "Valuing Care: Turn-of-the-Century Conflicts Between Charity Workers and Women Clients," *Journal of Women's History* 10, no. 3 (Autumn 1998): 33.

15. Simi Linton, *Claiming Disability: Knowledge and Identity* (New York: New York University Press, 1998), 118.

16. Adriana Petryna, "Biological Citizenship: The Science and Politics of Chernobyl-Exposed Populations," *Osiris* 19 (2004): 250–65; Petryna, *Life Exposed: Biological Citizens After Chernobyl*, 2nd ed. (Princeton, N.J.: Princeton University Press, 2013).

17. Of all the categories listed, freakery has been studied the most. See Rosemarie Garland Thomson, ed., *Freakery: Cultural Spectacles of the Extraordinary Body* (New York: New York University Press, 1996); and Robert Bogdan, *Freak Show: Presenting Human Oddities for Amusement and Profit* (Chicago: University of Chicago Press, 1988).

18. Linker, "On the Borderland of Medical and Disability History." For a useful essay on the etymology of disability and its variants, see Douglas C. Baynton, " 'These

Pushful Days': Time and Disability in the Age of Eugenics," *Health and History* 13, no. 2 (2011): 43–64. The most comprehensive account of how disability figures into and defines the modern welfare state is Deborah A. Stone, *The Disabled State* (Philadelphia: Temple University Press, 1984).

19. Peter Blanck and Chen Song, "Civil War Pension Attorneys and Disability Politics," *University of Michigan Journal of Law Reform* 35 (Fall 2001–Winter 2002): 1–81, 9.

20. Peter Blanck, "Civil War Pensions and Disability," *Ohio State Law Journal* 26 (2001): 109–249.

21. It is difficult to get an exact account of the amount of money paid out to Union veterans with consumption because secondary scholarship on the subject is virtually nonexistent. We deduced this number from Larry M. Logue and Peter David Blanck, *Race, Ethnicity, and Disability: Veterans and Benefits in Post–Civil War America* (New York: Cambridge University Press, 2010), 74–75. Logue and Blanck categorize pension applicants by certain disease categories. We took "pulmonary" complaints to be consumption, although other conditions could fall under the "pulmonary" category. More research in this area needs to be undertaken.

22. Throughout World War I, tuberculosis was "the leading cause of discharge for disability, accounting for 13.5 percent of all discharges." See U.S. Army Medical Department, Office of Medical History, "Tuberculosis," accessed November 19, 2013, http://history.amedd.army.mil/booksdocs/wwii/PM4/CH14.Tuberculosis.htm.

23. George E. Bushnell, "Tuberculosis Epidemiology in the World War," *Transactions of the American Climatological and Clinical Association* 37 (1921): 147–63, 151.

24. Linker, *War's Waste*, 13. See also Carol R. Byerly, *Good Tuberculosis Men: The Army Medical Department's Struggle with Tuberculosis* (Fort Sam Houston, Tex.: Borden Institute, 2013).

25. K. Walter Hickel, "Entitling Citizens: World War I, Progressivism, and the Origins of the American Welfare State, 1917–1928" (Ph.D. diss., Columbia University, 1999), 136.

26. "Report of Conference in Regard to Proposed Tubercular Clinics," December 18, 1923, file Od#1821, files of the Los Angeles County Board of Supervisors, Hall of Administration, Los Angeles.

27. Becky M. Nicolaides, "The Quest for Independence: Workers in the Suburbs," in *Metropolis in the Making: Los Angeles in the 1920s*, ed. Tom Sitton and William Deverell (Berkeley: University of California Press, 2001), 83.

28. Scott Gelber, "A 'Hard-Boiled Order': The Reeducation of Disabled World War I Veterans in New York City," *Journal of Social History* 39, no. 1 (2005): 161–80, 168.

29. Linker, *War's Waste*.

30. *Thirty-Second Biennial Reprot of the Department of Public Health of California for the Fiscal Years from July 1, 1930 to June 30, 1932* (Sacramento: State Printing Office, 1932).

31. Emily K. Abel, "Viewing Tuberculosis within the Context of the New Disability History," paper presented at the annual meeting of the American Association for the History of Medicine, 2002.

32. Ibid.

33. Hermann M. Biggs, *The Administrative Control of Tuberculosis* (New York: New York City Department of Health, 1909), 21.

34. New York City Charity Organization Society, *Home Treatment of Tuberculosis in New York City: Being a Report of the Relief Committee of the Committee on the Prevention of Tuberculosis of the New York City Charity Organization Society* (New York: New York City Charity Organization Society, 1908), 16. For more on how the histories of tuberculosis and alcoholism became linked in the twentieth century, see Lerner, *Contagion and Confinement.*

35. Charles-Edward Armory Winslow, *The Life of Hermann Biggs, M.D., D.Sc., LL.D., Physician and Statesman of Public Health* (Philadelphia: Lea and Febiger, 1929), 198.

36. Rothman, *Living in the Shadow of Death*, 209.

37. For more on the societal aversion to dependency, see Fraser and Gordon, "Genealogy of Dependency."

38. Brad Byrom, "A Pupil and a Patient: Hospital-Schools in Progressive America," in Longmore and Umansky, *New Disability History*, 133–56.

39. "Tuberculosis—Monthly Reports," June 12, 1934, California State Archives, Sacramento.

40. "Tuberculosis—Monthly Reports," January 1935, California State Archives, Sacramento, Califoria.

41. *53,052 Lives: A Brief History of the Los Angeles Tuberculosis and Health Association, with a Report of Activities for 1936* (Los Angeles: Los Angeles Tuberculosis and Health Association, 1937). As in the military sector, charitable and public programs at the state level provided financial assistance to people with tuberculosis long before the federal government mandated such relief. In 1910, for example, the New York City Charity Organization Society reported that 12 percent of the 5,387 families on its roster had at least one member with tuberculosis. Cited in Community Service Society, "Educational Nursing Service—Educational Nursing for Family Health," 1948, page 17, box 67, CSS Archive, Columbia University, New York. Figures compiled by the Los Angeles County Department of Charities in 1926 revealed that "tuberculosis was a factor" in a high proportion of the relief cases. See *Mexicans in California: Report of Governor C. C. Young's Mexican Fact-Finding Committee* (State Building: San Francisco, October 1930), 187.

42. See Emily K. Abel, *Tuberculosis and the Politics of Exclusion: A History of Public Health and Migration to Los Angeles* (New Brunswick, N.J.: Rutgers University Press, 2007).

43. Amy L. Fairchild, *Science at the Borders: Immigrant Medical Inspection and the Shaping of the Modern Industrial Labor Force, 1891 to 1930* (Baltimore: Johns Hopkins University Press, 2002).

44. Baynton, "Disability and the Justification of Inequality in American History," 33.

45. Abel, *Tuberculosis and the Politics of Exclusion*.

46. *Annual Report of the Department of Health of the City of Los Angeles, California, for the Year Ended June 30, 1917* (Los Angeles: City Department of Health, 1917), 3.

47. Herbert I. Sauer, "The Permanence of Rehabilitation Efforts: A Study of Rehabilitation of the Tuberculous in Los Angeles County," March 29, 1941, 10. Unpublished report in the files of the Los Angeles County Board of Supervisors, Hall of Administration, Los Angeles.

48. See Clark Davis, "The View from Spring Street: White-Collar Men in the City of Angels," in Sitton and Deverell, *Metropolis in the Making*, 179–98.

49. Los Angeles Tuberculosis and Health Association, "Executive Secretary's Report," September 1933, George Pigeon Clements Papers, Collection 118, Department of Special Collections, Charles E. Young Research Library, University of California, Los Angeles.

50. This advice is discussed in more detail in Emily K. Abel, "Medicine and Morality: The Health Care Program of the Yew York Charity Organization Society," *Social Service Review*, 71, no. 4 (December 1997): 634–51.

51. "Tuberculosis—Monthly Reports," September 25, 1934, California State Archives, Sacramento, Califoria.

52. Bryder, *Below the Magic Mountain*, 233.

53. "Tuberculosis—Monthly Reports," April 10, 1939, California State Archives, Sacramento, Califoria.

54. "Report of Conference in Regard to Proposed Tubercular Clinics," 18.

55. "Tuberculosis—Monthly Reports," January 10, 1939, California State Archives, Sacramento, Califoria.

56. Stone, *Disabled State*, 82.

57. Ibid.

58. Paul Starr, *The Social Transformation of American Medicine: The Rise of a Sovereign Profession and the Making of a Vast Industry* (New York: Basic Books, 1982), 145.

59. "Report of Conference in Regard to Proposed Tubercular Clinics."

60. Roger Cooter, "The Disabled Body," in *Medicine in the Twentieth Century*, ed. Roger Cooter and John Pickstone (Amsterdam: Harwood Academic Publishers, 2000), 367–83, 378.

61. See Emily K. Abel, "Medicine and Morality."

62. Richard Scotch, *From Good Will to Civil Rights: Transforming Federal Disability Policy* (Philadelphia: Temple University Press, 1984).

63. This line of argumentation is similar to Linda Gordon's claim that women, especially single mothers, were marginalized in the framing of the Social Security Act. See Gordon, *Pitied but Not Entitled: Single Mothers and the History of Welfare, 1890–1935* (New York: Free Press, 1994).

64. Jacobus tenBroek, "Have Our Blind Social Security?," radio speech, National Federation of the Blind national convention, Wilkes-Barre, Pa., November 15, 1945; quoted in Floyd W. Matson, *Walking Alone and Marching Together: A History of the Organized Blind Movement in the United States, 1940–1990* (Baltimore: National Federation of the Blind, 1990), 13–15. The issue of how disability welfare assistance can sometimes make it impossible for a disabled person to be gainfully employed is most powerfully (and personally) explicated by Paul Longmore in *Why I Burned My Book, and Other Essays on Disability* (Philadelphia: Temple University Press, 2003), 32–40.

65. TenBroek, "Have Our Blind Social Security?," 14.

66. Susan Wendell, "Unhealthy Disabled: Treating Chronic Illnesses as Disabilities," *Hypatia* 16, no. 4 (2001): 17–33, 17; emphasis in the original.

67. See Elspeth Brown, "The Prosthetics of Management: Motion Study, Photography, and the Industrialized Body in World War I America," in *Artificial Parts, Practical Lives: Modern Histories of Prosthetics*, ed. Katherine Ott, David Serlin, and Stephen Minm (New York: New York University Press, 2002), 249–81. See also Heather Perry, "Re-arming the Disabled Veteran: Artificially Rebuilding State and Society in World War One Germany," ibid., 75–101.

68. For chronic fatigue syndrome understood as a disability, see Wendell, "Unhealthy Disabled."

69. The exception here, of course, is pulmonary tuberculars who underwent rib resections, which could be noticeable to the naked eye when a person was unclothed. See Ott, *Fevered Lives*, 152–54.

70. See Crnic and Connolly, "'They Can't Help Getting Well Here.'" The few works that address children with tuberculosis (although not necessarily bone tuberculosis) include Cynthia Connolly, *Saving Sickly Children: The Tuberculosis Preventorium in American Life, 1909–1970* (New Brunswick, N.J.: Rutgers University Press, 2008); and Richard Meckel, "Open Air Schools and the Tuberculous Child in Early 20th Century America," *Archives of Pediatric and Adolescent Medicine* 150 (1996): 91–96.

71. Mildred B. Duncan, "Study of the Medical, Educational, and Social Situation in Sixteen Cases of Bone Tuberculosis in Children in Pittsburgh, Pennsylvania" (thesis, Smith College of Social Work, 1924).

72. Gloria Paris, *A Child of Sanitariums: A Memoir of Tuberculosis Survival and Lifelong Disability* (Jefferson, N.C.: McFarland and Co., 2010), 11.

73. Ibid., 107.

74. Ibid., 40.

75. Some examples of histories of disability that take account of family and kinship are Daniel Wilson, *Living with Polio: The Epidemic and Its Survivors* (Chicago: University of Chicago Press, 2005); and Susan Burch, *Signs of Resistance: American Deaf Cultural History, 1900 to World War II* (New York: New York University Press, 2002).

76. Rayna Rapp and Faye Ginsburg, "Enabling Disability: Rewriting Kinship, Reimagining Citizenship," *Public Culture* 13, no. 3 (2001): 533–56.

77. Andrew Solomon, *Far from the Tree: Parents, Children and the Search for Identity* (New York: Scribner, 2012).

78. Following the lead of scholars in Deaf studies, we distinguish between "Deaf" and "deaf." The former refers to the community and culture in which the hearing-impaired person participates, whereas "deafness" refers to an actual biological impairment.

79. Burch, *Signs of Resistance*, 15.

80. Katharine Butler Hathaway, *The Little Locksmith: A Memoir* (New York: Feminist Press at the City University of New York, 2000), 16. Her autobiography was originally published in 1943.

81. A more thorough treatment of this theme can be found in Rosemarie Garland-Thomson, *Staring: How We Look* (New York: Oxford University Press, 2009).

82. Hathaway, *Little Locksmith*, 24 ("ghoulish pleasure"), 25 ("burlingly upstairs").

83. Susan M. Schweik, *The Ugly Laws: Disability in Public* (New York: New York University Press, 2009).

84. In 1915, surgeon Harry J. Haiselden of Chicago's German-American Hospital was called upon to treat a newborn known as "the Bollinger baby," an infant with severe physical anomalies. A eugenicist, Dr. Haiselden urged the parents to withhold treatment and let the baby die. Haiselden publicized the Bollinger baby case in sensational newspaper interviews and in a fictionalized 1916 silent film called *The Black Stork,* in which he himself appeared. For more, see Martin Pernick, *The Black Stork: Eugenics and the Death of "Defective" Babies in American Medicine and Motion Pictures Since 1915* (New York: Oxford University Press, 1996).

85. Hathaway, *Little Locksmith*, 14–15.

86. Ibid., 41.

87. Ibid., 42. Similarly, Jane Addams, who contracted bone tuberculosis at the age of four and lived with a "crooked back" thereafter, constantly worried that her family would not want to be seen with her in public because of her "ugly" looks. See Louise W. Knight, *Citizen: Jane Addams and the Struggle for Democracy* (Chicago: University of Chicago Press, 2005), 36–37.

88. Hathaway, *Little Locksmith*, 67.

89. Ibid.

90. See Katharine Butler Hathaway, *The Journals and Letters of the Little Locksmith* (New York: Coward-McCann, 1946), viii.

91. Paul K. Longmore and Paul Steven Miller, "'A Philosophy of Handicap': The Origins of Randolph Bourne's Radicalism," *Radical History Review* 94, no. 1 (2006): 59–83.

92. John Adam Moreau, *Randolph Bourne: Legend and Reality* (Washington, D.C.: Public Affairs Press, 1966), 165; quoted in Paul Longmore, "The Life of Randolph Bourne and the Need for a History of Disabled People," in *Why I Burned My Book*, 32–40, 36.

93. Frimley Follow-up Records, 1928, ii. 117, as quoted in Bryder, *Below the Magic Mountain*, 218. The Frimley Follow-up Records are held at the Surrey History Centre, Surrey, U.K.

94. Bryder, *Below the Magic Mountain*, 216.

95. Hathaway, *Journals and Letters of the Little Locksmith*, viii.

96. Longmore, "Life of Randolph Bourne," 36.

97. King Edward VII Sanatorium, Midhurst, Annual Report, 1910–11, 43; quoted in Bryder, *Below the Magic Mountain*, 223.

98. Douglas C. Baynton, "Defectives in the Land: Disability and American Immigration Policy, 1882–1924," *Journal of American Ethnic History* 24 (Spring 2005): 31–44, 35.

99. Ibid., 39.

100. Bryder, *Below the Magic Mountain*, 233.

101. For a more thorough discussion of the hierarchy of impairment in disability studies, see Mark Deal, "Disabled People's Attitudes Toward Other Impairment Groups: A Hierarchy of Impairments," *Disability and Society* 18, no. 7 (2003): 897–910.

102. Charles E. Rosenberg, "The Tyranny of Diagnosis: Specific Entities and Individual Experience," *Milbank Quarterly* 80, no. 2 (2002): 237–60, 237.

## Chapter 5. Screening Disabilities

This chapter draws on Faye Ginsburg's "Disability in a Digital Age." We gratefully acknowledge support from the Spencer Foundation and New York University's Institute for Human Development and Social Change. We also thank Rebecca Howes-Mischel, Amikole Maraesa, and Ayako Takamori for research assistance. As always, we owe a debt of gratitude to the many people who responded to our requests for interviews, answered our endless questions, and thought out loud with us about this important topic. We thank editors Nancy Hirschmann and Beth Linker and anonymous reviewers for their helpful comments. Finally, we thank our children, who have shown us worlds far more illuminating than we might ever have imagined.

1. Authors' transcript of a talk by Emily Kingsley at New York University, March 22, 2012. For more on Kingsley's activism, see Rayna Rapp and Faye Ginsburg, "Enabling Disability: Rewriting Kinship, Reimagining Citizenship," *Public Culture* 13, no. 3 (2001): 533–56.

2. For a full discussion of this study of disability in the media, see Inclusion in the Arts and Media of People with Disabilities, "Fact Sheet", 2008, accessed April 12, 2012, http://www.iampwd.org/fact-sheet.

3. See Rapp and Ginsburg, "Enabling Disability"; and Rayna Rapp and Faye Ginsburg, "Reverberations: Disability and the New Kinship Imaginary," *Anthropological Quarterly* 84, no. 2 (2011): 379–410.

4. Rayna Rapp and Faye Ginsburg, "Enlarging Reproduction, Screening Disability," in *Reproductive Disruptions: Gender, Technology, and Biopolitics in the New Millennium*, ed. Marcia Inhorn (London: Berghahn Books, 2007), 98–121.

5. On cultural citizenship, see Ariella Azoulay, *The Civil Contract of Photography* (New York: Zone Books, 2008); Aihwa Ong, *Flexible Citizenship: The Cultural Logics of Transnationality* (Durham, N.C.: Duke University Press, 1998); and Renato Rosaldo, "Cultural Citizenship and Educational Democracy," *Cultural Anthropology* 9, no. 3 (1994): 402–11.

6. Benedict Anderson, *Imagined Communities: Reflections on the Origins and Spread of Nationalism* (London: Verso Books, 1983); Carol Pateman, *The Sexual Contract* (Stanford, Calif.: Stanford University Press, 1988).

7. Mary Bouquet, "Making Kinship with an Old Reproductive Technology," in *Relative Values: Reconfiguring Kinship Studies*, ed. Sarah Franklin and Susan McKinnon (Durham, N.C.: Duke University Press, 2001: 85–115).

8. Susan M. Schweik, *The Ugly Laws: Disability in Public* (New York: New York University Press, 2009).

9. See Rapp and Ginsburg, "Enlarging Reproduction, Screening Disability."

10. Mel Levine, *All Kinds of Minds: A Young Student's Book About Learning* (Cambridge, Mass.: Educational Publishing Service, 1993).

11. Rayna Rapp and Faye Ginsburg, "Belonging Made Visible: Recognition Struggles over Children with Learning Disabilities," in *Contesting Recognition: Contemporary Cultural and Institutional Disputes*, ed. Janice McLaughlin (London: Palgrave, 2011), 166–86.

12. W. J. T. Mitchell, "Seeing Disability," *Public Culture* 13, no. 3 (2001): 391–97.

13. Rosemarie Garland-Thomson, *Staring: How We Look* (New York: Oxford University Press, 2009).

14. Doug Auld, "bio", accessed June 11, 2012, http://dougauld.com/bio.htm.

15. Chris Rush, quoted in Kathleen Vanesian, "Chris Rush's 'Stare' at Mesa Arts Center Puts Viewers Face-to-Face with the Disabled," accessed June 11, 2012, http://www.phoenixnewtimes.com/2010-04-22/culture/chris-rush-s-stare-at-mesa-arts-center-puts-viewers-face-to-face-with-the-disabled/.

16. Kevin Michael Connolly, artist's statement, accessed June 11, 2012, http://www.therollingexhibition.com/statement.php.

17. Garland-Thomson, *Staring*, 195.

18. Sharon L. Snyder and David T. Mitchell, "'How Do We Get All These Disabilities in Here?': Disability Film Festivals and the Politics of Atypicality," *Canadian Journal of Film Studies* 17, no. 1 (2008): 11–29.

19. Snyder and Mitchell draw from B. Ruby Rich, "Collision, Catastrophe, Celebration: The Relationship Between Gay and Lesbian Film Festivals and Their Publics," *GLQ: A Journal of Lesbian and Gay Studies* 5, no. 1 (1999): 79–84.

20. See Snyder and Mitchell, "'How Do We Get All These Disabilities in Here?," 12.

21. Marc Edelman, "Social Movements: Changing Paradigms and Forms of Politics," *Annual Review of Anthropology* 30 (2001): 285–317.

22. See Reelabilities, accessed April 12, 2012, http://www.reelabilities.org/.

23. See State of the Art, Inc., "Wretches and Jabberers," accessed April 12, 2012, http://www.wretchesandjabberers.org/.

24. Wikipedia, "Ocean Heaven," accessed June 11, 2012, http://en.wikipedia.org/wiki/Ocean_Heaven.

25. Nancy Fraser, *Justice Interruptus: Critical Reflections on the "Postsocialist Condition"* (New York: Routledge, 1992), 12.

26. See Disthis.org, accessed April 12, 2012, http://disthis.org/AboutUs.htm.

27. Arjun Appadurai and Carol Breckenridge, "Consuming Modernity in India," in *Consuming Modernity: Public Culture in a South Asian World*, ed. Arjun Appadurai and Carol Breckenridge (Minneapolis: University of Minnesota Press, 1995), 12.

28. Miguel Nicolelis, "Beyond Boundaries," accessed June 11, 2012, http://thedianerehmshow.org/shows/2011-12-30/miguel-nicolelis-beyond-boundaries-rebroadcast.

29. Leo Kanner, "Autistic disturbances of affective contact," *Nerv Child* 2 (1943): 217–50.

30. Georges Canguilhem, *The Normal and the Pathological* (New York: Zone Books, 1991).

31. Joanne Kaufman, "Campaign on Childhood Mental Illness Succeeds at Being Provocative," accessed June 11, 2012, http://www.nytimes.com/2007/12/14/business/media/14adco.html.

32. See "Including Samuel," accessed June 11, 2012, http://www.includingsamuel.com/home.aspx.

33. See "Facilitated Communication," accessed March 21, 2014, http://en.wikipedia.org/wiki/Facilitated_communication.

34. Amanda Baggs, "In My Language," YouTube, January 14, 2007, accessed June 11, 2012, http://www.youtube.com/watch?v=JnylM1hI2jc.

35. David Wolman, "The Truth About Autism: Scientists Reconsider What They Think They Know," *Wired* 16, no. 3 (February 25, 2008), accessed June 11, 2012, http://www.wired.com/medtech/health/magazine/16-03/ff_autism?currentPage=all.

36. Grammatical and punctuation errors are in the original.

37. Sanjay Gupta, "Finding Amanda," accessed June 11, 2012, http://thechart.blogs.cnn.com/2008/04/02/.

38. According to U.S. census numbers from 2010, the percentage of Americans with disabilities is 19 percent; See "Nearly 1 in 5 People Have a Disability in the U.S., Census Bureau Reports," accessed March 21, 2014, http://www.census.gov/newsroom/releases/archives/miscellaneous/cb12-134.html.

According to the US Department of Labor's February 2014 "Disability Employment Policy Resources by Topic," only 19.1 percent of people with disabilities are employed, accessed March 21, 2014, http://www.dol.gov/odep/.

39. See Seshat Czeret, accessed August 18, 2011, http://seshat-czeret.blogspot.com/.

40. Virtual Ability, Inc., "About Us," accessed August 18, 2011, http://virtualabil ity.org/aboutus.aspx.

41. Widget Whiteberry. "The Story of the Heron Sanctuary," *The Imagination Age*, January 24, 2008, accessed August 18, 2011, http://www.theimaginationage.net/2008 /01/story-of-heron-sanctuary.html.

42. From 2006 to 2010, Wellness Island provided a support center on SL, offering mental health resources, counseling, and education. It closed because of constraints of time and money. Wellness Island, accessed August 18, 2011, http://slhealthy.wetpaint .com/page/Wellness+Island.

43. Virtual Ability, Inc., "About Us," accessed July 25, 2011, http://virtualability .org/aboutus.aspx.

44. See, for example, University of Michigan Health Sciences Library, "Second Life International Disability Rights Affirmation Conference Overview," July 23–24, 2011, accessed August 18, 2011, http://etechlib.wordpress.com/2011/07/26/second-life -international-disability-rights-affirmation-conference-overview/.

45. Marta Russell, *Beyond Ramps: Disability at the End of the Social Contract* (Monroe, Maine: Common Courage Press, 2002).

46. Virtual Ability, Inc., "About Us," accessed July 24, 2011, http://virtualability. org/aboutus.aspx.

47. Gerard Goggin and Christopher Newell, *Digital Disability: The Social Construction of Disability in New Media* (New York: Rowman and Littlefield, 2003), 154.

48. See Eye to Eye, accessed March 21, 2014.,http://eyetoeyenational.org/.

49. Pierre Bourdieu, *Outline of a Theory of Practice*, transl. Richard Nice (Cambridge: Cambridge University Press, 1977), 159.

50. See the trailer from Jenni Gold's "Ready, Willing & Able," accessed June 11, 2012, http://www.youtube.com/watch?v=gdBV3BAhmYw.

51. See I AM People with Disabilities, accessed April 12, 2012, http://www.iampwd .org/.

52. Personal communication to the author from Anita Hollander. March 13, 2012.

53. See I AM People With Disabilities, accessed April 12, 2012, http://www.iampwd .org/fact-sheet.

54. See Wolman, "Truth About Autism," 4–5.

55. From authors' transcript of a talk by Emily Kingsley at New York University, March 22, 2012.

56. Beth Haller, "Profitability, Diversity, and Disability Images in Advertising in the United States and Great Britain," *Disability Studies Quarterly* 21, no. 2 (2001), accessed June 11, 2012, http://dsq-sds.org/article/view/276/301.

57. For interesting interventions in advertising campaigns by disability activists, see Xian Horn's call for the Dove beauty campaign to include women with disabilities, accessed June 11, 2012, http://www.youtube.com/watch?v=8xM7Y7kbioc. Holly Norris's "American Able" offers a parody of American Apparel's campaign that claims to

represent average American women. As Norris writes on her website, she wants to use spoof to "reveal the ways in which women with disabilities are made invisible in advertising and mass media. I chose American Apparel not just for their notable style, but also for their claims that many of their models are just 'every day' women who are employees, friends and fans of the company." Norris, "American Able," accessed June 11, 2012, http://hollynorris.ca/americanable#h39067524.

58. Faye Ginsburg and Rayna Rapp, "The Social Distribution of Moxie: The Legacy of Christine Sleeter," in "Special Topic: Learning Disabilities," ed. David J. Connor and Beth A. Ferri, special issue, *Disability Studies Quarterly* 30, no. 2 (2010), http://www.dsq-sds.org/article/view/1239/1284.

## Chapter 6. Social Confluence and Citizenship

1. Michael Dregni, *Django: The Life and Music of a Gypsy Legend* (Oxford: Oxford University Press, 2004), 45–49.

2. Benjamin Givan, "Django Reinhardt's Left Hand," in *Jazz Planet*, ed. E. Taylor Atkins (Jackson: University Press of Mississippi, 2003), 19–20.

3. Alex Lubet, *Music, Disability, and Society* (Philadelphia: Temple University Press, 2011), 45–51.

4. Ibid., 1–2, 10–11. Arjun Appadurai, *Modernity at Large: Cultural Dimensions of Globalization* (Minneapolis: University of Minnesota Press, 1996). Mark Slobin, *Subcultural Sounds: Micromusics of the West* (Hanover, N.H.: University Press of New England, 1993).

5. Lubet, *Music, Disability, and Society*, 1–13.

6. *Lubet v. University of Minn.*, March 2, 2002, accessed November 25, 2013, http://mn.gov/workcomp/2002/Lubet-03-12-02.htm.

7. Gertrude Stein, *Everybody's Autobiography* (New York: Random House, 1937), 289.

8. Americans with Disabilities Act Amendments Act of 2008, accessed November 9, 2013, http://www.eeoc.gov/laws/statutes/adaaa.cfm.

9. Christopher Small, *Musicking: The Meanings of Performing and Listening* (Wesleyan, Conn.: Wesleyan University Press, 2011). Henry Kingsbury, *Music, Talent, and Performance: A Conservatory Cultural System* (Philadelphia: Temple University Press, 1988). Bruno Nettl, *Heartland Excursions: Ethnomusicological Reflections on Schools of Music* (Urbana: University of Illinois Press, 1995).

10. Jack Black, *School of Rock*. Film, directed by Richard Linklater. Hollywood, Calif.: Paramount Pictures, 2003.

11. Lubet, *Music, Disability, and Society*, 14–41.

12. Carole LaRochelle, "Leon Fleisher Uses Rolfing® SI and Botox® to Return to Playing Piano With Both Hands," San Francisco Redwood Empire Rolfing® SI, 2014, accessed March 23, 2014, http://redwoodempirerolfing.com/leon-fleisher-uses-rolfing-and-botox-to-return-to-playing-piano-with-both-hands/.

13. Neil Lerner, "The Horrors of One-Handed Pianism: Music and Disability in *The Beast with Five Fingers*," in *Sounding Off: Theorizing Disability and Music*, ed. Neil Lerner and Joseph Straus (New York: Routledge, 2006), 75.

14. John Henderson, *A Directory of Composers for Organ*, 3rd ed. (Swindon, U.K.: John Henderson, 2005), 280.

15. Lubet, *Music, Disability, and Society*, 51–56; Alex Lubet, "(Paralyzed on One) Sideman: Disability Studies Meets Jazz, Through the Hands of Horace Parlan," *Critical Studies in Improvisation/Études Critiques en Improvisation* 6, no. 2 (2010), accessed November 9, 2013, http://www.criticalimprov.com/article/view/1268.

16. Natalie Kononenko, *Ukrainian Minstrels: And the Blind Shall Sing*. (Armonk, N.Y.: ME Sharpe, 1998); Miles, M. "Disability on a Different Model: Glimpses of an Asian Heritage." *Journal of Religion, Disability & Health* 6, nos. 2–3 (2002): 89–108.

17. Maurice Ravel, *Piano Concerto for the Left Hand*, Leon Fleisher, piano, Sergiu Commissiona, conductor, Spanish Radio and Television Orchestra, Madrid, Teatro Monumental, November 10, 1995, accessed November 10, 2013, https://www.youtube.com/watch?v=Jgj6jScPWK8.

18. Noola K. Griffiths, "The Fabric of Performance: Values and Social Practices of Classical Music Expressed Through Concert Dress Choice," *Music Performance Research* 4 (2011): 30–48.

19. Hannah Furness, "'Sex Sells' in Classical Music, Dame Jenni Murray Says," *Telegraph*, June 11, 2013, accessed November 10, 2013, http://www.telegraph.co.uk/culture/music/classicalmusic/10111477/Sex-sells-in-classical-music-Dame-Jenni-Murray-says.html.

20. Tom Huizenga, "Lara St. John: A Little Skin, Lots of Violin," *NPR Music*, July 29, 2010, accessed November 10, 2013, http://www.npr.org/templates/story/story.php?storyId=128820860.

21. Vivien Schweitzer, "After Adversity, a Passion Unchecked: Years After a Calamity, Rachel Barton Pine Prospers," *New York Times*, June 21, 2013, accessed November 10, 2013, http://www.nytimes.com/2013/06/23/arts/music/years-after-a-calamity-rachel-barton-pine-prospers.html?_r=0.

22. "Virtuoso Voices—Evelyn Glennie (Playing Barefoot)," accessed March 23, 2013, https://www.prx.org/pieces/13401-virtuoso-voices-evelyn-glennie-playing-barefoo%3E.

23. Alex Lubet, "Tunes of Impairment: An Ethnomusicology of Disability," *Review of Disability Studies* 1, no. 1 (2004): 141.

24. Lubet, *Music, Disability, and Society*, 51–56; Lubet, "(Paralyzed on One) Sideman"; Don McGlynn, Jimmi Pedersen, Norma Parlan, and Celia Zaentz, *Horace Parlan by Horace Parlan* (DVD) (Chatsworth, Calif.: Image Entertainment, 2002).

25. David Tarnow, "Oscar Peterson," *NPR Jazz Profiles*, accessed November 10, 2013, http://www.npr.org/programs/jazzprofiles/archive/peterson.html; Oscar Peterson, *A Night in Vienna* (Santa Monica, Calif.: Verve, 2004), DVD.

26. Sherrie Tucker, *Swing Shift:"All-Girl" Bands of the 1940s* (Durham, N.C.: Duke University Press, 2000), 59–63.

27. "Ella Fitzgerald: The Official Website of the First Lady of Song," accessed November 10, 2013, http://www.ellafitzgerald.com/about/biography.html.

28. "Ella Fitzgerald Complete Discography," accessed November 25, 2013, http://ellafitzgerald.altervista.org/discography_gen.htm.

29. "Diane Schuur," accessed November 10, 2013, http://www.dianeschuur.com.

30. "Andrea Bocelli Official Website," accessed November 10, 2013, http://www.andreabocelli.com/en/#!/home.

31. Emanuel E. Garcia, "Frederick Delius: Devotion, Collaboration and the Salvation of Music," presentation, the Philadelphia Ethical Society, October 23, 2005, accessed November 10, 2013, http://thompsonian.info/delius-garcia.html.

32. Susan Feder, "Hausserman, John (William)," in *The New Grove Dictionary of Music and Musicians*, 2nd ed. (New York: Grove's Dictionaries, Inc., 2004).

33. Morning Concert: The Music of John Haussermann. Archived broadcast, RadiOM, San Francisco, July 2, 1980, accessed March 26, 2014, http://radiom.org/detail.php?omid=MC.1980.07.02.A.

34. Kononenko, *Ukrainian Minstrels*; Miles, "Disability on a Different Model"; Lubet, *Music, Disability, and Society*, 69–88; Lubet, Alex, "Music and Blindness," in *Encyclopedia of Disability*, 3rd ed., ed. Gary Albrecht (Thousand Oaks, Calif.: Sage, 2006) 1123–25.

35. Lubet, *Music, Disability, and Society*, 19–20, 38–39.

36. Thomas Quasthoff, *The Voice: A Memoir* (New York: Pantheon Books, 2008), 88.

37. Christie Garton, "Itzhak Perlman: We Are 'This Close' to Ending Polio for Good This World Polio Day," *USA Today*, October 24, 2011, accessed November 10, 2013, http://yourlife.usatoday.com/mind-soul/doing-good/kindness/post/2011/02/itzhak-perlman-says-we-are-this-close-to-ending-polio-for-good/141014/1.

38. "Vancouver Adapted Music Society (VAMS)," accessed November 10, 2013, http://www.vams.org.

39. "Drum'n'bass Veteran DJ Fresh and Julien Castet Help Disabled Music Fans Make Tracks 'Using Only Their Minds,'" *Fact Magazine*, June 4, 2013, accessed November 10, 2013, http://www.factmag.com/2013/06/04/drumnbass-veteran-dj-fresh-and-julien-castet-help-disabled-music-fans-make-tracks-using-only-their-minds/; "Smirnoff Mindtunes: Meet DJ Fresh," accessed November 10, 2013, https://www.youtube.com/watch?v=wLP5LGUt55E; "Smirnoff Mindtunes: Meet Julien," accessed November 10, 2013, https://www.youtube.com/watch?v=9eIjviXLi28.

40. "Smirnoff Mindtunes: Meet Andy," accessed November 10, 2013, https://www.youtube.com/watch?v=nzhnSD-ajok; "Smirnoff Mindtunes: Meet Jo," accessed November 10, 2013, https://www.youtube.com/watch?v=HlcWEyzKXU4.

41. "Smirnoff Mindtunes: Meet Mark," accessed November 10, 2013, https://www.youtube.com/watch?v=tnCdoEjLQQw.

42. "DJ Fresh & Mindtunes: A Track Created Only by the Mind (Video documentary)," accessed November 10, 2013, https://www.youtube.com/watch?v=PgfxKZiSCDQ.

43. "Drum'n'bass Veteran DJ Fresh," 1.

44. "Smirnoff Mindtunes: Meet DJ Fresh."

45. "DJ Fresh & Mindtunes."

46. Ibid.

47. Sara Gates, "Breaking the Myth of the Female DJ in Electronic Dance Music," *Huffington Post*, October 4, 2013, accessed November 10, 2013, http://www.huffingtonpost.com/2013/09/19/female-djs-edm-electronic-music-women_n_3873434.html; Gates, "For Women in Electronic Dance Music, It's About Beats, Not Gender," *Huffington Post*, September 20, 2013, accessed November 10, 2013, http://www.huffington post.com/2013/09/20/women-in-edm-female-djs-stereotypes-sexism_n_3948705 .html; McLeod, Kembrew, "Genres, subgenres, sub-subgenres and more: Musical and social differentiation within electronic/dance music communities," *Journal of Popular Music Studies* 13, no. 1 (2001): 59–75.

48. Lubet, *Music, Disability, and Society*, 43, 69–88.

49. Gates, "Breaking the Myth."

50. K. H. Woldendorp and W. van Gils, "One-Handed Musicians—More than a Gimmick," *Medical Problems of Performing Artists* 27, no. 4 (2012): 231–37.

51. Deke Dickerson, *World of Weirdness: Armless Musicians*, accessed November 10, 2013, http://www.dekedickerson.com/weird-armless.php.

## Chapter 7. Our Ancestors the Sighted

I have shared versions of this essay with numerous individuals and groups over the past decade, to the point that I do not dare to offer a list, mortified that I will leave out the most important; to those who have engaged with me on this topic, I give heartfelt thanks. That said, I must single out two key people: Nancy Hirschmann and Hoëlle Corvest. Without them, the present essay would never have been possible.

1. C. Bessigneul and Collectif, *Des clés pour bâtir* (Paris: Cité des Sciences et Industrie, 1991).

2. Ibid., 2–3.

3. On the role of physicians in modern French politics, see Jack D. Ellis, *The Physician-Legislators of France: Medicine and Politics in the Early Third Republic, 1870–1914* (New York: Cambridge University Press, 1990). Simi Linton, *Claiming Disability* (New York: New York University Press, 1998) offers a clear delineation between the "medical" and "social" models of disability throughout, although more and more scholars question this division. See Susan Burch and Michael Rembis, eds., *Disability Histories* (Urbana: University of Illinois Press, forthcoming).

4. Catherine Kudlick, "Disability History: Why We Need Another 'Other,'" *American Historical Review* 108, no. 3 (June 2003): 763–93.

5. I argue that French health officials helped create this cross-disability category when they tried to gauge the effectiveness of smallpox vaccinations: Catherine Kudlick, "Smallpox, Disability and Survival: Rewriting Paradigms from a New Epidemic Script," in Burch and Rembis *Disability Histories*.

6. Lynn Hunt, *Inventing Human Rights: A History* (New York: W. W. Norton, 2008).

7. Nicholas Mirzeoff has written a number of important works that explore this visual culture, beginning with *Silent Poetry: Deafness, Sign, and Visual Culture in Modern France* (Princeton, N.J.: Princeton University Press, 1995). No longer focusing on disability or even France, his subsequent scholarship nevertheless offers key contributions. See, for example, *An Introduction to Visual Culture* (New York: Routledge, 2009); and *The Visual Culture Reader* (New York: Routledge, 1998). Despite its promising title for the purposes of this chapter, his most recent book, *The Right to Look: A Counterhistory of Visuality* (Durham, N.C.: Duke University Press, 2011), does not engage blind people as potentially colonial subjects.

8. See the United Nations Convention on Human Rights (1948) and recent discussions of these rights being expanded into the UN Convention on the Rights of Persons with Disabilities, accessed April 6, 2014, http://www.un.org/disabilities/convention /conventionfull.shtml.

9. The 1980s and 1990s generated a rich scholarly discussion of French bourgeois culture, which I survey in my book *Cholera in Post-revolutionary Paris: A Cultural History* (Berkeley: University of California Press, 1996), 23–26. Sarah Maza's *The Myth of the French Bourgeoisie: An Essay on the Social Imaginary, 1750–1850* (Cambridge, Mass.: Harvard University Press, 2003) generated renewed discussion, summarized by Jan Goldstein in "Of Marksmanship and Marx: Reflections on the Linguistic Construction of Class in Some Recent Historical Scholarship," *Modern Intellectual History* 2, no. 1 (April 2005): 87–107. For the expansion of human rights as a concept, see Henry Shue, *Basic Rights: Subsistence, Affluence, and U.S. Foreign Policy* (Princeton, N.J.: Princeton University Press, 1996). J. P. Daughton's forthcoming book from Oxford University Press, *Humanity So Far Away: Violence, Suffering, and Humanitarianism in the Modern French Empire*, is sure to offer valuable insights into these questions in the context of colonial and postcolonial France.

10. My aim in this essay is not to engage with the exciting and rich scholarship about French colonialism and postcolonialism that took off in earnest with Alice Conklin's *A Mission to Civilize: The Republican Idea of Empire in France and West Africa, 1895–1930* (Stanford, Calif.: Stanford University Press, 1997), but rather to use these insights as inspiration and to invite reflection on possible connections. English-language avenues for future exploration might be found in the theme issue "Writing French Colonial Histories" that Conklin coedited with Julia Clancy-Smith in *French Historical Studies* 27, no. 3 (Summer 2004), and in works by J. P. Daughton, Clifford

Rosenberg, and Sarah Curtis, among others. Regarding missions within France's own borders, see Janet Horne, *A Social Laboratory for Modern France: The Musée Social and the Rise of the Welfare State* (Durham, N.C.: Duke University Press, 2002), 109–13. On immigration, Gerard Noiriel's influential *The French Melting Pot: Immigration, Citizenship, and National Identity* (Minneapolis: University of Minnesota Press, 1996) shares the stage with a number of comparative studies: Adrian Favell, *Philosophies of Integration: Immigration and the Idea of Citizenship in France and Britain* (Hound-smills, U.K.: Palgrave, 1998); Donald L. Horowitz and Gerard Noiriel, *Immigrants in Two Democracies: French and American Experiences* (New York: New York University Press, 1992); and *Parallel Views: Education and Access for Deaf People in France and the United States* (Washington, D.C.: Gallaudet University Press, 1994), which serves more as a primary source.

11. Mark Sherry offers a thoughtful critique of how scholars in disability studies and postcolonial studies have largely failed in their attempts at analogies, "(Post)colonizing Disability," *Wagadu* 4 (Summer 2007): 10–20. Fully aware that this connection is problematic for both sides of the equation, I persist with this thought experiment because it offers an opportunity to unpack some of the mechanisms at work behind assimilation. For a more in-depth theoretical exploration of the relationship, see Clare Barker and Stuart Murray, eds., "Disabling Postcolonialism: Global Disability Cultures and Democratic Criticism," special theme issue, *Journal of Literary and Cultural Disability Studies* 4, no. 3 (2010).

12. Harlan Lane, *The Mask of Benevolence: Disabling the Deaf Community* (New York: Vintage, 1992). Here I follow Lane, who capitalizes "Deaf" to refer to the community and culture of hearing-impaired people. Sherry, "(Post)colonizing Disability," 12, criticizes Lane for not really situating deaf people within a disability context and embodiment and not engaging with what makes colonialism a unique form of power.

13. Martin Jay, *Downcast Eyes: The Denigration of Vision in Twentieth-Century French Thought* (Berkeley: University of California Press, 1993); Guy Debord, *The Society of Spectacle* (Detroit: Black & Red, 2000); Vanessa Schwarz, *Spectacular Realities: Early Mass Culture in Fin-de-Siècle Paris* (Berkeley: University of California Press, 1999); Christopher Prendergast, *Paris and the Nineteenth Century* (Cambridge, Mass.: Wiley-Blackwell, 1995); David Harvey, *Paris: Capital of Modernity* (New York: Routledge, 2005).

14. The prefaces of many nineteenth-century novels mention this trope. See also Anne Therese O'Neil-Henry, "Parisian Social Studies: Positivism and the Novels of Balzac, Paul de Kock and Zola" (Ph.D. diss., Duke University, 2011).

15. I am deeply grateful to Amelia Lyon for introducing me to Father Ghys and the *Cahiers Nord-Africains*, in her 2004 dissertation that has been published as *The Civilizing Mission in the Metropole: Algerian Families and the French Welfare State During Decolonization* (Stanford, Calif.: Stanford University Press, 2013).

16. For reasons outside the scope of this essay, disability has remained largely apolitical and understood as undertheorized by many scholars interested in other forms

of marginality. See Alison Kafer's excellent discussion of this throughout her book *Feminist, Queer, Crip* (Bloomington: Indiana University Press, 2013).

17. Henri-Jacques Stiker, *Corps infirmes et sociétés* (Paris: Aubier Montaigne, 1982), translated as *A History of Disability*, trans. William Sayers (Ann Arbor: University of Michigan Press, 2000), 128, 132. All quotations and page numbers are from the English edition.

18. Ibid., 137.

19. Valentin Haüy, *Essai sur l'éducation des aveugles* (Paris: Imprimé par les Enfants-Aveugles, sous la direction de M. Clousier, Imprimeur du Roi, 1786; repr., Paris, Editions des Archives Contemporaines, 1985).

20. Pierre Henri, *La vie et l'oeuvre de Valentin Haüy* (Paris: Presses universitaires de France, 1984).

21. Zina Weygand, *The Blind in French Society from the Middle Ages to the Century of Louis Braille*, trans. Emily-Jane Cohen (Stanford, Calif.: Stanford University Press, 2009).

22. Ibid., esp. chap. 5.

23. Haüy, *Essai*, v–vi.

24. Ibid., 36–37.

25. Ibid., 37–38.

26. Sophia Rosenfeld, *A Revolution in Language: The Problem of Signs in Late Eighteenth-Century France* (Stanford, Calif.: Stanford University Press, 2001).

27. Haüy, *Essai*, 39–40.

28. Eugen Weber, *Peasants into Frenchmen: The Modernization of Rural France* (Stanford, Calif.: Stanford University Press, 1976). Although Weber's thesis has been successfully challenged, it presents an extreme-case scenario of acculturation to offer one way of thinking about the education of France's blind citizens. For a history of reading and writing that does not include the blind, see Martyn Lyons, *Reading Culture and Writing Practices in Nineteenth-Century France* (Toronto: University of Toronto Press, 2013).

29. Weygand, *Blind in French Society*, 281–90.

30. A history of daily life in nineteenth- and early twentieth-century schools for the blind remains to be written. For a contemporary meditation on secrecy, see Patrick White, "Sex Education; or, How the Blind Became Heterosexual," in *GLQ: A Journal of Lesbian and Gay Studies* 9, nos. 1–2 (2003): 133–47.

31. The battle over which writing system would win out also awaits its trained historian. For now, the story lives on through various service and advocacy organizations for the blind. Robert B. Irwin, "The War of the Dots," American Foundation for the Blind, 2009, accessed April 6, 2014, http://www.afb.org/warofthedots/book .asp.

32. Helen Keller, *The World I Live In* (New York: The Century Co., 1908), 42.

33. Constance Classen, *The Deepest Sense: A Cultural History of Touch* (Urbana: University of Illinois Press, 2012); Mark K. Smith, *Sensing the Past: Seeing, Hearing,*

*Smelling, Tasting, and Touching in History* (Berkeley: University of California Press, 2008). Neither scholar grapples substantially with blind people's ways of knowing.

34. Yvonne Eriksson, *Tactile Pictures: Pictorial Representations for the Blind, 1784–1940*, (Göteborg: 1998). In the fall of 2013, Heather Tilley curated an exhibition, *Touching the Book: Embossed Literature for Blind People in the Nineteenth Century*, at Birkbeck College, University of London, accessed April 6, 2014, http://blogs.bbk.ac.uk /touchingthebook/. This exhibit showcases a number of important innovations.

35. The discoveries generated much attention in the popular press. See Gregory Curtis, *The Cave Painters: Probing the Mysteries of the World's First Artists* (New York: Knopf, 2006).

36. Eriksson, *Tactile Pictures*, chap. 4.

37. On the ingenuity of blind people, see Catherine Kudlick and Zina Weygand, eds., *Reflections: The Life and Writings of a Young Blind Woman in Post-revolutionary France* (New York: New York University Press, 2002). For people with disabilities more broadly, see David M. Turner, *Disability in Eighteenth-Century England: Imagining Physical Impairment* (New York: Routledge, 2012); and Peter White, "Disability: A New History," BBC radio broadcast, January–May 2013, accessed April 6, 2014, http://www .bbc.co.uk/programmes/b01sm70w.

38. Albert Memmi, *The Colonizer and the Colonized* (Boston: Beacon Press, 1965), 120.

39. Ibid., 138.

40. Andrew Potok, *A Matter of Dignity: Changing the World of the Disabled* (New York: Bantam, 2001), 13.

41. For a list of the museum's other publications, including one on procreation that should probably be the subject of a future study, visit http://www.cite-sciences.fr /fr/cite-des-sciences/contenu/c/1248135853611/editions-en-relief/; to purchase a copy, visit http://www.boutiquesdemusees.fr/fr/librairie/des-cles-pour-batir/6725.html.

42. Special issue on literacy, *Journal of Vision Impairment and Blindness* 90, no. 3 (May–June 1996); National Federation of the Blind, "The Braille Literacy Crisis in America: Facing the Truth, Reversing the Trend, Empowering the Blind; A Report to the Nation by the National Federation of the Blind Jernigan Institute," March 26, 2009.

## Chapter 8. Citizenship and the Family

1. Eva Feder Kittay, "Forever Small: The Strange Case of Ashley X," *Hypatia* 26, no. 3 (2011): 610–31.

2. For a discussion of parent activism and education, see Allison C. Carey, *On the Margins of Citizenship: Intellectual Disability and Civil Rights in Twentieth-Century America* (Philadelphia: Temple University Press, 2009); David Goode, *And Now Let's Build a Better World: The Story of the Association for the Help of Retarded Children,*

*New York City, 1948–1998* (New York: AHRC, 1998); Kathleen W. Jones, "Education for Children with Mental Retardation: Parent Activism, Public Policy, and Family Ideology in the 1950s," in *Mental Retardation in America*, ed. Steven Noll and James W. Trent, Jr. (New York: New York University Press, 2004), 351–70; and Larry A. Jones, *Doing Disability Justice* (lulu.com publishers, 2010).

3. T. H. Marshall, *Citizenship and Social Class* (London: Pluto, 1950; repr., London, Pluto, 1992).

4. Many scholars have promoted a relational view of rights. Within the field of disability, see Carey, *On the Margins of Citizenship*; David M. Engle and Frank W. Munger, *Rights of Inclusion: Law and Identity in the Life Stories of Americans with Disabilities* (Chicago: University of Chicago Press, 2003); Jennifer Mason, "Personal Narratives, Relational Selves: Residential Histories in the Living and Telling," *Sociological Review* 52, no. 2 (2004): 162–79; and Solveig Magnus Reindal, "Independence, Dependence, Interdependence: Some Reflections on the Subject and Personal Autonomy," *Disability and Society* 14, no. 3 (1999): 353–67. For key works on citizenship and relationality outside the field of disability studies, see Seyla Benhabib, *Situating the Self: Gender, Community, and Postmodernism in Contemporary Ethics* (New York: Routledge, 1992); Susan Moller Okin, *Justice, Gender, and the Family* (New York: Basic Books, 1989); Margaret Somers, "Rights, Relationality, and Membership: Rethinking the Making and Meaning of Citizenship," *Law and Social Inquiry* 19, no. 1 (1989): 63–112; and Selma Sevenhuijsen, "The Place of Care: Relevance of the Feminist Ethic of Care for Social Policy," *Feminist Theory* 4, no. 2 (2003): 179–97.

5. Harlan Hahn, "Civil Rights for Disabled Americans: The Foundations of a Political Agenda," in *Images of the Disabled, Disabling Images*, ed. Alan Gartner and Tom Joe (New York: Praeger, 1987), 181–204; Martha Minow, *Making All the Difference: Inclusion, Exclusion, and American Law* (Ithaca, N.Y.: Cornell University Press, 1990); Reindal, "Independence, Dependence, Interdependence."

6. Will Kymlicka, *Multicultural Citizenship: A Liberal Theory of Minority Rights* (Oxford: Clarendon Press, 1995), 4–5.

7. Okin, *Justice, Gender, and the Family*.

8. Joseph T. Weingold and Rudolf P. Hormuth, "Group Guidance of Parents of Mentally Retarded Children," *Journal of Clinical Psychology* 9, no. 2 (1953): 118–24, 118.

9. Jane Bernstein, *Loving Rachel: A Family's Journey from Grief* (Urbana: University of Illinois Press, 1988; repr. Urbana: University of Illinois Press, 2007), 45.

10. Address by Governor George M. Leader at the sixth annual convention of the PA Association for Retarded Children, Penn-Harris Hotel, Harrisburg, Pa., May 18, 1956, George Leader Official Papers, MG 207, 9-0260, carton 59, folder 1, subject index - Pennsylvania Association for Retarded Children, 1955–1959, Pennsylvania State Archives, Harrisburg.

11. Sara Ryan and Katherine Runswick-Cole, "Repositioning Mothers: Mothers, Disabled Children and Disability Studies," *Disability and Society* 23, no. 3 (2008): 199–210.

12. Interviewee in Susan Schwartzenberg, *Becoming Citizens: Family Life and the Politics of Disability* (Seattle: University of Washington Press, 2005), 8.

13. Nicola Schaefer, *Does She Know She's There?* (Markham, Ontario: Fitzhenry and Whiteside, 1999), 42.

14. Gail Landsman, *Reconstructing Motherhood and Disability in an Age of "Perfect" Babies* (New York: Routledge, 2009).

15. Linda M. Blum, "Mother-Blame in the Prozac Nation: Raising Kids with Invisible Disabilities," *Gender and Society* 21, no. 2 (2007): 202–26. See also Susan L. Neely-Barnes, Heather R. Hall, Ruth J. Roberts, and J. Carolyn Graff, "Parenting a Child with an Autism Spectrum Disorder: Public Perceptions and Parental Conceptualizations," *Journal of Family Social Work* 14, no. 3 (2011): 208–25. Given the tremendous external pressures and prejudices, mothers often internalize these sentiments as self-blame. See Jessica Gill and Pranee Liamputtong, "'Walk a Mile in My Shoes': Researching the Lived Experience of Mothers of Children with Autism," *Journal of Family Studies* 15, no. 3 (2009): 309–19; and Kristin D. Mickelson, Minhoi Wroble, and Vicki S. Helgeson, "'Why My Child?': Parental Attributes for Children's Special Needs," *Journal of Applied Social Psychology* 29, no. 6 (1999): 1263–92.

16. Jenny Morris, "Disabled Children, the Children Act and Human Rights," presented at "Young and Powerful" conference, organized by Disability North, May 26, 1999, accessed July 15, 2011, http://www.leeds.ac.uk/disability-studies/archiveuk/morris/Disabled%20children,%20the%20Children%20Act%20and%20human%20rights.pdf.

17. Sue Swenson, "UN Experts Examine Disability Issues, Family Support," *European Coalition for Community Living*, posted May 16, 2007, accessed July 15, 2011, http://www.community-living.info/index.php?page=233&news=185&pages=5&archive=1.

18. Letter to Governor John S. Fine by Ruth S. Hayes, September 25, 1952, John S. Fine Official Papers, 1951–1955, MG 206, 9-0031, carton 29, folder 20, subject index - Mental Health 1951–54, General Correspondence, Pennsylvania State Archives, Harrisburg.

19. Letter to Governor George M. Leader by Mrs. Philip Elkin, August 2, 1957, George Leader Official Papers, MG 207, 9-0260, carton 59, folder 1, subject index - Pennsylvania Association for Retarded Children 1955–59, Pennsylvania State Archives, Harrisburg.

20. Luther Youngdahl, "Speech at the First Convention of the National Association of Parents and Friends of Mentally Retarded Children," 1950, quoted in Gunner Dybwad, "Farewell Address," paper presented at the Annual Convention of the National Association for Retarded Children, Disability History Museum, Washington, D.C., 1963, accessed May 10, 2006, http://www.disabilitymuseum.org/lib/docs/2233card.htm.

21. Sam Golden, "All About Anne Golden," Voice of the Retarded History Project, accessed June 6, 2006, http://www.vor.net/Anne%20Golden.html.

22. Valerie Leiter and Marty W. Krauss, "Claims, Barriers and Satisfaction: Parents' Requests for Additional Special Education Services," *Journal of Disability Policy Studies* 15 (2004): 135–46; Valerie Leiter, *Their Time Has Come: Youth with Disabilities on the Cusp of Adulthood* (New Brunswick, N.J.: Rutgers University Press, 2012).

23. Katherine Castles, "'Nice, Average Americans': Postwar Parents' Groups and the Defense of the Normal Family," in Noll and Trent, *Mental Retardation in America*, 351–70.

24. Letter to Governor George M. Leader by Wm. M. Armstrong, November 14, 1955, George Leader Official Papers, MG 207, Subject: Mental Health General Correspondence, 9-0180, carton 34, subject index - Mental Health General Correspondence, Pennsylvania State Archives, Harrisburg.

25. For studies of eugenics and its impact on families, see Edwin R. Black, *War Against the Weak: Eugenics and America's Campaign to Create a Master Race* (New York: Four Walls Eight Windows, 2003); Daniel Kevles, *In the Name of Eugenics: Genetics and the Uses of Human Heredity*, 2nd ed. (Cambridge, Mass.: Harvard University Press, 1998); Edward J. Larson, *Sex, Race, and Science: Eugenics in the Deep South* (Baltimore: Johns Hopkins University Press, 1996); Nancy Ordover, *American Eugenics: Race, Queer Anatomy, and the Science of Nationalism* (Minneapolis: University of Minnesota Press, 2003); Diane Paul, *Controlling Human Heredity* (Atlantic Highlands, N.J.: Humanities Press, 1995); Nicole H. Rafter, *White Trash: The Eugenic Family Studies, 1877–1919* (Boston: Northeastern University Press, 1988); Rafter, "The Criminalization of Mental Retardation," in Noll and Trent, *Mental Retardation in America*, 232–57; and James W. Trent, Jr., *Inventing the Feeble Mind* (Berkeley: University of California Press, 1994).

26. For a discussion of professional ideologies and eugenics, see Paul, *Controlling Human Heredity*; Martin Pernick, "Eugenics and Public Health in American History," *American Journal of Public Health* 87, no. 11 (1997): 1767–72; and James W. Trent, Jr., "To Cut and Control: Institutional Preservation and the Sterilization of Mentally Retarded People in the United States, 1892–1947," *Journal of Historical Sociology* 6 (2003): 56–73.

27. For social histories of the rise of institutions, see Philip M. Ferguson, *Abandoned to Their Fate: Social Policy and Practice Toward Severely Retarded People in America, 1820–1920* (Philadelphia: Temple University Press, 1994); and Trent, *Inventing the Feeble Mind*.

28. Letter to Governor James H. by Mrs. J. V. Fackiner, May 1, 1950, James H. Duff Official Papers, MG 190, GM1445, carton 25, subject index - Mental Health, Pennsylvania State Archives, Harrisburg. The archive also contains two earlier letters written by Mrs. Fackiner in 1948 concerning her institutionalized child.

29. Many letters written by parents or relatives seeking assistance in securing the release of their institutionalized children or relatives are held in the Pennsylvania

State Archives, Harrisburg. The following are a few examples: letter to Governor Leader by Mr. and Mrs. Beulah, February 14, 1955, George M. Leader Official Papers, MG 207, 9-0188, carton 31, folder 1, subject index - Laurelton State Village Investigation; letter to Governor Raymond P. Shafer by Thelma Gringich, November 19, 1969, Raymond P. Shafer Official Papers, MG 209, 9-1109, carton 75, folder 5, subject index - Pennhurst and PA state schools and hospitals; letter to Governor Raymond P. Shafer by Sarah Martino, n.d. (received July 25, 1968), Raymond P. Shafer Official Papers, MG 209, 9-1109, carton 75, folder 5, subject index - Pennhurst and PA state schools and hospitals; and letter to Governor James Duff by Mrs. Yamtorn, June 9, 1949, James H. Duff Official Papers, MG 190GM1447, carton 26, subject index - Pennhurst State School Investigation, 1948–49.

30. Allison C. Carey, "Parents and Professionals: Parent Reflections on Professionals, the Support System, and the Family," in *Disability Histories*, ed. Susan Burch and Michael Rembis (Urbana: University of Illinois Press, forthcoming); Shelly Tremain, ed., *Foucault and the Government of Disability* (Ann Arbor: University of Michigan Press, 2005).

31. Chrissie Rogers, "Mothering and Intellectual Disability: Partnership Rhetoric?," *British Journal of Sociology of Education* 32, no. 4 (2011): 563–81.

32. Bernstein, *Loving Rachel*; Josh Greenfeld, *A Place for Noah* (San Diego: Harcourt Brace, 1978).

33. Blum, "Mother-Blame in the Prozac Nation"; Amy Sousa, "From Refrigerator Mothers to Warrior-Heroes: The Cultural Identity Transformation of Mothers Raising Children with Intellectual Disabilities," *Symbolic Interaction* 34, no. 2 (2011): 220–43.

34. Carey, "Parents and Professionals."

35. Okin, *Justice, Gender, and the Family*; Carol Pateman, *The Sexual Contract* (Stanford, CA: Stanford University Press, 1988); Anne Phillips, *Engendering Democracy* (University Park: Pennsylvania State University Press, 1991); Iris Marion Young, *Justice and the Politics of Difference* (Princeton, N.J.: Princeton University Press, 1990).

36. Rose Galvin, "Challenging the Need for Gratitude: Comparisons Between Paid and Unpaid Care for Disabled People," *Journal of Sociology* 40, no. 2 (2004): 137–55. The dichotomy of caregiver and care recipient also disregards parents' broader experiences and narratives that typically stress the rewards they receive through parenting, such as those discussed by Sara Green, "They Are Beautiful and They Are Ours: Swapping Tales of Mothering Children with Disabilities Through Interactive Interviews," *Journal of Loss and Trauma* 8 (2003): 1–8.

37. Lisa C. McGuire, Lynda A. Anderson, Ronda C. Talley, and John E. Crews, "Supportive Care Needs of Americans: A Major Issue for Women as Both Recipients and Providers," *Journal of Women's Health* 16, no. 6 (2007): 784–89.

38. Galvin, "Challenging the Need for Gratitude."

39. See, for example, Marjorie L. Devault, *Feeding the Family: The Social Organization of Caring as Gendered Work* (Chicago: University of Chicago Press, 1991); Paula England, "Emerging Theories of Care Work," *Annual Review of Sociology* 31, no. 1 (2005): 381–99; Hee-Kang Kim. "Analyzing the Gender Division of Labor: The Cases of the United States and South Korea," *Asian Perspective* 33, no. 2 (2009): 181–229; and Jennifer L. Hook, "Gender Inequality in the Welfare State: Sex Segregation in Housework, 1965–2003," *American Journal of Sociology* 115, no. 5 (2010): 1480–1523.

40. Albert Deutsch, *The Shame of the States* (New York: Harcourt, Brace, 1948), 118–20; Greenfeld, *Place for Noah*, 29–30.

41. Fern Kupfer, *Before and After Zachariah* (Chicago: Academy Chicago, 1988), 110, 167.

42. See Gina Di Giulio, "Sexuality and People Living with Physical or Developmental Disabilities: A Review of Key Issues," *Canadian Journal of Human Sexuality* 12, no. 1 (2003): 53–68; Marita P. McCabe, "Sexual Knowledge, Experience, and Feelings Among People with Disability," *Sexuality and Disability* 17 (1999): 157–70; and Shana Nichols and Audrey Blakeley-Smith, "'I'm Not Sure We're Ready for This . . .': Working with Families Toward Facilitating Healthy Sexuality for Individuals with Autism Spectrum Disorders," *Social Work in Mental Health* 8, no. 1 (2010): 72–91.

43. Greenfeld, *Place for Noah*; Schaefer, *Does She Know She's There?*

44. Kittay, "Forever Small."

45. Scholarship on the politics of marriage and parenthood illuminates the ways in which laws concerning marriage, adoption, and custody uphold a heteronormative, ableist culture. Many states continue to restrict marriage on the basis of labels associated with mental disabilities. Similarly, parents with disabilities are still disadvantaged in terms of retaining their parental rights. See Terrell Carver and Véronique Mottier, *Politics of Sexuality: Identity, Gender, Citizenship* (London: Routledge, 1998); Helen Meekosha and Leanne Dowse, "Enabling Citizenship: Gender, Disability, and Citizenship in Australia," *Feminist Review* 57 (1997): 49–70; Elzbieta H. Olesky, ed., *Intimate Citizenships: Gender, Sexualities, Politics* (New York: Routledge, 2009); Robert McRuer and Anna Mollow, eds., *Sex and Disability* (Durham, N.C.: Duke University Press, 2012); Emily Russell, *Reading Embodied Citizenship: Disability, Narrative, and the Body Politic* (New Brunswick, N.J.: Rutgers University Press, 2011); and Tom Shakespeare, Kath Gillespie-Sells, and Dominic Davies, *The Sexual Politics of Disability* (London: Cassell, 1996).

46. *Olmstead v. L. C.*, 527 U.S. 581 (1999).

47. Steven J. Taylor, "Caught in the Continuum: A Critical Analysis of the Principle of the Least Restrictive Environment," *Journal of the Association for the Severely Handicapped* 13, no. 1 (1988): 41–53.

48. Kymlicka, *Multicultural Citizenship*, 7.

49. Nancy J. Hirschmann, "Difference as an Occasion for Rights: A Feminist Rethinking of Rights, Liberalism, and Difference," *Critical Review of International Social and Political Philosophy* 2, no. 1 (1999): 27–55.

## Chapter 9. Cognitive Disability, Capability Equality, and Citizenship

I am grateful to Nancy Hirschmann and Beth Linker, for the invitation to contribute to this publication. I am also very grateful to Nancy Hirschmann and two anonymous reviewers for their helpful comments and suggestions.

1. Liberal egalitarian theories of justice are centered on the idea of "distributive justice," and hence their main concern is how to distribute resources fairly.

2. Recent debates in political philosophy have explored the distinction between ideal theory and the nonideal circumstances that characterize policy making. Ideal theory is generally concerned with the value of idealized assumptions for issues of justice.

3. John Rawls, *A Theory of Justice* (Cambridge, Mass.: Belknap Press of Harvard University Press, 1971).

4. Jonathan Wolff, "Cognitive Disabilities in a Society of Equals," in *Cognitive Disability and Its Challenge to Moral Philosophy*, ed. Eva F. Kittay and Licia Carlson (Oxford: Wiley-Blackwell, 2010), 147.

5. Licia Carlson has defined the demands of cognitive disability as the "philosopher's nightmare" in *The Faces of Intellectual Disability: Philosophical Reflections* (Bloomington: Indiana University Press, 2010), 1. See also Licia Carlson and Eva F. Kittay, "Introduction: Rethinking Philosophical Presumptions in Light of Cognitive Disability," in Kittay and Carlson, *Cognitive Disability*, 1.

6. These questions parallel the debate in disability studies concerning models of disability and are presented in the Introduction to this volume.

7. Elisabeth Anderson, "What Is the Point of Equality?," *Ethics* 109, no. 2 (January 1999): 287–337.

8. Carlson and Kittay, "Introduction," 1.

9. Amartya Sen, "Equality of What?," in *The Tanner Lectures on Human Values* (Salt Lake City: University of Utah Press, 1980), 1–6; Sen, *Resources, Values, and Development* (Cambridge, Mass.: Harvard University Press, 1984); Sen, *Inequality Reexamined* (Oxford: Clarendon Press, 1992); Sen, *Development as Freedom* (Oxford: Oxford University Press, 1999); Sen, "Capabilities, Lists and Public Reason: Continuing the Conversation," *Feminist Economics* 10, no. 3 (2004): 77–80; Sen, *The Idea of Justice* (London: Allen Lane, 2009); Sen, "The Place of Capability in a Theory of Justice," in *Measuring Justice: Primary Goods and Capabilities*, ed. Harry Brighouse and Ingrid Robeyns (Cambridge: Cambridge University Press, 2010), 239–53.

10. Martha C. Nussbaum, *Women and Human Development: The Capabilities Approach* (Cambridge: Cambridge University Press, 2004); Nussbaum, *Frontiers of Justice:*

*Disability, Nationality, Species Membership,* The Tanner Lectures on Human Values (Cambridge, Mass.: Harvard University Press, 2006); Nussbaum, "The Capabilities of People with Cognitive Disabilities," in Kittay and Carlson, *Cognitive Disability,* 75–96.

11. See, among others, Anderson, "What Is the Point of Equality?"; and Elisabeth Anderson, "Justifying the Capability Approach to Justice," in Brighouse and Robeyns, *Measuring Justice,* 81–100.

12. Sen, "Place of Capability in a Theory of Justice," 241.

13. Ibid., 242.

14. Ibid.

15. Sen, *Idea of Justice,* 253.

16. Ibid., 254.

17. Ibid., 253.

18. See, for instance, Sen, *Development as Freedom,* 75.

19. Sen, *Idea of Justice,* 253.

20. Ibid., 33. The aim of this example is simply to highlight the importance of individual differences in the conversion of resources into functionings and hence into valued activities. Other factors that might influence such differences (for example, personal choice or cultural norms) are accounted for in the conception of human diversity.

21. Sabina Alkire, *Valuing Freedoms: Sen's Capability Approach and Poverty Reduction* (Oxford: Oxford University Press, 2002), 4.

22. See Lorella Terzi, "Vagaries of the Natural Lottery? Human Diversity, Disability and Justice: A Capability Perspective," in *Disability and Disadvantage: Re-examining Issues in Moral and Political Philosophy,* ed. Kimberley Brownlee and Adam Cureton (Oxford: Oxford University Press, 2009), 96–104; and Terzi, "What Metric for Justice for Disabled People? Capability and Disability," in Brighouse and Robeyns, *Measuring Justice,* 164, for a more elaborated account of equality in the approach; see also Terzi, "Disability and Civic Equality: A Capability Perspective," *Italian Journal of Disability Studies* 1, no. 1 (2013): 25–40.

23. Sen, *Idea of Justice,* 258.

24. Ibid., 253, 258.

25. Ibid., 258.

26. See in particular Nussbaum, *Frontiers of Justice*; and Nussbaum, "Capabilities of People with Cognitive Disabilities."

27. This conceptualization of disability draws on my previous work, in particular Terzi, "Vagaries of the Natural Lottery?"; and Terzi, "What Metric for Justice for Disabled People?"

28. See in particular Mozaffar Qizilbash, "Disability and Human Development" (paper read at the 2006 International HDCA Conference, Groningen, the Netherlands, August 29–September 1, 2006), accessed March 31, 2012, http://www.hdca.org.

This concept is expressed in more detail in Terzi, "What Metric for Justice for Disabled People?"

29. Carol Spears, *Rising to New Heights of Communication and Learning for Children with Autism* (London: Jessica Kingsly Publishers, 2010), 38.

30. For a more in-depth discussion of this issue, see Terzi, "Vagaries of the Natural Lottery?"

31. Sen, *Idea of Justice*, 307.

32. Anderson, "What Is the Point of Equality?"

33. Ibid.

34. Carlson and Kittay, "Introduction"; Nussbaum, "Capabilities of People with Cognitive Disabilities"; and Michael Bérubé, "Equality, Freedom, and/or Justice for All: A Response to Martha Nussbaum," in Kittay and Carlson, *Cognitive Disability*, 97–109.

35. An opportunity is generally defined as a chance to get something, providing that one wants to get it. Positions on equal opportunities are roughly considered to relate to equality of inputs and differ from positions on equality of outcomes.

36. Anderson, "What Is the Point of Equality?," 316.

37. Nussbaum, "Capabilities of People with Cognitive Disabilities," 78–80.

38. See, for example, Sen, "Capabilities, Lists and Public Reason," 78.

39. Anderson, "What is the Point of Equality?," 288.

40. Ibid., 289.

41. Ibid., 316.

42. Anderson, "Justifying the Capability Approach to Justice," 83.

43. Lorella Terzi, *Justice and Equality in Education: The Capability Approach to Disability and Special Educational Needs* (London: Continuum 2008), 123.

44. James C. Harris, "Developmental Perspective on the Emergence of Moral Personhood," in Kittay and Carlson, *Cognitive Disability*, 56.

45. For a philosophical critique of the social model of disability, see Lorella Terzi, "The Social Model of Disability: A Philosophical Critique," *Journal of Applied Philosophy* 21, no. 2 (2004): 141–57.

46. For an interesting and compelling discussion of these considerations, see, for instance, Daniel Wikler, "Cognitive Disability, Paternalism, and the Global Burden of Disease," in Kittay and Carlson, *Cognitive Disability*, 183–201.

47. Bérubé, "Equality, Freedom, and/or Justice for All," 107. See also Sophia Wong, "Duties of Justice to Citizens with Cognitive Disabilities," in Kittay and Carlson, *Cognitive Disability*, 127–46.

48. Michael Bérubé, "Equality, Freedom, and/or Justice for All," 98, 104–6.

49. The setting of specific conditions for citizenship is critiqued both by some scholars within the social model of disability and by philosophers such as Eva Kittay and Michael Bérubé. See, for example, Eva F. Kittay, *Love's Labor* (New York: Routledge, 1999); and Bérubé, "Equality, Freedom, and/or Justice for All."

50. See Wolff, "Cognitive Disabilities."

51. See Kittay and Carlson, Introduction, *Cognitive Disability*; but also see Leslie P. Francis and Anita Silvers, "Thinking About the Good: Reconfiguring Liberal Metaphysics (or Not) for People with Cognitive Disabilities," in Kittay and Carlson, *Cognitive Disability*, 237–60.

52. Carlson and Kittay, "Introduction," 13.

53. See the contributions of these scholars to Kittay and Carlson, *Cognitive Disability*: Martha Nussbaum, "Capabilities of People with Cognitive Disabilities", 75–95; Michael Bérubé, "Equality, Freedom, and/or Justice for All: A Response to Martha Nussbaum," 97–109; Eva F. Kittay, "The Personal Is Political Is Philosophical: A Philosopher and Mother of a Cognitively Disabled Person Sends Notes from the Battlefield," 393–413.

54. Bérubé is cautious about the case for jury service and more concerned with ensuring essential functionings in society for individuals with cognitive impairments.

55. Eva F. Kittay, "The Personal Is Philosophical Is Political: A Philosopher and Mother of a Cognitively Disabled Person Sends Notes from the Battlefield," in Kittay and Carlson, *Cognitive Disability*, 393–413.

56. Nussbaum, "Capabilities of People with Cognitive Disabilities," 90.

57. Bérubé, "Equality, Freedom, and/or Justice for All," 105.

58. I am grateful to Nancy Hirschmann for raising this problem and pressing for a more articulated discussion of the point.

59. Bérubé, "Equality, Freedom and/or Justice for All," 103.

60. Nussbaum, "Capabilities of People with Cognitive Disabilities," 91.

61. Sen, *Idea of Justice*, 348–49.

62. But see, for example, the powerful critique by Linda Barclay, "Cognitive Impairment and the Right to Vote: A Strategic Approach," *Journal of Applied Philosophy* 30, no. 2 (2013): 146–59.

## Chapter 10. Invisible Disability

This chapter was written under a grant from the National Endowment for the Humanities and further developed at the Center for Human Values at Princeton. Earlier drafts were presented at Emory University, Princeton University, Columbia University, Brown University, the Penn Humanities Forum, and the University of Virginia. I thank colleagues at these universities, particularly Beth Linker and Mara Mills, for their suggestions and encouragement.

1. I use the term "they" in reference to both disabled and able-bodied individuals not to imply anything about my own physical state but for facility of expression.

2. Susan M. Schweik, *The Ugly Laws: Disability in Public* (New York: New York University Press, 2009).

3. Ellen Samuels, "My Body, My Closet: Invisible Disability and the Limits of Coming-Out Discourse," *GLQ* 9, nos. 1–2 (2003): 244.

4. See, for instance, N. Ann Davis, "Invisible Disability," *Ethics* 116, no. 1 (October 2005): 153–213.

5. Samuels, "My Body, My Closet," 236, 244.

6. Martin Jay, *Downcast Eyes: The Denigration of Vision in Twentieth-Century French Thought* (Berkeley: University of California Press, 1994), chap. 1.

7. Lennard Davis, *Enforcing Normalcy: Disability, Deafness, and the Body* (New York: Verso, 1995), 12. See also Rosemarie Garland-Thomson, *Staring: How We Look* (New York: Oxford University Press, 2009).

8. Tanya Titchkosky, *Disability, Self, and Society* (Toronto: University of Toronto Press, 2003), esp. 81–84.

9. Rosemarie Garland Thomson, *Extraordinary Bodies* (New York: Columbia University Press, 1997), 41. The idea that the disabled are "the ultimate other" is similarly argued by Mairian Corker, "Sensing Disability," *Hypatia* 16, no. 4 (Fall 2001): 34–52.

10. Tobin Siebers, *Disability Theory* (Ann Arbor: University of Michigan Press, 2008), 48.

11. Harlan Hahn, "Introduction: Disability Policy and the Problem of Discrimination," *American Behavioral Scientist* 28, no. 3 (1985): 307.

12. Thomson, *Extraordinary Bodies*, 43.

13. Susan Wendell, *The Rejected Body: Feminist Philosophical Reflections on Disability* (New York: Routledge, 1997). Similar analyses are offered by John Hockenberry, "Public Transit," in *Voices from the Edge: Narratives About the Americans with Disabilities Act*, ed. Ruth O'Brien (New York : Oxford University Press, 2004): 137–53; and Tom Shakespeare, Kath Gillespie-Sells, and Dominic Davies, *The Sexual Politics of Disability: Untold Desires* (London: Cassell, 1996).

14. Martha C. Nussbaum, *Hiding from Humanity: Disgust, Shame, and the Law* (Princeton, N.J.: Princeton University Press, 2004), 219.

15. Nicholas Watson, "Enabling Identity: Disability, Self and Citizenship," in *The Disability Reader: Social Science Perspectives*, ed. Tom Shakespeare (London: Cassell, 1998), 161.

16. John Locke, "Essay on the Poor Law," in John Locke, *Political Essays*, ed. Mark Goldie (London: Cambridge University Press, 1997); Nancy J. Hirschmann, "Freedom and (Dis)Ability in Early-Modern Political Thought," in *Recovering Disability in Early Modern England*, ed. Allison Hobgood and David Wood (Columbus: Ohio State University Press, 2013); Schweik, *Ugly Laws*.

17. I discuss the ways in which hatred and hostility toward disability are a mask for fear at greater length in Nancy J. Hirschmann, "Queer/Fear: Disability, Sexuality, and the Other," *Journal of Medical Humanities* 33, no. 3 (December 2012): 139–47.

18. Lennard Davis, *Enforcing Normalcy*, 8.

19. Judith Butler, *Bodies That Matter: On the Discursive Limits of "Sex"* (New York: Routledge, 1993). See also Ellen Samuels, "Critical Divides: Judith Butler's Body Theory and the Question of Disability," *NWSA Journal* 14, no. 3 (Fall 2002): 58–76.

20. Lennard Davis, *Enforcing Normalcy*, 8.

21. Ibid., xvi.

22. Anita Silvers, "Reconciling Equality to Difference: Caring (f)or Justice for People with Disabilities," *Hypatia* 10, no. 1 (Winter 1995): 30–55; Deborah A. Stone, *The Disabled State* (Philadelphia: Temple University Press, 1984), chap. 2.

23. See, for instance, the Equal Employment Opportunity Commission's definition, accessed August 14, 2007, http://www.eeoc.gov/policy/docs/902cm.html.

24. For more on this topic, see Susan Wendell, "Unhealthy Disabled: Treating Chronic Illnesses as Disabilities," *Hypatia* 16, no. 4 (Fall 2001): 17–33.

25. Karen Elizabeth Jung, "Chronic Illness and Educational Equity: The Politics of Visibility," *NWSA Journal* 14, no. 3 (Fall 2002): 178–200.

26. Marissa C. Cortes, Christine Hollis, Benjamin C. Amick III, and Jeffrey N. Katz, "An Invisible Disability: Qualitative Research on Upper Extremity Disorders in a University Community," *Work* 18 (2002): 315–21.

27. See Wendell, *Rejected Body*; also Watson, "Enabling Identity."

28. Keith Morris and Jan Morris, "Easy Targets: A Disability Rights Perspective on the 'Children as Carers' Debate," *Critical Social Policy* 15 (1995): 36–57.

29. Wendell, *Rejected Body*, 25, 26.

30. Erving Goffman, *Stigma: Notes on the Management of Spoiled Identity* (Englewood Cliffs, N.J.: Prentice-Hall, 1963), 48.

31. Although Foucault dates "the great confinement" of the insane, which often included individuals with only physical impairments, to the seventeenth century, Roy Porter maintains that in England the mentally disabled were not institutionalized in great numbers until the late eighteenth century and more likely the nineteenth. Michel Foucault, *Madness and Civilization: A History of Insanity in the Age of Reason*, trans. Richard Howard (New York: Pantheon Books, 1965); Roy Porter, "Foucault's Great Confinement," *History of the Human Sciences* 3, no. 1 (1990): 47–54.

32. Peter L. Tyor and Leland V. Bell, *Caring for the Retarded in America: A History* (Westport, Conn.: Greenwood Press, 1984); David J. Rothman and Sheila M. Rothman, *The Willowbrook Wars: Bringing the Mentally Disabled into the Community* (New York: Transaction Books, 2005). See page 5 of the present volume.

33. Immanuel Kant, *Groundwork of the Metaphysics of Morals*, trans. H. J. Patton (New York: Harper and Row, 1964).

34. Danny Hakim, "A Disabled Boy's Death, and a System in Disarray," *New York Times*, June 5, 2011.

35. Silvers, "Reconciling Equality to Difference," 43. For a more positive view of nursing homes, see Jane Brody, "Nursing Homes That Belie the Bad Image," *New York Times*, October 6, 2009. But even in outstanding settings (by American standards), such as Het Dorp residential facility in the Netherlands, Irving Zola describes a climate in which residents are second-class human beings. Irving Kenneth Zola, *Missing Pieces: A Chronicle of Living with a Disability* (Philadelphia: Temple University Press, 1982).

36. Christina Cogdell, *Eugenic Design: Streamlining America in the 1930s* (Philadelphia: University of Pennsylvania Press, 2004).

37. See Nicholas Agar, *Liberal Eugenics: In Defence of Human Enhancement* (Malden, Mass.: Blackwell, 2004).

38. Mary Johnson, *Make Them Go Away: Clint Eastwood, Christopher Reeve and the Case Against Disability Rights* (Louisville, Ky.: Advocado Press, 2003), describes how Eastwood, who launched a vigorous defense against an ADA lawsuit to make his tourist ranch handicap accessible, also conducted a famous public relations campaign against the act, generally claiming "I like disabled people" and stating that it was their lawyers who were creating all the trouble, as if disabled individuals themselves were actually perfectly happy to be excluded.

39. Silvers, "Reconciling Equality to Difference," 35–36; Peter Ubel, George Loewenstein, and Christopher Jepson, "Whose Quality of Life? A Commentary Exploring Discrepancies Between Health State Evaluations of Patients and the General Public," *Quality of Life Research* 12, no. 6 (2003): 599–607. See also P. Brickman, D. Coates, and R. Jano-Bulman, "Lottery Winners and Accident Victims: Is Happiness Relative?," *Journal of Personality and Social Psychology* 36 (1978): 917–27, which shows that levels of happiness among people who had recently been made paraplegics by car accidents were no different from those of people who had recently won the lottery once the initial shock (whether positive or negative) had been absorbed.

40. Wendell, *Rejected Body*, 105.

41. For my own views on abortion, see Nancy J. Hirschmann, "Abortion, Self-Defense, and Involuntary Servitude," *Texas Journal of Women and The Law*, 13, no. 1 (2003): 41–54; and *The Subject of Liberty: Toward a Feminist Theory of Freedom* (Princeton, N.J.: Princeton University Press, 2003), 1, 34, 38, 87, 98, 142, 182–83, 199, 234–35, 237–38, 239nn1, 4.

42. Rosemary Garland-Thomson, "Integrating Disability, Transforming Feminist Theory," *NWSA Journal* 14, no. 3 (Fall 2002): 16. See also Alison Davis, "Women with Disabilities: Abortion and Liberation," *Disability, Handicap and Society* 2, no. 3 (1987): 275–84.

43. Tim Booth and Wendy Booth, *Parenting Under Pressure: Mothers and Fathers with Learning Difficulties* (Buckingham, U.K.: Open University Press, 1994).

44. Ralph Ellison, *The Invisible Man* (New York: Vintage, 1995), 3.

45. Wendell, *Rejected Body*, 12, 3.

46. Ibid., 122. See also N. Ann Davis, "Invisible Disability," 207–8.

47. David Hume, *A Treatise of Human Nature*, ed. L. A. Selby-Bigge, 2nd ed., rev. P. H. Nidditch (Oxford: Oxford University Press, 1978), 316.

48. Elaine Scarry, *The Body in Pain: The Making and Unmaking of the World* (New York: Oxford University Press, 1985).

49. See Ruth O'Brien, "Introduction," *Voices from the Edge: Narratives About the Americans with Disabilities Act*, ed. Ruth O'Brien (New York: Oxford University Press, 2004): 3–27.

50. Nancy Weinberg, "Another Perspective: Attitudes on People with Disabilities," in *Attitudes Towards People with Disabilities*, ed. Harold D. Yuker (New York: Springer, 1988), 141–53; Beatrice A. Wright, "Attitudes and the Fundamental Negative Bias," 3–21.

51. Wendell, *Rejected Body*, 22, 40.

52. Carole-Anne Tyler, "Passing: Narcissism, Identity, Difference," *Differences* 6, nos. 2/3 (1994): 212; Samuels, "My Body, My Closet," 240.

53. See Tobin Seibers's discussion of "masquerade" in *Disability Theory*, esp. at 96, 105.

54. Darlene Clark Hine, "Rape and the Inner Lives of Black Women in the Middle West: Preliminary Thoughts on the Culture of Dissemblance," in *Signs: Journal of Women in Culture and Society* 14, no. 4 (1989): 912, 915.

55. Sedgwick suggests that this idea may not apply to disability as well as it does to homosexuality, but I believe that she is mistaken; Eve Kosofsky Sedgwick, *Epistemology of the Closet* (Berkeley: University of California Press, 1990), 75.

56. Lisa Walker, *Looking like What You Are: Sexual Style, Race, and Lesbian Identity* (New York: New York University Press, 2001), 10.

57. Schweik, *Ugly Laws*, chap. 3.

58. Zillah R. Eisenstein, *The Female Body and the Law* (Berkeley: University of California Press, 1990).

59. That blindness is not what most sighted people think is the central point made by Georgina Kleege in *Sight Unseen* (New Haven, Conn.: Yale University Press, 1999).

## Chapter 11. Disability Trouble

1. Judith Butler, *Gender Trouble: Feminism and the Subversion of Identity* (New York: Routledge, 1990; repr., 1999), xxvii–xxix.

2. On complex embodiment and the epistemological value of disability identity, see Tobin Siebers, *Disability Theory* (Ann Arbor: University of Michigan Press, 2008), 22–27.

3. Allan Bloom, *The Closing of the American Mind: How Higher Education Has Failed Democracy and Impoverished the Souls of Today's Students* (New York: Simon and Schuster, 1987), 74–75.

4. Ibid., 86.

5. Ibid.

6. Ibid., 92, 95.

7. Christopher Lasch, *The Culture of Narcissism: American Life in an Age of Diminishing Expectations* (New York: Warner Books, 1979), 30, 116.

8. Ibid., 252

9. Ibid., 253.

10. Joan W. Scott, "The Evidence of Experience," *Critical Inquiry* 17 (1991): 773–97.

11. Wendy Brown, *States of Injury: Power and Freedom in Late Modernity* (Princeton, N.J.: Princeton University Press, 1995), 71–72.

12. Ibid., 74.

13. Judith Butler, *The Psychic Life of Power: Theories in Subjection* (Stanford, Calif.: Stanford University Press, 1997), 104.

14. Sigmund Freud, "On Narcissism: An Introduction," in *The Standard Edition*, ed. James Strachey, 24 vols. (London: Hogarth Press, 1953–74), 14:82.

15. Ibid.

16. Sigmund Freud, "Some Character-Types Met with in Psychoanalysis," in *The Standard Edition*, ed. James Strachey, 24 vols. (London: Hogarth Press, 1953–74), 14:314–15.

17. For an extended analysis of the part played by narcissism in attacks on identity politics, see Siebers, *Disability Theory*, 34–52.

18. Katha Pollitt, "Show Him the Money," *Nation*, November 6, 2006, accessed October 3, 2007, http://www.thenation.com/doc/20061106/pollitt.

19. Walter Benn Michaels, *The Trouble with Diversity: How We Learned to Love Identity and Ignore Inequality* (New York: Metropolitan Books, 2007), 80.

20. Ibid., 173.

21. Ibid., 172.

22. Ibid., 5.

23. Ibid., 166–69.

24. Brenda Jo Brueggemann, *Deaf Subjects: Between Identities and Places* (New York: New York University Press, 2002), 68.

25. Michaels, *Trouble With Diversity*, 91.

CONTRIBUTORS

**Emily K. Abel** is research professor at the UCLA Fielding School of Public Health. She was written several books on chronic disease, including *Hearts of Wisdom: American Women Caring for Kin, 1850–1940* (2000); *Suffering in the Land of Sunshine: A Los Angeles Illness Narrative* (2006); *Tuberculosis and the Politics of Exclusion: A History of Public Health and Migration to Los Angeles* (2007); *After the Cure: The Untold Stories of Breast Cancer Survivors*, with Saskia Subramanian (2008); and *The Inevitable Hour: A History of Caring for Dying Patients in America* (2013). She currently is writing a history of patients with terminal chronic diseases since 1965.

**Douglas C. Baynton** is an associate professor of history and American Sign Language at the University of Iowa. He is the author of *Forbidden Signs: American Culture and the Campaign Against Sign Language* (1996), a cultural history of debates over American Sign Language and the meaning of deafness; and coauthor with Jack Gannon and Jean Bergey of *Through Deaf Eyes: A Photographic History of an American Community* (2007), an exploration of American history from the perspective of the Deaf community and companion volume to a PBS documentary film. He is currently writing a book on the concept of "defective persons" in the making of American immigration policy since the nineteenth century.

**Susan Burch** is an associate professor of American studies and former director of the Center for the Comparative Study of Race and Ethnicity at Middlebury College. She is the author of *Signs of Resistance: American Deaf Cultural History, 1900 to World War II* (2002). She has also coedited *Women and Deafness: Double Visions* (2006) with Brenda Jo Brueggemann; *Deaf and Disability Studies: Interdisciplinary Approaches* with Alison Kafer (2010); and *Disability Histories* with Michael Rembis (2014). She and Hannah Joyner coauthored *Unspeakable: The Story of Junius Wilson* (2007). Burch served as editor in chief of the three-volume *Encyclopedia of American Disability History* (2009). With Katherine Ott she has curated *Every Body: An Artifact History of Disability in America*, an online exhibition sponsored by the Smithsonian National Museum of American History (2013).

**Allison C. Carey** is an associate professor of sociology and director of the interdisciplinary minor in disability studies at Shippensburg University. She is the author of *On the Margins of Citizenship: Intellectual Disability and Civil Rights in Twentieth-Century America* (2009), and coeditor of *Disability and Community* with Richard Scotch (2011) and *Disability Incarcerated: Disability and Imprisonment in the United States and Canada* with Liat Ben-Moshe and Chris Chapman (2014).

**Faye Ginsburg** is the David B. Kriser Professor of Anthropology at New York University, where she is also the director of the Center for Media, Culture and History and the codirector of the NYU Council for the Study of Disability. Recipient of MacArthur and Guggenheim awards, among others, she is the author or editor of four books, including the multiple-award-winning *Contested Lives: The Abortion Debate in an American Community (1989)*; *Conceiving the New World Order: The Global Politics of Reproduction* (with Rayna Rapp) (1995); and *Media Worlds: Anthropology on New Terrain* (with Lila Abu Lughod and Brian Larkin) (2002). Since 2007, she has been working with Rayna Rapp on a joint research project, "Cultural Innovation and Learning Disabilities." She is also president of the Dysautonomia Foundation.

**Nancy J. Hirschmann** is a professor of political science at the University of Pennsylvania. She has written articles on disability's relation to the concepts of freedom, rights, and justice; on disability in the work of John Rawls, John Locke, and Thomas Hobbes; and on the intersectionality of disability, gender, and sexuality. She is also the author of several monographs, including *The Subject of Liberty: Toward a Feminist Theory of Freedom* (2003), which won the Victoria Schuck Award from the American Political Science Association for the best book on women and politics and *Gender, Class, and Freedom in Modern Political Theory* (2008). She is currently working on a book on disability in political theory.

**Hannah Joyner** is an independent historian in Takoma Park, Maryland. She is the author of *From Pity to Pride: Growing up Deaf in the Old South*

(2004) and, with coauthor Susan Burch, *Unspeakable: The Story of Junius Wilson* (2007). Currently she spends most of her time with her son, a home-schooled high-school student.

**Catherine Kudlick** is professor of history and director of the Paul K. Long-more Institute on Disability at San Francisco State University, and affiliated professor, Université Paris VII (Diderot). She is author of *Cholera in Post-revolutionary Paris: A Cultural History* (1996) and with Dr. Zina Weygand, *Reflections: the Life and Writing of a Young Blind Woman in Post-Revolutionary France* (2001), as well as numerous articles on disability history and disability studies, including "Disability History: Why We Need Another Other" in the *American Historical Review* (2003). Trained as a historian of modern France, she works at the intersection of disability history and history of epidemics.

**Beth Linker** is an associate professor in the Department of the History and Sociology of Science at the University of Pennsylvania. She is the author of *War's Waste: Rehabilitation in World War I America* (2011), as well as over a dozen articles and reviews that pertain to the history of disability, gender, health policy, the body, and medicine. She is currently researching two book projects—*Slouch: The Rise and Fall of American Posture* and *Making the Cut: Excess Surgery in the United States*.

**Alex Lubet** is Morse Alumni/Graduate and professional distinguished teaching professor of music at the University of Minnesota, with additional appointments in Jewish studies, American studies, and cognitive sciences. He is the author of *Music, Disability, and Society* (2011) and dozens of articles and reviews, mostly concerning disability issues within and beyond music. His current areas of research include essays on the poststroke career of jazz pianist Oscar Peterson, the social construction of aging, "adaptive music" and physical disability, and a monograph on Bob Dylan from a disability studies perspective. He is also a composer and multi-instrumentalist; his album *Spectral Blues: New Music for Acoustic Guitar* was chosen by noted jazz critic Ted Gioia as one of the "Best Albums of 2013."

**Rayna Rapp** is a professor and associate chair of the Department of Anthropology at New York University. Her books include the coedited *Conceiving the New World Order* (1995) and *Testing Women, Testing the Fetus:*

*The Social Impact of Amniocentesis in America* (2000). Along with Faye Ginsburg, she has been conducting research on cultural innovation in learning disabilities, focusing on the existential gap between how neuroscientists and other biological researchers see childhood brain differences and how parents describe family life when a child receives a diagnosis of cognitive difference. Her many articles on gender, the politics of reproduction, and disability can be found on her university homepage.

**Susan M. Schweik** is a professor of English, associate dean of Arts and Humanities, and codirector of the Disability Studies Program and the Disability Research Cluster at the University of California at Berkeley. She is the author of *A Gulf So Deeply Cut: American Women Poets and the Second World War* (1990) and *The Ugly Laws: Disability in Public* (2009). She is currently at work on a project on Agent Orange representation in the United States and Vietnam and on a book tentatively titled *Lost and Found: How a Ward of Women in a State Institution Taught Us to Teach to the Test.*

**Tobin Siebers** is V. L. Parrington Collegiate Professor of Literary and Cultural Criticism and professor of English language and literature and art and design at the University of Michigan. He is author of many books, including *Morals and Stories* (1992), *Cold War Criticism and the Politics of Skepticism* (1993), *The Subject and Other Subjects: On Ethical, Aesthetic, and Political Identity* (1998), *Disability Theory* (2008), and *Disability Aesthetics* (2010); the editor of *The Body Aesthetic: From Fine Art to Body Modification* (2000); and the author of over fifty articles on a wide variety of topics, including disability, aesthetics, art, and pain.

**Lorella Terzi** is professor of philosophy of education at the University of Roehampton, London. She is the author of *Justice and Equality in Education* (2008), the winner of the 2011 Nasen Award "The Special Educational Needs Academic Book," which applies Amartya Sen's capability approach to the contentious question of just provision for students with disabilities; and the editor of *Special Educational Needs: A New Look*, by Mary Warnock and Brahm Norwich, which has also been translated into Japanese. Her articles have appeared in the *Journal of Applied Philosophy*, *Theory and Research in Education*, the *Journal of Philosophy of Education*, and the *Journal of Special Education*. She is the author of numerous book chapters published in international edited collections.

# INDEX

## ACKNOWLEDGMENTS

This volume would not have been possible without generous support from various departments, schools, and programs at the University of Pennsylvania. Of particular assistance in making publication of this volume possible were a Mellon Cross-Cultural Contacts Grant, administered through the Dean of Arts and Sciences at Penn; the Penn Provost's University Research Fund; the Penn Program on Democracy, Citizenship and Constitutionalism; the Department of Political Science; and the Department of the History and Sociology of Science. We are grateful to all for their support and their participation. Thanks also to the Philadelphia Area Center for History of Science.

Several colleagues also deserve special recognition. Mara Mills and Sigal Ben-Porath played a vital role in the initial stages of planning this volume. We are grateful for their collegiality and willingness to share their expertise in disability and citizenship studies. Series editor Rogers Smith has been encouraging from the start and offered invaluable feedback. We are grateful to our anonymous reviewers for their suggestions and criticisms and believe that they enabled us to make this a better book. Finally, we are grateful to the family members, friends, and colleagues who have encouraged us to translate our various personal experiences with disability into our research and publishing.

This book is available both in hard copy and as an e-book, which is deposited with bookshare.org because, like us, the University of Pennsylvania Press believes that it is important not just to talk about disability access but to model it and to put our thoughts into action. We hope that this volume makes a contribution to the exciting and emerging field of disability studies, and we welcome readers to contact us with questions, reactions, and thoughts.